cation

LLER
g Editor

LINGAME

Secondary Edu

VAN M
Consulti

NEW YORK • BUF

in the United States

LINDLEY J. STILES
Dean, School of Education
University of Wisconsin

LLOYD E. McCLEARY
Associate Professor of Education
University of Illinois

ROY C. TURNBAUGH
Assistant Superintendent
J. Sterling Morton High Schools and Junior College
Berwyn, Illinois

HARCOURT, BRACE & WORLD, INC.

Preface

THE MOST critical question confronting the United States today is not, as some believe, whether we can produce more, better, and bigger satellites than Russia. Rather it is the deeper consideration: Can a system of democracy continue to stand against a despotic communism that is directed by the master plans of a few and that can command the development and use of talent? The outcome of this global contest, which has as its audience the free people of the world, depends primarily upon the relative success of the educational programs of the two political systems.

Awareness of the vital role of education in this struggle has prompted widespread concern throughout the United States about the goals, quality, structure, and processes of education—particularly at the secondary school level. Desire to adapt and to strengthen high schools to serve both our new national purposes and the requirements of individual youth has ignited a series of explosive criticisms and recommendations that are shaking the foundations of secondary school functions, organization, and teaching theory and practice. Through the storm clouds of conflict and uncertainty that have been raised, one beam of agreement seems to prevail: all are convinced that our schools, and secondary schools especially, must bear the burden of freedom. There is much disagreement as to how this responsibility can be best met. The central point of contention seems to be whether our schools can be adapted to face new challenges without sacrificing the values and functions distinctive to the American way of life.

To help answer this question is the central purpose of this book. The authors have sought to identify the forces that now bear upon junior and senior high schools and to analyze the new responsibilities these schools are asked to assume in terms of their unique character and long-established functions in a democratic nation. Pertinent data are presented and issues and trends are examined in relation to such basic questions as the following: What is the present status and character of secondary education? What are its unique characteristics as well as its essential and lasting attributes and accomplishments? What are the historical functions secondary schools have been called upon to assume? What new educational responsibilities must they undertake in the years ahead? How are high schools adapting their organizational patterns, programs, and services? What use is being made of human and material resources to meet new demands? What are the key crucial issues and challenges that confront secondary education today and what solutions are being offered to meet them?

To provide insight and possible answers to these and other significant questions the authors have pooled their experience and scholarship. The aim has been to produce a book that would reflect a unified, objective, and comprehensive treatment of secondary education without evading controversial issues, espousing partisan dogma, or advocating either untested theories or accepted practices. In this spirit, both the old and the new have been analyzed without endorsing either the "sacred cows" of established procedures or the newly advanced panaceas of critics of contemporary secondary schools. Forthright efforts have been made to penetrate beyond popular theories, current procedures, and pedagogical slogans to identify the bedrock of secondary education for the United States in the last half of the twentieth century.

This book deals with secondary education in the broad spectrum of complex relationships and responsibilities to the individual, the community, and state, as well as to the nation in a world in which freedom is in danger. Because the reader is assumed to possess a substantial acquaintance with high schools, some topics dealing with the minor details of internal organization and practice have been consciously slighted to permit the treatment in depth of more crucial issues and subjects about which knowledge is not commonly available. For example, content not customarily included in books on secondary education will be found particularly in the chapters dealing with population trends, strengthening the common heritage, laying the foundations for scholarship, discovering talent, developing values, the school plant, the gifted, the handicapped, nonpublic schools, and competition from abroad. The references suggested at the end of each chapter were selected to facilitate the penetrating study of unique or restricted ideas and problems rather than to serve as documentation for the material presented. The aim throughout has been to stimulate and extend the scholarship of the reader, rather than to accentuate the obvious or to recount the known.

The authors are optimistic about the future of secondary schools. They see evidences of changes and adaptability that attest to the ability of high schools to assume greater responsibility for intellectual and moral leadership to the nation while maintaining universal educational values and necessary services to individuals in local communities. They appraise the leadership and teachers of junior and senior high schools as alert, competent, and responsive to the times. The picture herein of secondary education in the United States is an actual reflection of schools as they are coming to be. New practices described are not visionary; they are already under experimentation in selected school systems from Maine to Hawaii and Alaska to Texas. Traditional values and procedures highlighted are not out of date; they have stood the tests of time and controversy to win continuing endorsement.

Secondary Education in the United States is presented by the authors with the hope that prospective teachers and those in service, high school administrators and supervisors, as well as others interested in this important phase of education, will find in its pages sound analyses of educational issues, usable data pertinent to key educational questions, creative ideas for strengthening established programs, and reliable guides to the understanding and interpretation of junior and senior high schools of this country.

Numerous individuals and agencies have contributed to the development of *Secondary Education in the United States*. Its genesis came from William C. Ferguson, formerly president of the World Book Company, who in 1955 urged the senior author to prepare such a book. To Dr. Van Miller, consulting editor for World Book Company and Professor of School Administration at the University of Illinois, goes credit for the organization of an effective writing team with complementary strength and balances, as well as for his advice and encouragement during the development of the book. The Universities of Wisconsin and Illinois and the J. Sterling Morton High Schools have in various ways made it possible for the authors to undertake this project. Colleagues in these institutions, too numerous to mention, have shared ideas, research, and other resources. Appreciation is expressed specifically to Dr. Rick Heber, Research Professor at the University of Wisconsin, who gave advice on the preparation of Chapter 18, and to Dr. Harold Hand, Professor of Education, University of Illinois, for the release of unpublished data from research he was directing for the State Department of Public Instruction in Illinois. A debt of thanks is due, also, to officials in State Departments of Public Instruction of all fifty states and Washington, D.C., various religious associations that sponsor schools, the United States Office of Education, the National Education Association, and numerous school systems for data they supplied. Appreciation is expressed as well to other authors and publishers for permission to use quoted material. To the wives of the three authors, Marguerite C. Stiles, Marcella McCleary, and Zora Turnbaugh, special gratitude is felt not only for their patience and forebearance while the work was in progress but also for help in the typing and reading of parts of the manuscript in its various stages of development. Thanks are due to Evelyn L. Brown who assisted with the final editing of the book, the checking of proofs, and the preparation of the index; and to Mary Husting who typed the final draft of the manuscript.

LINDLEY J. STILES
LLOYD E. MCCLEARY
ROY C. TURNBAUGH

Contents

Preface   vii

PART I: THE SETTING

1 *Changing Emphases and New Perspectives*   3

SECONDARY EDUCATION—CENTER OF CONTROVERSY · INTERNA-
TIONAL RELATIONSHIPS · TECHNOLOGICAL DEVELOPMENTS · THREE
GOALS: UNIVERSALITY, QUALITY, AND EFFICIENCY

2 *Population, Mobility, and Enrollments*   19

EXPANDING POPULATION OF THE UNITED STATES · MOBILITY AND
HIGH SCHOOL ENROLLMENTS · ATTENDANCE AND RETENTION

3 *Public Education in the United States—*
  A Survey   33

PUBLIC EDUCATION—FOR THE COMMON GOOD · STRUGGLE FOR
FINANCIAL SUPPORT · CONTINUING CONTROVERSIES · PUBLIC SEC-
ONDARY SCHOOLS—A UNIQUE EDUCATION VENTURE · SEARCH
FOR PURPOSE AND DIRECTION · THE CONTEMPORARY SECONDARY
SCHOOL

PART II: PURPOSES AND FUNCTIONS

4 *Functions of Secondary Education*   59

DIVERGENT OLD WORLD ROOTS · EARLY AMERICAN SECONDARY
SCHOOLS: REVOLUTIONARY FUNCTIONS · TWENTIETH-CENTURY

FUNCTIONS OF SECONDARY EDUCATION · FUTURE FUNCTIONS OF
SECONDARY EDUCATION: THE WISHES OF THE PEOPLE

5 *Strengthening the Common Heritage*   81

A UNIQUE HERITAGE: DEMOCRACY AS BOTH POLITICAL THEORY
AND WAY OF DAILY LIFE · DANGER ON TWO FRONTS: AT HOME AND
ABROAD · SECONDARY EDUCATION: MAJOR MOBILIZATION AGENCY
FOR DEMOCRACY · PRESENT PROBLEMS AND THE HERITAGE

6 *Laying the Foundation for Scholarship*   103

INTELLECTUAL DEVELOPMENT—THE PRIMARY OBJECTIVE · NA-
TURE OF SCHOLARSHIP · DISCOVERY AND USE OF KNOWLEDGE ·
CONDITIONS REQUIRED FOR SCHOLARSHIP

7 *Discovering and Developing Talent*   125

EQUALITY AND UNIFORMITY · CULTIVATION OF TALENT—A
NATIONAL NECESSITY · OBSTACLES TO TALENT DEVELOPMENT ·
NATURE OF TALENT · TASK OF THE SECONDARY SCHOOL

8 *Developing Values*   149

CONCEPTIONS OF VALUES · IMPACT OF CONTEMPORARY FORCES
ON VALUES · FACTORS IN VALUE DEVELOPMENT · THE SECONDARY
SCHOOLS AS AN AGENCY FOR VALUE DEVELOPMENT

PART III: ORGANIZATION AND PROGRAM

9 *Organization of Secondary Schools*   175

SETTING FOR SCHOOL ORGANIZATION · ELEMENTS OF ORGANIZA-
TIONAL THEORY · GROWING COMPLEXITY OF ORGANIZATION ·
TEACHERS AND ORGANIZATION · EMERGING TRENDS IN ORGANI-
ZATION

10 *Planning and Development of the Curriculum* 199

MEANING OF CURRICULUM · CURRICULUM STRUCTURE · PLANNING
THE CURRICULUM · STATUS OF CURRICULUM OFFERINGS · OVER-
ALL DESIGN OF THE SECONDARY SCHOOL PROGRAM

11 *Instruction in Secondary Schools*   227

ORGANIZATION OF INSTRUCTIONAL RESOURCES · INSTRUCTIONAL
PROCEDURES · ASPECTS OF INSTRUCTION · EVALUATION OF IN-
STRUCTION · RECOGNITION OF QUALITY TEACHING

12 *Programs of Guidance*   247

GUIDANCE RATHER THAN COMPULSION · THE GUIDANCE PROGRAM
IN SECONDARY SCHOOLS · RELATIONSHIP OF GUIDANCE TO IN-
STRUCTION · PROBLEMS CONFRONTING GUIDANCE PROGRAMS

13 *Student Activities*   273

NATURE OF STUDENT ACTIVITIES · DEVELOPMENT OF STUDENT
ACTIVITIES · ORGANIZATION OF PROGRAM OF ACTIVITIES · VALUES
PROMOTED BY STUDENT ACTIVITIES · THE TEACHER AND STUDENT
ACTIVITIES · FUTURE OF STUDENT ACTIVITIES

PART IV : HUMAN AND PHYSICAL FACILITIES

14 *Leadership for the Secondary School*   299

NATURE OF LEADERSHIP · DIFFERING CONCEPTIONS OF LEADER-
SHIP · NEW DEMANDS ON LEADERSHIP · DILEMMAS OF LEADERSHIP
· NEW LEADERSHIP ASSIGNMENTS IN THE SECONDARY SCHOOL ·
THE PROFESSIONAL PRINCIPALSHIP · TEACHER'S ROLE IN LEADER-
SHIP

15 *The Secondary School Teacher*   325

TEACHER: KEY TO QUALITY EDUCATION · ATTRACTING THE MOST
ABLE · THE BEST SHOULD TEACH · CHOICE OF SECONDARY SCHOOL
TEACHING · SOME ASPECTS OF TEACHING AS A CAREER

16 *Secondary School Buildings*   347

ACCUMULATED SHORTAGES OF FACILITIES · DEVELOPMENT OF A
PHILOSOPHY FOR THE SECONDARY SCHOOL PLANT · PLANNING
THE HIGH SCHOOL · CURRENT TRENDS IN ARCHITECTURAL TREAT-
MENT OF EDUCATIONAL DEVELOPMENTS

PART V : CURRENT CONCERNS IN SECONDARY EDUCATION

17 *Challenging the Gifted Student*   387

URGENT EDUCATIONAL GOAL · CHARACTERISTICS OF THE GIFTED
SECONDARY SCHOOL PROGRAMS: ADAPTATIONS FOR THE GIFTED ·
EVALUATION OF PROVISIONS FOR THE GIFTED

18 *Providing Educationally for the Handicapped* 415

SOCIETY'S CONCERN FOR THE HANDICAPPED · RESPONSIBILITIES OF THE SECONDARY SCHOOLS FOR THE HANDICAPPED · INSTRUCTIONAL PROVISIONS FOR THE HANDICAPPED · FACTORS PERTINENT TO THE SECONDARY SCHOOL'S PROGRAM FOR THE HANDICAPPED · PROBABILITIES

19 *School-Community Relationships* 439

PUBLIC EDUCATION REQUIRES AN INFORMED PUBLIC · CONSCIOUS CULTIVATION OF HEALTHY COMMUNITY RELATIONSHIPS: A SCHOOL RESPONSIBILITY · AGENCIES AND INSTRUMENTS · SCHOOL-COMMUNITY RELATIONS: CHALLENGE TO EDUCATION

20 *Nonpublic Secondary Schools* 465

SCOPE AND GROWTH OF NONPUBLIC SECONDARY SCHOOLS · THE GROWTH OF NONPUBLIC SECONDARY SCHOOLS · SPECIAL PURPOSES ON NONPUBLIC SCHOOLS · STRENGTHS OF THE NONPUBLIC SCHOOLS · OBJECTIONS TO NONPUBLIC SCHOOLS · REGULATION OF NONPUBLIC SCHOOLS

21 *Competition from Abroad* 493

COMMITMENTS TO EDUCATION · ORGANIZATION OF SECONDARY SCHOOLS · STRENGTH OF CURRICULUM · CHALLENGE TO THE UNITED STATES

Index 515

PART I

The Setting

Secondary schools in the United States and Russia are responding to the space age by increased emphases on scholarship.

CHAPTER I

Changing Emphases and New Perspectives

SECONDARY education has assumed a crucial position of responsibility in the schools in the United States. Its vital role has been created by forces largely external to the school itself—the power of newly discovered knowledge, the changes taking place in industry and science, and world-wide tensions and developments.

Awareness is growing that excellence in education at each level depends heavily upon the effectiveness of high school programs. Some students find these years of schooling "make or break" periods in their lives. Parents, as well as citizens in general, are coming to realize that our total system can be no stronger than its middle section—the secondary school. Its strength and well-being, therefore, are the concern of all.

SECONDARY EDUCATION—CENTER OF CONTROVERSY

Public interest in secondary education has reached an all-time high as citizens see the heavy responsibilities that education must bear in an age that makes brain power the nation's most important resource, both for individual attainment and happiness and for national security and well-being.

Interest in education generally, and in high schools particularly, is so keen that only the subject of cancer has been accorded a higher priority by the press, popular periodicals, and radio and television news services. Such leading public figures as former Harvard President James B. Conant, Naval Vice-Admiral Hyman G. Rickover, and others have studied the functions and organizations of high schools.[1]

Attitudes regarding secondary education range from the demand for almost total change to vigorous defenses of the *status quo*. Pressures on school officials and teachers have become so strong in many places that courses and graduation requirements have been changed without adequate study, just to quiet outspoken critics. As a result, there is uncertainty and uneasiness, in community after community, about the emphases and perspectives of the secondary school.

Criticism of High Schools

Some critics of present-day high schools claim that the curriculum is "too soft," that difficult subjects are not offered, or that the elective system permits students to choose easy courses. Others charge that standards are set for average pupils and thus represent little challenge to those preparing for college. It is claimed that students in the United States are poorly motivated, that the practice of automatically passing or promoting all enrolled has destroyed drive, initiative, and competitive spirit. Widespread agreement prevails that, whatever may be said for the program of "education for all," academically talented youth have not made maximum educational progress as compared to their contemporaries in other nations.

Buildings and Ball Games

The expansion of secondary education during the past half-century has been phenomenal. As more young people have attended high schools, public interest and support have multiplied. Communities and states have taken pride in the percentages of youth of high school age in school, while the high school diploma has become almost a prerequisite to employment of any kind above unskilled labor jobs.

The general public endorsement of secondary education, which has made possible its incomparable growth, has been the result more of civic pride and competition between communities—the kind of spirit that also builds new courthouses, city halls, sewage disposal plants,

---

[1] James B. Conant, *The American High School Today*, New York (McGraw-Hill), 1959. Hyman G. Rickover, *Education and Freedom*, New York (Dutton), 1959. Devereux C. Josephs and others, *The Pursuit of Excellence: Education and the Future of America*, Garden City, N.Y. (Doubleday), 1958.

and paves streets and roads—than a deep dedication to the values of education. The strength of schools has been reckoned more in such quantitative terms as size and cost of buildings and the competitive success of extracurricular groups than it has by qualitative educational success. In fact, school officials have been so busy finding ways to house expanding enrollments and communities have been so infatuated with the interscholastic competition of high schools that the past fifty years might well be called, for purposes of educational reference, a period of buildings and ball games.

Small Schools—Poor Results

Further cause for dissatisfaction with secondary education on the part of critics has been the number of high schools that are too small to produce good results.[2] The small school is limited in the quality of teachers it can attract and retain, by the number of courses it can offer, by the academic standards it can enforce, and by the provisions it can make to meet individual differences among students.

Resisting state departments of public instruction, legislative inducements, and encouragement from educational leaders, many rural and small-town communities cling to their small high schools. Local pride and independence have been largely responsible for this resistance to reorganization into schools of sufficient size to assure quality programs.

Opposition to Democratic Schools

Although the majority of the people of the United States maintain solid faith in, and dedication to, a system of public schools free to all youth, various small, yet often influential, minorities do not share such a commitment. Some people would restrict enrollments to segments of the adolescent population based on such factors as intelligence, educational plans, academic interests, and in some states on race or religion; others oppose public schools because they are too selfish to help bear the costs; still others find, in their dedication to parochial or private schools, a conflict with the conception of public education; and a few criticize American schools because of the differences they represent in contrast to those in certain foreign nations.[3]

Comprehensive or Differentiated

Substantial controversy has developed in recent years over whether secondary schools should be organized on a comprehensive or differ-

[2] Conant, *op. cit.,* pp. 37-38, 77-85.
[3] Rickover, *op. cit.,* pp. 29-30, 131-57, 185-86.

entiated basis. Those who support the comprehensive high school, Dr. Conant for one,[4] hold that a single, relatively large school can give maximum educational service to all youth, the academically talented as well as those with other abilities and aptitudes, while simultaneously providing for the intermingling and intercultural enrichment of pupils from different backgrounds in ways compatible to American traditions.

Supporters of the differentiated secondary school claim that quality in education suffers when the population becomes too heterogeneous.[5] They advocate that selected high schools be developed as academic, college-preparatory institutions, with enrollments limited to youth of high intellectual ability and outstanding academic promise. Other young people would be assigned to nonacademic schools to prepare for the trades and for their citizenship responsibilities.

INTERNATIONAL RELATIONSHIPS

A growing influence on the emphases and perspectives of the secondary school program is the new role of the United States as the leader of the free world. Intensified competition between the United States and the Soviet Union has highlighted the educational differences between the two nations and increased concern for the quality of education.

Back of this concern is the sober realization that our only hope for survival as a free people—in an age when scientific, technological, political, psychological, and medical competence are at a premium—is to conserve and develop the intellectual resources of all more effectively.

Leadership of the Free World

The suddenness with which leadership of the free world was thrust upon the United States intensified demands for experts—in politics, economics, health, science, sociology, and business, as well as in all phases of education. Efforts to recruit and develop competent individuals turned the spotlight on the quality of education at all levels. Weaknesses were revealed not only in the areas of specialization in which experts were sought, but also in such fields as foreign languages, world history, geography, mathematics, and science, as well as in the technical skills of communication.

The increase of national participation in world affairs, particularly

[4] Conant, *op. cit.*, pp. 11-40.
[5] Rickover, *op. cit.*, 124-25.

in the United Nations, involved Americans in decisions that required substantial knowledge about the world and its people. General education for citizenship responsibilities in a democratic nation began to be inspected in terms of the wider responsibilities of individuals who, by their votes, choose representatives to help decide the direction of world affairs.

Spotlighted before other nations were all our national institutions, including our particular system of free public schools that is identified in the minds of many throughout the world as a major instrument of freedom and self-government. The focus of such interest falls heavily upon the secondary school inasmuch as it represents a sharp divergence from education for adolescents as carried on in many other countries. Its characteristics that attract interest are: its comprehensive features, which include academic and vocational education within the same building; the heavy emphasis upon general education as an upward extension of the common schooling required for all; the practice of automatic admission of any pupil who has completed the elementary school; a system of electives that permits students to choose courses to study; programs of guidance aimed at helping students to plan their own educational careers; and extensive emphasis on extracurricular activities.

As foreign observers, including exchange teachers and students, appraised the merits of the secondary school in the United States, and as representatives of this country studied schools abroad, comparisons of existing differences raised questions relative to the strengths and weaknesses of various systems of secondary education.

The Cold War

The struggle for supremacy of two conflicting ways of life—democracy and communism—tests the strengths, and reveals the weaknesses, of all our vital institutions. Pitted against Russian Communism, with its avowed policy of dominating the world through intrigue and infiltration and of competing for the affiliation of numerous newly freed countries, both large and small, all of whom need help, the United States upholds the rights of humanity.

This test of strength against a nation committed to authoritarian rule in a planned society requires that we excel not only in politics, production, and science, but in education as well. The audience for this drama of world leadership is composed of the uncommitted masses of the world whose fate may well be decided by who wins this test. In this encounter the demand is for knowledge to counteract ignorance; for values that will stand against demagoguery, prejudice, and oppression; for human understanding which will create relationships of trust and confidence; for commitments to peace and world happiness as goals; and for democratic behavior between people.

In this struggle it is knowledge imparted in large measure in our schools which will decide how well our citizens handle concepts, skills, and values. It is possible that the foundation for victory will be laid in the victor's classrooms. At the very least, what occurs in the classroom can be an important source of strength. Students enter the secondary school still on the edge of childhood, they graduate on the threshold of adulthood. For this reason much of the current general interest in the quality of education has focused upon the secondary schools in particular. Blemishes in high school programs are caught in the glare of the same floodlights that are turned on the drama of the cold war. No longer can they be passed over as minor flaws, of importance only to local communities; every weakness is cause for public concern.

Satellite Competition

A new phase of the competition between the United States and Russia that set off a barrage of criticisms of secondary schools began with the orbiting of Sputnik I. Russia's achievement in successfully launching the first object into space has been explained as being due to U.S. policy decisions not to go all-out in the field of satellite research and testing, while Russia began intensive research immediately after World War II. Despite this, the loss of prestige and humiliation experienced by many citizens caused them to find fault with high schools for failing to emphasize sufficiently the study of science.

The controversy grew more intense as Russia continued to send objects into space. While the actual solid contributions to science were largely the product of U.S. space research, the contest between the two countries on the newspaper headline level favored the Russians. As a result there were widespread efforts to reorganize the programs of mathematics and physics, from high school through college, and to add to the secondary school program such subjects as Russian history and language. In addition, programs designed to identify and challenge academically talented students gained support as greater emphasis was placed on the sustained study of such subjects as mathematics, science, history, and a foreign language, as well as English.

Another direct result of the satellite race was the passage by the

United States Congress of the National Defense Education Act, in 1958, which provided federal assistance to high school programs that were judged to be vital to the interests of national security. This legislation gave financial support to the preparation of teachers in such fields as mathematics and science, as well as certain underemphasized foreign languages. It also aided programs for the training of guidance counselors to work with gifted students and it established support for research aimed at making greater use of television in teaching. Although the major assistance provided by the act is to train teachers, grants are also made available to schools for improving science laboratories. States are allocated funds, on a matching basis, for testing programs to inventory student abilities.

The total impact of the satellite competition on secondary education has been an emphasis on quality and the study of basic subjects. By-products that are already providing changing emphases and new perspectives in high schools include: differentiated programs for gifted students; provisions for acceleration of the academically talented, including early admission to college, e.g., at the end of the tenth grade; the inclusion of honors courses for college credit in some high schools; and the use of advanced placement examinations on a nation-wide basis.

Human Relations

Whereas most of the recent emphasis on the high school program has been on the physical sciences, considerable concern has been evidenced for greater attention to the humanities and the behavioral sciences—fields that relate to the quality of man's relationships to himself and his fellows. In general, the people of the United States, in spite of demands for additional emphasis in science, have recognized that the fears, tensions, and aggressions that divide people will not be resolved through scientific discoveries and technological advances alone. Consequently, the conviction is held by many that better human relations depend upon the emphasis placed in school programs on the study of such subjects as history, geography, literature, language, sociology, economics, and ethics, and on the contribution such studies make to the values and commitments of people.

Conflicts of national, ethnic, racial, religious, and political groups, both at home and afar, generate inquiries into the values that school programs seek to develop in pupils. The prevalence of prejudices, distrust, and lack of understanding and cooperation among people suggests that greater emphasis is needed in schools on training to develop sound moral and spiritual principles to guide human behavior. In short, breakdowns in relationships among people, whether within or between nations, underscore the importance of schools giving greater attention to promoting higher standards of morality and citizenship.

TECHNOLOGICAL DEVELOPMENTS

The emphases and perspectives of secondary education are being changed by the technological developments that are impinging upon almost every phase of life in the United States. Scientific discovery has opened new prospects to man; but to inherit these prospects he must acquire greater knowledge and technical skill in science. The full exploitation of the benefits of science demands not only education of all to minimum levels of scientific knowledge but the high-level specialization of those individuals who possess the interests and the qualities of intelligence required for basic scientific research and highly technical work.

An Age of Science

The new knowledge that is being produced cannot be fitted into traditional course and curriculum patterns. For example, the demand for increasing the mathematical base for the study of science, in terms of new conceptions and emphases in content, as well as the changes taking place in the subject matter of physics and chemistry, have made curricular reorganization essential in these fields from elementary school through college and graduate school.

Likewise, the rapid growth of scientific knowledge about human behavior and relationships necessitates changes in the courses in social studies and the humanities. The complexities of life in a world in which scientific invention brings people of different lands closer together, through both transportation and communication, produce forces that impinge on what is taught in *all* fields of the secondary school curriculum.

The amount of knowledge required to instruct gifted students in depth in any field suggests that teachers need longer periods of preparation, with more specialization in their teaching fields. Inevitably, high school teachers will, in the future, be pressed for intense specialization in one teaching field, with possibly considerable training in closely related subjects. It is coming to be realized, for example, that it is no longer possible to prepare one individual, during four years of college, to teach all the branches of science, including mathematics, that are usually offered by high schools. Instead, a teacher can today master no more than two closely related or supportive fields, such as mathematics and physics, or mathematics and chemistry.

Impact of Automation

Since the beginning of time, man has sought to invent machines to do his work for him. Whether it be the lever or the automated production line, the effect has been to increase the amount of production while reducing the amount of labor. Inevitable dislocations and temporary unemployment have occurred, but in the end increased production has led to even more jobs. At the present machines are lightening not only the labor in factories but the drudgery in offices. For instance, modern machines calculate statements, address them, and mail them, and in research problems which formerly required many repeated, routine calculations computers have taken over. Even in the home, machines now take up a major share of what was another generation's hard labor.

With machines doing practically all the manual jobs of yesterday and many of the semiskilled and skilled jobs of today, it is obvious that the demand in the future will be for much more highly trained technical and professional personnel. By 1975, it is estimated, jobs requiring advanced technical training will have increased by 75 per cent. While automation makes some jobs obsolete, experience is proving that in the long run it creates more jobs than it eliminates; each new job, however, often demands a higher level of training and broader competence.

In the past, much attention has been given to designing specialized training programs, beginning usually in high school. The objective has been to prepare young people for particular types of employment. The rapid changes that result from automation make it imperative that programs of education help students develop such traits as adaptability, creativity, technical ingenuity, and capacity to visualize and solve intricate new problems. Lifelong learning and continuous change in job assignments may characterize the successful worker of the future.

General and Specialized Emphasis in Science

To supply the necessary number of high-level specialists who are broadly educated to meet the complexities of a technological and scientific future, high schools are taking steps to identify gifted students early and to provide motivation, as well as the type and quality of educational programs they require to achieve their maximum potentials. At the same time, it is recognized that efforts must not be slackened to help every student make the most of his talents. Furthermore, all must be prepared to function as citizens in an age that demands decisions about the uses that will be made of scientific discoveries and technological instruments. The citizen needs to understand much about science just to be able to discharge his responsibilities for self-government. He needs, in addition, to be better educated for consumption of goods and services in an age when technological developments have produced bonanzas of competing products, many of which are being marketed through exaggeration, innuendo, and emotional appeal.

With the increased emphasis upon greater technical and scientific specialization comes a demand for more and better general education for all students. Leaders in business, industry, and the professions are seeking employees whose broad liberal education has laid the foundation for the development of high proficiency in specialized fields. They recognize that the individual whose preparation is narrow and highly concentrated is ill equipped to cope with the rapid changes. Few can predict what they will be doing ten years hence. Trade and vocational preparations are already beginning to lean more heavily upon general education. Programs to prepare for college are moving away from early specialization.

Automation and the revolution wrought in production by science have touched and are changing many aspects of education. Many time-tested career clusters, with their related programs of preparation, have been made invalid. Youth who plan to follow the careers of their fathers, or to take over family businesses, find their decisions must be changed because of the shift in the types of businesses and creation of new careers. Business and industrial corporations have taken over products and services once supplied by small business, thus reducing the opportunities for the individual to make a place for himself as an independent producer or business owner. In some instances change has been so rapid the industries themselves have had to establish their own educational programs.

A further impact on secondary schools of the increased demands for both specialized talent and broader and greater depth of general education is the necessity of extending formal schooling for more young people beyond the twelfth grade. This factor promises to emphasize more the preparatory function of secondary school programs, while reducing the terminal obligations that have demanded so much attention in the past.

Electronics and Learning

The manpower shortage touches all fields, especially those requiring professional competence, and ways, therefore, must be found to increase the efficient use of available talent. This problem is becoming acute in secondary schools as the rapid population expansion that began around 1940 increases enrollments.

Education finds itself, at all levels, lagging far behind other fields in adapting the results of scientific discoveries to the problems of instruction. Medicine, particularly in hospitals, has become much more efficient in recent years. More patients receive better care in a shorter time than ever before and yet the number of doctors has not risen greatly. Much of this is derived from new machines and techniques that did not even exist before World War II. In some areas such as engineering severe shortages of fully qualified specialists have forced programs of conservation. The skilled do only that work which requires skill; levels of skill are identified and correlated with the skill of the labor available. Yet in elementary and secondary schools the best-qualified specialists are still used as part-time clerks and room attendants. Certainly today's teaching is different from that of a generation ago but not nearly so much as the difference in medical practice.

Recent educational experiments have sought ways to adapt the products of scientific discovery, particularly electronic devices, to teaching and learning. Television is being used to extend the services of outstanding teachers to students throughout a school or group of schools in an area. Teaching machines have been developed that make learning possible without the close attention of an instructor. Talking records are helping children learn to read in elementary schools and to expand their literary appreciations at the high school level. Tape recordings have proved valuable in adapting instruction to individual differences in fields such as foreign language, shorthand, and speech, in which material and dictation must be presented to groups. Films and slides are being employed in creative ways to enrich large group instruction as well as to further independent study. The telemation techniques that produced 9 per cent more learning in 30 per cent less time when used in educational programs of the armed forces are being tested for public school use.

The new applications of electronic devices to extend the benefits of instruction to more students and to improve individual learning may be expected in the years to come. Such resources may well encourage the differentiation of professional competencies to permit greater excellence in teaching. They may break the lock step of traditional secondary education, making possible programs of instruction that will be better adapted to the learning rates and abilities of individual pupils.

THREE GOALS: UNIVERSALITY, QUALITY, AND EFFICIENCY

Against the background of its historical development, and in the light of new forces that are changing educational emphases, three goals for secondary education are clearly indicated: universality, quality, and efficiency. These three objectives promise to shape the character of secondary schools in future years.

Universality

Out of past commitments to the dignity and worth of the individual, i.e., the conviction that each person is deserving of a fair chance to make the most of his talents, comes the objective of *universality* in secondary education. Not all youth, to be sure, will graduate from high school; not all can. Yet today, more than three-fourths of the young people of secondary school age are in school. Additional numbers may be expected to stay in high school longer, as it becomes evident that a scientific and technical age has little place for the unskilled or poorly educated. With the exception of those handicapped by limited intelligence, poor emotional stability, or physical disabilities that require special schooling, the secondary school may be expected in the future to be called upon to serve practically all young people.

The objective of universality in education is constant; it is not subject to change as long as freedom and self-government are cherished. The progress that has been made toward this goal in high school education is unmatched in the history of the world. Perhaps we are closer to the fulfillment of this goal than to the other two. The ability to provide for large numbers of students, with wide deviations in aptitudes and potentialities, is fairly well developed by most schools. Yet, the increase in enrollments at the secondary school level, the exigencies of the manpower shortage, and the changing emphases that are being demanded in courses and curriculums, promise to challenge the ingenuity of both teachers and laymen to maintain secondary schools as educational agencies for all young people.

Quality

The demand for excellence in education at all levels increases as citizens recognize that the trained mind is today our most dependable source of national defense. In a highly industrialized world, it is recognized, too, that education is essential to our advancement economically. Many find the goal of excellence conflicts with universality. However, in a democratic society one should not be sacrificed to the other; both must be attained if free government and private enterprise are to be preserved.

The achievement of excellence demands quality programs of education. Provision must be made for academically talented students to advance in both depth and breadth of their preparation, as rapidly as possible. Such students must not only be provided the proper courses, they should be given the incentive of maximum achievement goals, as contrasted with the attainments that classmates of average ability may be able to achieve. The gifted, contrary to educational folklore that assumed they could shift for themselves, are the best investments in instructional time and skill. They can carry on many learning tasks independently, to be sure, but the maximum development of their mental powers requires intensive instruction by highly competent teachers who themselves are keen intellectually and are sound and creative scholars in their fields of specialization.

But, quality programs of education must also be attuned to the educational requirements of the average and the below-average student. The demands of the time are for better-prepared personnel in all fields as well as for citizens with adequate preparation to share in self-government and the responsibilities of life. The test of excellence, most people agree, must be met by educational service to all students, with the extent to which each realizes his maximum intellectual potentialities being the paramount criterion by which the worth of a school is judged.

The goal of greater quality in secondary schools can be expected to dictate changed priorities in program emphases as well as in pupil activities. It is possible that it may force schools to restrict their efforts to encompass only those educational functions and services that are uniquely appropriate to their resources and basic objectives. In any case, as secondary schools reach for even greater quality, significant changes are due to take place in the traditional high schools as viewed by most teachers and parents.

Efficiency

Public education has never faced the criterion of efficiency as squarely as have private business and industrial organizations. Such an assertion should not be taken to imply that schools have irresponsibly wasted public funds. This is not the case. It suggests, rather, that schools have not been as sensitive as will be necessary in the future to the achievement of maximum efficiency. Greater attention will have to be given to such matters as the utilization of teaching talents, the promotion of maximum learning by pupils in minimum time, and the design as well as use of buildings and facilities. In the future schools will have to *teach more of the essential skills and content, in less time, yet with greater permanence and usefulness.*

The goal of efficiency is related to the costs of education. The expanding expense of schools, along with financial burdens on taxpayers for other aspects of living and government, place a special obligation on those in charge of school programs to give strict attention to the costs of education. Such an objective, in and of itself, compels the testing of ways in which efficiency can be increased by the utilization of such developments as educational television, self-teaching devices, and the potentialities of other types of audio-visual aids to improve instruction.

The test of efficiency depends on the cost of imparting given amounts of learning; it cannot be measured solely by comparisons with previous tax rates or size of school budgets. Some educational procedures, such as the use of closed-circuit television, are initially more expensive, but they may actually produce greater quantities of learning at less per unit costs. They may also make possible higher salaries for outstanding teachers, an accomplishment that would be, itself, an efficiency gain.

Coordinating Competing Forces

The three goals of universality, quality, and efficiency, it will be recognized, incorporate objectives that represent, to a degree, opposing forces. Universality, in the minds of many, is counteracted by an emphasis on excellence. Both these goals, if taken together, may reduce efficiency; while the latter, if stressed apart from the first two, may distort their attainment. To assume that any one of the three may be discarded in favor of the other two, however, is to ignore the total mission of secondary education in the United States.

The obligation of those responsible for secondary education in the future is to find suitable ways to coordinate the competing goals of universality, quality, and efficiency. As this task is pursued, the public must be helped to understand the importance of each of the basic objectives that our way of life and new international relationships, as well as scientific and technological developments, are setting for schools. The controversies that develop from community to community and enlist nation-wide interest must be viewed with maturity and objectivity in terms of what high schools ought to accomplish in the years ahead, not with what they have accomplished in the past.

Secondary schools in the United States are a unique social and political, as well as educational, venture. That they should be the center of controversy about education in general is due to a growing awareness by citizens that secondary education has assumed a crucial position of responsibility in our educational system. Of necessity, they must fulfill the tripart mandate, the attainment of universality, quality, and efficiency, if individual freedom and happiness and national security and well-being are to be preserved.

SELECTED REFERENCES

BABIAN, HAIG, ed. *The American Economy: An Appraisal of Its Social Goals and the Impact of Science and Technology.* New York: Joint Council on Economic Education, 1958.

CONANT, JAMES B. *The American High School Today.* New York: McGraw-Hill, 1959.

GIDEONSE, HARRY D. *On the Educational Statesmanship of a Free Society.* New York: Woodrow Wilson Foundation, January 1959.

HOLTON, GORDON, ed. "Education in the Age of Science." *Daedalus,* Winter 1959.

JOSEPHS, DEVEREUX C., AND OTHERS. *The Pursuit of Excellence: Education and the Future of America,* Garden City, N.Y.: Doubleday, 1958.

STRAUSS, LEWIS L., AND HYMAN G. RICKOVER. *Freedom's Need for the Trained Man,* West Orange, N.J.: Thomas Alva Edison Foundation, 1955.

THAYER, V. T. *The Role of the School in American Society.* New York: Dodd, Mead, 1960.

The one-room school serves a population area characterized by sparsely settled rural regions, slow growth, and low mobility.

Densely populated suburban areas require new schools, more teachers, and curricular adaptations—continuous adjustments to expanding and mobile school enrollments.

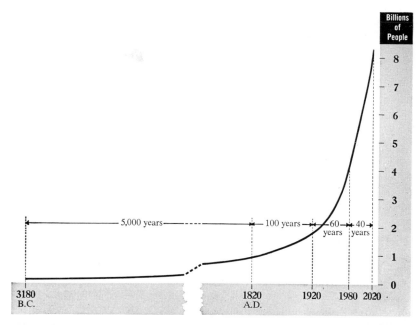

Fig. 2–1. *Projected Increase in World's Population Based on Present Pattern of Growth*

Of course, that day will never come. The problem will be solved before that. The question is, will it be solved by man or will it be solved by itself, that is, by war, pestilence, and famine? A solution by man will require his best effort in all the fundamental fields of human endeavor—morality, productivity, and knowledge. A problem so huge touches all fields.

To education it presents a challenge: as the number of young people increases, the job of education grows. But the challenge is far more than one of providing for a growing quantity. Population growth creates problems which only a trained population can solve and that training must be done well and thoroughly.

It is against this world-wide background that we can view the United States and its growing numbers of citizens and, more to the point, the nature of secondary education in relation to population.

EXPANDING POPULATION OF THE UNITED STATES

The history of the United States has been a story of people in migration. Early settlers fled the crowded countries and oppressive govern-

CHAPTER 2

Population, Mobility, and Enrollments

THERE is no doubt that the world faces a population crisis. Even in the United States, a land long noted for its "wide open spaces," one hears more and more complaint about overcrowding. Conditions, however, are mild here compared to some areas where population growth can only be termed catastrophic. Starvation, political unrest, social turmoil, disease, and oppression are the consequences.

It was not until 1820 that the world's population reached one billion (see Figure 2-1). In 1920 it was two billion; by 1980, at present growth rates, it will be four billion. It is not only that the population is increasing, but the rate of growth is also rising. The world-wide annual rate from 1650 to 1750 was 0.3 per cent. This rose to 0.5 per cent during the period 1750-1850 and to 0.8 per cent for 1850-1950. During the 1950's the rate was 1.7 per cent.[1]

Anyone adept with the slide rule can project today's growth figures to a point in the not too distant future when there will literally be no more room on the earth's land areas for a man to stand.

[1] Population Reference Bureau, "Population Inflation Shrinks the Earth," *Population Bulletin*, June 1958.

ments of Europe in search of freedom, opportunity, and space. In a new land with an abundance of virgin resources, additional immigrants were welcome—and often recruited. In a growing country, expanding westward, as space, adventure, and material wealth were sought, almost ideal conditions prevailed for rapid population increases.

Absorption of the Frontier

Thomas R. Malthus described the United States, at a time when the numbers of people were small, as an outstanding example of population growth under optimum conditions. It took about a century for the early colonists to extend their sparse settlements a distance of one hundred miles inland from the Atlantic coast line. Once this base was established, immigration, large families, and westward movement changed the face of the continent at an increasing tempo.

The first census of the United States, in 1790, showed slightly under four million inhabitants; this was fewer than half the number who came as immigrants in the single decade 1900-1910 when the peak of new arrivals was reached. Each decennial census until the war

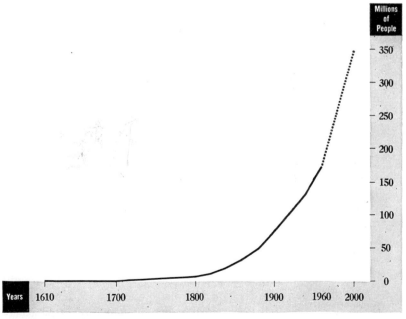

Fig. 2–2. *Population Increase in the United States Projected on Present Pattern (not a prediction)*

decade, 1860-1870, showed an increase exceeding 30 per cent. Not until the decade of World War I did the percentage of increase drop below 20 per cent. The census of 1920 was the first one to show a reduction in percentage increase over a previous census; yet its gain was nearly 15 per cent, and the added numbers of people were almost fourteen millions. In 1930 a new record growth in total numbers was reported, seventeen million, the percentage of increase being 16 plus. Figure 2-2 shows the pattern of population of the United States projected on the basis of present rates to 2000 A.D.

During much of the nation's history the frontier was advancing so rapidly that even the tremendous population expansion had little effect on density of settlement. In 1850 the number of people per square mile had not doubled over the first census, although the country's population was nearly six times as great. Since that time, the growth in density has kept pace approximately with the growth in numbers, with the national frontier being dropped from Bureau of the Census reports in 1890.

There have been times in the nation's history when war or transitory economic conditions have temporarily slowed immigration and native increase. Two new influences affected population trends dramatically in the twenties and thirties. The first of these was the introduction of tightly restrictive immigration quotas, beginning in 1921 and becoming increasingly effective as the years went by. During the 1930's the number of immigrants was only a trickle by earlier standards. Special quotas for displaced persons, established after World War II, had little effect on the national population—whatever their temporary impact may have been on communities where new arrivals concentrated.

The second major influence on population was the depression, beginning with the market crash of 1929. Far-reaching economic adjustments had an immediate effect upon the number of marriages and, consequently, on the number of births. Not until 1941 did the birth rate return to predepression levels.

Prediction of "Leveling-Off"

The limitation of immigration following World War I, the apparently well-established downward trend in births influenced substantially by economic conditions, and theories about population growth painstakingly derived from data from the United States and other countries with high levels of education, industrialization, and urbanization—all led demographers to predict a stabilized population as an immediate prospect. The Bureau of the Census as well as independent analysts looked upon the 1940 census as marking a major turning point toward population stability which they believed had gradually but consistently been developing during previous decades. It was freely predicted, for example, that the number of persons in the nation might never exceed 175 million, or even 150 million, with a decline in numbers by no means unlikely.

It seems unbelievable now, in a period when population increases are swelling school enrollments and taxing economic resources, that throughout the postdepression decade careful sifting of the evidence led to the conclusion that population growth in the advanced countries of the world was nearing or had reached an end. The conspicuous increase in births already recorded was viewed only as a temporary response to war conditions and economic recovery.

Such forecasts naturally affected school planning. During the two decades that these interpretations were being placed on population trends, school budgets were drastically reduced, first by the economic depression and then by wartime emergency measures; later, they were in effect cut further as the postwar inflation reduced the value of the dollar. In the face of long-range predictions that the population spurt would level off and enrollments would become stabilized, few school boards had sufficient confidence to project major expansions. Even in those communities where obsolescent physical plant, expanding school population, or bold leadership forced careful local appraisal of enrollment trends, the wealth of warning data from population experts had the effect of forcing conclusions that were too cautious and conservative.

Present Mushrooming Growth

As more reliable knowledge of upward population trends accumulated, predictions of future patterns were revised. Statistics revealed, for example, that the decade 1950-1960 produced the largest percentage of increase in rate of growth (17 per cent) experienced since the 1900-1910 decade when the recorded high was a consequence of the immigration of over eight million people. This new rate, which represented by far the largest increase in total numbers ever achieved in a single ten-year period in the United States, suggested that the pattern of population increases resulting from births is different from that caused by migration. "In prosperity, what follows a wave of births is a larger wave of births, and then a still larger one, indefinitely."[2]

Reappraisal of older theory has led to a new theory—the annual rate of increase in the United States may well equal or exceed 1.5 per cent in the foreseeable future.

Studies of the composition of the growing population have revealed, also, a significant change in the sizes of families. Differences based on such factors as urban or rural residence, high and low income, educational level, or religious affiliation are beginning to narrow.[3] This new tendency reflects the willingness of parents who are able to offer great advantages to their children because of high educational and economic levels to welcome family responsibilities.

The new trends also promise eventually to erase the imbalance in the age composition of the population, which is currently producing a manpower shortage. Births in the United States remained fairly constant at around two and one-half million per year from 1931 to 1940. This figure was over a quarter-million lower than the number achieved and maintained from 1910 to 1930. In 1940 the trend reversed. The number of births reached well over three million a year by 1943, three and one-half million by 1947, and over four million by 1954. This increase, taken together with the low rates of the 1930's and scientific discoveries that are extending the life expectancy of adults, has produced a bimodal distribution of the population. As shown in Figure 2-3, the population is concentrated in two age groups: older adults, many of whom are moving into their less productive years or into retirement; and children and youth of school age. The 1960 population aged 20-35 was actually less than the population in that age group in 1950. This imbalance in population will, until the new pattern of births can produce its own group of adults, produce manpower shortages in all critical fields. The schools, along with industry, business, and other agencies, are faced with shortages of teachers at a time when enrollments are growing in unprecedented numbers.

[2] John Rader Platt, "The Delicate Question of Population," *New Republic,* September 2, 1957.

[3] Ronald F. Freedman, Pascal K. Whelpton, and Arthur A. Campbell, "Family Planning in the U.S.," *Scientific American,* April 1959, pp. 50-55.

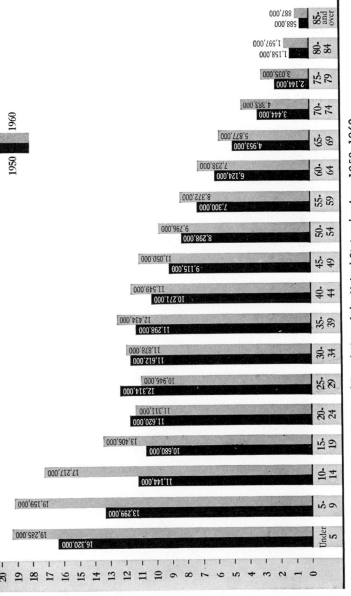

Fig. 2–3. *Total Population of the United States, by Age, 1950–1960*

Secondary schools are just beginning to feel the upward swing in population that began gradually in 1940 but took its first big jump upward in 1946, when the number of births per year increased from 2,360,000 to 3,289,000. Children born that year entered the seventh grade in 1958, thereby ending the long enrollment lag that high schools had experienced since about 1940. As the birth rate continues to increase, the upward swing in secondary enrollments also continues without any leveling-off yet in sight. By 1965, the new wave of population will reach the colleges, but not before 1969 can it be expected to produce any noticeable increase in teachers to help with the increase in enrollments in secondary schools that will already exist. Such considerations force efforts to find new ways to staff schools without sacrificing quality. They suggest that ways must be found to extend the contributions of outstanding teachers by reorganizing the pattern of instruction in high schools.

The dramatic increases in high school enrollments are shown in Figure 2-4. Not reflected in this portrayal are the significant increases

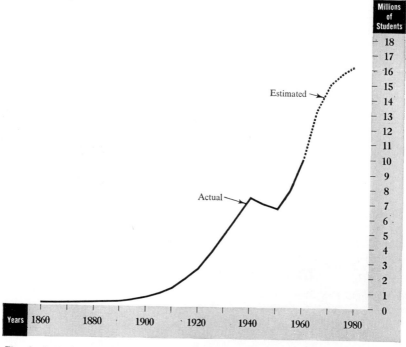

Fig. 2—4. *High School Enrollment, 1860–1960, with Projected Enrollment to 1980*

in the proportion of adults gainfully employed, a factor that has considerable bearing upon the ability of the adult population to support the expansion of school services.

MOBILITY AND HIGH SCHOOL ENROLLMENTS

Mobility is a characteristic of the people of the United States. They move from one section of a city to another, from farm to town, and from state to state. The impact of this mobility upon school programs, particularly at the secondary school level, as well as on the educational development of individual students, is frequently drastic.

Mobility—An American Characteristic

The settling of the frontier brought about a westward movement of families, many of whom had already come as immigrants from other lands. This westward movement shifted the center of population from Baltimore, Maryland, in 1790 to Centralia, Illinois, in 1960.

Closing of the frontier by no means arrested the migration of Americans. Opportunity continued to draw people to particular regions of the nation. The major direction of movement continued to be westward. During the 1950's the West, as a region, showed a gain of more than 32 per cent, nearly double the national gain of 17 per cent. The smallest regional gain was in the Northeastern states. The South was characterized by contrasting population changes, with Florida growing by more than 70 per cent and Arkansas losing nearly 9 per cent.

The forces producing mobility of population on a regional basis have exerted even more significant influences on smaller areas. Perhaps the most important of these has been the general shift from rural to urban, brought on by the simultaneous mechanization of agriculture and growth of large-scale manufacturing. The process of urbanization, which started in the nineteenth century, has accelerated in recent years.

A second migrational trend now developing is what one economist has called a "search for the sun."[4] It is reflected in the recent influx into Florida and the Southwest. The third main stream of movement has taken place within the urban structure itself as families have forsaken cities for the suburbs.

In some instances, these forces have affected the population struc-

---

[4] Charles L. Leven, "Population Migration and Regional Economic Development," *Current Economic Comment*, November 1959, pp. 31-42.

ture in ways other than the change in numbers. For example, the shifts have left large proportions of older people in rural areas, while children and youth have been concentrated in cities and suburban communities.

The Impact of Mobility

The force of population movement has been reflected most vividly in suburban developments that have utilized the techniques of mass production to provide, in short periods of time, living accommodations for families. Cities such as Levittown, New York, Park Forest, Illinois, and Port Charlotte, Florida, have grown up almost overnight.

In addition to the changes taking place in regions experiencing rapid growth, some communities whose rates of growth are average or less than average are experiencing changes in population composition as established residents move away to be replaced by new arrivals of different backgrounds. School districts, in general, are confronted with constantly changing populations. Each year, large numbers of students are forced to adjust to new schools, new communities, and new geographic regions. Schools must not only assimilate these newcomers into existing educational programs. Often, procedures and standards have to be adjusted to accomodate pupils whose backgrounds are different from those of the existing population. Mobility also imposes on school officials and teachers the burden of interpreting educational goals to incoming parents and taxpayers.

The problems involved in coping with changing populations range from those confronted by New York City, where the yearly immigration includes 30,000 Puerto Ricans and 10,000 Negroes—both groups coming from widely different cultural backgrounds—to Farmersville, California, which experiences an increase of more than 100 per cent in school population each year during the harvest season as the children of migrating workers enter school for short periods of time. Even secondary schools in relatively stable communities like Madison, Wisconsin, though their migratory problems are less extreme, often experience an annual change in pupil population of up to 20 per cent as part of a normal pattern of mobility among families.

ATTENDANCE AND RETENTION

The population spiral, mobility patterns, demands for higher levels of educational preparation for employment, and greatly expanded school offerings are combining to skyrocket enrollments in secondary schools in many communities. Two factors, the added numbers of youth going to high school and the increase in years of attendance per student, have combined to expand secondary education.

Multiplication of Secondary School Enrollments

As secondary education assumed the responsibility of providing for all young people, and of extending common schooling upward, it broadened its program to include courses designed for citizenship education as well as for vocational preparation. The amazing increase in productivity per worker has made it possible for young people not to have to go to work in their teens, thus freeing them for an education. At the same time the increased productivity per worker has required a greater skill and knowledge from that worker, making more education necessary.

The impact of this two-way relationship between productivity and education on school attendance and retention is by now well known. While the senior high school-age population (14-17 years) was increasing by 71.2 per cent from 1890 to 1956, enrollments in grades nine through twelve were multiplying almost 34 times.[5] This impressive record stands as an undisputed tribute to the commitment of Americans to universal secondary education as well as to the ingenuity of educational officials who provided buildings, teachers, and learning materials for enrollments that were doubling almost every decade from 1890 to 1940.

Retention of Youth in High School

Favorable parental attitudes toward schooling, compulsory attendance laws, industrial demands for better-trained personnel, campaigns to reduce dropouts, the appeal of extracurricular programs, and broadened offerings adapted to varying abilities and interests—all have combined to keep high school-age youth in school for more years, if not until graduation. Two means are employed to measure the holding power of secondary schools: the percentage of the total high school age group (years 14-17) enrolled in school, and the percentage of youth who enter and remain in school until graduation.

[5] U.S. Department of Health, Education and Welfare, "Statistics of State School Systems: 1955-56," *Biennial Survey of Education in the United States— 1954-56,* Washington, D.C., pp. 10-11.

In terms of the first measure of retention, only about 11 per cent of the young people of high school age were reported to have been attending school in 1900; by 1956, the proportion had risen to 84.2 per cent.[6] The increase in retention according to the second measure has been equally impressive. On the average, 67.3 per cent of the pupils who entered the ninth grade in 1952-53 continued in high school to graduation in 1956.[7] The retention to graduation ratios ranged from a high of 93.1 per cent in Wisconsin to a low of 43.4 per cent in Mississippi.[8] The rate of retention to graduation has grown steadily. During the 1940's, for example, when high school enrollments dropped nearly 700,000 pupils, the number of graduates held constant with previous high-enrollment years because the proportion of those remaining in school to graduation increased from 49.5 per cent in 1932 to 61.6 per cent in 1948. Only in 1944, due to war conditions as well as dropping enrollments, did the rate fall.[9]

Implications of Population Changes and Mobility Patterns

The secondary schools of the United States must serve, now and in the coming years, ever larger numbers of students. But it should be realized that the proportions of the increases are by no means unprecedented. The history of the high school has been, above all else, a story of expansion to accommodate greater numbers and variations in individual differences.

The major impact of the changing composition of the student population has already been felt, but not yet completely absorbed. Schools and teachers have experienced nearly the full range of capacities and problems that the high school-age population will present, although the full range has not been retained in most schools through graduation. The schools face a strong challenge in adjusting programs and methods to the necessity of retaining nearly all youth to age 16 or 17 or beyond, while at the same time the total numbers in the high school age group are increasing rapidly. This task must be accomplished while continuing to improve the quality of learning.

[6] Rose Marie Smith and W. Vance Grant (with Louis H. Conger, Jr.), *Statistical Summary of Education: 1955-56*, Washington, D.C. (U.S. Department of Health, Education and Welfare), 1959, p. 30.

[7] *Ibid.*, p. 31.

[8] National Education Association, *Rankings of the States*, Washington, D.C. (Research Division, NEA), April 1959, p. 16.

[9] Smith and Grant, *op. cit.*, p. 31.

SELECTED REFERENCES

BOGUE, DONALD J. *The Population of the United States.* Glencoe, Ill., The Free Press, 1959.

DEEVEY, EDWARD S., JR. "The Human Population." *Scientific American,* September 1960.

FREEDMAN, RONALD F., PASCAL K. WHELPTON, AND ARTHUR A. CAMPBELL. "Family Planning in the U.S." *Scientific American,* April 1959.

HAUSER, PHILIP M. "The Census of 1960." *Scientific American,* July 1961.

MALTHUS, THOMAS R. *An Essay on Population.* Vol. I, London: J. M. Dent and Sons, 1914.

"Population Inflation Shrinks the Earth." *Population Bulletin,* June 1958.

SAX, KARL. *The Population Explosion.* Foreign Policy Association Headline Series, No. 120, November-December 1956.

Statistical Abstract of the United States: 1957. Washington, D.C.: U.S. Bureau of the Census, 1957.

"The Speed-Up in Population Growth." *Population Bulletin,* June 1952.

TURNER, FREDERICK J. *The Frontier in American History.* New York: Henry Holt, 1920.

United Nations. *The Future Growth of World Population.* New York: U.N. Department of Economic and Social Affairs, 1958.

Opportunity to learn has been a recognized
human right since colonial times. Shown is the
original schoolhouse, built in 1763 and recon-
structed in 1938, of the first boarding school in
America, South Byfield, Massachusetts.

CHAPTER 3

Public Education in the United States—A Survey

TO UNDERSTAND the character of secondary education in the United States, it is necessary to study it in its social setting—as a phase of public education in a democratic nation. The long struggle for financial support and certain continuing controversies, concerning education generally as well as the secondary schools, are other factors that must be considered. Finally, the unique venture of secondary education—its search for purpose and direction as well as its present level of maturity as an educational institution—helps complete the image of the character of secondary schools.

PUBLIC EDUCATION—FOR THE COMMON GOOD

From its inception, organized education in the United States has served to strengthen our way of life. Public concern and support have centered on the school's ability to prepare citizens for civic, economic, and moral responsibilities. Deeply imbedded in American thought is the belief that the common good is best served when each individual has the opportunity to realize fully his potentialities within a social system dedicated to the preservation and extension of human freedom.

A New Nation: Nurtured by Education

The leaders who guided the Revolution and established the Con-stitution were deeply interested in public education. George Wash-ington said, "Knowledge is in every country the surest basis of public happiness. . . . The time is therefore come, when a plan of universal education ought to be adopted in the United States—exigencies of public and private life demand it." John Adams wrote, "Education is more indispensable, and must be more general under a free govern-ment than any other—in a free government knowledge must be gen-eral, and ought to be universal." James Madison made this often quoted statement, "A popular government, without popular informa-tion or the means of acquiring it, is but a prologue to a farce or a tragedy; or, perhaps both."[1] This remarkable group of men—and few, if any, other periods of history have been blessed with such able stu-dents of politics—turned unanimously to public education as the means of maintaining popular government.

Despite the efforts of national leaders, there was no great public response to the early calls for universal education. Even when public education became widely accepted, in the generation following the Revolution, elementary schooling was believed to be sufficient for the common welfare. The later extension of free education into the sec-ondary school grades and the inclusion of large proportions of youth were delayed by social forces and conflict over support and by general failure to endorse the need for universal secondary education.

State Responsibility—Intention or Oversight

Legal responsibility for the establishment and operation of public schools rests with individual states. Whether the lodging of control of education with the state instead of with the federal government was done intentionally or merely through oversight by the framers of the Constitution of the United States is not clear. No mention of education is made in this historic document. Only through the disclaimer pro-visions of the Tenth Amendment, which assigns to the states all powers not specifically delegated to the federal government, is responsibility for providing and supervising schools assigned to state jurisdiction. On this subject Edwards and Richey have observed:

[1] These and other quotations may be found in numerous sources; however, they all appear in the John Dewey Society First Yearbook, *The Teacher and Society,* William Kilpatrick (ed.), New York (Appleton-Century), 1937, pp. 6-9.

The failure of the Constitution to mention education in express terms probably does not reflect the intention of the founding fathers to make public education a function of the state governments; it probably reflects the widespread sentiment of the time that education was a private, religious, or philanthropic function. Moreover the authority conferred upon Congress to promote the general welfare may have appeared to many to be entirely adequate, as was actually the case, to enable the national government to support a program of education.[2]

Despite these doubts about its origin, the right of each state to control education stands today as an unassailable legal principle.

It is clear that education in the early stages of the nation was viewed as a personal matter. State governments actually left education largely in the hands of local communities. Of sixteen states in existence by 1800, the constitutions of nine failed to mention education. Those of Massachusetts, Vermont, and New Hampshire contained provisions charging the legislature to encourage education, public and private, while giving the legislature powers to grant "rewards and immunities" to this end. Education during this early period apparently was left largely in the hands of parents who relied heavily upon the church or other locally initiated arrangements to provide schooling for children.

Local Control

With state governments unconcerned about developing a system of education, and with education looked upon as a special privilege to be provided by parents out of their own personal resources or by the church for children from poor homes, local control of schools evolved out of practice. The doctrine of local autonomy and responsibility was, therefore, born more out of accident than created by intent. Over the years, however, it has been firmly welded, by the social conditions and political movements of the Western frontier, into an established educational philosophy.

From our viewpoint the early schools were humble and seemingly poor in quality. Each church, private corporation, and, in some cases, community which built and maintained a school did so in an isolated manner. There were no general standards, no state-wide systems. But in terms of the times each of these crude starts was a revolutionary act. Behind them lay the Middle Ages and its pandemic illiteracy, the class division and autocratic despotism of Europe, the generations that had

[2] Newton Edwards and Herman Richey, *The School in the American Social Order*, Boston (Houghton Mifflin), 1947, p. 240.

resigned themselves to poverty and ignorance. Just learning to read, write, and figure was an enormous accomplishment. These are the minimum skills of citizenship, and these our early schools sought to provide. True, there were no common standards, and curriculums were haphazard, but a beginning was made because the people wanted education.

At the end of World War II there were over 100,000 separate school districts operating either elementary or secondary schools, or both.[3] By 1960 this number had been cut in half by concentrated state programs of consolidation and reorganization.

In its early stages the school district was the central power in public education. States had not yet assumed control of schools. As the welfare of states and the nation indicated a need for a centralized organization for educational programs, local control was often so firmly entrenched that progress in promoting state responsibility was inhibited. Although technically a state legislature could establish state control, leadership, and support by simply passing laws, such action required the endorsement of the electorate—in this case, of people whose loyalties were with the local school district. Consequently, what appeared to be a simple problem of natural growth actually became very difficult to solve. Advocates of local control, employing the old Jeffersonian adage, argued that the best government governed least. They claimed, therefore, that it was dangerous to permit educational policy to fall into the hands of the central state government.

Local-State Partnership

Opposition to the district control of education developed during the first half of the nineteenth century. Educational statesmen such as Horace Mann, Henry Barnard, Caleb Mills, Calvin Wiley, and others, fought for general supervision of schools by the state. These educators and politicians waged a continuous battle for such goals as free textbooks, a reasonable length of school year, teacher certification standards, minimum required courses, and a reasonable local tax effort. In the 1820's the New England states (with the exception of Rhode Island), along with New York, formulated a concept of public education for elementary schools. Throughout New England, state laws were passed prescribing that school buildings should be

[3] Rose Marie Smith and W. Vance Grant (with Louis H. Conger, Jr.), *Statistical Summary of Education: 1955-56*, Washington, D.C. (U.S. Department of Health, Education and Welfare), 1959, p. 23.

provided, specifying the subjects to be taught, setting standards of qualification for teaching positions, providing funds for local communities, permitting school districts to levy "rate bills," and establishing the length of the elementary school term. Such laws provided the beginning of state systems of education and reflected the partnership that was ultimately to flourish between local communities and the state. They also established a precedent for the later development of public secondary education.

Problems of local-state relationships in education still exist today. Fortunately, educators now speak of the local-state *partnership* rather than the local community *versus* the state in providing education. By and large, states are assuming more responsibility for the general supervision and the financing of schools. Nevertheless, the amounts of control and support that should be left to the local district are still subjects of heated debate in most states.

The principal advantages of a large degree of local autonomy are that it facilitates adaptations to local conditions, fosters wide community participation in educational affairs, and allows experimentation and innovation at the local level. Some important arguments against local control are that inequalities between districts are perpetuated; that education should not remain oriented primarily to the local community, or even to the state in a period of national crisis; and that efficient operation requires more standardization than is now possible.

Federal Participation in Public Education

Although the federal government has no direct legal control over public education, its machinery and resources have been used to aid schools in numerous ways. Before the ratification of the Constitution, generous grants of public lands were made to aid schools. In a later period, under Jefferson's presidency, an accumulated surplus of the Treasury was distributed to the states to be used to support education. Eventually, almost every branch of the federal government has participated in one educational program or another that today affects directly almost every local school district. There is no single source of information about these programs, nor does any central agency coordinate or control them. Some programs are as small as the one that provides payment of tuition to a few local districts by the Bureau of Indian Affairs, under a plan by which Indian youth on reservations receive their education at nearby public schools. Others are as large as the school lunch program administered by the Department of Agriculture in which surplus foods and some money are distributed to all but a few local school districts. This program alone cost more than $227 million in 1959-60.

The 1954-56 Biennial Survey of Education in the United States, published in 1959, revealed that the amount of federal support for elementary and secondary education increased from more than $161 million in 1949-50 to more than $574 million in 1955-56.[4] Federal participation in the support of education has increased substantially since that time with the passage of the National Defense Education Act of 1958 which provided more than a billion dollars to be spent over a four-year period to strengthen programs in certain areas judged critical to the national security.

Support is growing for the federal government's assuming a greater responsibility for education, as a partner with states and local districts.[5]

STRUGGLE FOR FINANCIAL SUPPORT

The quest for adequate means of financing public education has been a long and bitter one; many aspects of the problem do not yet offer hope of easy solutions. The ideal of free public secondary education did not become a firmly established principle of public policy until after 1874. In that year the well-known Kalamazoo case established the legality of the use of public funds (raised by general taxation) to provide education beyond the elementary grades. Before this legal decision secondary education was not viewed as being an institution of public responsibility for which public funds could be expended, and many ridiculously feeble provisions were made for financing education.

Early Reliance upon Permanent Funds

Legislatures, which were unable to pass general taxes for educational purposes, were able to use indirect taxes and sales of public lands to establish permanent school funds. The income from such sources appeared, for a time, to offer adequate support. Twenty-two of the twenty-six states in the Union in 1825 provided such funds. The distribution of the federal surplus moneys and the extensive sale of

4 *Ibid.*, p. 20.
5 A majority of participants in the White House Conference, in 1956, which was concerned with problems of elementary and secondary schools, favored this position. Included were key leaders from all walks of life as well as professional educators.

public lands lent confidence to the view that these funds might provide a solution to the problem of state school finance. However, income from these sources soon proved insufficient to meet increasing needs and mounting costs. In the end, such funds only served to retard the use of general taxes, even to the extent of causing local districts to cancel taxes that had been levied for public education.

Rate Bills and Permissive Legislation

The rate bill was a tuition charge levied upon the parent and based upon the number of children sent to school. Intense political fights resulted from controversy over the rate bill, although many educational leaders at the time felt that it was the only means of obtaining financial support. Cities generally sought the elimination of the rate bill in favor of direct state taxation, but legislatures, dominated by representatives from rural areas, repeatedly refused to enact tax laws, even when referendums were passed with large majorities. The legislative procedure followed by many states in order to bypass public demands for state-wide taxation for educational purposes was the enactment of permissive legislation. Such acts ranged from laws permitting counties or districts to levy property taxes to laws allowing the taxation of property upon written consent of the owner. Rate bills were being abolished by the time of the 1874 Kalamazoo decision and states were acting to provide more dependable systems of support.

Local-State Partnership in School Finance

The fact that legislatures began to recognize the responsibility of the state to provide programs of free public education far from ended the struggle for adequate or equitable financing of education. Early state-supported plans relied solely upon the use of the flat grant and matching funds. The flat grant provides for the states to pay a fixed amount for each pupil in attendance (usually computed upon the basis of average daily attendance); the matching fund involves matching amounts raised at local levels with state funds, on a ratio basis. The flat grant is used to provide an equal amount of money to every district in terms of the number of pupils served, while the matching funds represent a type of reward for local effort. Matching funds are used to stimulate school districts to provide certain programs or services; wealthy districts have always been able to profit most from such plans. Flat grants have tended to equal only a small fraction of the cost of education; consequently, they serve little more purpose than to remind the local districts that such funds exist. In each case, inequalities are maintained and amplified; the total amounts of such funds have been inadequate.

The foundation principle has proved to be a reasonably satisfactory means of equalizing educational opportunity without sacrificing local effort. It provides for a state subsidy to raise equated contributions of local districts to an established level of support. First, a unit of cost per pupil which the state can afford and which finances a minimum educational program is established. Next, a reasonable level of local tax effort is set; this is called the qualifying rate. Under this plan, if the amount of taxes yielded per pupil, based upon the qualifying rate, falls below the foundation figure, the state supplies the amount necessary to equal the foundation figure. For example, in Illinois, the 1960 foundation level was $252 per pupil; the qualifying rate for a unit district was $.067 per dollar of assessed valuation. If a local district taxed itself at this rate, and if this rate yielded only $200 per pupil, the difference, $52.00, was paid to the local district by the state. The state thus guaranteed an educational program up to the foundation level.

Under the foundation plan, the local district may tax itself beyond the qualifying rate without loss of the equalization funds. The foundation is treated as a floor, not a ceiling, to financial arrangements. Local effort can raise funds beyond the foundation level, and state funds, apart from equalization funds, may be provided for special programs and services.

Although the foundation principle is considered a sound one, it does not in itself solve all fiscal problems. In some cases the foundation figure may be set too low, or it may become inadequate because of economic changes. The tax base for the foundation program is the property tax. The problem of obtaining satisfactory and equitable assessment of real property throughout a state has not been solved, and in many states the property tax is inadequate to produce sufficient revenue. In some states, local districts are left to their own devices to provide programs and facilities not covered by foundation funds. In general, states that have sound financial systems provide a balanced combination of funds and have a periodic appraisal of their plans. A sound program of state finance must equalize educational support at a reasonably high level, require local effort which does not overburden the poorest local district, and provide separate funds to maintain special services and encourage desirable new programs.

Despite the slow progress that has been made and the difficulties inherent in developing a sound and equitable plan for state participation in the support of local schools, the amount of state aid has increased substantially during the past half century. In 1959–60, for example, of all the revenues collected for school purposes, 56.4 per cent came from local sources while 40 per cent came from the state; the remaining 3.6 per cent was contributed by the federal government. The ratio between local, state, and federal participation in the support of schools, when considered for the nation as a whole, remained fairly constant during the 1950's.[6]

Hidden Costs—A Barrier to Free Education

The struggle for free public education, although well accepted in principle, has yet to be completely accomplished in fact. Since World War II many investigations have been concerned with the problems of high school "dropouts." These were made to test the generally held belief that boys and girls withdraw from school largely because they cannot profit from the program offered and, consequently, are "better off" in some gainful employment. The results of these studies show that many who leave school early have sufficient academic ability to be successful, and often are, in fact, experiencing no scholastic difficulties at the time of withdrawal. Furthermore, the youth who drop out of school are not "better off." Jobs are not open to them, and the enforced leisure they encounter often leads to antisocial actions. Such evidence has led researchers to look for other reasons why boys and girls leave school. Among those identified, inability to meet the financial cost of secondary education proved to be a major one.

In spite of the proud boast that public education in the United States is free, hidden costs in books, supplies, fees, and special equipment such as band instruments and physical education uniforms, as well as the expenses of clothing and extracurricular activities, make high school attendance prohibitive for some students. The cost of attending school varies, depending upon the individual and the community, but studies conducted in the early 1950's placed the hidden costs of secondary education as high as $450 per pupil, per year.[7]

[6] National Education Association, *Estimates of School Statistics, 1959-60,* Washington, D.C. (Research Division, NEA), December 1959, p. 14.

[7] Harold C. Hand has conducted some of the pioneering work in the study of hidden costs. A summary of the research and a discussion of its implications appear in his book *Principles of Public Secondary Education,* New York (Harcourt, Brace & World, Inc.), 1958, pp. 79-113.

CONTINUING CONTROVERSIES

The character of education is shaped by a number of basic and continuing controversies that provoke heated debate and often divide support for public schools. Most of these issues have roots as deep historically as the concept of public education itself. Often they touch various facets of community life, as well as the program of education.

Separation of Church and State

Religion was a dominant concern in the lives of the early colonists. In most of the settlements, officials of the prevailing church possessed considerable civil authority. Education, in this period, was accepted generally as a function of the church. Even though secular interests became dominant in political affairs by the beginning of the eighteenth century, education remained within the province of the churches.

Close association of church and state in the New England colonies actually facilitated the assumption of control of education by the state and local governments. In Massachusetts particularly, the church and the political government were, in effect, identical throughout its colonial history. Here the state enacted laws and conducted civil affairs in the name of the established church. Education was an important feature of the Puritan religion; consequently, as early as 1642, the General Court of the Company of Massachusetts Bay enacted a law pertaining to the education of the children of the colony, "especially of their ability to read and understand the principles of religion and the capital laws of this country." Through the civil authorities, taxes were levied to provide this kind of education. As the influence of the church upon political matters declined, and as state and local governments assumed control of men's affairs generally, the schools and the traditional arrangements for their provision were transferred automatically into the hands of civil authorities.

The legal formulation of the principle of the separation of church and state is in the First Amendment of the federal Constitution. Subsequent court decisions have upheld its validity. As late as 1948, the Supreme Court of the United States, in ruling on the McCollum case stated, "The First Amendment has erected a wall between church and state. That wall must be kept high and impregnable. We could not approve the slightest breach." The denial of the use of the facilities and the machinery of public education to foster sectarian religious indoctrination is a clearly established legal principle.

Separation of church and state has not been completely adhered to with respect to financial aid to children in church schools. Textbooks, transportation, and lunches have been paid for with federal funds. Aid in the form of health services, in addition, has long been provided in the interests of public safety and welfare. Seventeen states have approved state-subsidized transportation for children in parochial schools. In most cases, these states have also provided support for the purchase and distribution of textbooks. Nonpublic schools may participate in the federal lunch program in all states. Arguments for such aid hold that it is given to benefit pupils, not the school. The counterposition is that aid to pupils is, in fact, assistance to the school. This aid represents costs which would have to be borne by the school, inasmuch as schools cannot exist without pupils. Such financial support, in effect, does aid the school. Nevertheless, strong support currently prevails for the extension of pupil welfare aid to church schools, and the opponents of aid fear that such grants may lead to general federal financial support for nonpublic schools.

Legal provisions, ranging from court decisions to legislative restrictions attached to budget bills, help to spell out the relationship of public education to other social institutions. Such provisions represent formal expressions of public policy. Philosophical and educational principles underlying such issues as the relationship of public education to religion, and to the federal, state, and local governments, help to influence both official policy and popular attitudes toward such problems as the separation of church and state.

The Issue of Federal Aid

Over the years, various proposals have been made to permit the distribution of federal funds to local schools for general educational uses. Although specific programs in such fields as vocational and agricultural training have long enjoyed grants at the national level, public endorsement for federal aid to general education has not been of sufficient force to win favorable congressional action. As yet, each effort to appropriate funds for such items as teachers' salaries and school construction has been beaten by controversy over the classic issues of federal control, aid to sectarian schools, racial integration, and states' rights.

The National Defense Education Act of 1958 has provided financial support to strengthen school programs in certain fields judged to be vital to national security. Over a billion dollars in federal funds were earmarked to be spent during a four-year period upon twelve different programs. The allotment of funds to states and localities was based upon the traditional relationships of the U.S. Office of Education with the state agencies and with colleges and universities. The programs for which funds could be used range from guidance and the improvement of instruction for the talented to improvements in the instructional programs of science, mathematics, and foreign languages and to the use of mass mediums in teaching. Commenting upon the National Defense Education Act of 1958, Lawrence Derthick, U.S. Commissioner of Education, said:

> The National Defense Education Act is regarded by many as the most comprehensive and important educational legislation ever passed by Congress. None of the Federal educational programs enacted through the years has held greater potential for the young people of our country than this Act.[8]

Racial Segregation

Developments in the Southern states following the freeing of the slaves resulted in a system of schools segregated on the basis of race. Readmission to the Union was achieved under the mandate that the states should develop and maintain public schools. For most of the seceded states, this stipulation brought about the development of state systems of schools which included public high schools; these had not previously existed in most of the states involved. Although the new state systems of education included many admirable features— the large county unit as a basis of organization, provision for substantial state aid, professional leadership, strong state departments of public instruction, and state courses of study and established standards—their dual schools for white and Negro children became a social, economic, and political burden that counteracted many of their other strengths.

The blight of segregation in schools has continued to undermine quality in education in the Southern states and in some communities in other parts of the nation where an influx of Negro children has led to forms of segregation. The depth of this challenge to public education is illustrated by the attempt by several Southern states to abandon their system of public schools rather than comply with the rulings of

[8] Lawrence G. Derthick in a report to the Forty-third Annual Convention of the National Association of Secondary School Principals. "The Proceedings," *The Bulletin,* April 1959, pp. 343-44.

the United States Supreme Court, in 1954, against compulsory school segregation.

Private versus Public Schools

Generalities about the relationship between private and public schools are, at best, difficult to make. While it is true that some private schools only pretend to uphold high standards and others maintain extreme positions on such matters as discipline and academic preparation, there are many excellent private schools. The roots from which they spring are various. Some parents require private schools for purely social reasons. Others have groundless fears about their public schools and, with some urban populations in extreme flux, some parents quite reasonably can question the public school's present ability to serve children whose educational levels differ widely. As a result private schools exist for those parents willing, in effect, to pay "double taxation" for their children's education. For more on the relationship between public and nonpublic schools and the potential conflict between the two see Chapter 20.

PUBLIC SECONDARY SCHOOLS—A UNIQUE EDUCATIONAL VENTURE

Although the antecedent of the high school of today was not to appear until 1821, forty years after the American Revolution, the plans and hopes for public education were spelled out in almost prophetic detail within the two or three years following independence. The Revolution marked the successful establishment of a new political system. As we have seen, the leaders of the time understood with remarkable clarity the function required of education in a democratic society. George Washington, Thomas Jefferson, Noah Webster, Samuel Knox, Robert Coran, Benjamin Rush, and others debated extensively all facets of public education. Their objective was to conceive of a system of schooling that would maintain the level of literacy and provide for the dissemination of information required for each citizen's participation in self-government.

In 1795, the American Philosophical Society offered a prize for "the best system of liberal education and literary instruction . . . a plan for instituting and conducting public schools in this country, on the principles of the most extensive utility."[9] This stimulus released a flood

[9] O. A. Hanson, *Liberalism and American Education in the 18th Century,* New York (Macmillan), 1926, pp. 23-24.

of widely circulated plans. Nearly all of the important proposals included a national system of public education from elementary school through college, universal and tax-supported. They provided for public education to teach citizenship, prepare youth for suitable vocations, instill democratic principles, ensure the general level of happiness and well-being, adapt science to the problems of daily life, and help men learn to live together cooperatively. Running through many of the plans was the thought that a scientific spirit, with full freedom of thought and debate, should permeate the educational system. Some plans suggested, also, that the same educational opportunities should be offered to both girls and boys. Of all the features of these proposals, perhaps the basic and most influential, in terms of its impact on all the others, was the notion that free public education should be extended to include secondary education and perhaps college. The idea that high schools should be free, open to all, and responsible for preparing young people for life and citizenship led later to the development of one of the most unique educational ventures the world has known—public secondary education.

Born in Protest of the Common People

The high school, like the academy before it, came into being as a protest against unsatisfactory existing secondary schools. Benjamin Franklin's dream that the academy he founded in Philadelphia, in 1751, would be a school of the people, open to girls as well as boys, and concerned with preparing for "the important business of living" as well as for college, had begun to fade by the turn of the century. Before his death, Franklin himself criticized his creation for giving too much status to the classical and college-preparatory aspects of its program and for slighting citizenship and work preparation.

Against the background of secondary schools that catered to those who could afford the tuition and were preparing for college and the professions, the public high school was born to serve the educational needs of the common people. This development testifies both to the rigidity of the established schools and to the determination of parents to develop a truly public high school—one that would provide for the educational needs of all youth within a single program.

That the high school came in protest against an educational aristocracy, to serve the children of all the people, particularly the common people, is one key to the competition that has prevailed down through the years between independent and public schools. In the early

days, only children of the poor attended public schools, which were
called pauper schools in some states. Colgate W. Darden, Jr., former
Governor of the State of Virginia, who also served with distinction as
President of the University of Virginia and who was a staunch friend
of public education, delights in recalling how, as a boy, he and others
who attended public schools were taunted as "free cats" by students in
the private academy. Such distinctions still exist today, more so in
Eastern seaboard states than in the Midwest and West where the
growth of public high schools paralleled the westward movement of
people.

Intellectual Development—With Social Responsibility

Prior to Franklin's academy there existed the Latin grammar school
(the first was founded in Boston in 1635), which was strictly an
intellectual institution, dedicated to preparing young men, who aspired
to professional careers and cultural sophistication, for college. Although
the academy attempted to provide a dual program that incorporated
an emphasis on citizenship education, its dependence upon tuition
income, combined with the force of tradition, soon turned it into an
extended image of the Latin grammar school.

With the establishment of public high schools, the dual objectives—
intellectual development and social responsibility—were again established. The emphasis on intellectual development centered in early
secondary programs, as it does today, on the study of such basic fields
as English, foreign language, mathematics, history, and science; the
assumption of social responsibility by schools has taken the forms
of practical emphasis for citizenship preparation, training for trades
and vocations, programs in manual and physical education, art, and
musical activities, as well as a variety of courses to prepare for homemaking and leisure-time pursuits.

Doors Open to All

The powerful influence of the masses—expressed in Jacksonian
democracy, the industrial revolution, urbanization, and the rising
importance of the West—called attention to the need for universal
education beyond the elementary school. Social conditions and political
responsibility demanded enlightened citizens. The concept of equality
of opportunity plus the requirements for more highly trained personnel
for business and industry added to the demands that public high schools
should be open to all. The belief in the importance of education to the

community and state, as contrasted to the older view that education was a personal privilege, helped establish the principle that parents should no longer be left to educate their children entirely according to their own desires. Gradually, all these forces brought communities and states to recognize that universality in education was a social necessity, rather than an individual luxury.

A Slow Beginning

Despite the familiarity of many of the early proposals for public secondary schools—familiar because they are more or less commonplace today—most of them were not incorporated into educational practice for over a century after they were first advanced. As Charles and Mary Beard observed:

> There was in America no Prussian monarch to impose a compulsory system on the people for reasons of state. Consequently the project of universal free education had to be evolved gradually in a democratic fashion, under the leadership of men and women with vision, who realized that they could move only as fast as knowledge of the ideal could be disseminated and practical interests enlisted for its support. When the task was seriously undertaken, at the middle of the nineteenth century, the stamp of American nationality was clear upon it.[10]

Fear of government, opposition to taxes, and the practice of reserving education for the parent and the church, were the major factors responsible for the slow growth of public education. Free tax-supported public education did not leap into existence upon the heels of the Revolution; it grew slowly, often against bitter resistance.

SEARCH FOR PURPOSE AND DIRECTION

The search for purpose and direction in public education that goes on continuously, with various groups and individuals—official and unofficial—seeking to influence what is taught, centers primarily in secondary schools. Although debates may flare about procedures or standards in elementary schools, rather common agreement prevails regarding their function—the teaching of the basic skills of learning and the introduction of all children to the study of the various fields of knowledge. At the secondary level, controversy continues about

[10] Charles and Mary Beard, *The Rise of American Civilization*, New York (Macmillan), 1930, p. 486. Quoted by permission of The Macmillan Company.

such matters as who should be educated, the central objectives of education, major emphases in the educational program, courses that should be offered, standards that should be maintained, teaching procedures, organization, preparation of teachers, and the meaning of graduation.

That disagreements about secondary education should have continued to exist over such a long period of time is to be expected because of the nature of a democratic society and the decentralized system of public education that prevails in the United States. Everyone is free to influence public education: Local boards of education; state departments of public instruction; legislatures, as official bodies; and any group or individual with citizenship status. In addition, accrediting agencies, institutions of higher learning, professional organizations of teachers and administrators, school board associations, parent-teacher associations, and other bodies concerned directly with education exert substantial influence. The absence of a national system of education with a ministry of education to set policy (existing in many nations, see Chapter 21), plus the extremely loose organizations that prevail in many states, leave the determination of purposes and direction largely to local decisions.

Decentralization and Lay Control

Historical suspicion of the national government, as well as fear of control by either the clergy or politicians, have supported the decentralized system of public education. Furthermore, resistance by citizens to domination by professional educators has maintained a strong dedication to lay control. The attitude prevails that, as the armed forces are too important to be placed in the hands of the militarist, education is too vital to the welfare of the nation to be left to the jurisdiction of the educator. For the same reasons, efforts are made to prevent any special interest from gaining undue influence over educational programs. As a result, procedures for determining the purposes and direction of public education are kept open and responsive to the will of all the people. Confidence in this process, cumbersome as it is at times, has developed through the experiences over the years that have kept public schools free from domination by any group—political, religious, commercial, trade, or educational. This unique feature of education in the United States has stood the test of history, as Conant has pointed out:

> When one tells a foreign visitor that we have tens of thousands of local school boards with vast powers over the elementary and the

high schools, he is apt to say, 'this is not a system but a chaos.' To which I always reply, 'But it works; most of us like it; and it appears to be as permanent a feature of our society as most of our political institutions.'[11]

Continuing Concern

No grounds exist for believing that discussion and debate about public education will cease or that controversy will diminish. Change, of course, is of the nature of life. To stand still would only invite retrogression and disaster. This is true of education as it is of every other facet of life. As we experience deep and pervading cultural changes at an ever-accelerating rate, education must adapt itself to the conditions imposed by change or our society will fail.

The age we entered at the moment an atomic reaction was controlled is one in which new dimensions have been added to the problems of the adjustment of education to cultural change. These new dimensions present frightening challenges to the average citizen who must make decisions about educational goals for an atomic age. First, change is now so rapid that for the first time in history an oncoming generation must be educated for a life which is not likely to resemble that of the generation that must provide the education. Second, rapid transportation and communication have intensified the physical and philosophical differences between us and other people of the world while at the same time they force upon us the need for resolution and accommodation. Third, the impelling problems require solutions at levels so remote from the average person that he feels helpless and inadequate to contribute to their solution. If the people of the United States are to survive and to continue to progress as a nation, means must be found constantly to reconstruct programs of public education and to do so through the intelligent participation of the citizenry. To give over this task to one group in society or to attempt to find stability by reverting, through fear, to a mythical program of the past would bring disaster.

THE CONTEMPORARY SECONDARY SCHOOL

The character of secondary education in high schools today is based upon various trends and emphases which have grown out of the past. Three factors are readily recognizable as typical of most public second-

[11] James B. Conant, *The American High School Today,* New York (McGraw-Hill), 1959, p. 8.

ary schools: the comprehensive type of organization; the inclusion of both junior and senior high school divisions; and a diversified program.

The Comprehensive High School

A long-standing goal of the public high school has been the provision of an educational program sufficiently differentiated in its emphases, standards, and course offerings to serve all youth within one comprehensive school. Although a few cities have experimented with separate vocational and academic high schools, the usual pattern is the single school in which various programs of study are provided.

The rapid expansion of high schools following the turn of the century, with a growing emphasis on vocational and citizenship training, raised questions about the feasibility of accomplishing the multiple objectives of secondary education within one organization. In 1918, the Commission on the Reorganization of Secondary Education threw its weight behind the comprehensive school organization by recommending it as "the standard type of secondary school in the United States."[12]

The general notion underlying the concept of the comprehensive high school is that this pattern of organizing public secondary schools can provide an effective program of education to all the youth of a given community. Its advocates believe that such a school can best resist the forces operating to stratify and to divide society, and that it can instill democratic principles as a part of daily living and maintain the widest possible number of alternatives for personal development and vocational choice. The rapid increases in the percentages of youth who complete a secondary education over the past decades and the "holding power" of the high schools give a crude indication of the effectiveness of the comprehensive high school to provide a challenging educational program fitted to the purposes and the abilities of youth.

Recent concern for excellence in education has raised proposals that academic and vocational work be placed in separate high schools. Again the comprehensive organization has been given strong endorsement after careful study by Dr. Conant in his personal appraisal and recommendations for the American high school.[13] The conviction that

[12] National Education Association, Commission on Reorganization of Secondary Education, *Cardinal Principles of Secondary Education*, Bulletin 1918, No. 35, Washington, D.C. (Government Printing Office), 1918.

[13] Conant, *op. cit.*, pp. 10-40.

Welfare,[14] from which Figures 3-1A and 3-1B were drawn, revealed that the total number of secondary schools in the United States has changed only slightly since 1930. In the peak year, 1938, there were 25,000 high schools; in 1959, there were 24,000. The consolidation of small schools into larger units is being offset by the new schools that are being created to care for expanding enrollments.

Diversified Programs

Characteristically the programs of contemporary secondary schools include emphasis on general education, provision for specialized training, a wide range of pupil activities, availability of guidance services, and special training for handicapped students.

General education. Out of the emphasis on citizenship preparation, plus the support for liberal training in the United States, has grown a relatively heavy emphasis on general education in secondary schools. Such work typically comprises about half of the offering of the secondary school.

The problem of defining general education has challenged both individuals and national committees.[15] The Harvard report, prepared by a distinguished committee of scholars representing various disciplines, refers to general education as the "part of a student's whole education which looks first of all to his life as a responsible human being and citizen."[16] Almost all such statements include in general education the common attitudes and knowledges that each individual must attain in order to achieve an effective personal life and to practice good citizenship.

The basic portion of the program that is devoted to general education is required of all students. At the high school level it is often referred to as the common learnings. The minimum content generally includes three or four years of English language, two years of social studies (one year devoted to the study of American history), one year of mathematics, one year of science, and four years of some combination of physical education and health. Although separate subjects are

[14] Edmund A. Ford, "Organizational Pattern of the Nation's Public Secondary Schools," *School Life,* May 1960, pp. 2-4.

[15] See especially, Will French and associates, *Behavioral Goals of General Education in High School,* New York (Russell Sage Foundation), 1957. And, Harvard Committee on the Objectives of a General Education in a Free Society, *General Education in a Free Society,* Cambridge, Mass. (Harvard Univ. Press), 1945.

[16] *General Education in a Free Society,* p. 51.

the standard organization of instruction, other patterns include core, fused, or unified fields, and correlated subjects. General education has been referred to as being "common to all" and "required," but the implication should not be drawn that the content is identical for all students within the same school or even within the same classroom.

Specialized education. The program of special education typically comprises at least half of the high school offering. The time allotment and the number of specialized education courses offered increases sharply as the student moves from grade to grade through the junior and senior high schools. These offerings are of two kinds: well-defined sequences of preparation for a vocation or for advanced study and personal-interest courses. The two kinds of offerings comprise the elective portion of the program. In theory, this offering should be as varied as the needs and interests of the students of a given school. In practice, it is limited to the facilities, to the resources within the staff, and to the numbers of students enrolling in a given area of study. Taking the country as a whole, the size of our schools and the adequacy of counseling services seem to be two critical factors in the success of the specialized education programs of secondary schools.

Student activities. Outside of the scheduled school day each secondary school conducts a program of student activities. This program includes activities which permit each student to pursue worthwhile personal interests and to develop unique talents and skills. It also includes activities which help students to learn to plan and conduct projects of common interest and concern to the school community. This latter purpose of school activities, through student government, intramural programs and the like, gives students the opportunity to learn to live together cooperatively and to understand and appreciate the attitudes, interests, and wishes of others.

Guidance services. Complex patterns of individual abilities, interests, and goals become forcefully apparent as education widens the differences between individual students. The secondary school offering is complex because of these differences. The school's guidance program is concerned with helping the student make wise choices. Each teacher understands adolescents and has a personal interest in them, but the counselor has special skills and knowledge and is in a position to aid students to make a success of their total school life. The counselor is concerned about such matters as each student's adaptation to school, his future plans for a vocation or his choice of a college, and the personal problems which may affect his success in school. Some members of the guidance staff are regularly assigned to conduct studies of the nature of the school population, gather information about students who have left or graduated, administer a program of standard tests, operate a job-placement service, conduct career conferences, meet with college representatives and groups of college-bound students, consult with teachers concerning student problems, and many other specific tasks. Some schools employ psychologists, psychiatrists, and social workers as part of their counseling staffs.

Programs for the handicapped. Most secondary schools of moderate to large size (enrollments of four hundred or more) have some special programs for handicapped youth (see Chapter 18). These programs are different from the ability-groupings now widely employed in larger schools. The handicapped generally take as much schoolwork within the regular school program as is practical but spend some part of each day with specially trained teachers. In addition to the educational goals of normal youth, the handicapped receive special instruction and counseling to minimize the effects of their handicap. Special teachers are employed for such groups as the mentally retarded, the blind, deaf, the orthopedically handicapped, and the speech handicapped.

SELECTED REFERENCES

American Association of School Administrators. Thirty-sixth Yearbook. "The High School in a Changing World." Washington, D.C.: the Association, 1958.

BEACH, FRED F., AND ROBERT F. WILL. *The State and Education.* Washington, D.C.: U.S. Department of Health, Education and Welfare, 1958.

EDWARDS, NEWTON, AND HERMAN G. RICHEY. *The School in the American Social Order.* Boston: Houghton Mifflin, 1947.

FITZWATER, C. O. *School District Reorganization: Policies and Procedures.* Washington, D.C.: U.S. Department of Health, Education and Welfare, 1957.

GOOD, H. G. *A History of American Education.* New York: Macmillan, 1956.

MILLER, VAN, AND WILLARD SPALDING. *The Public Administration of American Schools.* 2nd ed. Tarrytown, N.Y.: World Book Company, 1958.

SCOTT, C. W., AND C. M. HILL. *Public Education Under Criticism.* Englewood Cliffs, N.J.: Prentice-Hall, 1954.

STANLEY, WILLIAM O., AND OTHERS. *Social Foundations of Education.* New York: Dryden, 1956.

PART II

Purposes and Functions

Preparation
for citizenship
has made stu-
dents active
participants in
the process of
learning with
teacher serv-
ing as guide.

Limited functions of a century ago placed emphasis on teacher-centered
drill and recitations.

CHAPTER 4

Functions of Secondary Education

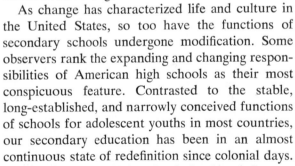

THE FUNCTIONS of education are always determined by forces outside the school. They are
defined by the moral, intellectual, cultural, social,
political, and economic values held by a particular
people at a specific time. Essentially, the functions
of secondary schools grow out of the nature and
extent of knowledge and its use.

As change has characterized life and culture in
the United States, so too have the functions of
secondary schools undergone modification. Some
observers rank the expanding and changing responsibilities of American high schools as their most
conspicuous feature. Contrasted to the stable,
long-established, and narrowly conceived functions
of schools for adolescent youths in most countries,
our secondary education has been in an almost
continuous state of redefinition since colonial days.

The American high school developed from a
variety of parent institutions in response to the
hopes, dreams, and ambitions released by the
opportunities of a new continent and a new republic supported by the revolutionary ideals of
freedom and equality for all. The responsibilities
assigned to educational institutions changed as
the nation struggled to advance the frontier westward. More recently dramatic advances in knowledge, industrial progress, and widened concerns

for man's social, physical, and emotional well-being have pressed additional duties on educational institutions. Today, international forces engaged in the struggle for the dignity and freedom of the individual man—wherever he may be—have stimulated a reappraisal of the functions and emphases in high school programs.

Behind the changes that have taken place in the functions of secondary schools has been the *will of the people*. American high schools have always been, and continue to be today, the kind of institutions citizens demand—or tolerate. When changes have been urged, schools have responded; or new institutions have been created that will provide the kind of educational programs desired. In effect, secondary education reflects a clear picture of the composite educational wishes of the American people, as expressed in local communities, as well as at the state and national levels.

DIVERGENT OLD WORLD ROOTS

American colonists, as did the later immigrants, brought with them institutions and values. Their reasons for coming often determined the priorities they followed when re-establishing themselves in the new environment. Because most sought freedom and opportunity, schools were considered vital to their goals.

To New England came Puritans seeking religious and political freedom; education was needed for both moral and intellectual ends. The belief of certain groups that each man should be able to achieve direct communication with God, and therefore needed to interpret the Bible for himself, meant that at least he would be able to read, a skill which required some schooling.

In Virginia, South Carolina, and North Carolina grants of land to favored families established an aristocracy whose allegiance was to the Anglican church and its system of selective sectarian education. As a result, public education—particularly secondary schools— developed slowly in the South. In fact, some deficiencies in high school programs that exist today can be traced to colonial conceptions.

Although New York was dominated originally by the Dutch Reformed Church, it soon turned to material interests in trade and commerce and allowed a variety of faiths to become established. Pennsylvania and Delaware, under the influence of the Quakers, who were tolerant of other religions, had to assimilate the ideas and faiths of German and Swedish Lutherans, Mennonites, Moravians, and Scotch-

Irish Presbyterians. New Jersey, Maryland, Rhode Island, and Georgia attracted more homogeneous religious groups, each with its own inheritance of educational perceptions. Whatever the colony, its people faced the problem of adapting Old World views of education to the new environment.

Two Predominant European Influences: English and German

Studies of the early origins of secondary schools in the United States favor the English influence. Equally important, however, has been the German heritage, much of which was introduced at a later stage through the leadership of such men as Horace Mann and Henry Barnard. Until recent years, England and Germany exercised strong influences upon American high schools and, even today, some point to the programs of these two countries as guides in the improvement of secondary schools here.

English backgrounds. Seventeenth-century England, out of which American colonists came, experienced religious conflict, economic change, and scientific awakening that affected her patterns of secondary education. Cromwell's sympathy with religious freedom and the strength his protectorate gave to the independents bolstered education for all faiths. After Cromwell's death, Charles II, reversing the national policy of religious toleration, expelled 2,000 dissenting clergymen from their parishes and excluded dissenters from schools and universities. This repression stimulated the development of a new type of secondary school in England.[1] The dissenters were accustomed to the study of the Bible, prayer books, and secular material in English, rather than Latin (the language of the "private" schools and universities). On being excluded from these institutions, they established terminal schools, where instruction was often given in English.

The predominant school of England, however, continued to be the private "public school"—boarding institutions in most cases—in which many of Britain's leaders and statesmen were trained. These secondary schools, whose origins were in the Italian Renaissance, professed to educate children in the "knowledge and fear of God . . . [and] good Christian life and manners." They prepared selected students for the ministry, statesmanship, and the cultural pursuits of the nobility. The universities to which their graduates went—only Oxford and Cambridge until 1836—concerned themselves principally with the

---

[1] Paul Monroe, *A Brief Course in the History of Education,* New York (Macmillan), 1907, p. 250.

classics and theology. Law and medicine did not receive professional emphasis until the nineteenth century. This narrow focus in higher education tended to restrict the curriculums of secondary schools.

One dissenter, John Milton, did have some effect on English education. A follower of Cromwell, Milton strongly advocated the separation of church and state in his writings. With Puritan fervor he advanced the educational aim of "regaining to know God aright." The program outlined in his treatise *Of Education* encompassed instruction in Latin, Greek, Italian, Hebrew, and other languages, as well as in science, mathematics, agriculture, manual training, history, ethics, politics, economics, and theology. In this ambitious curriculum no subjects were to be elective. In addition to broadening the interpretations given to the traditional objectives of moral and intellectual training, he clearly favored education to develop social qualities—such as civic participation and vocational professional competence—and felt that education should have some concern for physical development, at least as related to manual dexterity. The English academies that developed after 1665 reflected Milton's ideas to some extent, although their main purpose still was preparation for the ministry. A century later these ideas were adapted to a substantially broader student population in the academies founded in America.

John Locke's opposition to the traditional grammatical and linguistic curriculum, expressed in his *Thoughts on Education,* 1693, influenced both English academies and leaders in America. Another kind of secondary education that started in England and thrived in the new continent was the simple, practical education developed by the Quakers.

German backgrounds. German influence on secondary education has been substantial in other parts of the world as well as in the United States. The Protestant Reformation broadened the functions of secondary education. Lutheranism advocated a "priesthood of all believers"; this equality before God logically led to the translation of the Bible into the vernacular and supported the concept of universal education.

Luther, Melancthon, and other Germans of their circle developed an educational program that was supported by sympathetic civil authorities. They not only urged the German princes to establish schools and to compel attendance; they also made concrete proposals for the improvement of the education of their time—many of which were put into effect. German grammar schools were criticized by Luther for teaching "only enough bad Latin to become a priest to read Mass . . . and yet remain all his life a poor ignoramus fit neither to cackle nor to lay eggs."[2]

In contrast to the sectarianism and stratification of English education, the German system offered a wide variety of courses. Its philosophical orientation was toward politics and economics rather than religion. Consequently, education was made more widely available, and organization, methods, and standards were attuned to intellectual and civic development. Barnard's translations of Luther's sermons on education and Melancthon's plan for education in Saxony, as well as reports on the early school systems of Württemberg and Saxe-Coburg-Gotha, provided a pattern for the American state-school systems.[3] Among the features adopted were the German system of education from grammar schools through the gymnasiums (high schools) and the university, and the emphasis was placed on the education of leaders for all the learned callings, including political leadership and training for commercial activities. In effect, Germany offered the example of a state system of education, nonparochial in its emphasis, with high standards of scholarship, improved teaching procedures, and comprehensiveness of functions.

EARLY AMERICAN SECONDARY SCHOOLS: REVOLUTIONARY FUNCTIONS

Although the Latin grammar school developed first and most extensively in New England, it thrived in the Middle Colonies and the South as well. Because of an interesting tendency of religious and ethnic groups to establish colleges first and secondary schools thereafter, the early high schools typically came into existence to prepare pupils for specific colleges. This sequence prevailed not only throughout the colonies but in the new territories and states as each was settled.

Latin grammar schools, although closely related to particular colleges at first, actually were independent of them in most instances. According to Dr. Conant, this situation—plus the autonomy that each college enjoyed—accounts for the fact that the educational revolution, which began in England during the seventeenth century, flourished only in the United States while becoming abortive in all other English-speaking countries.[4]

2 Martin Luther, *Works,* Vol. IV, Philadelphia (Muhlenberg Press), 1943, p. 156.

3 Henry Barnard, *American Journal of Education,* Vol. IV, 1858, *passim.*

4 Conant, *Education and Liberty,* Cambridge (Harvard Press), 1953, pp. 29-54.

The Latin grammar school was defined more easily than it was developed. New England town life was more favorable to secondary education than were the feudal estates of Dutch New York, the raw farming areas of the Middle Colonies, or the plantation states of the South. Growth was more rapid in New England; yet, even there, secondary schools developed slowly. While the avowed purpose of Latin grammar schools was to prepare for godly living and entrance into college, their students frequently failed to live up to either of these high goals. Similar conditions prevailed, no doubt, in England itself; but in America new opportunities and the near absence of social class made formal education at the secondary school level less a required steppingstone to success. William Penn argued that "the surest way of serving God and attaining happiness in this and the next world is by laboring diligently in some honest trade." He criticized schools for making youth "scholars but not men, to talk rather than to know," and advocated more attention to "mechanical, physical, or natural knowledge."[5] Penn's views foreshadowed a Quaker influence that was to be later magnified, throughout their scattered academies, out of all proportion to the numbers of students. This influence lasted well into the twentieth century.

Benjamin Franklin: "The Important Business of Living"

As the colonies moved toward independence, a distinctively American spirit—born of the religious and philosophical ideas of sixteenth- and seventeenth-century Europe and nurtured in the stimulating atmosphere of a new continent—rapidly intensified. Benjamin Franklin translated these smoldering revolutionary ideals into educational theory. Unimpressed with the famous Boston Latin Grammar School in which he spent only a year, Franklin educated himself in letters, politics, science, and business; he was one of the most conspicuously successful men of his time. In addition to his many other interests, he formulated a theory about the teaching of foreign languages. In it he proposed that the study of Latin should follow, rather than precede, the development of proficiency of French, Italian, and Spanish.[6]

Franklin's major contribution to secondary education was the founding in 1751 of the Philadelphia Academy to carry out his edu-

---

[5] Louis B. Wright, *The Cultural Life of the American Colonies, 1607-1763,* New York (Harper), 1957, p. 107.

[6] Benjamin Franklin, *Autobiographical Writings,* Carl Van Doren (ed.), New York (Viking), 1945.

cational ideas. Contrasted to the Latin grammar school with which it competed, this was the first attempt to shape an institution to the variety of people, the political and economic conditions, and the spirit of freedom that represented colonial America. The program for the academy was developed to suit the wide variety of mid-eighteenth-century Philadelphians. It was adapted to the practical Quakers, the Germans and Mennonites, the educationally conscious Moravians, and the morally righteous Anglicans. Franklin's goal was to develop an institution that would serve all since he believed that "The good education of youth has been esteemed by wise men in all ages as the surest foundation of the happiness both of private families and commonwealths."[7]

Teaching young people "the important business of living" was a central function envisioned for this nonsectarian academy, which later grew into the University of Pennsylvania. Because it was not possible to teach everything of value, concentration was to be upon the "most useful and most ornamental." The curriculum, while as broad as that proposed by Milton in England almost a century before, was to have different content and emphases; some subjects such as the classics were to be elective. Drawing and perspective, arithmetic, accounts, geometry, astronomy, history, geography, morality, oratory, natural history with a practical agricultural slant, and the English language were to be the fields of study. The school was to be placed in an appropriate location and provided with a library and suitable maps and scientific apparatus. Students were to be given plain and frugal food and regular exercise to keep them healthy and vigorous.

Important to the character of the academy was the emphasis planned for the study of English—style, reading, and pronunciation—and the perusal of other subjects in the vernacular. Franklin urged the study of history in such a fashion as to show the wisdom of joining in societies and governments, the advantages of liberty, and the "mischiefs of licentiousness." The variety of other revolutionary emphases in secondary education that many academies originally sought to develop is shown in Table 4-1. As is true of any schools where state control is absent, differences in academies prevailed. Some were sectarian and differed little from the Latin grammar schools. Preparation for college, often for a particular college, frequently dominated other objectives. Other institutions had other goals, as did the Kents Hill School in

[7] David Excelmons Cloyd, *Benjamin Franklin and Education,* Boston (D. C. Heath and Company), 1902, p. 73.

Table 4-1. *Revolutionary Emphases in Secondary Education Advocated for the Academy*

Nonpartisan control
Tax support
Nonsectarian
Differentiated curriculum
Elective subjects
Books and teaching in English language
Citizenship education
Applied subjects
Modern foreign languages
Marketable skills
Coeducational
Audio-visual aids
Emphasis on science
Advance placement college courses
Campus-type school
Physical fitness
Universality

Maine that was established "for the purpose of affording instruction to youth in the principles of Experimental Christian Religion, Theology, Religious Literature, and in a practical knowledge of Agriculture and Mechanic Arts."[8] Some of the academies were coeducational; others had both male and female divisions. Girls frequently were given only the "polite branches" of study—embroidery, painting, drawing, and courtesy. Advanced college placement programs, as they are called today, existed in a number of academies that gave some college courses that were recognized by institutions of higher learning. Gardiner Lyceum in Maine established an agricultural school in 1821 which received state aid for ten years.

Had Franklin's academy, and the others that eventually enrolled as many as 250,000 students by 1850, lived up to the goals they originally sought, the public high school would not have come into being. Such an achievement was too much to expect, however, in the face of the entrenched supporters of religious sectarianism and classical scholarship. The Philadelphia Academy's first provost was a classicist and a religious partisan, William Smith, who did not promote the English program, or "school." As a result, the Latin school soon became the prestige program; only students of lesser ability elected the

[8] Harriet Webster Marr, *The Old New England Academies,* New York (Comet), 1959, p. 10.

other. Throughout his later life, Franklin periodically restated his philosophy for the academy and expressed his disappointment that the English school was starved and neglected and instruction in English, scientific studies, and the useful arts was not developed. Similar distortions took place in other academies; most eventually abandoned the revolutionary functions for which they had been founded and returned to the classical emphasis of the Latin grammar school. Typical of the regressive developments in the academy that were made in the mid-nineteenth century was the trend at Exeter. Its English department was discontinued in 1848 because, as the trustees reported: "Those students whose bad habits or want of capacity prevent them from success in Latin, usually desire to finish their academic course in the English Room—in this way the English Room is liable to be filled with the idle and stupid."[9]

Mr. Jefferson: Talent and Democracy

As Franklin advocated educational emphasis on the useful and scientific, so Thomas Jefferson proposed a system of schools which would permit no intellectual talent to go undeveloped and which, through the general diffusion of knowledge, would "render the people safe, as they are the guardians of their own liberty." Jefferson's Plan for Education in Virginia, first advanced in 1779, proposed a system of district, county, and regional elementary and secondary schools leading to an educational capstone—the state university. Its functions were to be twofold: to provide a literate, informed, and competent citizenry, and to provide the best possible leadership in politics and other intellectual spheres. Jefferson advocated selectivity, based on merit, to a degree that has never been attempted in the United States. Scholarships were to be provided for able but needy students to make certain that ability alone would be the criterion for advancement.

Although Jefferson's plan of education was initially rejected in Virginia—even in his beloved home county of Albemarle, later to become the seat of his University—it gradually gained adoption throughout the South[10] and exerted strong influence on the territories that were being settled and developed west of the Appalachian Mountains. Jefferson's influence on secondary education itself was largely indirect, being exerted through the establishment of state universities

9 *Ibid.,* p. 169.
10 Charles William Dabney, *Universal Education in the South,* Chapel Hill (Univ. of North Carolina Press), 1936.

that in turn helped to shape the public high schools. Here again, as in colonial times, the founding of institutions of higher learning preceded the creation of secondary schools. By 1825, eight states—six in the South, and Ohio and Indiana—had made provisions for state universities modeled after Jefferson's "capstone" dream. These institutions, along with the independent colleges, have been the key influence in developing the distinctive character of the American high school. Of them and their relationship to secondary schools Turner commented:

> The most obvious fact about these universities, perhaps, lies in their integral relation with the public schools, whereby the pupil has pressed upon him the question whether he shall go to college. By this means the State offers to every class the means of education, and even engages in propaganda to induce students to continue. It sinks deep shafts through the social strata to find the gold of real ability in the underlying rock of the masses. It fosters that due degree of individualism which is implied in the right of every human being to rise in whatever directions his peculiar abilities entitle him to go, subordinate to the welfare of the state. It keeps avenues of promotion to the highest offices, the highest honors, open to the humblest and most obscure lad who has the natural gifts, at the same time that it aids in the improvement of the masses.[11]

Functions of First Public High Schools

The first public secondary school, established in Boston in 1821 and called, first, the English Classical School and later, simply the English High School, took a good part of its approach from Franklin and Jefferson. According to its first report published in 1823: "This school was established by a vote of the town in 1820, expressly for the purpose of affording to lads, intending to become merchants or mechanics, better means of instruction than were provided at any of the public schools."[12]

Preparation for college was already available in the Latin grammar schools and academies. The English high school as a new institution took on a new responsibility, one of urgent importance to the expanding commercial and industrial enterprises of New England seaports— the terminal education of noncollege-bound youth. By 1827, the

[11] Frederick Jackson Turner, *The Frontier in American History,* New York (Henry Holt), 1920, p. 283.
[12] Ellwood P. Cubberley, *Readings in the History of Education,* Boston (Houghton Mifflin), 1920.

Massachusetts High School Law provided these schools with legal endorsement of the curriculum which emphasized preparation for life and work, including instruction in good behavior. Hence, the social function of the secondary school, including the development of marketable skills, was established.

The new English high school developed slowly during the mid-nineteenth century. In many places these schools added to their programs the classical subjects that would prepare the students for college so that they could compete for students with the flourishing academies and the remnants of the Latin grammar schools. After 1850, the public high school began to move toward the dominant position that it finally assumed during the first half of the present century. Unlike the academy, the public high school—although it has often undergone rigorous pressures—has not departed from the mission of serving all kinds of young people with their many different educational goals.

TWENTIETH-CENTURY FUNCTIONS OF SECONDARY EDUCATION

Since the 1890's, when the high school became a major institution, many deliberate efforts have been made to define its functions and to standardize its programs. Such attempts to define the responsibilities of secondary schools have been undertaken by national organizations of educators, accrediting bodies, representatives of colleges and universities, and citizen groups, as well as by individuals. Their objectives have ranged from specifying the high school's program for college preparation,[13] defining its comprehensive functions,[14] or emphasizing new obligations—such as social development, vocational training, and physical efficiency—[15] to analyzing the needs of adolescent youths and their roles in civic and vocational affairs,[16] or delineating the

[13] Report of the Committee on Secondary School Studies, Washington, D.C. (Government Printing Office), 1893; and, Report of the Committee on College-Entrance Requirements, National Educational Association Proceedings, 1899, pp. 632-817.

[14] Commission on Reorganization of Secondary Education, *Cardinal Principles of Secondary Education*, Bulletin 35, U.S. Bureau of Education, Washington, D.C. (Government Printing Office), 1918.

[15] Leonard V. Koos, *The American Secondary School*, Boston (Ginn and Company), 1927, and Educational Policies Commission, *The Purpose of Education in American Democracy*, Washington, D.C., 1938.

[16] Hollis Caswell, et al., *The American High School: Its Responsibility and Opportunity*, New York (Harper), 1946. Also, U.S. Office of Education, *Life Adjustment Education for Every Youth*, Washington, D.C. (Government Printing Office), undated, pp. 18-19.

priorities and organizational relationships that should prevail with respect to its comprehensive functions.[17]

Basis and Definition of Functions

Differences in the functions advocated for secondary schools by various individuals and groups often result from the fact that different backgrounds are referred to as the basis for the delineation of high school goals. The backgrounds most often referred to are:

(a) Human traits and capacities
(b) Educational and vocational utility
(c) Societal demands
(d) Individual needs
(e) Developmental tasks

Often a taxonomy of functions will be found to have been drawn from several different backgrounds, as were the famous Cardinal Principles of Secondary Education. In some classifications, two or more advocated functions may overlap somewhat, e.g., human relationship and civic responsibility.[18] Oddly enough, some widely publicized statements of functions have omitted entirely certain traditional responsibilities of the high school on the basis, presumably, that they should be taken for granted.[19] The sequence in which functions are listed has been taken by some authorities as the recommended order of priority. For example, the National Association of Secondary School Principals listed as the first of ten "imperative needs" of youth: "saleable skills and those understandings and attitudes that make the worker an intelligent and productive participant in economic life."[20] Not until tenth did it list "ability to think rationally, to express their thoughts clearly, and to read and listen with understanding."

The unclarities, imbalances, and distorted priorities of these statements are more easily explained than defended. These presentations of educational responsibilities of schools are often formulated by spe-

[17] James B. Conant, *The American High School Today,* New York (McGraw-Hill), 1959.

[18] Educational Policies Commission, *op. cit.*

[19] Koos, *op. cit.,* made no mention of intellectual development, or even of "command of the fundamental processes" when he listed civic-social-moral; training for recreational and aesthetic participation and appreciation; training for vocation; and training for physical efficiency.

[20] Committee on Curriculum Planning and Development, *The Imperative Needs of Youth,* Washington, D.C. (National Association of Secondary School Principals), 1949, p. 4.

cial committees, whose members are either elected or appointed to represent particular professional or citizen bodies. Such groups typically undertake, within a limited period of time, the preparation of statements for presentation to and adoption by the authorizing organization. The work is largely done in committee meetings, without scholarly assistance, with ideas and vocabulary subjected to the pressures of vested interest, popular theories, and the latest professional jargon. Sometimes ultimate approval by the entire organization involves changes made in open meetings, without reference to the total context. These procedures, democratic though they may be, can hardly be expected to produce carefully reasoned, logical, and precisely ordered statements. Unfortunately, these statements once made have the prestige of the formulating group behind them. They gain nation-wide publicity and wide acceptance before their shortcomings are identified. They sometimes become models for educational programs and practice. Even some individuals who undertake to prepare personal proposals, or who write professional textbooks for educational personnel, will refer frequently to these committee formulations. In this way they become a permanent part of the literature on education, valueless though many of them may be.

Basic Functions

The basic functions that secondary schools have assumed are best understood, perhaps, in relationship to the various human traits and capacities for which education is prescribed. Historically, high schools have been called upon, for example, to provide moral training— either of a sectarian religious nature or through the study of non-sectarian ethics and values. This was the primary function of the Latin grammar schools, which were established to promote and extend organized religions. Similarly, intellectual development has always been a function of secondary education, since refined mental ability is essential to all other objectives.

Social proficiency, including both civic and vocational preparation, is a function that has grown out of the concern for group life, self-government, and materialistic success in the United States. This responsibility of secondary schools was advocated by Franklin, as well as Jefferson; it was the primary motive behind the creation of both the academy and the public high school.

Other functions that have received attention in most secondary schools are the promotion of physical development and well-being and emotional stability. These two objectives grow out of recent concern for the individual, his needs, adjustment, recreational pursuits, and entertainment.

The relationship between basic functions and various emphases that have been related to them, as well as the outcomes that have been sought, and selected examples of oversimplified aims that are often endorsed are shown in Table 4-2. This table illustrates the difficulty

Table 4-2. *Functions, Emphases Developed, Outcomes Sought, and Oversimplified Aims in Secondary Education*

BASIC FUNCTIONS	EMPHASES DEVELOPED	OUTCOMES SOUGHT	OVERSIMPLIFIED AIMS
MORAL TRAINING:	Religion Moral values Ethics Democratic ideals	Religious commitments Ethical behavior Sound value judgments	Religious indoctrination
INTELLECTUAL DEVELOPMENT:	Skills of communication and scholarship Cultural transmission Liberal arts Subject specialization	Disciplined intelligence Scholarship skills and inclinations Acquaintance with cultural gains of civilization Introduction to primary fields of knowledge Propaedeutic emphasis Aesthetic interests	Mental discipline College preparation Early specialization Basic education
SOCIAL PROFICIENCY:	Civic affairs and structure Family life Group relationships Vocational preparation	Effective citizenship Responsibility to family Vocational efficiency Effective human relations	Social experiences Life adjustment Marketable skills Needs of youth
PHYSICAL WELL-BEING:	Health knowledge and habits Physical skills and poise Manual dexterity	Freedom from disease Physical strength and vigor Wholesome recreational habits	Formal calisthenics Group sports Interscholastic athletics
EMOTIONAL STABILITY:	Personal adjustment Developmental activities Counseling	Sound mental health Emotional balance Personal fulfillment	Activity as therapy Laissez-faire relationships

involved in clarifying the responsibilities of high schools when confusion prevails between conceptions of functions and the means of their attainment.

Moral training. Moral training in colonial days was often based upon the assumption that sectarian religious instruction forms the only reliable base for developing sound moral values and acceptable behavior. This premise lay behind the church-controlled colonial schools. It survives as the major justification for present-day parochial schools and furnishes, conversely, a key argument against nonsectarian education.

Recent years have seen attacks against public education on the ground that, without religious training, moral behavior is impossible. Opposing the constitutional provisions for separation of church and state, advocates of sectarian religious training indict public schools as "Godless institutions," while pleading the cause for church-controlled secondary schools. They oppose the premise that morality may have plural sanctions and that, therefore, nonsectarian secondary schools can develop sound moral and spiritual values, and consequent ethical behavior in students, while respecting the religious convictions of all.[21] Supporters of public schools hold that through appropriate emphases on generally accepted moral, ethic, and democratic values, ethical behavior and sound value judgments can be taught in public schools.

Intellectual development. Agreement that intellectual development is a primary function of secondary education prevails. Sharp and bitter conflicts often develop, however, not only over the priority and emphasis to be accorded to this objective, but over its very definition. The aims associated with it have been oversimplified by those who view the responsibility of high schools in terms of narrowly defined intellectual tasks.

The major debates over the high school's intellectual role have centered on the argument that the expansion of such functions as the teaching of social proficiency, physical well-being, and emotional stability has reduced the emphasis on the training of the mind in preparation for college and the professions. The "Basic Education" versus "Life Adjustment" quarrel and the "mind or hand training" arguments are examples of the bitter verbal battles that have been fought over this issue. In actuality, both sides in this argument are over-

[21] For a good discussion of this subject, see V. T. Thayer, *The Role of the School in American Society,* New York (Dodd, Mead), 1960, pp. 404-27.

simplified, and proponents of either side attempt to advance their own cause by distorting the intent of the other. The real issue at stake is whether the secondary school should be permitted to have, as a major responsibility, any function other than intellectual development.

Another kind of disagreement involves the emphasis within the function itself. One position holds that secondary education should concentrate first on perfecting the skills of communication and scholarship as ways to sharpen mental proficiency.[22] This position stresses the study of English, foreign language, and mathematics ahead of other fields. Its objective is to promote a high level of literacy. Critics of this point of view contend that study should range over a variety of courses. Some critics argue for more emphasis on cultural transmission and the liberal arts—basic subjects—while others would promote early specialization. Some see the high school as an agency for toughening the mind through mental exercise in much the way that muscles are developed through physical exercise. By this view it makes little difference what students study, as long as the subjects are difficult. Current protests against "soft" courses spring in part from this approach to mind training.

College preparation, long a basic aim of secondary schools, actually is, in itself, an oversimplified goal. The wide variations in types of colleges, differences in their programs and students, as well as the evidence that almost any field of study seriously pursued can contribute to college success, disprove the assumption that any one pattern of high school subjects can best prepare all students for all colleges.

Social proficiency. Practically all statements of function for secondary education that have been made since the formulation of the famous Cardinal Principles[23] by the National Association of Secondary School Principals in 1918 have given high priority to social proficiency. Some have centered almost exclusively on this cluster of responsibilities.

Social proficiency covers those adaptations that human beings must make in order to live in groups. It includes preparation for citizenship, both civic and economic; political knowledge; attitudes and behavior conducive to "worthy home membership"; respect and acceptance of others; skill in working with human beings; and preparation for making a living.

This emphasis on developing social proficiency in the secondary schools is unique. Visitors from other democratic countries are fre-

---

[22] Conant, *op. cit.,* pp. 41-76.
[23] Commission on Reorganization of Secondary Education, *op. cit.,* pp. 1-32.

quently most interested in this program, especially its citizenship phases. German educators, who generally feel that their schools do a better job of intellectual development—particularly for brighter students—admit freely that they must look to the United States for a workable plan of civic instruction. The progress achieved in retaining greater numbers of young people in school is often attributed to the values and satisfactions boys and girls find in a program which provides opportunities to prepare for life itself.

Social proficiency is the key target for opponents of the comprehensive high school. They argue that no special training is needed for participation in civic and community affairs, nor for family membership. These attainments, they claim, will be by-products of a high school program that concentrates on developing scholarship in the basic liberal arts subjects, without reference to their application. Vocational preparation, particularly, is condemned by such critics as a nonintellectual, applied activity that belongs in industry rather than in the secondary school.

As is true with intellectual development, some disagreements about the function of training for social proficiency are rooted within the function itself. Its relative newness and the wide variety of untested theories about it have produced disturbing examples of superficiality and distortion of basic objectives. Also, the results in individual students often can be measured only in the most subjective ways, even though these results may affect the entire community. The obvious fact that the secondary school, despite its terminal responsibility to many youths, cannot hope to complete the job of developing social proficiency—in civic, family, and vocational enterprises—leads to a lack of confidence in the school's aims and a consequent reluctance to invest educational time and energy in it.

Here, too, certain oversimplifications have become popular, such as the value of social experience for its own sake; the assumption that a specific program for "life adjustment" can be designed; the suggestion that marketable skills can be developed when business, industrial, and agricultural changes are making skills obsolete before they can be used; and the exclusive stress given to the needs of youth.

Physical well-being. Physical training to develop strong and healthy bodies has been endorsed as desirable from the time of ancient Greece to the present. Never, however, has it been such an integral function of the secondary school as it has become during the past forty years.

Following World War I, the awareness that some soldiers had not been physically fit prompted the introduction into high schools, often by state legislation, of required physical training. The objective was to develop sound health habits, physical strength and vigor, and the kind of hand-and-eye coordination essential for manual dexterity. A subsequent increase in leisure time encouraged the emphasis on physical recreation.

Oversimplification and distortion of this function have produced, in different times and situations, widespread attention to formal calisthenics; an overabsorption with group or team sports, in informal extracurricular programs as well as in required courses; and preoccupation with interscholastic athletics. As a consequence, many observers of the American high school believe that the emphasis on sports— under the name of physical well-being—threatens to throw the entire secondary school program out of balance. This point is epitomized by recent evidence that physical fitness programs in junior high schools are being used as training grounds for senior high school athletic teams.[24]

Emotional stability. The most recent function to receive attention in secondary schools is the promotion of emotional stability. Coming out of a growing concern for mental health and efforts to aid students in achieving personal fulfillment, it emphasizes personal adjustment, activities that foster emotional growth, and counseling services.

This function is sometimes distorted by aims that treat activity as justified in and of itself, for the sake of its therapeutic values.

Emphasis on Basic Functions by Different Types of Secondary Schools

The expanding functions of secondary education can be illustrated by the emphasis given to each by the various types of high schools that have served colonial America and the United States. Table 4-3 indicates the extent to which each kind of institution has given great, some, or no emphasis to the various basic functions. It must be recognized that such a tabulation, of necessity, is arbitrary in some respects. Practices in particular schools may well not conform to the indicated emphasis. The object here is to reflect the central concerns of each type while at the same time indicating when some attention is also accorded to other functions.

Not all public high schools, even those that profess to be comprehensive in scope, give great emphasis to each of the five functions as

[24] *Time,* February 29, 1960, p. 97, reporting on an address before the American Association of School Administrators by James B. Conant.

Table 4-3. *Emphasis on Functions Typically Given by Various Types of Secondary Schools*

Great emphasis: √√ Some emphasis: √ Little or no emphasis: 0

FUNCTIONS	LATIN GRAMMAR SCHOOL	ACADEMY	PUBLIC HIGH SCHOOL	INDEPENDENT PREPARATORY SCHOOLS	PAROCHIAL HIGH SCHOOLS
MORAL TRAINING	√ √	√	√ √	√	√ √
INTELLECTUAL DEVELOPMENT	√ √	√ √	√ √	√ √	√ √
SOCIAL PROFICIENCY	0	√ √	√ √	√	√
PHYSICAL WELL-BEING	0	0	√ √	√	√
EMOTIONAL STABILITY	0	0	√ √	√	√

shown. For particular institutions in given communities some functions receive only secondary attention. Here again the classification represents the general pattern, or the philosophy, of public secondary education more than the practice in individual situations.

FUTURE FUNCTIONS OF SECONDARY EDUCATION: THE WISHES OF THE PEOPLE

Currently the United States is enmeshed in the exciting venture of charting the course for secondary education in the future. This enterprise, which had long enlisted the efforts of professional educators, became a public passion subsequent to the launching of the first Russian satellite in the fall of 1957. The realization by the American people that a competing nation had achieved the distinction of being the first to project a man-made object into orbit around the earth provoked bitter and intemperate attacks against schools—particularly high schools. The following parable calls attention to the relationship that will always prevail in a democratic nation between the functions that schools serve and the wishes of people.[25]

> There developed in the Twentieth Century a people, strong in spirit and talents, kind of heart, and dedicated to liberty. They grew and flourished in a land of rich resources, aided by youthful imagination and daring, until they were known throughout the world.
> Among these fortunate people was placed a lamp of learning. They

[25] Lindley J. Stiles, "The Parable of the Lamp," *Nation's Schools*, March 1958.

were told by the genie who presided over it: 'Attend this lamp well and it will grant you wishes beyond your fondest dreams. It has the magic power to heal the sick, to harness the forces of nature or to make all the world beautiful and good. But remember, the lamp cannot wish for you; this you must do for yourselves. And if the wish is truly the desire of all the people, it shall be granted.'

Being young and headstrong, many of the people did not respect the power of the lamp. Some questioned its reputed magic. They impudently asked how a lamp with such a tiny, flickering flame could be so powerful. The genie was ridiculed and abused and assigned to low status among them. When they did agree upon wishes for the lamp, like Aladdin of old, they asked for an abundance of food, magnificent dwelling places, wealth and scientific baubles for their comfort and entertainment.

One day as the people reveled in their push-button wonderland of automatic appliances, high-powered automobiles, and dreams of grandeur, they were startled by the appearance of a new star moving rapidly across the heavens. When they realized that this magical wonder was the gift of the lamp to the people of another land, they were filled with fear and apprehension that their freedom was in danger. In anger they began to cry out indignantly that they had been cheated by the lamp of learning. They cursed the genie for not making them wish for such a wonderful scientific achievement. Some threw sticks and stones to drive away the faithful few who had endeavored to attend the lamp. Many who previously ridiculed the genie began to fight among themselves for his favor. Each proclaimed loudly that others were to blame for the loss of face before the world. Committees were appointed to find a suitable scapegoat to compensate for their damaged pride.

Above the din and confusion could be heard one distinct and persistent sound: an ominous, intermittent radio signal emitting from the new man-made miracle encircling the globe. It reminded all that the magic lamp of learning, if properly attended, has power to grant wishes beyond man's fondest dreams. It echoed the advice of the genie that the lamp cannot wish for a people. This they must do for themselves.

Secondary education in America indisputably is able to experiment, add, drop, and alter responsibilities. This receptiveness to change is one of its strengths. The increasingly complex American social organization, our deepening involvement in world affairs, and the accelerating demands of technology, clearly make it impossible to narrow the functional role of the high school. Public concern over the challenge from a competing system and ideology coincident with a re-examination brought on by an educational profession aware of the gap between ideal and practice in the high schools together point to the need for a re-evaluation and clearer assignment of priorities.

New functions can hardly be expected to come from the new and more consciously realized challenges now confronting secondary schools. A different concept of comprehensiveness, sharper differentiation, greater efficiency, and firmer emphasis must be developed. The major stress must be upon:

(a) Strengthening the common heritage
(b) Laying the foundations for scholarship
(c) Discovering and developing talent
(d) Developing values

The important minor emphases belong upon those goals and methods that contribute most to these four central functions. The subsidiary, though indispensable, concerns of the high school include such separate matters as developing guidance functions and providing the material environment in which the student can mobilize his best efforts. High schools must operate in heightened awareness that their functions in American democracy stem from the wishes of a people whom they help to make ever more dedicated to exercising freedom wisely.

SELECTED REFERENCES

BRIDENBAUGH, CARL, AND JESSICA BRIDENBAUGH. *Rebels and Gentlemen—Philadelphia in the Age of Franklin.* New York: Reynal and Hitchcock, 1942.

BUTTS, R. FREEMAN, AND LAWRENCE A. CREMIN. *A History of Education in American Culture.* New York: Henry Holt, 1953.

CUBBERLEY, ELLWOOD P. *The History of Education.* Boston: Houghton Mifflin, 1920.

DABNEY, CHARLES WILLIAM. *Universal Education in the South.* Vol. I, Chapel Hill, N.C.: Univ. of North Carolina Press, 1936.

KEATS, JOHN. *Schools Without Scholars.* Boston: Houghton Mifflin, 1958.

KOOS, LEONARD V. *The American Secondary School.* Boston: Ginn and Company, 1927.

MARR, HARRIET WEBSTER. *The Old New England Academies.* New York: Comet Press Books, 1959.

THIRRING, HANS. "Education for the Age of Science." *Bulletin Atomic Science,* September 1959.

WERTENBAKER, THOMAS JEFFERSON. *The Puritan Oligarchy.* New York: Scribner's, 1947.

Students from the Middle East and Southeast Asia are introduced to the common heritage of the United States during a visit to the C. J. Scott High School in East Orange, New Jersey.

CHAPTER 5

Strengthening the Common Heritage

THE COMMON heritage supplies both the spirit and the conscience of a democratic United States. From it are drawn the ideals, values, beliefs, and commitments that make possible self-government and individual liberty. The political structure; an economic system that incorporates private enterprise, organized labor, and governmental services; wide variety in social and religious organizations, public institutions, and family life—all are nourished by this heritage that is a unique endowment from past generations.

Public education, especially at the secondary level, is the major instrument by which the common heritage is transmitted from one generation to the next. How well schools perform this responsibility determines in large measure how strong the heritage will remain. From early national days to the present, the problem of developing and maintaining unity among peoples of diverse racial, religious, ethnic, social, and political backgrounds has persisted. In the past, a young and developing nation found that adversity bound men together and gave them the will and power to survive. Ironically, now that the United States has achieved success, prosperity, and world leadership, there is evidence that the common faith in democratic traditions and institutions, and in the American system of life—

indeed, in the very processes of democracy—may be weakening. To check this erosion of ideals and morality, both personal and social, as well as to strengthen faith in freedom and self-government, the nation must turn to its schools.

A UNIQUE HERITAGE: DEMOCRACY AS BOTH POLITICAL THEORY AND WAY OF DAILY LIFE

The common heritage, as herein used, refers to that conception of democracy in political affairs and private life which is unique to the United States. It was born in the struggle for independence of the original thirteen colonies, nurtured by the vision and foresight of the founding fathers, and matured by a people determined to make freedom and self-government survive. For almost two hundred years it has served as an ideal that provided direction, stability, and character to the social, political, and economic life of a new and ambitious nation.

Nature

The common heritage might be defined as the operational agreements that specify the goals, ideals, values, and relationships by which the people of the United States have chosen to live. Basically, these are national in scope and application rather than regional, state, or local. They regulate political policies and procedures, shape economic theories, and influence social institutions, as well as guide human relationships.

A distinction is made between the common heritage—a possession of one nation—and the "cultural heritage" which includes the knowledge, creations, inventions, and ideas that civilized man has accumulated and made available to people everywhere. For example, the English language is a part of the cultures of several nations; mathematics belongs to the cultures of all countries. Artistic and musical creations, inventions, and such social institutions as the family or church, also overlap national boundaries. Similarly, self-government and personal freedom are values many nations enjoy and are potentially available to all. On the other hand, the form of self-government and the quality of individual freedom in the United States are unique; hence these are examples of the "common heritage."

Sources

The sources of the common heritage of the United States are diverse. They represent a number of historical ages and events and are founded upon three basic philosophical or religious theories: the Hebraic-Christian ethic, the Athenian theory of political democracy, and the more recently developed conception of the scientific method.

The agreements that constitute the heritage are enunciated in *The Declaration of Independence,* the *Constitution of the United States of America* with its appended *Bill of Rights,* and various subsequent acts of Congress. Interpretations and clarifications have been added throughout the years by various decisions of the Supreme Court. In addition, these basic agreements have been supplemented by such historic statements as George Washington's *Farewell Address,* Thomas Jefferson's *Letters,* and Abraham Lincoln's *Gettysburg Address.* Through the years they have been dramatized and disseminated in prose, poetry, picture, drama, and song by the nation's leading creative geniuses.

Components

A distinguishing feature of the common heritage is its dual role as a philosophy of government and as a system of values to guide man's private life. Of these, Gunnar Myrdal, a visiting Swedish scholar observed that "America, compared to every other country in Western civilization, large or small, has the most explicitly expressed system of general ideals in reference to human interrelations. . . . This body of ideals is more widely understood and appreciated than similar ideals are anywhere else."[1]

Myrdal recognized a system of values that is written into basic historic documents, laws, and literature and is widely taught and understood. He noted that inconsistencies exist in isolated places with respect to particular situations and problems. He recognized, however, that the American people use their ideals as a frame of reference against which to judge social conflicts. This frame of reference he called the "American Creed." Such a title is justified inasmuch as the common heritage often functions as what might be called the national conscience; it constitutes the values that people cherish and use as criteria for evaluating individual and group behavior.

[1] Gunnar Myrdal, *An American Dilemma,* New York (Harper), 1947, p. 3.

Possibility of Self-Destruction

Democracy possesses within itself the possibility of self-destruction. Such a fate may result from neglect by its citizens—their failure to vote, to support social institutions, and to defend their values against aggressive actions, either from within or from abroad. It could come from selfish, vested interest which might violate the concept of the brotherhood of man that underlies democracy. Conflicts between subgroups, provoked, for example, by devotion to religious doctrines, economic policies, racial segregation, labor or business interests, or class status, could be the destroying force if these conflicts were to deteriorate into violence. The freedom allowed to competing ideas and beliefs—to minority opinions, the toleration of error in the conviction that truth rather than force should be used in its counteraction, the fact that the process of transmitting the common heritage, itself, is left to voluntary actions—all hold the potential of helping to weaken national commitments if the nation allows the enemies of freedom to use these freedoms for their own destructive purposes. Finally, self-government provides the means by which its entire structure may be changed or discontinued in response to the will of the people. If the people lose their belief in freedom, their government will soon turn to tyranny.

The ideals that comprise the heritage of democracy are seldom realized completely in any situation. Even in the United States, the operation of democracy is far from perfect, but the citizens of this country continue to hold fast to their faith in democracy. Related to this point is a pertinent observation by Vice-Admiral Rickover who, although his educational proposals are hotly debated, is widely applauded as a patriot and designer of atomic submarines.

> It is often said that democracy is on trial. To my mind it is not democracy but democracy's ability to handle certain basic problems that is on trial. The Soviet Union and the United States are competing for the best solutions to these problems . . . only our own stupidity and selfishness could lose us the race. If we saw to it that democracy prevailed throughout our private and public life we should inevitably be more efficient than the Russians. The free individual always out-creates the bound individual—provided, of course, the two are equal as human beings, equally well-educated and equally patriotic.[2]

[2] H. G. Rickover, "Don't Hamstring the Talented," the *Saturday Evening Post,* February 13, 1960, p. 30.

DANGER ON TWO FRONTS: AT HOME AND ABROAD

Events during the last twenty years have thrust the mantle of leadership for the free countries of the world upon the United States. At the same time an enemy has arisen that threatens that leadership and the values it holds.

The decline of colonialism following World War II released millions of the world's people to pursue their own destinies. Large numbers of these are desperately in need of help to combat poverty and disease. They are aware of the scientific discoveries and technological developments that theoretically make possible adequate standards of living for all and they are determined to share such benefits. To gain this goal they are often willing to form alliances with any nation, regardless of its political, economic, or ideological commitments.

Signs of Internal Decay

The strength of the United States has been doubted, challenged, and tested many times since independence was first won. Its political and economic systems have been called confused, cumbersome, and inefficient. Nevertheless, each time the nation has seemed in danger of faltering, the common heritage has served as a basis for rallying new strength to safeguard democratic values.

Today, there are signs that suggest a lessening of devotion to the democratic way of life. Some view these tendencies as nothing more than normal fluctuations in individual and group behavior; others see them as danger signs that call for study and counteraction. Eugene Kinkead, after a study of the behavior of United States military prisoners during the Korean conflict, concluded that the nation's youth reflect a "wholesale moral dissolution," that individual "weakness" of character is primarily responsible, and that the fundamental social institutions must carry the responsibility for this "collapse."[3] Other students of the problem of "brainwashing" disagree with Kinkead's conclusions, but they recognize the danger involved and the need to attend to the development of clearer individual commitment to national goals.[4]

Devotion to the basic principles of political, economic, religious,

[3] Eugene Kinkead, "The Study of Something New in History," the *New Yorker,* October 26, 1957, p. 102.

[4] Raymond A. Bauer and Edgar H. Schein (eds.), "Brainwashing," *Journal of Social Issues,* Vol. 13, No. 3, 1957.

and personal freedom, as well as enthusiasm for the responsibilities of democracy, have all seemed less widespread in the behavior of American citizens in the postwar years. Perhaps this loss of confidence had its start in the disillusionment that followed World War I when it became apparent that the "war for democracy" had fallen short of achieving its goals. The depression of the 1930's raised doubts about the conscience and integrity of private enterprise and spurred steps toward greater state control. The conflict between Russia and the free world ranges from cold to actual warfare and causes some people to doubt whether America will be able to realize its ambitious, unofficial goal of extending democracy to all people throughout the world.

Loyalty oaths for teachers and federally aided students are evidences of the loss of confidence, as are the vigorous efforts of certain groups to force religious instruction into the public schools. So, too, are some of the more intemperate attacks against social institutions, particularly the schools. The intense efforts of congressional committees to uncover damaging leaks in the government's security dikes reflect, also, the fear that has pervaded the nation. Closely associated with these actions have been efforts to require citizens to testify publicly as to their allegiance, or be labeled traitors.

The outward signs of internal decay are difficult to interpret. That their basis is fear seems clear. The difficulty lies in judging how much of the fear is rooted in the very real presence of a real enemy out to destroy our way of life and how much is sheer hysteria. A distinction must be made between the two if their impact on national strength is to be accurately appraised.

Perfect democracy has not yet been achieved in the United States. Nevertheless, until recent years, this objective has been realistically cherished and vigorously pursued. A tendency is developing, however, for the imperfections in democratic life not to be endured as temporary obstacles to improvement, but rather rationalized as unavoidable, if not desirable, concomitants of freedom.

Respect and acceptance of differences, basic ideals of democratic life, are no longer being accorded to extreme intellectual positions. The range, for example, between the liberal and conservative in politics has sharply narrowed within and between both major parties. A middle-of-the-road philosophy has become predominant. The effect has been to reduce the exercise of freedom of speech and thought to conform with the opinions of the timid.

Outright flaunting of the principles and procedures of democracy and its institutions by widely acclaimed public figures is another sign of decay. Regrettably, the public press has in some cases championed the demagogue while ridiculing the conscientious and loyal who call attention to his desecration of the common heritage. The condemnation of religious bodies and colleges and universities as communist-infested, the accusation that the public schools are godless, and the attacks on the integrity of the Supreme Court are examples of the issues used by demagogues to win support from the public.

Reductions or breakdowns in communications between groups is evident in racial relations, labor-management negotiations, religious interdenominational conflicts, and educational conflicts and controversies, as well as in economic and political affairs. When communication stops, the processes of democracy are impaired.

Many Americans find the self-centered, comfort-conscious outlook on life that exists in the United States unsatisfying. They are not content to attain high standards of living for themselves in a world where starvation, disease, and unhappiness grip so many human beings. Evidence of this concern is found in support for the Marshall Plan, the Point Four programs, and various other foreign-aid plans that have been developed since World War II. These, in aggregate, have added up to billions of dollars of aid to underdeveloped nations. The most recent indications are found in the eagerness of young people to volunteer for the Peace Corps, even though it means hard work without pay at standards of living far below those to which participants are accustomed.

On the other hand, some people look to the past—even to colonial days—for simple convictions about religion, education, and community life that will give them comfort and a feeling of security in a rapidly changing world. They yearn to return to an age when life was simpler, more understandable, and subject to individual control.

World-Wide Attitudes and Forces

The distorted image the United States exports of itself often conflicts with the ideals and values of the common heritage.

Testifying before the United States Senate Subcommittee on National Policy Machinery in March 1960, Mr. Abercrombie Lovett, former Under Secretary of State and later Defense Secretary, said: "The country's security lies in fields that embrace things other than sheer military end-products themselves—our position in the world, the psychological image which we present to the world as a whole. I feel that we are doing less than our best."[5]

Negative attitudes have been produced, for example, by the shock to the human conscience that occurred the world over when the first atomic bomb was exploded at Hiroshima—a mass massacre of civilians to gain military advantage. The picture of a leading democratic nation as an agent of atomic destruction is difficult for many to reconcile with the American respect for human life and property. There is an obvious difficulty in explaining why a nation would outlaw the use of poison gas as too brutal in combat and then turn to equally inhumane and much more destructive devices.

Materialism, diplomatic immaturity, and international paternalism are other images that are being exported by both public officials and civilians. These confuse foreign people who otherwise would join eagerly with the United States to gain the benefits of democracy. Such faults, of course, are often exaggerated by propaganda designed to weaken democratic influence; nevertheless, they add to the problems that confront the country in its new responsibilities in international relations.

Increasingly, the American heritage of freedom is being challenged, openly and defiantly, by advocates of the communistic planned society. Russian spokesmen present the communist ideology as an efficient system for developing a well-organized, strong, and prosperous state. The weaknesses and dangers of communism have not always been apparent to people in economically deprived regions, particularly in those countries with no democratic traditions and a low level of general literacy. Communist leaders have developed effective procedures for creating and exploiting unrest and dissatisfaction. The confidence Russia feels that her planned society will ultimately win over democracy's freedom of choice was expressed by Nikita Khrushchev on his official visit to Indonesia in 1960. Reporting an interview, the United Press commented: "Mr. Khrushchev is firmly convinced that the people of the United States are amateurs at the 'art of revolution,' a phrase which refers to the struggle between East and West to win the peoples of the world to their side."[6]

[5] *Time,* March 7, 1960, p. 11.

[6] United Press International, Washington, D.C. Dispatches of Tuesday, March 8, 1960, reporting an interview with Soviet Premier Nikita Khrushchev, during his tour of Indonesia.

The United States has been embarrassed by the success of Russia in the space satellite race. In reality, however, important as this success is scientifically, it is partially a power demonstration in the political arena—like the strutting of the peacock—to impress underdeveloped nations. The real satellite race is being run not in space, but on the earth's surface. Its goal is to win the political allegiance of unattached nations whose wealth of human and physical resources is vital to world leadership. Russia seeks to win by intrigue and seduction if possible, while implicitly threatening the use of force; the United States, along with the rest of the free world, must depend upon the strength of its ideals, the power of truth, and the invitation to freedom, reserving its military strength for defense.

Reinforcement of Heritage Needed

The survival of democracy requires more than the continuation of the mechanisms of self-government, important as these are. It necessitates each citizen's translating the spirit of mutual respect and shared responsibility into the entire pattern of his life. In addition, world leadership imposes an obligation to place such behavior on exhibit, so to speak, as an example to other countries. Furthermore, inasmuch as international interdependence has created governmental problems that involve other nations, Americans must be informed about the world, as well as about state and national conditions.

President Kennedy sounded a ringing reinforcement to the national heritage in his *Inaugural Address:*

> Let the word go forth from this time and place, to friend and foe alike, that the torch has been passed to a new generation of Americans—born in this century, tempered by war, disciplined by a cold and bitter peace, proud of our ancient heritage—and unwilling to witness or permit the slow undoing of those human rights to which this nation has always been committed, and to which we are committed today.[7]

With these words, a new President ushered in a new administration that called upon the people of the world to work together to preserve the freedom of man. The urgency of reinforcing the national heritage and sharing it with other nations that seek similar goals is critical. To

[7] John F. Kennedy, *Inaugural Address,* January 20, 1961.

strengthen it is vital in understanding the force and factors that tend to weaken the common heritage.

Change itself can be a threat to the common heritage when the change is so rapid that the problems it raises cannot be solved quickly enough. For instance, when the population shifts so as to leave cities as centers primarily for business and slums while the encircling suburbs house the more prosperous, the traditional approaches to local government and taxation may have to change if the city is to remain viable. Experts may know exactly what should be done, yet it is difficult to persuade all concerned to change their customary ways. Often when a course of action is finally taken, it comes too late. The delay between the arising of a problem and its solution has been loosely identified as "cultural lag."[8] Under the pressure of such problems people, impatient for relief, may abandon the approaches implicit in common heritage and turn to methods that contradict the American scheme of values. George Counts explains the cultural lag in this way:

> It [the cultural lag] is certainly the underlying source of the more powerful and disrupting tensions to be observed both within our American society and among the nations of the world. Today a great gulf stands between many of the stubborn realities of our industrial civilization and our customs, loyalties, understandings, and outlooks— between our closely integrated economy and our competitive spirit, between our shrunken world and our traditions of isolation, between our knowledge in almost every field and our ways of life.[9]

In addition to being assigned the basic functions that relate to the development of individuals for life in a democratic society, public schools are now being called upon to assume the educational mission of overcoming the cultural lag. The school is coming to be regarded as a focal point for community interest in, and concern about, any kind of problem—local, state, national, or international. Beyond the direct responsibilities the school assumes for American youth, it is called upon to sponsor or encourage such international services as exchange of cultural information, placing programs on display for foreign visitors, improving the training of teachers of other nations, helping with student and teacher exchange programs, and providing educational consultation to underdeveloped nations.

[8] William F. Ogburn, *Social Change,* New York (Viking), 1922.
[9] George S. Counts, *Education and American Civilization,* New York (Bureau of Publications, Teachers College, Columbia Univ.), 1952, p. 185.

SECONDARY EDUCATION: MAJOR MOBILIZATION AGENCY FOR DEMOCRACY

The major educational agency for transmitting the common heritage to successive generations of citizens has come to be the secondary schools. They are charged with developing unity out of diversity, resolving the conflicting concepts for teaching the heritage, perfecting effective approaches to teaching and school organization, and providing curricular content appropriate to these goals.

Developing Unity Out of Diversity

The high school assembles in one building students with divergent religious beliefs, racial origins, and economic statuses. Their home backgrounds reflect different vocational and professional fields; often, their previous elementary schooling has been dissimilar. In addition, these pupils possess varied interests, capacities, and educational and career plans.

This means that the school must serve two ends at once: It must encourage the worthwhile and discourage the irrational without hurting the individual's self-pride. Individuality is a prime value; it is no solution to regiment students into some caricature of the common heritage. That heritage itself contradicts such an approach. Yet there are certain values all should learn, values that sometimes conflict with views held by individuals, and that are often transferred to the school uncritically from the individual's background. Wrong views can lead to racial prejudice, religious intolerance, wrong career choices, wrong self-evaluations.

By the time youth reach high school, their loyalties and commitments to democracy and its processes have been at least intuitively established. The home, church, and elementary school, as well as the entire community, have provided training by precept and example in the principles, values, and behaviors appropriate to the common heritage.

It remains for the secondary school, however, to raise these intuitions to a level of reason and maturity that will assure their permanence. This assignment falls primarily on the high school for two reasons: first, adolescence is the period of development most conducive to such instruction; and second, the high school is the last level of the school system virtually all youth will experience.

Controversy is the key to democratic progress. Only when it is permitted is freedom of thought and expression possible. Yet the spirit of democratic cooperation may tend, in itself, to discourage dissent. The concept of loyalty, too, if held at a superficial level, may coerce agreement. The high school faces the challenge of teaching all young people genuine respect and appreciation for the common heritage without, at the same time, destroying such a basic element of democracy as the toleration of controversy. In effect, the task is to develop freedom and initiative. Respect for agreements must be taught without developing intolerance for minority opinions that may question them. The school must teach the capacity to live with controversy—a mark of democratic maturity.

The United States is a nation of plural cultures—national, racial, religious, and ethnic. Democracy requires that these rich multiple resources be respected, preserved, and utilized in the interest of national strength and the preservation of individual happiness. No one cultural pattern has priority; all are viewed as worthwhile to the extent that they give support—or do not conflict with—the ideals, values, and goals of the common heritage. The task of identifying tenets within these various cultures that accord with the goals of society as a whole falls on the secondary school.

Conflicting Concepts of Transmittal

Both citizens and educators disagree over the proper way to transmit the common heritage in schools. The major methods advocated are the following:[10]

1. *Indirect teaching of values as a concomitant of the study of basic subjects.* The belief that values cannot be taught but must be "caught," plus the assumption that intellectual development itself represents the best safeguard to the common heritage, support the concept of teaching values indirectly. Schools that follow this procedure make no provision for teaching the tenets and practices of democracy. Instead, they trust to such subjects as literature and history to develop the kind of intellectual competence that will discover, for itself, the ideals and social practices characteristic of the nation.

2. *Indoctrination.* This method is the same as that used in authoritarian societies, namely, teaching the unequivocal acceptance of speci-

---

[10] For a recent study of this problem see Franklin Patterson, *High Schools for a Free Society,* Glencoe, Ill. (The Free Press), 1960.

fied ideals and practices without logic or evidence to support their validity. Under this procedure the "accepted" point of view is presented for mastery. An underlying assumption is that, inasmuch as the common heritage represents basic agreements that have been reached by the nation regarding its political structure and group life, they are not subject to question by students; consequently, indirect and comparative procedures are a waste of time and may weaken loyalties.

3. *Study of noncontroversial problems.* A procedure somewhat akin to indoctrination permits the study only of noncontroversial matters. This concept allows the comparison of certain ideals and social and political practices, but rules out consideration of such controversial subjects as racial integration, separation of church and state, competing economic systems, labor-management differences, or the strengths and weaknesses of democracy and communism. The particular issues avoided often differ from one region to another and over periods of time. The theory behind this exclusion of two-sided issues from school study is that high school youth are too young to face such conflicts without endangering their commitments to democracy.

4. *Objective comparisons of conflicting values and competing systems of life.* This approach assumes that it is best for students to discover for themselves the ideas and ideals of the heritage. They are encouraged to examine and compare the strengths and weaknesses of democracy and communism.

Until recently, public sentiment opposed permitting students to learn about communism. Teachers who discussed communism in class were often under attack. Such sentiment grew out of fear and insecurity, often encouraged by political leaders who equated knowledge about Russia with disloyalty. Gradually, however, many Americans have come to realize that ignorance is not the safest way to maintain the common heritage, and they are willing to have their children compare competing ways of life.

This comparative approach has been given support in some school systems by boards of education who establish statements of principles on the handling of controversial issues in classrooms. Such policies help educate the community and also to protect teachers.

Process Approaches

In some secondary schools both vicarious and firsthand experiences are used to make the common heritage real. To implement these two approaches certain courses are required for all students and at the same time opportunities are created for students to learn democracy by experiencing it in school. For instance, the student gains both theoretical and practical knowledge of democratic processes by being required to study certain courses and by observing, and participating in, school government.

1. *Academic study of required courses.* Courses in American history, civics, literature, and the problems of American democracy are often required because they contribute to the transmittal of the common heritage.

2. *Teaching procedures.* In order to develop democratic behavior, teaching procedures have been created that emphasize teacher-student cooperation in planning, executing, and evaluating the learning activities in formal courses. Laboratory techniques also stress independence in thought and self-direction in learning. Group discussion provides opportunities for students to consider questions together, to bring facts to bear on issues, and to appraise the validity of various positions— much as they will ultimately do in life situations.

3. *Climate of school life.* The American high school has in the main sought to maintain within itself a climate representative of the best examples of democratic ideals and procedures. Heterogeneity—that is, a student population representing all types of backgrounds, abilities, and interests—has been defended on the ground that young people need to learn to respect differences in their fellow men. Those who oppose grouping students on the basis of intellectual capacity do so because they believe such arrangements promote an undemocratic class system. One of the major arguments for the comprehensive high school is the opportunity it provides for all young people to live and work together within a common school community while pursuing their individual goals.

4. *Experiences in democracy.* One agency for teaching students the principles and processes of democracy is student government. Although practices differ widely, the objective is to encourage students to learn shared responsibility by actual experiences in self-government. The extent of student participation in the management of a school often depends upon faculty convictions, community support, and successful experiences by students. Home-room organizations, student councils, and agreements between students in classes and clubs are vehicles for such student participation. The areas of student participation and the

extent of their responsibilities are usually defined by agreements between the faculty and the student body. Where student councils are formally organized, charters or constitutions usually set these limits. It is estimated that between two-thirds and three-fourths of the secondary schools in the United States provide for some participation by students in school management.[11]

5. *All-school interpretation of the common heritage.* In addition to involving students in the management of school affairs, most schools conduct special programs aimed at developing feelings of loyalty to the school, community, and nation. Such activities include the following:

(a) Ceremonies involving the flag salute and the singing of the national anthem and other popular national songs

(b) Assembly programs commemorating historical events, e.g., Washington's Birthday and Veterans Day

(c) Home-room programs and discussions on current local, state, or national issues, social and civic problems, and individual and group behavior

(d) School and community service projects which may range from "clean up days"—the educational value of which some question—to community investigations or surveys of particular problems

The theory behind these activities is that as the individual participates in cooperative experiences with his peers, he gains a sense of responsibility which can be transferred to new circles of civic and social associations. Such feelings of involvement with and responsibility to the group are viewed as essential if youth is to develop cooperative traits and the willingness to sacrifice for the welfare of others.

Although simple loyalties to small groups can often be developed largely through experience, the establishment of commitments to ideals and procedures that function at the state, national, and world levels requires greater emphasis on rational thought processes. Thus, the establishment of loyalty is seen as a process of helping the individual translate satisfying firsthand experiences into an acceptance of broader, less personally satisfying situations.

Curricular Treatment

Three areas of the curriculum have carried major responsibility for transmitting the cultural heritage: history and the social studies, the humanities and the arts, and, to some extent, the sciences.

[11] Franklin Patterson, *op. cit.,* p. 45.

History and the social studies. History and the social studies bear, perhaps, the heaviest responsibility for transmitting the facts, developments, and agreements of the common heritage. The social studies courses in high school, particularly those in civics and problems of democracy, have aimed directly at citizenship training. History courses generally are concerned with providing an academic background to support the more applied treatment of the social studies. The teaching of the history of non-Western areas is becoming more prevalent. At least one state, Pennsylvania, requires the inclusion of such content in the programs of all students.

The emphasis on history and social studies in high school curriculums can be seen from a recent survey of the courses most frequently offered at each grade level of the secondary school program.[12] The placement of different courses is shown in Table 5-1.

Traditional social studies courses have been criticized for neglecting the history of this nation and its government, Western civilization, the

Table 5-1. *Courses in History and Social Studies Typically Offered in U.S. Secondary Schools*

GRADE	COURSES MOST FREQUENTLY OFFERED
SEVEN	Selected people and nations
	Geography
	United States history
	Social studies
EIGHT	United States history
	Civics
	Social studies
NINE	Civics
	Orientation
	State history
TEN	World history
	Modern history
ELEVEN	United States history
TWELVE	Contemporary problems

[12] Richard Gross and Leslie Zeleny, *Educating Citizens for Democracy: Curriculum and Instruction in Secondary Studies,* New York (Oxford Univ. Press), 1958, p. 70.

common heritage as a force in contemporary problems, and such subjects as economics, geography, and anthropology; for emphasizing extraneous matters, such as vocational guidance, personal problems, e.g., personality development or marriage; and for the lack of vitality and effectiveness in the quality of instruction.

Humanities and the heritage. Literature bears an especially heavy responsibility for helping students understand and appreciate the events, values, hopes, and ambitions of past generations that formed the fabric of democracy. It holds the potential, if properly organized and well taught, of both conveying knowledge and stimulating loyalties to the ideals that have given man freedom. Through the poetry of Walt Whitman, the stories of Thomas Paine, the essays of Oliver Wendell Holmes, the dramas of Maxwell Anderson, and the speeches of Patrick Henry or Abraham Lincoln the heritage may be brought to life for every student.[13] How well literature serves the common heritage depends partly on the focus given to human values.

Fine arts strengthen heritage. Many students who have difficulty with abstract concepts gain vital understanding of the ideals and spirit of democracy through the arts. Others who are adept at verbal learning benefit from the reinforcement that comes through active experiences in art, music, and the dance.

The role of the fine arts in helping to convey, interpret, and give reality to the heritage has been seen as: "first, the reception of the heritage from the past; second, the reaction of the individual mind upon this heritage with a view to the enhancement of present experiences; third, the opening of the eyes of the mind outward to the universal realm of value."[14]

Science and the heritage. Science is most frequently identified with the great technological developments of our times. It has long been integrally related to the heritage of democracy, however, through the procedure it offers for the discovery of truth—the "scientific method." For the scientist truth is something objectively verifiable by anyone. The truth is open to all who seek it. The assertion of truth by authority

[13] During World War II the College English Association sponsored the publication of an anthology of literature that presents the ideas of freedom and democracy: see, George F. Reynolds and Donald F. Connors (eds.), *Freedom Speaks*, New York (Ronald Press), 1943.

[14] Committee on Objectives of a General Education, *General Education in a Free Society,* Cambridge, Mass. (Harvard Univ. Printing Office), 1945, pp. 128-29.

is opposed to the spirit of science and democracy. Recent scientific discoveries emphasize the importance of every citizen's knowing more about both the method and the applications of scientific knowledge to the affairs of men. Solutions of international problems, the extension of the benefits of freedom to people in underdeveloped nations, the prevention of war—all depend in some degree upon the use made of science. This point is stressed by Francis Friedman, a distinguished scientist from the Massachusetts Institute of Technology:

> We all know that science is a human endeavor . . . our picture of the physical world is one of the triumphs of thought. Both the present picture and the story of how we came to it and how we are extending it are an essential part of our culture. We need some (commonly shared) understandings of both the state and the process of science to live effectively in our world.[15]

Weaknesses in high school science programs include the presentation of science as the study of technological processes rather than as a distinct type of intellectual activity; attempts to teach science without adequate mathematical foundation; and laboratory procedures that stress recipe-following rather than logical analysis and creative discovery.

PRESENT PROBLEMS AND THE HERITAGE

Some of the present problems confronting the secondary school grow out of the accelerated pace of life today; others are by-products of the increased dependence on formal educational programs to prepare youth for democratic participation. Still others arise from those who oppose the public secondary school or would limit its freedom. Finally, there is the problem of participation by the school in the life of the community, which is essential to the effective transmission of the common heritage.

The amazing technological progress of this century has produced the paradox of maintaining stability in the face of change. Traditional ideals and values, as well as the democratic processes, must be maintained while adaptations are made to accommodate new developments in communication, transportation, and production.

[15] Francis L. Friedman, "A Blueprint," *First Annual Report of the Physical Science Study Committee,* Washington, D.C. (National Science Foundation), 1958, p. 26.

Established governmental policies, such as the Monroe Doctrine, are undergoing re-evaluation as the United States joins with other countries to strengthen the United Nations as a force for international cooperation. New internal forces, e.g., the growing strength of the federal government, compel readjustments; at the same time they must not be permitted to undermine the heritage of stability that the past offers.

Knowledge and Values

Conflict often results between the fact-oriented standards of scholarship, in the social studies as well as the sciences, and the religious position that faith should guide the selection and interpretation of knowledge. The issue strikes at the heart of the church and state controversy. Supporters of the parochial school hold that knowledge gained outside the framework of the moral and spiritual values of organized religion is dangerous. Occasionally, some of the more extreme of these supporters attack the public schools and advocate a change in the system that would allow religious training in the schools. When such an attack occurs, defenders of public secondary education must keep in mind that the separation of church and state is a fundamental part of our heritage written into the Constitution. Behind it lies not only the force of custom but also the force of law.

Another problem arises from the tendency of people to live by their emotions and prejudices, rather than by the facts. In effect, this is the age-old contest between ignorance and intelligence; in operation, it often finds the prejudices of people winning over rational intelligence.

Some politicians are quick to capitalize on the emotions of their constituents. As a result, many controversial problems are kept alive long after their time by appeals to the emotions rather than to the dependable guidance that facts can provide.

Although it is the objective of education in support of the common heritage to promote the application of knowledge, ideals, and beliefs, school programs do not always implement this principle. Too often schools have fostered the separation of school and community life; they have avoided also some controversial issues that could give reality, as well as motivation, to study in formal subjects. A study conducted for the Tufts University Civic Center led to this conclusion:

> The great issues of public affairs, about which free citizens should know and in whose resolution they should participate, can excite the

curiosity, interest and hard work of youth. But in practice some of the most important areas of economic, political and social concerns tend to be avoided by the high school as objects of study.[16]

The solution to this problem of isolation lies in pushing intellectual considerations to the stage of application. Application, unsupported by sound scholarship, is rarely useful; the problem of the school is to provide opportunities for students to translate their scholarship into practical civic and human relationships.

SELECTED REFERENCES

BEATTY, JOHN L. *Heritage of Western Civilization.* Englewood Cliffs, N.J.: Prentice-Hall, 1958.

CHALMERS, RANDOLPH C. *The Heritage of Western Culture.* Toronto: Ryerson Press, 1952.

COMMAGER, HENRY S. *Education in a Free Society.* Pittsburgh: Univ. of Pittsburgh Press, 1960.

GROSS, RICHARD E., LESLIE D. ZELENY, AND ASSOCIATES. *Educating Citizens for Democracy: Curriculum and Instruction in Secondary Studies.* New York: Oxford Univ. Press, 1958.

HAVIGHURST, ROBERT J., AND BERNICE L. NEUGARTEN. *Society and Education.* Boston: Allyn and Bacon, 1957.

JONES, HOWARD MUMFORD. *American Humanism: Its Meaning for World Survival.* New York: Harper, 1957.

MAYOR, FREDERICK. *A History of Educational Thought.* Columbus, Ohio: Charles E. Merrill, 1960.

MULLER, HERBERT J. *Issues of Freedom: Paradoxes and Promises.* New York: Harper, 1960.

President's Commission on National Goals. *Goals for Americans.* Englewood Cliffs, N.J.: Prentice-Hall, 1960.

SHUSTER, G. N. *Education and Moral Wisdom.* New York: Harper, 1960.

SPINDLER, GEORGE D., ed. *Education and Anthropology.* Stanford: Stanford Univ. Press, 1955.

THAYER, V. T. *Role of the School in American Society.* New York: Dodd, Mead, 1960.

[16] Franklin Patterson, *op. cit.,* p. 69.

Audio-lingual aids in language laboratory help students to advance at maximum rates through independent study and practice.

Students lay a sound foundation for scholarship by learning to use reference books in a good high school library.

CHAPTER 6

Laying the Foundation for Scholarship

SECONDARY education is an intellectual enterprise. This is true whether students are preparing for college, seeking to master marketable skills, or simply readying themselves for adult responsibilities. Regardless of the particular learning tasks—having students master the binomial theorem, write a historical essay, or design and construct a table —the school is concerned with developing skills, responses, and knowledges that require the use of mental powers. Educators generally agree on this premise. Nevertheless, they frequently disagree about how intelligence is best developed, the nature and amount of scholarship required at the secondary school level, and the means of the discovery of knowledge and its use, as well as the proper conditions for scholarship.

The responsibility of the secondary school for laying the foundation for scholarship has been confused by the enrollment of many boys and girls who possess little interest in, or aptitude for, academic work. Efforts to adjust curricular offerings and instructional procedures to such pupils have resulted in an emphasis upon firsthand experiences and activity projects that often seem to accord priorities to the physical and emotional rather than to the mental, the contemporary in place of established knowledge, and to superficial social relationships rather than basic understandings and appreciations.

The struggle to adapt instruction in secondary schools to the wide range of student abilities, aptitudes, interests, and motivations, while still according priority to intellectual development, has been complicated by two factors. First, although mature scholarship is readily recognizable, no simple standards are available to judge progress toward such an attainment in immature learners. Second, the programs of colleges and universities are so diverse that no uniform standards exist to provide scholarship goals for the secondary school.

INTELLECTUAL DEVELOPMENT—THE PRIMARY OBJECTIVE

The primary objective of education, at all levels, is to equip man to live by his intelligence. This premise applies equally to the individual who works with his hands and to the academic scholar. Also, it is of special significance in a democratic nation that challenges each citizen to think independently in affairs of government and to chart his personal and economic destiny. Intellectual development must be the central goal of the secondary school inasmuch as it deals with young people at a time in their lives when mental processes can be refined to maximum sharpness.

Intellectual development in the secondary school has been influenced by such forces as the search for the meaning of intelligence; the theory of aggregate response of capacities; an emphasis on behavior outcomes; efforts to relate processes of learning to achievement; and continuing conflicts over priorities in the school program.

Search for the Meaning of Intelligence

The history of civilization is the story of man's use of his intelligence to understand, to control, and to change the natural forces of his environment. Within the past century, concentrated efforts have been made to identify the meaning of intelligence so that it may be better developed. These efforts range from exhaustive studies of the history of ideas[1] to scientific attempts to measure mental powers.[2]

[1] For example, see John Herman Randall, Jr., *The Making of the Modern Mind*, Boston (Houghton Mifflin), 1940.

[2] Pioneering studies were conducted by Alfred Binet, Lewis M. Terman, E. L. Thorndike, Wolfgang Koehler, and others. See George D. Stoddard, *The Meaning of Intelligence*, New York (Macmillan), 1944.

Explorations into the meaning of intelligence have dealt with groundless beliefs and age-old superstitions as well as scientific debates about the relative contributions of heredity and environment to mental capacity and its development. They have been concerned, also, with the nature of the thinking process, including the skills, sensory responses, and internal changes that it involves. Attention has been given to the various factors that make up intelligence, the role of memory in intelligence, the retention of knowledge and skill, and to adaptability or transfer of intellectual attainments. Scholars have sought to learn how to predict at an early age such traits as high intellectual capacity, creativity, or skill in fields such as mathematics, science, or language.

Despite the efforts to discover the meaning of intelligence, the quest remains in its embryonic stages. In the absence of facts to document hypotheses, theorists debate the nature of mental powers and speculate how they may best be cultivated. The secondary school must carry on its efforts to prepare young people for a future that will make greater intellectual demands than has the past, without conclusive directives for its mission.

Aggregate Response of Capacities

Two important generalizations about intelligence are influencing programs of education in secondary schools today. One holds that the total capacities of the individual—mental, emotional, physical—respond in aggregate to total patterns of stimuli. This theory replaces the ancient belief that mind and body functioned separately from, and often in competition with, each other. The thesis that intelligence is the aggregate response of all capacities makes possible the formulation of concepts of behavior as related to environment. Such observations can lead to a concept of intelligent behavior, or rational responses to particular situations.

The second premise holds that intelligence, itself, is more than the sum total of abilities and capacities.[3] Thus the measurement of traits possessed by an individual may not reflect fully the degree of intelligence possessed. Rather, the impact of intelligence is achieved not only by the aggregate strength of various capacities, such as memory, verbal facility, and ability to perceive relationships; it is influenced as well by the configuration achieved as traits combine at a given time, the inter-

[3] See especially, David Wechsler, "The Meaning of Intelligence," *Wisdom,* May 1957.

est and the drive of the individual toward a goal, and by the balance of capacities that prevails.

What is called intelligent behavior thus becomes a product of both capacity and coordination of abilities to respond to particular situations. The problem of predicting accurately the behavior of an individual when confronted with variable stimuli, and the inadequate knowledge of the aggregate processes involved, have led to deep-seated disagreements regarding the education best suited for producing intelligent behavior.[4]

Emphasis on Behavior Outcomes

The relationship between programs of education and the production of desired forms of behavior has long been the concern of curriculum experts at the secondary school level. The appraisal of intellectual development in terms of behavior outcomes focuses on how well students respond to environmental situations. Attitudes, values, insights, judgments, reasoning, use of symbols, analyses of reactions— all are studied when measuring an individual's behavior under specific circumstances.

This emphasis is responsible for curriculum and instructional developments in the secondary school which aim at making knowledge function more effectively in the lives of students. Opposing the view that mental training is preparation for a distant, adult world, it utilizes contemporary examples of behavior as samples of what might be expected in the future. The emphasis on behavior outcomes contributes both in reducing the compartmentalization of knowledge by the development of fused or correlated courses and in supporting experiments with the core curriculum that enable students to work on clusters of related problems.

Relationship of Processes to Achievement

Another trend toward the development of intelligent behavior, as opposed to mind training, is the experiments that have been conducted to ascertain the relationship between the method of learning and the

[4] See Robert M. Hutchins, *The Higher Learning in America*, New Haven (Yale Univ. Press), 1936. Also, Arthur Bestor, *The Restoration of Learning*, New York (Knopf), 1955. Also, B. O. Smith, William Stanley, and Harlan Shores, *Fundamentals of Curriculum Development*, Tarrytown, N.Y. (World Book Co.), 1957.

results achieved. The effect has been greater emphasis on methods of teaching in secondary schools.

In general, studies of this type have led to a reduction in those teaching and learning procedures that stress mastery of skills and content as ends in themselves. They have supported instructional approaches that require problem-solving, experimentation, creative production, analysis and interpretation of data and situations, and the practical use and communication of knowledge. Extensive utilization of audio-visual aids and dependence upon firsthand learning experiences, often outside the classroom to take advantage of community resources, have characterized such teaching procedures. Typical, also, have been attempts to help young people to face their personal problems intelligently as training for more complicated situations they will later confront.

Conflict over Priorities

The developing theories of intelligence, particularly with the emphasis they place on aggregate responses and behavioral outcomes, have upset traditional conceptions of the nature of intellectual development in secondary schools. They compete with entrenched practices that treat the mind more or less as a muscle, to be developed by rigorous, routine exercise, with the mastery of content its sole objective.

At the same time, in the confusions resulting from a multiplicity of experimental programs and procedures, values and priorities have yet to be established. In some situations, activity, as an end in itself, has replaced emphasis on mental discipline. In addition, schools meet confused advice about the behavioral outcomes secondary schools should achieve. Preparing students for college is a goal that has advocates of conflicting opinions that range from faith in the study of certain basic subjects as the only way to develop intelligence, to the theory tested by the Eight-Year Experiment of the Progressive Education Association that interest, application, creativity, approach, and initiative in study are more important for intellectual development than the particular subjects mastered.[5]

NATURE OF SCHOLARSHIP

To develop the intellectually free and independent scholar is the end of education. The secondary school has the responsibility of helping

[5] Wilford M. Aikin, *The Story of the Eight-Year Study*, New York (Harper), 1942.

young people to integrate the skills of learning and to expand interests in various subject fields (initiated at the elementary level) into a solid foundation for continuing scholarship. To accomplish this objective, the ability to organize, master, and put knowledge to use must be cultivated in all students. The ideal result is the high school graduate who is an independent scholar, whether he continues his formal study or enters immediately into a vocation.

Meaning of Scholarship

Scholarship requires that an individual attain a high level of achievement in one or more subject fields. In a broader sense, it designates the process of applying intellectual power to the discovery, organization, and use of all knowledge. It depends on the individual's adeptness in the use of the basic language skills—reading, organizing, writing— by which information is gathered and recorded, and proficiency in the symbols—mathematics, formulas, designs, language—pertinent to a field of inquiry. Over and above the ability to acquire knowledge, scholarship requires the development of intellectual processes such as insight, reasoning, interpreting, analyzing, deducting, judging of values, formulating hypotheses, creating new concepts, and acting on conclusions.

After analyzing autobiographical statements of various learned men, creative writers, and artists, Ghiselin Brewster concluded:

> Even the most energetic and original mind, in order to reorganize or extend human insight in any valuable way, must have attained more than ordinary mastery of the field in which it is to act, a strong sense of what needs to be done, and skill in the appropriate means of expression. It seems certain that no significant expansion of insight can be produced otherwise.[6]

With fields of knowledge becoming more complex, it is imperative that high school students lay sound foundations for scholarship. The key to such a beginning is interest in an area of study. Unless the student finds in his early acquaintance with a field an intellectually challenging, stimulating, and enjoyable experience, he is not likely to pursue it to the point of satisfactory scholarship. Concerning this point Alfred North Whitehead observed:

[6] Brewster Ghiselin (ed.), *The Creative Process: A Symposium,* Berkeley (Univ. of California Press), 1952.

There can be no mental development without interest. Interest is the sine qua non for attention and apprehension. You may endeavor to excite interest by means of birch rods, or you may coax it by the incitement of pleasurable activity. But without interest there is no progress. Now the natural mode by which living organisms are excited towards suitable self-development is enjoyment.[7]

The secondary school helps young people to understand the nature and importance of scholarship and introduces them into fields of knowledge that offer exciting invitations to lifelong study.

Development and Maturation of Learning Skills

The basic skills of reading, spelling, writing, arithmetic, use of references and audio-visual resources, as well as outlining, summarization, and note-taking, will have been fairly well developed by most pupils by the time they reach the secondary school. Certain processes, however, require concentrated attention at this level; for others, continued practice and reinforcement are necessary to maintain peak efficiency.

The use of symbols. The symbols of language, mathematics, art, music, and the sciences are the means by which thinking and communication take place. Systems of symbols permit levels of abstraction ranging from simple, single images or concepts to the most complex, multidimensional abstractions. Common language has general usage, being adapted to communication at the popular level in various fields. Specialized language symbols that relate only to specific fields permit scholars to exchange intricate, precise knowledge that is beyond the comprehension of the novice or layman. The more complex the system of symbols, the greater the abstraction involved in their use.

Recently, experts have criticized the secondary school for its failure to teach the symbols essential for scholarship, particularly in science. They point to the fact that the emphasis in the high school curriculum has been on the literary, humanistic, and social, rather than on the mathematical and scientific. As evidence, they cite the preponderance of nonscientific books in school libraries and the historical and literary reading programs for high school students. They also note the number of schools that do not provide advanced courses in science, foreign language, or mathematics.

[7] Alfred North Whitehead, *The Aims of Education*, New York (Macmillan), 1929, p. 42. Quoted by permission of The Macmillan Company.

Study skills. A command of symbols frees the student to search for information, to weigh evidence, to organize and record knowledge, to draw deductions, to project hypotheses—all of which are skills essential to study. To employ such processes effectively, the student needs to understand the general structure of a field of knowledge, the primary theories and discoveries around which its organization is built, and the methods of investigation most appropriate to it.

Instruction in subject fields at the secondary school level should aim to help students perceive the scope of knowledge, the basic facts that should be committed to memory to facilitate study, the general procedures that should be followed to master critical content, and the most promising ways of attacking the unknown. Various fields require different approaches in scholarship and, even within a subject field such as mathematics, the techniques of study are changing as increasing emphasis is being placed on the theoretical probabilities of spatial relationships. In sum, study skills depend upon the ability to think clearly and objectively. The scholar must also be able to communicate his thoughts to others.

"Study habits" refers to the orientation of an individual to the dimensions of a field of inquiry and to his use of tested procedures for its investigation. Actually, the term "habit" is unfortunate; it implies that study is a process that becomes routine. True scholarship, in contrast, is just the opposite. Perhaps one reason why beginning students in a field sometimes find their work laborious and uninteresting is the emphasis placed upon study *habits*. It is true that investigation requires the perfecting of certain skills to the level of habitual operation; nevertheless, the inquiry itself, if conducted properly, involves the learner, at each step of his progress, in the exciting intellectual venture of searching for and judging evidence, finding relationships, exploring possibilities, developing deductions—all in the search for truth. The challenge of pushing students to the skill of thinking is one that faces the secondary school today.

Knowledge—Its Organization, Mastery, and Function

Disagreements about the organization, mastery, and function of knowledge in the process of education have led to deep schisms among theorists of secondary education. One group of distinguished scholars[8]

[8] James D. Koerner, *The Case for Basic Education*, Boston (Little, Brown), 1959.

holds that the initial stages of scholarship should be concerned almost exclusively in high school with the mastery of the accumulated knowledge, wisdom, and culture of the human race as incorporated in the basic subject fields of history, mathematics, science, and language. The object of such study, it is held, is both mental development through the mastery of organized knowledge, and initiation into habits of scholarship that will be advanced in subsequent collegiate programs of instruction.

The other position, supported by equally distinguished scholars,[9] recognizes the importance of students' becoming acquainted with the characteristics of various basic fields of knowledge but places greater emphasis upon the process of scholarly inquiry itself. It supports the proposition that high school students should join in the quest for truth, even before they have mastered the accumulated knowledge of the race. This theory rejects the passive approach to scholarship held by representatives of the "basic education" group. Instead, it urges that students be given problem-solving assignments that challenge them to engage in the collecting, organizing, and interpreting of information with immediate objectives as incentives. One outstanding advocate of this position, Alfred North Whitehead, stated his belief thus:

> I have no hesitation in denouncing it [passive learning] as one of the most fatal, erroneous, and dangerous conceptions ever introduced into the theory of education. The mind is never passive; it is a perpetual activity, delicate, receptive, responsive to stimulus. You cannot postpone its life until you have sharpened it. Whatever interest attaches to your subject-matter must be evoked here and now; whatever possibilities of mental life your teaching should impart, must be exhibited here and now. That is the golden rule of education, and a very difficult rule to follow.[10]

Holders of these two positions find further conflict in the subjects they would require to be taught in secondary schools. Proponents of the basic education philosophy maintain that all students should study

[9] Francis S. Chase and Harold Anderson (eds.), *The High School in a New Era,* Chicago (Univ. of Chicago Press), 1958. This book is a collection of papers presented at the Conference on the American High School which was held at the University of Chicago. The papers give a view of the need for preparing pupils for college and/or leadership roles in science.

[10] Alfred North Whitehead, *op. cit.,* p. 18. Quoted by permission of The Macmillan Company.

the same subjects, while their opponents support the partial-elective system as best for laying a foundation for scholarship.

Careful observers of this conflict see evidences of extremism on both sides. They point out that the knowledge that should be mastered by high school students must be defined in terms of individual abilities, as well as educational and vocational goals. They stress also the necessity for the secondary school to assume greater responsibility for giving academically talented students sound preparation in such basic fields as English, mathematics, and foreign language—skill subjects for learning in all fields—as well as science. History and the social studies are also viewed as basic—not only for scholarly values but for the contribution they make to citizenship. At the same time, these neutral observers point to the urgency of inducting young people into the full processes of scholarship—data collecting, experimenting, interpreting, and drawing conclusions, in short, thinking,—as well as memorizing and reciting the accumulated knowledge assembled by established scholars.

An example of efforts to increase the emphasis of the secondary school on projects that require students to exercise thought processes is entitled Project for the Improvement of Thinking.[11] One facet of this experiment, carried on in three pilot schools, sought to ascertain whether the principles of logic and semantics can be systematically taught at the secondary school level. Teachers of mathematics, science, social studies, and English incorporated principles and concepts of logic and semantics into both teaching units and evaluation instruments. Careful observations were maintained to supplement the measured results of the instruction. Those responsible for the study concluded that pupils in the experimental groups were better acquainted with the skills essential to thinking, applied these skills more effectively after the instruction than before, and performed significantly better in thinking exercises than did their counterparts in the control groups. The evidence seemed to suggest that students in the experimental groups also learned the content of the courses more effectively and efficiently. In addition, teachers reported that members of the experimental groups improved noticeably in the quality of their questions, and in discussion.

[11] A report of this investigation is contained in B. O. Smith, *A Study of the Logic of Teaching,* Urbana, Illinois (College of Education, Bureau of Educational Research), 1960.

The Ultimate Goal

Thus, it can be seen that the ultimate goal of all educational efforts is the creation of the independent scholar. Only through such attainment is education able to free the individual mind. Intelligent behavior—whether in business, community affairs, or highly technical scientific research—requires independence in assembling facts and information, in their analysis and interpretation, and in judgment and subsequent action.

Because the secondary school still represents the last stage of formal education for more than half the population, it faces a particular responsibility for aiding young people to achieve intellectual independence. This responsibility conflicts with the educational tradition that experience in independent scholarship be postponed until university undergraduate or graduate study. It is often made difficult by the immaturity and lack of self-direction and self-discipline of individual boys and girls. Nevertheless, secondary education must endeavor to raise students to levels of intellectual development and independent scholarship that permit them to think and to act in an intellectually responsible manner.

DISCOVERY AND USE OF KNOWLEDGE

Within the past thirty years, secondary education has experimented with experience-centered programs of instruction, programs involving the fusion of content from related fields, and programs focused on life problems. Although each of these developments has contributed something to the character of high schools, the basic pattern of organization for learning has remained largely subject-centered. Experiments with new ways of organizing the high school program have resulted in a shift in emphasis from the simple acquisition of knowledge to the involvement of students in its discovery and use.

The revolt against the presentation of knowledge to high school students as highly organized, separate entities to be learned, rather than used, has characterized this period. Although efforts to reorganize content into more functional categories have met with only moderate success in areas such as the social sciences and general science, the main outcome, perhaps, has been a broadening of the approaches or avenues to knowledge that are employed in programs of high school teaching. Gains, too, have been made in using knowledge to promote wise behavior by the individual and by groups in our democratic society.

Revolt Against Inert Mastery of Knowledge

The tradition of requiring students to master logically organized subject fields, without reference to their use or to other fields of content, has long plagued education at all levels. It has met with resistance in secondary schools in recent years. Since half the population looks forward to immediate entry into work and life activities, interest tends toward utilitarian skills and content. For those going to college, knowledge mastered in high school is often found to be out of date in such rapidly changing fields as science, history, and geography, thus undermining general confidence in the "cold-storage" theory of curriculum. The emphasis on detail, based on the assumption that memorization of facts develops mental powers, often obscures the broad principles and understandings essential to thinking.

The revolt against the inert mastery of knowledge has produced a reorganization of the content and instruction in the basic subject fields of the secondary school curriculum. In general, the organization of knowledge now utilized is characterized by the following five criteria:

1. The organization is developed in terms of specific units that provide the material of study and define the areas of inquiry, i.e., in geography: soils, rivers, mountains; in mathematics: measures, shapes, and number systems; in physics: light, sound, electrons, and energy.

2. Relationships within the units and their properties are the focus of study, i.e., cause-and-effect relations in history, or laws in physics.

3. The generally accepted theories, hypotheses, and concepts of the subject are employed.

4. Techniques and methods of investigation characteristic of the field are used.

5. Factual data relative to the above four elements are studied but not as ends in themselves.

There are, of course, dilemmas and difficult choices involved in the unit system. All pupils do not attain mastery of the subject. Even the degree of attainment of able students often fails to satisfy the specialist. Then, the choice of units to be included in a given subject leaves grounds for disagreement. Teachers are often frustrated by the necessity of omitting details that they feel are essential in their particular field. Problems also arise in measuring and appraising the learning of pupils who have not all covered the same content at the same rate of progress.

Avenues to Knowledge

The major avenues to knowledge have long been known: firsthand experience, historical reference, theoretical projection, analytical treatment, classical reasoning, and scientific experimentation. Concern for scholarship at the secondary school level is opening these avenues for student use. Such practice rests on the assumption that sound scholarship is developmental, that the student learns the kind of investigational procedures he practices. For this reason, teacher-centered lectures and recitations, with the student required to absorb and reproduce assigned materials, have lost ground to those methods that open more avenues for the student to pursue knowledge.

Some high schools provide for students who are interested and talented in fields such as science to carry on independent research, with help from the teacher as needed. Such ventures are important advances toward the development of the highly trained scientific talent now needed by the nation.

Attitudes, Understandings, and Values—Bolstered by Knowledge

The admonition, "with thy knowledge, get understanding," reflects the possibility of learning stopping short of such a goal. Not so often stressed is the fact that attitudes, understandings, and values may not always be bolstered by knowledge. Secondary education has undergone its share of experimentation with the premise that attitudes, understandings, and values can be developed out of experiences alone, without the underpinning that only established truth can supply. It has endeavored, for example, to teach respect for human personality merely by providing wholesome, satisfying experiences between youth of different races, religions, and economic classes. Impressive as such ventures may appear at the time, they often prove to be superficial and ineffective when actual conflicts challenge basic beliefs.

If high school youth are to be prepared to preserve the ideals of democracy and to defend the rights of freemen everywhere, if people with differences are to maintain a way of life that permits the pursuit of happiness for all, programs of education aimed at developing suitable attitudes, understandings, and values must be based upon knowledge. They must aim at helping individuals live by their intellects rather than by emotions and habits. They must replace ignorance with fact, prejudice with respect, intolerance with acceptance, and aggression with cooperation.

Achievement of Wisdom

The generally accepted assumption that only the better educated and the old can be wise operates against efforts at the high school level designed to translate knowledge into its highest form of utility— wisdom. That this belief is often erroneous is clear to anyone who has either observed the foolhardy acts of some highly schooled adults or witnessed the intelligent behavior of youths of lesser educational attainments. The ability to extract from knowledge the truth that we call wisdom is more the result of the nature of learning experience than it is of how much knowledge is mastered. The student who learns to *live by his knowledge* soon becomes wise beyond his years. Similarly, a program of instruction in the secondary school that encourages pupils to use learning in their daily decisions and future plans promotes the kind of responses that are described as wise.

Use of Knowledge by Groups

Group decisions and actions have become important facets of life in the United States. Even highly technical research is no longer always conducted by individuals working alone. Instead, teams of investigators, whose skills and knowledges complement each other, plan and carry out carefully coordinated experiments that may exceed individual capabilities. Whether a person functions as a citizen or a specialist, his skill in working with others is important if his knowledge is to be properly and effectively used.

The appeal to reason by members of a group is often a complex and difficult process. Involved are communication skills required for presentation, discussion, and debate, procedures for group consideration and action, and the emotions that may be stirred by differences of opinion. Group action requires the validation of knowledge at levels that can be understood by all. Objectives often must be clarified before suitable decisions can be made. Frequently complex conflicts of values occur to negate the use of knowledge or to distort goals.

Secondary schools not only must teach individuals to become independent scholars, capable of thinking and acting for themselves, but they must develop in students the skills of group cooperation that make possible the joint pursuit of truth and the shared use of the results of scholarship.

CONDITIONS REQUIRED FOR SCHOLARSHIP

Secondary education must provide certain conditions that are essential to good scholarship. These include the climate of support existing in the community, curricular offerings and instructional procedures, and the commitment of individual students to the satisfactions they derive from intellectual efforts.

Climate of Support

Development of scholarship in a high school depends, first of all, upon parental and community attitudes toward scholarly attainments. Students respond to the attitudes of parents and of other adults, and will devote their energies to activities that are most highly esteemed by those to whom they look for approval.

A community that applauds only extracurricular activities, such as interscholastic athletics, band performances, school dramatics, or debates, will find its high school students favoring these activities. If local newspapers and radio and television stations publicize such events and the individuals who excel in them, boys and girls will gravitate toward them. On the other hand, if a town or city has developed a strong endorsement for intellectual attainment, if young people who have distinguished themselves as scholars are held before their classmates as leaders, the school has a much better chance of laying sound foundations for scholarship for all students.

The development of a climate of support for scholarship is a problem facing communities in the United States today. Teachers and administrators can provide valuable assistance by helping parents and adults identify clearly the order of priorities in secondary education. Fortunately, the demands of the business and industrial world for highly educated personnel, and the international competition for pre-eminence in science are having a sobering effect on citizens who in the past have given only casual support to scholarship.

Curricular Provisions for Concentration in Depth

The development of scholarship requires curricular offerings that permit students to concentrate intensively in a subject field. One major weakness of the secondary school program—particularly in the thousands of small high schools with enrollments under five or six hundred —is the failure to provide sequences of courses in the same subject field that enable students to pursue the subject throughout high school. With the exception of English, in which a course in speech or dramatics is often counted as one of the four-year courses required in grades nine through twelve, only two or three years of work is offered in any one subject field.

The standard college preparatory curriculum followed in most high schools, although intended to lay a foundation for scholarship, has often failed to do so. Its pattern of prescribing two years of study in each of several fields, i.e., history, mathematics, science, and foreign language, in addition to four years of English, has tended to encourage students to spread themselves over many fields, rather than to concentrate upon one or two. Many pupils have neglected particularly to pursue such studies as mathematics and foreign language to a point of real proficiency.

Authorities now urge that high schools not only provide four years of study in the basic fields of the high school curriculum, but also that the content of the first-year college course be included in "honor-type" classes to permit academically talented students to make maximum progress by carrying more than a normal load of high school subjects each year.

Table 6-1 suggests the sequence of courses in four fields, social studies, science, mathematics, and art, in grades nine through twelve, necessary to provide the depth of scholarship appropriate to at least half the population of the senior high school.

Adaptations to Differences in Students

The wide range of pupil abilities requires that secondary schools adapt their programs to differences in pupils. In required general education courses, each student must be challenged to capacity and not held back by classmates. Specialized and advanced subject courses must be adapted to the extremely bright students.

Grouping of students according to ability, long out of favor with educators because of its purported undemocratic influence,[12] is again

[12] Norman Grunlund has studied the problem of ability grouping in relation to the development of the most desirable personal choices of pupils. He cites studies which indicate that such grouping does not violate democratic principles. See Norman Grunlund, *Sociometry in the Classroom,* New York (Harper), 1959, pp. 190-97.

coming to be one method of adapting courses to differences in ability. Such arrangements are now becoming more sophisticated, however, with the differentiation of students for each subject. Ability grouping is particularly useful in required subjects because it reduces the range of interests and aptitudes within each learning group. Homogeneity in specialized, advanced courses is usually achieved by having prerequisites and minimum levels of scholarship for admission.

Experiments with teacher teams are a promising recent development which permits variations in class size from large to very small and allows extensive individual tutoring. Likewise, the utilization of learning machines, tape recorders, records, and films permits individual

Table 6-1. *Curricular Provisions for Concentration in Depth*

GRADE	SOCIAL STUDIES	SCIENCE	MATHEMATICS	ART
NINE	History of civilization	Biology	Algebra[a]	Introduction to art[b]
TEN	World history or European history	1 Physical science[c] or chemistry	Plane geometry	General design; commercial art; sculpture; art appreciation; painting
ELEVEN	U.S. history	2 Physical science[c] or physics	Trigonometry; solid geometry; or advanced algebra	
TWELVE	American problems; world problems; U.S. history*; European history*	3 Physical science*[c] or biology; science seminar	Senior math or senior math*	Art studio

[a] The mathematics sequence is often labeled Math 1, Math 2, Math 3, and Math 4 in programs which integrate the content of the field. The principal substance of such integrated programs includes the areas listed here with the senior level covering at least the content of analytics and differential calculus.

[b] The art program is shown to indicate a sequence for talented pupils in an area which normally is not included in "academic" programs.

[c] The physical science sequence is a combined program in chemistry and physics so arranged that the pupil completes one year of college-level physics and chemistry in the senior year. Pupils electing college-level biology who do not wish to take both physics and chemistry may elect a regular physics or chemistry course in either grade ten or eleven.

* College level.

initiative in study that is often thwarted by group procedures. Such devices tend to counteract the rigid organization of classes, in both size and length of teaching period—arrangements that have tended to limit high school teaching, in many subject fields, largely to expository and demonstration types of instruction.

The Scientific Method

Independent scholarship will not result from methods of instruction, such as the lecture or recitation, that make the student dependent upon the teacher. Such procedures are useful only if they are employed appropriately. The lecture is valuable when the mode of instruction requires presentation; the recitation and discussion are useful in small groups to test mastery of basic concepts and knowledge, to clarify material which has been presented or assigned, or to facilitate exchanges of ideas. The development of sound approaches to scholarship, however, requires the involvement of students in the scientific method as a means of learning. Training in discovery and evaluation of information, and its use in solving problems, is essential to the development of scholarship in secondary schools.

Laboratory procedures in high school science are often a mockery of the scientific method. Like the lecture and the recitation, they direct the student—in cookbook fashion—through each stage of the discovery process, allowing little chance for independent thinking. They measure attainment in terms of ability to follow directions and memorize results instead of evidence of creative, logical thinking by the student. Experts in the teaching of science now believe that such superficial laboratory processes should be replaced by demonstrations, either by the teacher or students, to permit more time for actual experiences with the scientific method as the student gains some familiarity with the use of techniques and equipment. The test of laboratory courses, in terms of their contribution to scholarship, is the extent to which students actually function under their own brain power, with guidance rather than detailed direction from the teacher.

The scientific method is useful in courses other than science. Its emphasis on the search for facts and their organization, appraisal, and interpretation, and its focus upon the use of knowledge to resolve problems can be employed in any field, particularly in the advanced courses. The unit method which permits various types of "problems approaches" can utilize the scientific method. In fact, all procedures which require students to take responsibility for the planning, conducting, and evaluating of their study activities promote independence in scholarship.

High Standards

The development of sound scholarship demands that students be held to high standards. Of course, these standards must vary according to the levels of maturity, abilities, and educational potentialities of individual students; but they should impose the obligation on each pupil to "play over his head" intellectually.

Scholastic standards need to be framed in terms of quality of performance as well as quantity of work accomplished. They should take into account such matters as creativity, reasoning power, thoroughness, exactness, and objectivity, as well as skill in the organization, use, and communication of knowledge. Rather than rating accomplishment in accordance with the norm of all other students, each student should be judged by the degree to which he approaches mastery. Particular attention should be paid to the extent to which an individual is exceeding his expectation at a given time as well as to his ability to progress from one level of scholarship to another. Standards in scholarship should be applied so as to create healthy states of dissatisfaction in students when their efforts fall short of their potentialities. Such standards should become increasingly exacting as the learner grows in ability and maturity.

Guidance

In a democracy, guidance and persuasion are the means by which students are moved toward the goal of scholarship. Inasmuch as the school cannot compel the students to choose subjects appropriate either to scholarly development or individual aptitudes, it must provide adequate guidance services to help them arrive at sound choices for themselves.

Within individual courses, teachers find the techniques of guidance valuable in persuading students to make the most of their opportunities. This is particularly true with the more able boys and girls who accomplish the goals of a course with relative ease and who should be encouraged to push ahead on their own initiative.

Individual Commitment and Satisfaction

Scholarship demands individual commitment. If it is to be pursued, the student must experience such satisfaction with his efforts that he will continue them with minimum external motivation. The commitment of high school students to scholarly development has been limited in the past by anti-intellectual attitudes held by adults in the community. Scholarship received little impetus from the "something for nothing" philosophy of life that developed during the depression years of the 1930's. Assembly-line industrial jobs that require little preparation for success, collective bargaining practices that provide automatic (rather than merited) increases in salaries, personnel theories that equate skill in human relations above intellectual competence—all have de-emphasized the importance of scholarship in school. In addition, educational practices that stressed conformity, lock-step progress, and automatic passing and promotions, but failed to recognize priorities between the curricular and extracurricular programs of the school, tended to downgrade scholarship.

Although the need for satisfaction as a basis for promoting continued scholarship has been strongly endorsed by educators in the past forty years,[13] human learning attests to the fact that a commitment to scholarship will be maintained only if the satisfactions it returns to the individual are adequate to make him want to continue. Secondary school teachers, through their own examples as scholars and through the procedures they employ in teaching their courses, make major contributions to the attainment by students of the wholesome and rewarding satisfactions of scholarly activities.

SELECTED REFERENCES

CHASE, FRANCIS S., AND HAROLD ANDERSON, eds. *The High School in a New Era.* Chicago: Univ. of Chicago Press, 1958.
CONANT, JAMES B. *The American High School Today: A First Report to Interested Citizens.* New York: McGraw-Hill, 1959.

[13] In 1918, a small group of teachers founded the Progressive Education Movement as a protest against the teaching practices and conditions of the day. The original leaders of this movement sought to abolish rote and routine learning in favor of creative, intellectual, self-directed activities—the essence of scholarship. Unfortunately, the originally sound theory was put into practice by less competent leaders who frequently established procedures that did not result in high-level creativity, intellectual attainment, or responsible self-direction by pupils. Although the progressive movement is much maligned because of the "do as you please" fringe which was attached to it, the movement contributed a significant and sound body of theory and practice to education.

GHISELIN, BREWSTER, ed. *The Creative Process: A Symposium.* Berkeley: Univ. of California Press, 1952.

KOERNER, JAMES D., ed. *The Case for Basic Education: A Program of Aims for Public Schools.* Boston: Little, Brown, 1959.

National Society for the Study of Education. "The Integration of Educational Experiences." *Fifty-seventh Yearbook,* Part III, Chicago: Univ. of Chicago Press, 1958.

SMITH, B. O., WILLIAM O. STANLEY, AND J. HARLAN SHORES. *Fundamentals of Curriculum Development,* rev. ed. Tarrytown, N.Y.: World Book Company, 1957.

WHITEHEAD, ALFRED NORTH. *The Aims of Education and Other Essays.* New York: Macmillan, 1929.

Westinghouse science talent contests stimulate the development of talent among high school students.

Talent is a precious commodity. Its discovery requires opportunity for independent creative and research activities by students.

CHAPTER 7

Discovering and Developing Talent

THE DEDICATION to equality inherent in a democratic political philosophy tends to promote uniformity in all social services, including education.
This tendency, especially in secondary schools,
conflicts both with the national need for highly
refined talents and with individual inclinations to
develop abilities. In addition, the cultivation of
talent may be inhibited by social customs, family
traditions, and prejudices.

Success in discovering and developing talent
depends upon the preciseness with which specific
abilities can be identified and cultivated. Despite
the meagerness of dependable research in this field,
there are certain general principles which help to
define the task of the secondary school.

EQUALITY AND UNIFORMITY

In its broadest interpretation, the process of education is always concerned with the refinement of
talent. Yet in specific applications this function
may be obscured by the attention given to promoting relatively identical educational outcomes for all
pupils. The support for equality and uniformity in
educational services rests on the premise that in a
democracy everybody should have the same opportunities. This attitude is supported by the resistance

of citizens to any form of intellectual differentiation and by certain religions which teach that talent is a divine gift, and does not, therefore, need developing. The image of the self-made man that was popularized in the frontier communities, where success often depended more on luck and perseverance than on special and refined talent, further supported the belief that the main job of the secondary school was to provide an equal, more-or-less uniform start for all—a common mold from which each is free to go as far as his ingenuity and good fortune permit.

Historical Resistance to Differentiation

Thomas Jefferson envisioned for Virginia a system of education oriented toward the discovery and development of talent. He proposed that the more able youth should be identified in elementary school and sent through secondary school where finer screening would select the most gifted for admission to college.

Pundits and philosophers ask why the United States has so long ignored the wisdom of following such a plan when its benefits appear obvious. The clue to an answer lies in a seeming inconsistency between Jefferson's educational and political theories. With respect to education he urged that "the best genius will be raked from the rubbish annually, and be instructed, at public expense. . . ."[1] On the other hand, in the Declaration of Independence, Jefferson asserted "that all men are created equal, and that they are endowed by their Creator with certain inalienable rights, that among these are Life, Liberty and the pursuit of Happiness." There has been little disposition among Americans, at any time, to separate genius from rubbish—not even at the college level, and still less in the high schools. Americans have almost instinctively believed that the uneducated are handicapped in the pursuit of happiness. Time after time the basic principle of equal opportunities for all was established and reconfirmed as various states, territories, religious bodies, and communities struggled with their educational problems. Even privately endowed institutions normally waited until other institutions were available before exercising the prerogative of selection. In the most exclusive of the "prestige" collegiate institutions, rigorous application of selective standards is relatively recent.[2]

[1] Jefferson's Plan for Education in Virginia, in Ellwood P. Cubberley, *Readings in the History of Education,* Boston (Houghton Mifflin), 1920, p. 420.
[2] Lawrence Bloomgarten, "Our Changing Elite Colleges," *Commentary,* February 1960, p. 151.

In recent years Jefferson's educational theory has gained greater acceptance. By 1960 enterprising high school seniors considered it a dull Saturday when some institution or organization did not confront them with a battery of tests on which they were to reveal their worthiness for college or a scholarship or their ability to pursue specialized academic programs. The search for talent had become so intense, and so disruptive of school and individual schedules, that the National Association of Secondary School Principals, the American Association of School Administrators, and the Council of Chief State School Officers united efforts to find ways to simplify and to coordinate the mushrooming programs for the identification of talent.

Yet the current interest in "raking genius from the rubbish" still meets with resistance that is deeply rooted in educational practice as well as in political theory. Within a generally egalitarian atmosphere, of course, there has always been some selection, and even discrimination, based upon various criteria, consciously and unconsciously applied. High schools, while selecting a wider variety of students, were slow to differentiate curriculum and method. As a result many students found little to interest them and dropped out or failed. Only now are high schools able to retain to graduation a majority of the students who enter. Nonetheless, one of the striking characteristics of the public high school in the United States has been its efforts to provide equality of opportunity and at the same time to adapt to a universal student population and diversified student goals. This characteristic has not failed to capture the attention of Americans studying foreign school systems[3] and of modern educators from other countries studying the United States.[4]

American culture thus has gradually but consistently developed an ideal with an inner contradiction:

> We firmly believe that in a quite real sense one man is as good as another; and we believe quite as firmly that the man who can bat .300 is a great deal better than the man who can bat only .250— and that only in the pitcher can defensive skill quite make up for that deficiency. We very clearly believe that men are equal and that they are not equal. In the daily round of living we have no

[3] Paul R. Mort and Francis G. Cornell, *Adaptability of Public School Systems,* New York (Bureau of Publications, Teachers College, Columbia Univ.), 1938, pp. 4-5.

[4] Geoffrey Crowther, "English and American Education," *Atlantic Monthly,* April 1960, pp. 37-42.

trouble with the qualifying and saving 'in respect to—;' we are all equal in the eyes of the law, equal in the waiting line for tickets, equal at the supermarket, where there are no charge accounts, but not equal in the halfback position, or—let us be fair—not equal as candidates for Phi Beta Kappa. There remains, however, in our final moral summing up a troubled feeling that there is something unAmerican, even about so consecrated a formulation as 'many are called but few are chosen.'[5]

Concept of Divine Gifts

Religious beliefs play important roles in shaping attitudes about the development of talent. In a society of many faiths these attitudes often contradict one another. The concept that special talents are divine gifts is deeply ingrained in the feelings of many. Thus, some people think of intellectual capacity, artistic and musical ability, or skill in a specific activity as an endowment from a power beyond individual influence. As a result, they discount man's capacity to develop, or to improve upon his abilities.

On the other hand, some people are influenced by the Biblical parable that admonishes against burying one's talents. These people apply the lesson of the parable most frequently to those whose inheritance is unquestionably recognizable, rather than to individuals whose potentialities are less obvious. Many individuals, therefore, continue to "bury" their talents, or to develop them only partially and to use them poorly.

Image of the Self-Made Man

In a simpler day Americans held up as examples many men who owed little of their success to formal schooling—not only men of courage and daring like Daniel Boone and Kit Carson, but also giants of industrialization and technical progress such as Henry Ford and Thomas A. Edison, or political heroes like Abraham Lincoln and Sam Houston, as well as literary figures like Herman Melville and Walt Whitman. Their success helped to establish confidence in the ability of men to develop their talents without help. In fact, the disdain for dependence upon organized education has been strong in the attitudes of some people. The men in the ranks—the "common people"—often

[5] Crane Brinton, *A History of Western Morals,* New York (Harcourt, Brace & World, Inc.), 1959, p. 398.

have contempt for the college graduate in law, science, business, education, engineering, or agriculture. Similarly, the West Point or Annapolis graduate has, at times, been ridiculed for not having "come up through the ranks." The implication has been that those who bypass the long and difficult climb of the self-made man by riding the vehicle of formal education up the mountain of success were not only of the weaker sort, but actually were in some fashion cheating. For the past half century, however, realization has been growing that the attainment of American ideals increasingly rests upon development, through education, of the highest levels of capacity. The intricate social organization of a populous, preponderantly urbanized nation has demanded of its leaders a highly sophisticated understanding of its history and of problems of organization and communication, as well as of goals sought and means for their attainment. While there remain many roads to Rome, the maps become increasingly difficult to read without the help of thorough and continuing education.

Secondary School—A Common Mold

American ideals, as applied to high schools, have had an irresistible centripetal pull, seeking to involve and retain all youth in an identical experience—a common mold—of secondary education. In the midst of the financial chaos of the 1930's the most articulate spokesman for traditional scholarship, Robert M. Hutchins, examined the Jeffersonian concept of selectivity and concluded that it could only be applied at the university level, where, however, he recommended its most rigorous use.[6] All but the most irresponsible of present critics of secondary education similarly acknowledge an American consensus on this point.

The harmonization of the two simultaneously held ideas that all men are equal in rights—equal under the law and before God—but different and unequal in talent, drive, or desire for self-development or social contribution, cannot be achieved at the secondary school level by selectivity and exclusion. Neither can it be accomplished by a standardization with a denominator of accomplishment low enough to include the whole range of aptitude and its lack in all the aspects of talent indispensable to individual happiness and social progress.

[6] Robert Maynard Hutchins, *No Friendly Voice,* Chicago (Univ. of Chicago Press), 1936, p. 59.

CULTIVATION OF TALENT—A NATIONAL NECESSITY

Realization that the cultivation of talent is a necessity rather than a luxury predominates in educational planning today. Although the demand for highly developed scientific and technical skills has received the greatest publicity, expertness actually is at a premium in all fields. Competition for able students and for trained workers and professionals has become the major force in improving education and motivating individual students.

Specialization

The most important recent change that has taken place in all professions is that from the generalist to the specialist. Although some people look longingly at the past and deplore the demise of the general practitioner in such fields as medicine, engineering, industry, and teaching, the fact is that intellectual developments of the last half century have made obsolete the Jack-of-all-trades. In his place have developed teams of highly specialized practitioners whose talents and intensive scholarship are harmonized into cooperative forces. Interrelationships have become more complex and demanding, as Devereux C. Josephs has explained.

> In all occupations the level of competence required is constantly increasing. No scientist can hope to encompass more than a small sector of scientific knowledge. Military strategy is no longer only a matter for professional soldiers but rests importantly on the advice of scholars and technical experts. The conduct of government depends heavily on the talents of the economist, the agronomist, the public health officer, and similar experts.[7]

The story of the changes in aircraft design in one company over the past thirty years provides an interesting illustration of the growing complexity of the task and the increasing numbers of individuals with different talents needed to complete it. When the first all-metal, twin-engine transport plane was designed in 1932, twelve men worked on the project. The 1960 model, a transport plane built by the same company, was a project for nearly 1,000 engineers and designers. The aeronautical engineer in charge of both projects contrasted the one drawing detailing the entire electrical system in 1932 with the 1,000

[7] Devereux C. Josephs and others, *The Pursuit of Excellence: Education and the Future of America,* Garden City, N.Y. (Doubleday), 1958, p. 9.

drawings necessary in 1960; also, where one man had performed stress analysis in the 1932 design, 300 specialists were assigned to this one facet in 1960.[8]

Technology and Talent

Expanding technology requires increasing kinds and amounts of talent. The discovery of resources, production of goods, medical science, the field of communications—in fact, every field of human endeavor—demands more talent each year. A report by experts in mathematics education says:

> The new mathematics discovered and developed in this century exceeds by far all the mathematics previous to 1900. Its use and the need for mathematicians and mathematically trained persons have grown enormously, both in scientific and technical fields and in fields not ordinarily thought of as involving mathematics—such as translation.[9]

What is true of an established basic field like mathematics is multiplied throughout a mechanized and automated technological complex. A slight change in a key element in one field rapidly affects a whole series of related fields and, consequently, the talent required to service the new developments.

Competition for Talent

The competition for talent, of all types and degrees of usefulness, presses secondary schools to intensify efforts to identify, refine, and extend the abilities of youth. Educationally, the achievement of this goal requires intensive counseling as well as quality instruction. It challenges school officials, as well as adults in general, to interpret to the student the importance of preparing for a future that inevitably will accord highest rewards to the talented.

Adolescence: Opening or Closing Doors

The changes only briefly suggested in the foregoing make it increasingly unlikely that a man who spent his youth splitting rails will ever

[8] Robert J. Serling, "Father of the Electra," *Voyager,* March-April 1960, p. 22.

[9] Julius H. Hlavaty (ed.), *Mathematics for the Academically Talented Student in the Secondary School,* Washington, D.C. (National Education Association), 1959, p. 43.

again lead the nation in a critical period, nor, in this age, is a vast organization such as the Ford Motor Company likely to be founded by a man who never attended high school. Complexity and specialization raise multiple hazards for the individual who fails to recognize or is prevented from recognizing his abilities and from beginning to develop them before his life pattern is shaped. For a variety of reasons this danger has often not been clearly realized by the adult society even while it has been preached to secondary school youth. This is, perhaps, partly because of our stubborn belief in the tradition that "you can't keep a good man down," partly because of distortions of the point of view that American society will somehow take care of everyone. A post-World War II survey of the use and loss of talent led to the conclusion: "The point of most serious loss is at the level of high school graduation."[10]

Actually, high school graduation is merely the time at which it becomes obvious that a talented student is not pursuing his education. The decision to pursue or not to pursue was made at an earlier time. A study that may be taken as representative showed that of those who attended college 40 per cent had decided before entering ninth grade, 20 per cent in that year, 12 per cent in tenth grade, 9 per cent in eleventh grade, 12 per cent in twelfth grade, and only 6 per cent after leaving high school.[11]

The complexity of social and industrial organization makes it harder for the student to find his way, unassisted, to demonstrate outstanding competence independently. The high level of technology largely eliminates for youth beginning points leading onward to growth and challenge, except for those who have demonstrated competence as well as willingness. These same factors work to thwart institutions of higher education and employers as well as young people; their opportunity to fit youth with careers by trial and error is not so free as in earlier years. Experimentation is too costly; they must use more efficient methods. These complications need not force an early specialization, as is largely the case for European students, but they do intensify the high school's obligation to help the boy or girl to identify talents and to try them for scope and satisfaction.

[10] Educational Policies Commission, *Education of the Gifted*, Washington, D.C. (National Education Association), 1950, p. 20.

[11] Leslie E. Moser, "When Do Young People Make Decisions About College?" *School Review*, March 1955, p. 158.

OBSTACLES TO TALENT DEVELOPMENT

American society is distinctive in the variety of avenues it provides the able to exercise their abilities, even though equality of opportunity has not yet been accorded to all minority groups. The sheer quantitative expansion of the high school is one of the dramatic indicators of the spread of opportunity. Yet there are still barriers of various kinds to the fullest discovery and use of talent. Among the more important forces blocking talent development are social customs, family traditions, economic conditions, and racial, religious, and sex discrimination.

Social Customs

Level of education and social class are so closely associated that the first is one of the most reliable indexes of the second. Warner found a correlation coefficient of .78 between levels of school attainment and social class.[12] In America's fluid society, cause and effect are sometimes interchangeable. Education is one way to rise to a higher social class; more frequently, however, social class imprisons the student, especially in the lowest socioeconomic levels, so that pursuit of education is discouraged.

Through social customs some girls in high school are oriented to the select "finishing schools" and some boys associate education with attending particular institutions of higher learning. Social traditions in rural communities often lead more able students to think of college only in terms of "practical" curriculums, e.g., agriculture, home economics, or engineering. These customs are only a few of the social traditions which limit the student's opportunity. It is the high school's responsibility to help the pupil think of himself as an individual, identify his capacities, and find goals for himself without the handicap of social restrictions.

Family Traditions

Family traditions and social customs are obviously related. Family attitudes, however, play a more important role in determining whether youth will make maximum development of their talents. Not infrequently, parents seek to help their children overcome both family traditions and social customs that limited their own educational preparations. Examples of this type of parental ambitions for youth

[12] W. Lloyd Warner and others, *Social Class in America,* Chicago (Science Research Associates), 1949.

are often found among immigrant families whose traditions included limited educational opportunities. A contrasting influence of family traditions is found among certain ethnic and nationality groups in which it is not customary for children to rise above the educational levels of their parents. In Wisconsin, for example, the number of high school graduates going on to college from each community can be almost predicted by studying the types of national groups that make up the various communities.

A study by Little of the educational plans of all youth in Wisconsin who graduated from high school in 1957 revealed that "the socio-cultural background of the families, especially the educational attainments of parents, conditioned the educational aspirations and attitudes of high school graduates and is perhaps the most striking finding about factors which influence the decisions about college attendance."[13] The facts revealed by this study indicated that attitudes of parents toward college attendance, and their own level of educational advancement, were key determinants in the decisions of their children.

Thus family traditions may be either an asset or an obstacle to the development of talent. Yet, teachers and guidance counselors recognize that such influences are subject to modification. The objective the secondary school must pursue is the identification of family traditions in order to ascertain their impact upon plans of youth. Changes in parental influences must then be encouraged in those cases in which parental attitudes tend to limit the educational ambitions of their children.

Economic Conditions

Even in a culture with the world's highest material standard, economic limitations stifle talent in various ways. First, and perhaps most important, public support of the schools is not great enough to permit school programs, with the necessary equipment, materials, and teachers, sufficiently stimulating to arouse curiosity and free creativity in those whose home environment is intellectually sterile. Second, for some pupils financial problems set limits far below their innate potential. The National Youth Administration of depression years provided federally subsidized earning opportunities for high school and college

---

[13] J. Kenneth Little, *Explorations into the College Plans and Experiences of High School Graduates,* Madison (School of Education, Univ. of Wisconsin), 1960, p. 95.

students, and the G.I. Bill and Korean G.I. Bill provided outright subsidies to young veterans, some of which were used by students who returned to high school. These programs established far-reaching precedents. Although their purpose was to remove economic obstacles for students with a wide range of ability, they paved the way, perhaps, for state scholarships, underwritten by tax funds, and the various federal scholarships and fellowships.

As a high school education has become attainable for nearly all youth, the opportunities to continue education beyond high school become even more essential to talent development. Post-high school educational opportunities both influence the quality of high school programs and open the way to further development of talent.

Social tradition, family outlook, discriminatory practices, and economic limitations are mutually reinforcing. Their impact on the secondary school has lessened—in fact, their decrease in importance is one of the glories of America—but they remain factors to be dealt with in giving scope to all the talents of American youth.

Discrimination

In the main, Americans can take pride in the school treatment of minorities. Although the United States has been guilty of some exploitation of and discrimination against minorities, its accomplishment in assimilating minorities is unprecedented in history. The process of assimilation and adjustment continues, but honesty requires acknowledgment that discrimination still imposes a handicap on some groups. The penalty for imposing such a handicap is inherent; society loses to the extent talents are thwarted. Segregation of the American Indians on reservations has hindered their assimilation and doubtless contributed to a lack of achievement among the group. The complex and emotional situation of Negroes in American education has occupied the courts for years; literature on the subject could fill libraries. The recent recognition of Negro talent in intellectual and cultural fields as well as in athletics and public entertainment, however, indicates a wider, general acceptance of the Negro. Religious and racial discriminations in America now operate principally through the vestiges of "quota systems" in colleges and universities, including graduate schools, and through discriminatory employment.

In addition to its minorities, American society recognizes one majority source of talent that is being underutilized. In this sense, at least, there is "discrimination" against girls. In appraising the achievement of nearly 1,500 "geniuses" after thirty-five years of follow-up, Terman and Oden found that the careers of gifted women followed a quite different pattern from those of gifted men. After summarizing the record of the 700 women in professional recognition, publications, and other distinctions (including 5 patents) the authors observed:

> Our gifted women in the main, however, are housewives, and many who also work outside the home do so more to relieve the monotony of household duties or to supplement the family income rather than through a desire for a serious career. There are many intangible kinds of accomplishment and success open to the housewife, and it is debatable whether the fact that a majority of gifted women prefer housewifery to more intellectual pursuits represents a net waste of brainpower.[14]

The great increase in the number of women workers has not yet eliminated a dual system of incentives in the employment fields. Average earnings of women professionals remain below those of men. Only in teaching has the concept of "equal pay for equal work" made much headway—at the expense of low averages for men—and even there promotions and administrative responsibilities come more readily for men. The biggest untapped reservoir of talent in both critical occupations and artistic fields may well be the undeveloped aptitudes of girls.

Conformity

The people of the United States, and particularly high school students, place a premium on conformity. To be different is to court ridicule and rejection. Because adolescents are keenly interested in being accepted by their fellow students, they tend to shun activities that are not endorsed by members of their peer groups. This tendency toward conformity represents another obstacle to the development of talent. It has produced in secondary schools, and colleges as well, a glorification of the average student and a disdain for the gifted.

NATURE OF TALENT

No categories have yet been developed to classify the various types and degrees of talent individuals possess or society requires. Terms

[14] Lewis M. Terman and Melita H. Oden, *The Gifted Group of Mid-Life,* Stanford (Stanford Univ. Press), 1959, p. 145.

such as "able," "gifted," "talented," and "superior" have been used to refer to students with intellectual potential above the ordinary. The precision with which these have been used, and the meaning given to each, depends on the definition accepted by those employing them. Yet all dimensions of talent cannot be designated by such general references.

Efforts to define the nature of talent have been concerned with its relationship to intelligence; the extent to which it is a product of generalized or specialized capacities, or both; the developmental potentialities it presents; the amount of adaptability its owner possesses; and the use to be made of it.

Relationship to Intelligence

Current campaigns to discover and develop talent actually aim at what is often called academic ability. (See Chapter 17 for a more detailed treatment of this subject.) Such projects may assume that students who score above a specific point on a standardized scholastic test, e.g., in the top 10 per cent, are sufficiently talented to deserve special attention. The cutoff point in determining the talented may be as high as the ninety-ninth centile scores or as low as the norm. The North Central Association Project on Guidance and Motivation of Superior and Talented Students limited its population for study to individuals in the upper quarter in one hundred high schools as measured by various tests of scholastic aptitude.[15]

Disagreements about the amount of intelligence necessary to identify the talented are encouraged by results of observations and standardized tests that fail to find a high relationship between certain kinds of talent and intelligence. Studies have shown, for example, that artistic ability is not highly correlated with verbal intelligence, neither is musical talent; similarly, creativity in its various forms may not be highly correlated with intelligence quotients.

Getzels and Jackson of the University of Chicago examined the achievement motives, fantasy productions, school performance, and teacher preferences of two types of adolescents—those exceptionally high in creativity but not in I.Q., and those exceptionally high in I.Q. but not in creativity. They found there were no differences in need

---

[15] J. Ned Bryan and Bruce Shertzer, *An Interim Report on the NCA-STS Project,* Chicago (North Central Association of Colleges and Secondary Schools), 1959, p. 17.

achievement; there were significant differences in the fantasy productions, the creative group using more stimulus-free, humorous, and
playful themes; in spite of striking differences in I.Q., the two groups
were equally superior in school achievement; and the intelligent were
preferred to the creative ones by teachers.[16] The carefully performed
exploratory work of these psychologists raises serious questions about
the adequacy of procedures for identifying students who have the
potential to infuse the culture with new ideas, inventions, and works
of art.

Generalized and Specialized Capacities

Talent may well be composed of both generalized and specialized
capacities, many of which as yet defy precise measurement. Some experts on mental abilities believe that intelligence can be analyzed
into various separate factors. Others hold that mental ability is a general trait that functions as a total response. There is considerable reason
to believe that a broad stratum of the academically talented—say
20 per cent—includes most of those with the combination of general
intellectual capacity and specialized aptitude necessary to outstanding
accomplishment in any field. But those who have investigated this
subject most closely have encountered a number of signs that we are
still far from a complete understanding of what constitutes talent. Terman and Oden, for example, found that their sample, so rigorously
selected on general intellectual ability, did not fulfill their promise
in every area: "There are, however, a few fields, all dependent on
special talent, in which there has been a lack of outstanding accomplishment. These are the fine arts, music, and, to a lesser extent,
literature."[17]

The most promising approach to identifying talent, on the basis
of present knowledge, is to use a double-barreled identification procedure throughout the secondary school years. Those students with
academic ability can be reasonably well identified by using psychological tests supplemented by records of school achievement and other
readily available data. The second essential aspect is to search out

[16] J. W. Getzels and P. W. Jackson, "The Highly Creative and the Highly
Intelligent Adolescent: An Attempt at Differentiation," a paper presented at the
American Psychological Association Convention in Washington, D.C., August
1958.

[17] Terman and Oden, *op. cit.,* p. 150.

all those who possess a particular talent. Some of the talents to be found are:

(a) Intellectual ability and its variously defined components, such as reasoning or verbal facility

(b) Special aptitudes, such as scientific, mathematical, mechanical, or social leadership

(c) Creativity in the arts, such as music, painting, writing, and drama

Although theories are contradictory and evidence in support of either the generalized or specialized conceptions of talent is yet inadequate, it is generally agreed that certain traits and achievements are related to talent. Some of these are widely distributed among the population; others are possessed, or possible of attainment, to a useful degree by only a few individuals. Some seem to bear a causal relationship to others, while certain ones as yet seem to be less related. A hypothetical distribution of talent traits is suggested in Table 7-1 to illustrate the relationships that are generally now believed to exist.

Table 7-1. *Hypothetical Distribution of Talent Traits*

RARE TRAITS

Professional Potential	*Creativity*	*Managerial Ability*
Interests	Insight	Sociability
Aptitudes	Inventiveness	Organization
Motivations	Discovery	Leadership
Dedication	Conceptualization	Skill in com-
	Research	munication
	Idea development	Judgment

SPECIALIZED CAPACITIES

Specialized Abilities	*Scholarship and Use of Knowledge*
Manual dexterity, verbal facility, and artistic, musical, literary, linguistic, mechanical, or scientific tendencies.	Curiosity, habits and skills of study, mastery of basic and technical subjects.

WIDELY DISTRIBUTED QUALITIES

General Human Abilities	*Capability of Functioning at a Skill Level*
Intelligence, mental and physical health, character, self-direction, co-operativeness.	Maintenance, technical manipulation, uncomplicated intellectual tasks.

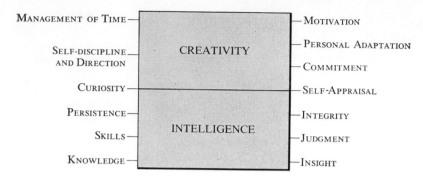

Fig. 7–1. *Factors Related to Talent Development*

A complete catalogue of talents would include all of the socially valuable talents, using the broadest possible base. Some of the simpler abilities, like the unusual finger dexterity of the most accomplished typist, would appear anyway as a natural outgrowth of instruction. The same can be said of the athletic skills already well identified in most schools. Identification, of course, implies a further purpose—development of the talents found. Development at this point in secondary education in the United States principally means gearing up in every direction to provide richer, deeper, more challenging educational experiences aimed at the ceiling of individual accomplishment as opposed to minimum or average or adequate standards.

Factors Related to Talent Development

Certain human activities or traits appear to be invariably related to all conceptions of talent and its development. These are suggested in Figure 7-1. The degree to which these are present and the harmony with which they supplement each other may well make the difference between what ultimately is recognized as a talented person and another whose potentialities are never realized.

Programs to identify and develop talented students, such as the state-wide one at the University of Wisconsin,[18] recognize the necessity of studying and encouraging the attainment of all these qualities. This program, which began in the College of Engineering in 1953, constantly widened its approach until when finally established in its own quarters in 1959, it was committed to a two-pronged program of

[18] "Research and Guidance Laboratory for Superior Students," Madison (Engineering Experiment Station, Univ. of Wisconsin), 1959.

research and guidance. This program contrasts with one launched in Illinois[19] in 1959, which was focused on enrichment, seeking to make University of Illinois resources available to talented high school students by permitting them to enroll in university courses, receive university credit, and, after graduation from high school, receive advanced placement.

Adaptability of Talent

The American secondary school must constantly keep before it the ideal of developing not some, or most, but all talents. Among the world's most gifted theorists in physics are men who had been educated and worked in other fields before switching to the field in which they earned fame. I. I. Rabi majored in chemistry in college, was employed as a chemist, worked in a bank, then returned to graduate study in physics. Emilio G. Segre left engineering to work with Fermi and establish a reputation as a physicist.[20] Americans studying Russian education are convinced that in the Russians' intensely directed educational program much talent is lost through inflexibility.

Nazi Germany is an example of a nation that tried with fanatical determination to educate its youth for a single purpose, the so-called "leadership principle." Competent German psychologists made tremendous efforts to identify and develop leaders. Their own experts at the Psychological Institute of the University of Würzburg concluded in 1940 that they were training predominantly "bureaucrats" rather than leaders.[21] A democratic society follows the wiser policy of permitting potential leaders to be identified by their peers and providing appropriate activities from which leaders can emerge and develop.

In all areas of talent, and at all levels of talent, it is extremely important to emphasize growth as well as identification. In emphasizing growth, it is equally important to provide opportunities for generative experiences, those that make it possible for a chemistry student to become a physicist, as Rabi did, or for a mathematician to become a philosopher, as did Whitehead. A society of men who are at the same time equal in right and unequal in talent needs all the talents of all the

[19] Unpublished report of the Dean of Admissions, Univ. of Illinois, Urbana, September 1959.

[20] Francis Bello, "Great American Scientists: The Physicists," *Fortune,* March 1960, pp. 113-19, 226-42.

[21] William Ebenstein, *The Nazi State,* New York (Farrar and Rinehart), 1943, p. 195.

people. A truly American system will develop not only the most talented but also talents of the second and third order. As the *Christian Science Monitor* remarked editorially, "In this era of attention to the 'gifted student' we are seriously pleased to hear an intelligent voice raised on behalf of dunces. . . .

"Emphasis on gifted students should never mean neglect of those whose gifts are unorthodox, late-blooming, or merely in need of uncovering."[22]

Use of Talent

Recent efforts to discover and develop talent have focused more on its use to society than to the individual. One such approach might be called the manpower concept. It is concerned with shortages and surpluses of talent as well as supply and demand, particularly in "critical occupations." In recent years it has been broadened to include "pure sciences"—biology, chemistry, physics, earth sciences, and mathematics, but it still emphasizes heavily the need to produce able engineers and applied scientists of various kinds. Exponents of the manpower point of view summarize their utilitarian conclusions as follows:

> The explanation of these shortages is essentially the same throughout the whole of the industrialized world: the accelerating pace of scientific, technological, and economic change in the modern world has produced demands greater than the more slowly growing supply has been able to meet.
>
> The only reasonable assumption for the future is that the pace of change will remain rapid and will probably speed up. Total demand, therefore, can be expected to continue at a high level. Three factors are of major importance: the need for teachers, the expected increase in research activities, and the expected continuation of a high rate of industrial production.[23]

The second concept which was consistently promoted by various individuals and organizations associated with institutions of higher learning and which was officially endorsed by the National Education

[22] "A Feather in the Dunce Cap," *Christian Science Monitor,* March 30, 1960, p. 20.

[23] Dael Wolfle, "Forecasting Surpluses and Shortages in Key Occupations," *Annals of the American Academy of Political and Social Science,* September 1959, p. 31.

Association in 1958, is the training of the academically talented.[24] The proponents of this concept urge special provisions for the top 15 or 20 per cent of high school youth as identified by various means—primarily scholastic aptitude tests. Many of the advocates of this approach are strongly influenced by the manpower concept.

A strong and growing minority voice is raised in favor of a more individual-centered and more culture-conscious concept of talent development. The supporters of this point of view abhor percentages and have no confidence in the planning commissions' ability to forecast the needs inspired by social change and scientific advance. They are particularly skeptical about the fate of the arts.

> Who can tell us, and by what powers of divination, how many poets we 'need' or how many we could 'absorb'? On an efficiency basis, the answer is clearly none. As Archibald MacLeish remarked, 'Homer has already sung.' A vast wealth of poetic literature is lying virtually unused. . . .
>
> It is part of the record of our society that poets are not always appreciated in their own day and generation. As with other artists, some achieve fame and rich rewards, material and immaterial, during their lifetime. But the general rule runs the other way. Should we plan on producing poets for our unborn generations?[25]

The same comment could be made about the other arts and about many other fields. There is no reliable way to identify all of the talented even among adults, much less in the secondary school. Even those who are most enthusiastic about singling out the "academically" talented take this difficulty partly into account.

TASK OF THE SECONDARY SCHOOL

In a good school system, talent identification and development begins when the child first enrolls in the elementary school. It continues throughout the child's total school experience. The secondary school not only must continue to develop the general talents discovered in elementary school but must also introduce intensive educational experiences appropriate to the development of certain specialized talents.

[24] James B. Conant and others, *Invitational Conference on the Academically Talented Secondary School Pupil,* Washington, D.C. (National Education Association), 1958.

[25] Henry M. Wriston, "Humanists and Generalists," *Annals of the American Academy of Political and Social Science,* September 1959, p. 15.

The attainment of this objective requires differentiation of curricular offerings as well as of instructional procedures. Finally, the secondary school is called upon to encourage the continuation of talent development in the post-high school years.

Identification

Because specialized abilities become more apparent during adolescence, the secondary school has a special responsibility to promote their identification. During the early years of secondary education the student is typically curious and eager both to discover his own potentialities and to learn. Educators attempt to capitalize on this natural tendency in the design of junior high school programs, which are very often exploratory.

The age of exploration, however, does not start and end at definite points on the age span, nor is exploration all of discovery. A systematic, "exploratory" course in art in the ninth grade may be followed by a more intensive experience in painting and drawing in tenth grade. The second course may be the one in which the student's imagination is caught, his powers tested. Involved more deeply in a richer experience, he may discover a new world of feeling and expression and a new dimension of himself.

Similarly, the general science student may become acquainted with some of the subject matter and techniques of science, but become excited about scientific method in a later course with more specialized content and more challenging problems. It may well be, as Anne Roe, one of the most distinguished investigators of this subject concludes, that the preschool years already determine the areas in which an individual's greatest satisfactions will lie.[26] Dr. Roe believes, nevertheless, that the high school program and the teachers a student encounters may do much to encourage and shape a predisposition. The school can help the youngster begin to see what it means to be a scientist, to understand the opportunities, challenges, and difficulties of science, and to see himself as a scientist.

Continuity of Emphasis

The more unusual a talent is in kind or degree, the less likely it is to be recognized or stimulated by the home or elementary school environment. In equipment, curriculum, and teaching staff the best

[26] Anne Roe, "Science Begins at Home," New York (Thomas Alva Edison Foundation), 1959.

comprehensive American high schools provide the elements necessary to the identification and motivation of a wide range of talents, as well as opportunity for their exercise. A lack of motivation and challenging opportunity at the high school level can be crucial. The adolescent is equipped with a craving for new experience and for status that must be gratified in individually satisfying and socially worthwhile ways, if it is not to be absorbed in trivial or undesirable activities.

A well-equipped and well-staffed school can provide in its libraries, laboratories, extraclass activities, and interpersonal relationships the opportunity for the student to discover himself in a way no other social agency can. Such discoveries change lives.

Comprehensive cumulative records for each student are essential to the provision of continuity in the development of talent. The information they provide to counselors and teachers makes possible the uninterrupted development of individual talents.

Differentiation

To the extent that the secondary school attempts to promote all kinds of talent, it must develop appropriate differentiation in its program. The traditional practice of providing multitrack curriculums, e.g., college preparation, business, vocational, and general, has been a step in this direction. The size of the school and the educational ambitions of the community help to determine the amount and nature of differentiation.

The vocational education movement itself arose from a nation-wide demand for a type of differentiation designed to prepare for skilled work in trades and industry. High school vocational training has taken the place of much of the apprenticeship training on the job. As technology grows more complex, programs of vocational education are being forced to concentrate on the development of higher levels of skill. Greater specialization in mathematics and the physical sciences is now required for those preparing for design, operational, and maintenance jobs in industry and business.

Another type of differentiation, new on the scene, concerns preparation for various types of specialization in college. Some contend, of course, that the college preparatory program should be substantially the same regardless of the potential aptitudes of students. Others believe that specialized abilities, whether they be mathematical, artistic, or literary, should receive appropriate attention in high school.

Conservation of Talents

Maximum conservation of talent requires priority attention by secondary school guidance personnel. Counseling services aim not only at helping students make the most of high school opportunities; they are concerned also with motivating post-high school talent development.

The greatest loss of talent occurs at the end of secondary schooling. About half of the top one-third of the population, intellectually, fail to enter college. Of those in the top one-third who do enroll in an institution of higher learning, three or four out of ten drop out before graduation. Similarly, many students allow mechanical ability, artistic talent, leadership potentialities, or inventive inclination to go undeveloped.

The challenge of conserving talent and encouraging its development in post-high school educational programs confronts all who serve in secondary schools. Although the problem is being attacked most vigorously in connection with the academically able student, it prevails generally. National security and well-being, as well as progress in all fields, require that both the creative genius and the generally good student be encouraged to achieve maximum development. It follows that individuals whose talents are less spectacular should not be permitted to bury them, only partially developed, at the end of their secondary school years.

SELECTED READINGS

DeHAAN, ROBERT F., AND ROBERT J. HAVIGHURST, *Educating Gifted Children*. Chicago: Univ. of Chicago Press, 1957.

DeHAAN, ROBERT F., AND JACK KOUGH. *Identifying Students with Special Needs*. Chicago: Science Research Associates, 1956.

Educational Policies Commission. *Education of the Gifted*. Washington, D.C.: National Education Association, 1950.

GARDNER, JOHN W. *Excellence: Can We Be Equal and Excellent Too?* New York: Harper, 1961.

The Identification and Education of the Academically Talented Student in the American Secondary School. Washington, D.C.: National Education Association, 1958.

National Education Association, and the National Association of Secondary School Principals. *Administration: Procedures and Practices for the Academically Talented Student in the Secondary School*. Washington, D.C.: National Education Association, 1960.

TAYLOR, CALVIN W. *The Second (1957) University of Utah Research Conference on the Identification of Creative Scientific Talent.* Brighton, Utah: Univ. of Utah Press, 1958.

TERMAN, LEWIS M., AND MELITA H. ODEN. *The Gifted Group at Mid-Life.* Stanford, Calif.: Stanford Univ. Press, 1959.

TRAXLER, ARTHUR E., ed. *Selection and Guidance of Gifted Students for National Survival.* Washington, D.C.: American Council on Education, 1956.

WITTY, PAUL, ed. *The Gifted Child.* Boston: D. C. Heath and Company, 1951.

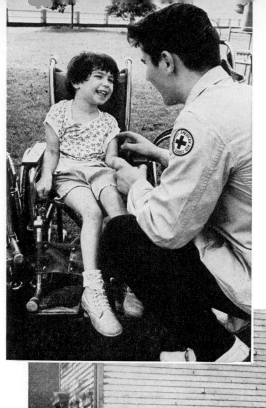

Values are produced by a variety of experiences. Volunteer work with handicapped children by high school student contributes positively to value development.

Idle hours in a poor environment can have a negative impact on values. Schools must help to counter-act such influences.

Developing Values

A FUNDAMENTAL belief which undergirds American public education was expressed in the official act incorporating the Northwest Territory in 1787: "Religion, morality, and knowledge being necessary to good government and the happiness of mankind, schools and the means of education shall be forever encouraged." This statement puts clearly the ends of cooperative human endeavor—good government and the happiness of mankind. It links religion, morality, and knowledge as the human attributes to be cultivated to produce those ends; and it implies a harmonious association between schools and other "means of education" in which schools, as public instruments, have primary place.

Protestant and deist philosophy were paramount in the formative period of the United States and there was a widespread conviction at that time that the person who knew how to read and had access to the means of education would arrive at his own valid religious conclusions and lead a moral life. This outlook did not survive the industrial revolution, the assimilation of streams of immigrants, the emergence of new, revivalistic religious sects and the splintering of old, and the impact of science on traditional values. Instead people turned to schools.

There is evidence, however, that when the first high schools were established, people still clung to the belief that youth who could read and who had had ordinary family training, probably including religious study and worship, would have an adequately developed character. The early high schools had three qualifications for entrance—age, character, and scholastic preparation. Barnard gives a typical example of entrance regulations in 1869.

> Pupils may be admitted to such departments of the schools as they are qualified to enter, but not later than three weeks after the commencement of a term, unless qualified to enter classes already organized. They must be twelve years old to enter the high school and have a certificate of good moral character. The president and four members of the board, the superintendent, and the principal of the high school constitute the committee of examination for admission to the high school. Detroit, 1867.[1]

One may wonder what the board of education would have recommended for the twelve-year-old morally unfit for high school. These policies should probably be read, however, as another indication of the school's concern for moral development and for making parent and child conscious that the school was as interested in his character as his intellect. At no time has the American secondary school been indifferent to values, although the values emphasized have changed and been questioned now and again.

CONCEPTIONS OF VALUES

The term "values" signifies those attributes an individual or a society desires to create, enhance, and preserve. The attempt to define and specify values is a central preoccupation of philosophy. Differing conceptions of values divide the world today as they have divided it in countless other generations. Disagreement over values also divides communities and enlivens faculty meetings in schools across the United States. Certain mutually held values make conflicting values tolerable and permit disagreements to be resolved or held in abeyance while instruction of the young goes forward.

Historical Emphases on Values

Historians, who work with the longest time perspectives, are most likely to perceive both the slowness with which value systems change

[1] Henry Barnard, "Digest of Rules and Regulations of Public Schools in Cities," *Barnard's American Journal of Education*, Vol. 19, 1869, pp. 417-64.

and the evolutionary process by which new values survive and are judged superior to the old. While the modern historian's confidence in improving value systems has been considerably shaken by two catastrophic world wars and the rise of monolithic totalitarian despotisms, these may be phases necessary to challenge men's value systems to the higher adaptations now called for by the advance of science. Durant stresses the evolutionary development of values.

> Conventions are forms of behavior found expedient by a people; customs are conventions accepted by successive generations, after natural selection through trial and error and elimination; morals are such customs as the group considers vital to its welfare and development. In primitive societies, where there is no written law, these vital customs or morals regulate every sphere of human existence, and give stability and continuity to the social order. Through the slow magic of time such customs, by long repetition, become a second nature in the individual; if he violates them he feels a certain fear, discomfort or shame; this is the origin of that conscience, or moral sense, which Darwin chose as the most impressive distinction between animals and men. In its higher development conscience is social consciousness—the feeling of the individual that he belongs to a group, and owes it some measure of loyalty and consideration. Morality is the cooperation of the part with the whole, and of each group with some larger whole. Civilization, of course, would be impossible without it.[2]

Not all can share Durant's optimistic outlook, even when the historical data demonstrate the stubborn persistence of ethical codes. Brinton says:

> Both as to formal philosophic ethical writing and as to folk notions of ethics incorporated in tradition, codes, aphorisms of folk wisdom, the three or four thousand years of our Western recorded history show an unmistakable constant element. Honesty, loyalty, kindness, self-control, industry, cooperativeness are virtues; lying, treachery, cruelty, self-indulgence, laziness, conspicuous and uncontrolled aggressiveness, and selfishness are vices. There are indeed in-group limitations; lying to an outsider, cruelty to an enemy, are vices only in lofty ethical systems which take in all humanity, not just Western man, let alone just the tribe, as the in-group.[3]

2 Will Durant, *Our Oriental Heritage,* New York (Simon and Schuster), 1954, p. 36.
3 Crane Brinton, *A History of Western Morals,* New York (Harcourt, Brace & World, Inc.), 1959, p. 417.

The best Brinton is willing to say is that it is too soon to predict the collapse of a moral system painfully arrived at and supported both by Christianity and the Enlightenment. He enters a mild but well-documented demurrer against the voices that say Western values are losing their force and contributing to the breakdown of Western civilization.

Toynbee is perhaps the best known of the modern historical philosophers who see a great cyclical movement in history in which civilizations build and accumulate driving force from cohesive systems of values. He warns that the West today shows increasing signs of losing confidence in its values—in his view a certain sign that a civilization is waning.[4]

Since World War I, popular books, magazines, and newspapers in the United States have printed a flood of alarm and analysis about loss of moral and ethical values in American life. Just which values are considered lost depends greatly on the point of view of the author and the audience for whom he writes. Among the most readable and intelligible of these treatises are two books by Frederick Lewis Allen.[5] Allen mirrors the effect of war, depression, and social change on peoples' beliefs and behavior. From his shorter-range, and perhaps more superficial, viewpoint, traditional American values have been disintegrating under the shock of wartime experiences, the disillusionment of the depression, the impact of science on traditional religious dogma, and Freudian interpretations of human behavior. The process has been accelerated by social and technological changes, especially the automobile and mass mediums of communications—movies, radio, television, magazines, and newspapers. Conceivably such changes in some American values can be for the better; however, majority opinion among both trained and lay observers seems to agree with Allen that there is a danger that the value system can be debased by change.

Sources of Values

The values Americans hold today have accrued from the experience of mankind. They are more like than different from the values of other men, yet there are certain ones which may be termed distinctively "American." Their sources are various.

Racial traditions and folklore. The anthropologist is able to learn a

[4] Arnold Toynbee, *A Study of History,* 6 vols. London (Oxford Univ. Press), 1946.
[5] Frederick Lewis Allen, *Only Yesterday,* New York (Harper), 1931. Also, *The Big Change,* New York (Harper), 1952.

good deal about values from the study of primitive societies. Certain values seem to be developed by most societies, even those far removed from each other in time, place, and environment. Moral codes develop from the need to adjust human nature to society. In a preliterate tribal society these codes are passed on as traditions and folklore, frequently reinforced by imagination in the form of myth. An advanced culture also has its folklore, passed on informally, principally by word of mouth.

Religion. While anthropologists no longer claim that religion is universal, they point out it is nearly so. Modern men who have officially dispensed with it often have seemed to clothe something else with mysticism and the status of divinity, such as the scientific method or dialectical materialism. It is not within the scope of a book on secondary education to enter into a critique of religious beliefs, but it is useful to observe that religion often is related to fear of death and awe at the unexplainable. Religious belief has been a rich source for human ideals and a lasting reinforcement for man's most lofty aspirations. It contributes to morality both by glorifying the desirable traits and actions and by creating taboos.

Philosophy. Since the time of the Greeks, men have attempted to employ thought to determine values. A wide range of conclusions has been reached by philosophers at different periods and in different cultures, as well as by men in the same general cultural framework. Although philosophy uses the methods of logic, among its most prominent disagreements are the proper places of thought, feeling, intuition, and experiment in arriving at value judgments. The importance of philosophy as a source of values for education is increased by the inclusion of education among the problems directly considered by philosophers and the growth of educational philosophy as a separate discipline for the preparation of educational workers.

Social and political theory. Just as religion and philosophy overlap, sometimes contradicting, sometimes reinforcing one another, so do both contribute to social and political theory. The schools of the United States and Russia, perhaps more than any others, have consciously justified their existence and orientation upon the basis of social and political theory and have sought to perpetuate values drawn from those fields. While the Russian value system has been nourished—or starved —on Marxist ideology, social and political theories in the United States have been more diverse, compatible with religion, and largely consistent with a philosophy of Christian idealism.

Science. Faith in utilitarian science is considered by both Americans and foreign observers to be the foremost American value. Science has been heralded as a bringer of good as well as an arbiter of values. It has been invested with a mystique of its own. But this phenomenon is neither as recent nor as distinctively American as many seem to believe. Since the time of Francis Bacon (1561-1626), of course, the inductive method of arriving at truth through experimentation and observation has been part of the intellectual tradition of the Western world. A mystical faith in the truth of science is also not confined to contemporary America. George Bernard Shaw tells a story that could happen today. His work as a reporter took him to cover a lecture by an eccentric who sought to convince his audience that the world is flat. Though the lecturer was confronted by indignation, his attackers possessed too little concrete geographical and astronomical knowledge to refute his position. Entering into the debate following the lecture, Shaw praised the data the lecturer presented but argued that it tended to prove that the world is a cylinder. Shaw reported that never had he been so deluged with letters of protest and indignation as he was for this playful scoffing at science. He concluded that "Mr. Everyman is often as credulous and bigoted in his modern scientific scepticism as his grandfather was in his Evangelicism."[6]

Scientists, of course, maintain that the usefulness of science rests not on faith in it but rather on its ability to demonstrate truth through techniques which, in turn, permit verification through objective repetition.

Mutually reinforcing sources. When an American says, "One man's as good as another," he is drawing upon folklore to bolster a demand for impartial treatment. When he repeats the doctrine that "All men are created equal," he usually interprets it to mean, in contradiction to science, that all men are equally endowed with talent. In support of his interpretation, he can point to the scientific evidence that no race or national stock is biologically inferior, although individuals differ. When he adds that each individual personality is unique and invested with dignity and worth, he sums up an American philosophy based upon folk experience, religious tradition, social theory, and science. Thus do all aspects of the American culture reinforce its most precious values.

[6] George Bernard Shaw, *Everybody's Political What's What,* New York (Dodd, Mead), 1945, pp. 360-61.

Plural Nature of Values

Values serve both personal and social purposes. One reason for today's uncertainties about values is in the increased emphasis on social values. In the traditional value system, the essential is a correct inner balance of virtue. According to Christian doctrine, this is to be achieved through a right relationship with God, from which flows a right relationship with one's fellows. A clear illustration is provided by a book used for instruction of the young by one of the Protestant denominations, explaining the Ten Commandments "as the head of the family should teach them in a simple way to his household." The Seventh Commandment is explained as follows:

> Thou Shalt not steal.
> *What does this mean?* We should fear and love God that we may not take our neighbor's money or goods nor get them by false ware or dealing, but help him to improve and protect his property and business.[7]

In today's complex society the traditional, individualistic religious values seem to have less hold, and values are derived more and more from the society. Indeed, the social psychologist sees at least some of each person's values as determined by communication within the social groups of which he is a member. A religious denomination, for instance, inculcates certain beliefs into its members in order to make them part of the group. Value development, therefore, is a process of socialization.

A major difficulty in the complex American social environment is the *variety* of group identifications. Even in a small town the adolescent today no longer finds among his high school peers, among his casual adult associations, among the cues he receives from the mass mediums of communication, or among the other stimuli of his social environment the consistent, clear, and explicit stress on values and ideals that existed in a simpler society.

A value system gives the individual both a sense of purpose and a sense of direction. It helps him to know what to expect of others and what to expect of himself. It builds the sense of right and wrong (although the traditional Christian idealist believes this is innate). It provides a basis of judgment and discrimination for the acts and qualities of individuals and the "worth" of things.

---

[7] *Dr. Martin Luther's Small Catechism: A Handbook of Christian Doctrine,* St. Louis, Mo. (Concordia Publishing House), 1943, p. 6.

In a group, a value system gives a common outlook and a basis for collective action. It helps a group to choose its leaders and assign other roles to its membership. It helps the group relate itself to the broader society and to mankind in general. Values guide the group in its judgmental activities, somewhat as they do the individual.

Figure 8-1 suggests various conceptions of values and illustrates the complexity of the problem of finding precise meanings with which to discuss this difficult subject.

IMPACT OF CONTEMPORARY FORCES ON VALUES

American secondary schools have periodically faced new tests growing out of new situations. There is widespread agreement that such a testing period is again in process and that values are at the center of the major stresses. As Clifton Fadiman has written from the traditionalist viewpoint:

> A crisis period is not necessarily marked by disaster or violence or even revolutionary change. It is marked by the absence of any

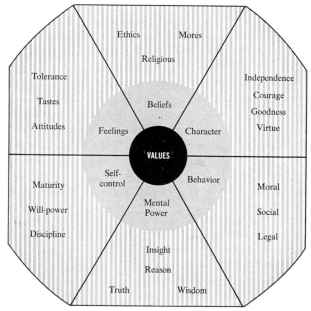

Fig. 8–1. *Various Conceptions of Values*

general, tacit adherence to an agreed-upon system of values. It is in such a crisis period that we live. . . . Our present educational system quite properly mirrors this uncertainty of the majority. It mirrors our mental chaos. There is nothing else it *can* do, for ours is a democratic society, and all our institutions are representative.[8]

Why is our value system described as chaotic? At least three major forces are behind the uncertainty and controversy. Continuing urbanization lessens face-to-face value transmission; accelerating scientific discovery widens the lag between traditional values and newly discovered truths; and multiple cultures and subcultures impinge upon one another more directly and more constantly.

Urbanization Encourages Anonymity

As urbanization and suburbanization have gone forward, the individual's identification with those close to him has weakened. The family that uproots itself from a rural or small-town environment and relocates in an urban or suburban area finds itself in new social, as well as new physical, surroundings. The patterns of living are unfamiliar, seem strange, and often ignore or deny the moral codes of the old home. New neighbors may be indifferent, or perhaps even hostile, to newcomers. Social reinforcement for behavior in line with values explicitly or implicitly held may be weakened. The practical grounds for behaving in an upright and trustworthy manner toward a "neighbor" one has never met can hardly be the same as for a neighbor whose parents one knew and whose children will preserve a community memory of how one behaved in tests of truth, responsibility, honesty, or sexual restraint.

Old city neighborhoods no longer are residential areas containing predominantly people of the same ethnic group, the same church membership, and similar occupation—often living relatively close to the place of employment. The newer suburbs, as well as the deteriorating city centers, conspicuously lack these features. The social structure of the family environment may be considerably weakened by the custom of the male head of the family commuting to work or traveling in connection with his work, so that in spite of a shorter workweek he has fewer hours to spend at home. The increasing trend toward employment of women, including mothers, also fragments families.

The effect of these and other similar changes has been to weaken or

[8] Clifton Fadiman, "Today's Lost Generation," *Saturday Review,* September 12, 1959, p. 13.

destroy group involvement in the old sense. At the same time, individual acts—as well as the effects of such acts—become blurred. An individual can violate the old code with less fear of being observed or "found out." Simultaneously the individual is substantially freed from having to deal with the effects of acts he knows to be counter to traditional or rational values. If he exploits the unwary in a commercial transaction, that transaction may be the first and last contact with the person who is victimized. "Am I my brother's keeper?" is still a meaningful question, but its meaning is less personal, more abstract than in other times.

Science—An Avenue to Truth

Since the Renaissance the method of science increasingly has become an arbiter of values. During this time the usefulness of science in an ethical sense has been obscured by the persistent capacity of some distinguished scientists (from Bacon to Fuchs) to lead unethical lives and to pronounce foolish judgments in fields outside their expertness. In this respect the record of scientists is probably not greatly different from that of theologians or politicians. Dewey observed:

> If the physician is careless and arbitrary because of overanxiety to get his work done, or if he lets his pecuniary needs influence his manner of judgment, we may say that he has failed both logically and morally. Scientifically he has not employed the methods at command for directing his act of judging so as to give it maximum correctness.[9]

Dewey and a host of his followers, along with many to whom his name is anathema, have looked to science as the instrument for social, moral, and material progress. At the risk of oversimplifying, it can be said that many of the best-informed and most educated people in the United States agree upon this pre-eminence of science. Dewey wrote of a "science of conduct":

> Such a science can be built up only through reference to cases which at the outset need explicit critical direction in judgment. We need to know what the social situation is in which we find ourselves required to act, so that we may know what it is right to do. We need to know what is the effect of some mental disposition upon our way of looking at life and thereby upon our conduct. Through clearing up

[9] John Dewey, "Logical Conditions of a Scientific Treatment of Morality," *Philosophy of Education*, Ames, Iowa (Littlefield, Adams and Company), 1956, p. 228.

the social situation, through making objective to ourselves our own motives and their consequences, we build up generic propositions: statements of experience as a connection of conditions, that is, in the form of objects. Such statements are used and applied in dealing with further problems. Gradually their use becomes more and more habitual. The 'theory' becomes a part of our total apparatus. The social situation takes on a certain form or organization. It is pre-classified as of a certain sort, as of a certain genus and even species of this sort; the only question which remains is dicrimination of the particular variety. Again, we get into the habit of taking into account certain sources of error in our own position as these affect our judg-ment of behavior, and thereby bring them sufficiently under control so that the need of conscious reference to their intellectual formu-lation diminishes. As physical science has brought about an organi-zation of the physical world along with an organization of practical habits of dealing with that world, so ethical science will effect an organization of the social world and a corresponding organization of the mental habits through which the individual relates himself to it.[10]

Thus Dewey not only urged science as the foundation of ethical values, but outlined a theory of the way science is to work in develop-ing character. In a penetrating analysis of the problems of values man now confronts, H. J. Muller takes a somewhat similar position, al-though he gives less emphasis to the immediate social context of be-havior. He points out that other animals "value" things—that is, strive for them as desirable. Only man classifies values and arranges them in hierarchies. From the biologist's viewpoint man is a relative newcomer, remodeling his behavior to meet his circumstances in a relatively crude manner, and thus subject to considerable conflict—inner and outer. This view of man holds in behavior, including desires and values, just as it does in the other functioning of the organism. He claims that man has a great number of unlearned predilections and aversions rang-ing from the purely sensory level to a perceptual and perhaps even conceptual level. Individuals differ in inheritable feelings, such as egotism and sociability. To a considerable degree natural selection has favored cooperative behavior (which furthers survival). Muller concludes:

> In recent times, however, human understanding and the conditions of human living and association have been changing so fast that

[10] *Ibid.,* pp. 246-47.

our systems of values and ethics, education, and social relations have fallen behind and are not well enough adjusted to our present needs and knowledge.

What kind of reorientation is needed? Obviously, one in which our motivations are reshaped in accordance with our modern knowledge of the world and ourselves.[11]

In this reshaping, science is forcing man to identify himself with humanity in general. It can build this identification through gratification of man's natural curiosity (seeking "truth for its own sake"), through the fulfillment of love in its varied aspects; through encouraging freedom (making one's own decisions); and through his desire for achievement, variety, adventure, and appreciation.

Merging Cultures

Rapid transportation, rising disposable incomes, and far-flung economic interests are intermingling the American people on a scale unprecedented in our history. When cultures and subcultures come in contact, variant values often conflict. From this conflict new values often are created which are acceptable to the conflicting parties. Sometimes in this cultural exchange a value rejected in an old environment is accepted in the new, though perhaps without enthusiasm. Whatever the specific process may be, the end result is a widening of perimeters.

World War I, the problems of postwar readjustment and depression, World War II, the Korean War, and the cold war are only the major landmarks in the growing recognition that all mankind must be included in any comprehensive system of moral directives. President Roosevelt's presenting to Congress and the nation an international program based upon the four "Freedoms," was a dramatic instance of making explicit for the nation a moral program to meet the realities confronting men on a shrinking planet who are divided by their conceptions of what is best for man.

The public high school is one institution in which differing value patterns merge. While elementary schools, usually of smaller enrollment, often still serve relatively homogeneous neighborhoods, this is rarely true of high schools. Increasingly, they take youth from all the diverse backgrounds society provides, with their different conscious and unconscious values. These youth arrive at a time in their own development when they are concerned about their relationships with

[11] H. J. Muller, "Human Values in Relation to Evolution," *Science*, March 21, 1958, p. 629.

others, with their own selves, and with abstractions such as happiness, justice, freedom, and responsibility. The high school has the opportunity of contributing to the construction and reconstruction of the value systems of its students. Ignoring the opportunity amounts to abdicating a responsibility to other agencies which will, in the main, be less interested and less qualified.

Direction of Transition in Values

Lately, because of the changes in society growing out of urbanization, the growth of science, and the merging of plural cultures, many observers feel that a great transition in values is in process. Whyte writes of this as a transition from a "work ethic" to a "social ethic";[12] Riesman describes it as a transition from the inner-directed man to the other-directed man.[13] Both of these careful studies explicitly consider education. Getzels has neatly presented a similar viewpoint.[14] In his opinion, Americans hold four values sacred—democracy, individualism, equality, and human perfectibility. They are held on a sufficiently high level of abstraction to allow considerable departure from them in practice, but people appeal to them when they wish to "legitimize action." Traditionally Americans have also held four major values on a less sacred level—the work-success ethic, a future-time orientation, independence, or the autonomous self, and Puritan morality. These less sacred values, he says, are changing toward sociability, present-time orientation, group conformity, and moral relativism. Getzels presents evidence to support these changes, to show that students adhering to traditional values do better schoolwork and are more likely to continue education and to prefer professional careers. He also suggests that seniors leave high school with the same values they brought as freshmen.

There are many reasons for concern about youth in a period when the adult society is unable to offer consistent patterns and to provide a unified dedication to a value system that would make models easy for youth to find and to follow. The dilemma in which youth finds itself is well represented by the problems of sex adjustment, where a power-

---

[12] William H. Whyte, Jr., *The Organization Man,* New York (Simon and Schuster), 1956.

[13] David Riesman, *The Lonely Crowd: A Study of the Changing American Character,* New Haven (Yale Univ. Press), 1950.

[14] Jacob W. Getzels, "The Acquisition of Values in School and Society," *The High School in a New Era,* Chicago (Univ. of Chicago Press), 1958, pp. 146-61.

ful instinct is stimulated by all the arts and devices of entertainment and advertising. Adults debate contradictory values on property, law, honor, and sex without taking a firm stand on a set of standards. There is no firm basis to which youth can orient themselves. A young alumna of a selective college for women writes:

> What or what not to do about sex is, these days, relative. It all depends. This is not to say that there are no longer any moral standards; certainly there are—the fact that sex still causes guilt and worry proves it. But moral generalizations seem remote and unreal, something our grandparents believed in.
>
> Today girls are expected to judge each situation for itself, a far more demanding task.[15]

This is hardly a description of an adequately functioning value system.

FACTORS IN VALUE DEVELOPMENT

In a period of value shifts and debates about the priorities of values, one could not expect to find a consensus about the ways values are to be inculcated into the younger members of society. Nor could one anticipate agreement upon the roles of authority, democracy, and individualism in value development.

Conflicting Points of View

Individuals and groups have differed on such matters as the use of compulsion as against self-direction in developing values, upon the importance of emotional as against factual grounding for values, upon the formation of habits as opposed to intellectual consideration in value decisions, and upon the importance of example as against indoctrination.

Imposition versus self-direction. Very early in the sparsely settled colonies differences of opinion appeared as to the position of compulsion in religious belief and opinion. Members of various religious sects worked out uneasy compromises to permit freedom of religion. They were influenced partly by Reformation doctrine holding that the Holy Spirit would work in each man through the Bible, and partly by the growing belief that each man was capable of using reason to control

[15] Nora Johnson, "Sex and the College Girl," *Atlantic Monthly,* November 1959, p. 59.

his own affairs, but chiefly, perhaps, by the realization that in a society where each sect was a minority, civil order demanded toleration. The idea that a man might hold unpopular beliefs, but speak and write freely about them, was accordingly incorporated in the Constitution of the United States as well as the constitutions of the early states. Firmly grounded was the notion that in areas of values each man was to be freed from outside compulsion. At the same time free men had an inner compulsion to see to their own souls and well-being. They were their own stern taskmasters. Such ideas were bound to affect children. Writing of the early days of the nineteenth century George Clay, a historian, reports:

> The stern standards of colonial child-training, with its emphasis on submission and self-denial, still had many supporters, even in the western settlements. But the frontier itself bred a toughness and independence in its children, which neither the fear of God nor New England parents could budge.
> 'As a child . . . I had unbounded confidence in myself,' remembered Henry Wright, who came from Connecticut to western New York in 1801. 'I did feel . . . that I was competent to be a church, a priesthood, a government, an empire, in myself, and I never could see any good reason why any created being should exercise authority over me.'[16]

Such ideas inevitably became incorporated into schooling, even at a time when control of student behavior in the school followed authoritarian methods. The schools usually thought of themselves as preparing for self-direction, so the question, as time went on, became one of how soon self-direction should begin and how to prepare for it.

Emotional or factual grounding. Totalitarian societies have usually been quick to exploit the emotional possibilities of scapegoats, of ceremony and pomp, and of mass identifications with causes and spectacles. In democratic societies appeals to feeling are less frequent and less pervasive since the basis of democracy rests not on emotion but on rational conviction. While some social and educational philosophers oppose emotional grounding for values, in practice much use of emotion is made. In fact, the more important any matter seems, the more likely it is that attempts will be made to associate emotion with it. This is true in national crises, important elections, and wherever controversial issues are considered.

[16] George R. Clay, "Children of the Young Republic," *American Heritage,* April 1960, p. 49.

In the schools emotion is more likely to be reserved for inter-scholastic athletic contests and the Senior Prom. To most people the use of emotion to build and reinforce values seems a denial of the educational function, which is usually thought of as being objective and disinterested. Nevertheless, it may be appropriate for students to learn that after the facts have been sought, considered, and evaluated, there may still be a place for the zeal and dedication associated with emotion.

Habits as opposed to intellectual decisions. About 1890 William James wrote a chapter on "Habit" which is excellent reading today. While he saw clearly the importance of memory, reasoning, and emotion, James observed:

> There is no more miserable human being than one in whom nothing is habitual but indecision, and for whom the lighting of every cigar, the drinking of every cup, the time of rising and going to bed every day, and the beginning of every bit of work, are subjects of express volitional deliberation.[17]

James thought of habit not as a result produced by discipline and forced on the learner but as a deliberate acquisition. He laid down three maxims for acquiring moral habits. First, one must launch the new habits as strongly and decidedly as possible. Second, exceptions must not be allowed to occur until the new habit is securely rooted. Third, one must act on a resolution as quickly as possible and on every emotional prompting. He concludes:

> The hell to be endured hereafter, of which theology tells, is no worse than the hell we make for ourselves in this world by habitually fashioning our characters in the wrong way. Could the young but realize how soon they will become mere walking bundles of habits, they would give more heed to their conduct while in the plastic state. We are spinning our own fates, good or evil, and never to be undone. Every smallest stroke of virtue or of vice leaves its never so little scar.[18]

With the advent of behaviorist psychology, habits came to be thought of in a narrower sense—as stimuli and responses locked together by associated repetition. Habits in this sense are valuable but hardly an adequate base for moral training since each habit must be

[17] William James, *Psychology,* Cleveland, Ohio (World Publishing Company), 1948, p. 145.
[18] *Ibid.,* pp. 149-50.

built up separately. Modern psychology has found it necessary to explain other aspects of learning values. Habits built through routine and repetition will serve for a limited range of values. They are necessary for very young children and those of limited mental ability, but normal youth of secondary school age can generalize in value situations where choices are involved. As Kingsley says:

> By way of illustration let us consider the ideal of *honesty*. Here the individual has an understanding of what it means to be honest; he feels that honesty is worthwhile, and purposes to be honest in all matters that come within the range of his ideal. His goal is to be an honest individual. His concept of honesty may be imperfect, in which case he is likely to be honest in some situations and not in others.[19]

There are thus two major problems in securing moral conduct. The first is to acquire an adequate understanding of what moral conduct is in the situations where one is required to act; the second is to internalize strong purposes. How are strong purposes developed?

Values "caught" rather than taught. Although there are many other factors that contribute to good character and moral behavior, example is almost surely the most important. The critical phase in the process of establishing an ideal is the actual adoption of the conceived standard of conduct as a goal. Example is more convincing than argument. For instance, to be most effective several conditions should be present. The individual who sets the example must be admired, the example should be consistent, it should be accompanied by evidence that the behavior exemplified is satisfying, and it should be reinforced by the approval of others. Obviously all of these conditions are difficult to meet, but it would be hard to overestimate, for instance, the influence of a driving teacher who consistently drives skillfully and safely, shows that his proficiency and consideration for others are a source of pleasure to him, and receives the frank approval of other adults and of students.

After a rather discouraging review of the influence of schools on values, Getzels concludes:

> But the fundamental mechanism by which we interiorize values, in school as elsewhere, is *identification*. As the child struggles to integrate and to maintain a stable self-image from among his piece-

[19] Howard L. Kingsley, *The Nature and Conditions of Learning*, Englewood Cliffs, N. J. (Prentice-Hall), 1946, p. 444.

meal perceptions of who he is and where he fits, he is led to view himself as at one with another person. The parents are the child's earliest objects of identification. Later he may add older siblings, favorite neighbors, community heroes, and, of course, school personnel. In making these identifications, the child not only assumes the outward manners and expressive movements of his 'significant figures' but attempts also to incorporate their values and attitudes.[20]

Levels of Response in Behavior

The secondary school-age student is in transition toward adulthood. His identification with his peers is heightened and complicated by a strong desire for belonging and by his efforts to remain independent *within* a social group. He is concerned with trying to find his "self"— to rank his purposes and goals, to recognize his powers and lacks.

Response to adult controls. For his own safety and well-being the young child must be directed in most of his behavior. While more enlightened parents and teachers provide reasons and explanations with their commands and give their instructions in courteous and considerate ways, showing respect for the child, the difference in experience and knowledge compels a situation in which the adult will prevails. Riesman maintains that in an earlier time the period of adult direction was so powerful in its influence that a psychological mechanism like a gyroscope was developed.[21] By this means the person was able to stay on course even when new demands were made upon him, and his behavior remained consistent.

No one doubts that this period is past. The difference of opinion now is about whether the passing is to be lamented. All seem agreed that the modern course must be to retain adult guiding influence through example and persuasion, to help young people make value choices through conviction rather than through compulsion. One of the hazards in this situation is that the influence of immature associates may be more powerful than that of adults no longer able to employ compulsion.

Response to peer groups. No one can work with American high school students without becoming aware of the power of the high school peer culture. Typically, the adolescent enters school seeking approval and acceptance. Sometimes the particular segment of his age-mates from whom he seeks acceptance is clearly defined, some-

---

[20] Getzels, *op. cit.*, p. 160.
[21] Riesman, *op. cit.*, p. 16.

times it is not. While a constant seeking for social approval and acceptance must be considered an immature level of behavior, it has tremendous import. It seems to be extremely difficult for the young person whose social needs are unsatisfied to develop adequate behavioral patterns. Frustration leads to rebellion and to conflict with the values of the culture. "Since they are not accepted in the social life of the adolescent peer culture, they make a life for themselves with other adolescents who are not accepted. This gives them a bad reputation, and they have more difficulty than ever in their relations with their school mates."[22] The normal course of development is from social acceptance to social deliberation and mutual agreement by young people and adults on the value issues young people must decide.

Response to self. Interaction with adults and one's age-mates is the principal method through which one builds a concept of self. Havighurst and Taba[23] classified the persons they investigated as self-directive, adaptive, submissive, defiant, and unadjusted. These terms are descriptive; the unadjusted person has not yet successfully established a relationship with his environment, but neither has he developed a self-concept as an individual hostile to society.

The individual who has developed a mental picture of himself has a beginning from which to work out an understanding of moral questions. With some of his more important goal identifications established he is able to classify himself roughly in reference to other individuals and group values.

THE SECONDARY SCHOOLS AS AN AGENCY FOR VALUE DEVELOPMENT

There is no more complex function of secondary education than its role in developing values. Since the tremendous forward step of secularizing education was accomplished as a necessary concomitant of unifying schools, indecision has marked the school's approach to values. Perplexity has increased rather than diminished in recent times with growing confusion and counterforces in the mores of the adult society in the United States. A part of the problem of understanding the school's function has stemmed from praiseworthy efforts to clarify it, for partisans of traditionalist or experimentalist philosophy have made the usual partisan error of oversimplifying. Traditionalists

[22] Robert J. Havighurst and Hilda Taba, *Adolescent Character and Personality,* New York (John Wiley), 1949, p. 39.

[23] *Ibid.,* pp. 103-75.

enthusiastically decry the false gods of the progressives, who in turn would demolish as outworn the dogmas of all who believe truth can be derived from any source except objective science.

The first thing the secondary school must do is recognize the importance of values, morals, and character. The second imperative is to recognize that the school is not the sole agent for character development and instilling values; its burden is shared with the home and other agencies of culture. This second recognition can go a long way toward eliminating one of its handicaps, the false opposition between the school's role as conservator of the past versus its role as leader for change. In helping to develop the values of a people, the school must be to some extent a conservator, for the sources of our values lie deep in our culture and often far in our past. When the founding fathers thought of "schools and other means of education," they meant not only schools, but churches, a responsible press, libraries, and voluntary societies of many kinds. They believed that such a plural approach could not help but foster "religion, morality, and knowledge" and that true religious, moral, and intellectual values would need neither a monolithic church nor an autocratic state.

With these recognitions the secondary school can operate in three areas of primary importance—in clarifying the value system, in increasing the range and depth of values, and in helping to translate ideals into moral behavior.

Clarifying the Value System

The schools' greatest asset is a substantial consensus that, for them at least, intelligence is the supreme virtue. This has increasingly come to mean that any important question can be freely dealt with in the school if the methods of intelligence are used. This makes it possible for students to learn through thinking about moral situations; they may examine various kinds of behavior to identify their possible and probable consequences. As they do this with the help of the teacher's experience and understanding, they can draw conclusions that affect their own present and future behavior. This process helps the student learn both a method of procedure for future use and moral principles to be applied in future situations.

One of the most important principles the school can teach is that the rapid change of society makes generalized moral principles more rather than less important, for change requires a person to make value decisions rather than merely follow habits that have been formed uncritically during static periods. The possibilities of learning such principles are endless in the school environment, if these possibilities are properly realized and planned. In economics, students who learn that wealth depends upon production can deduce the moral value of producing for oneself and others. In health class, learning the causes of disease can be followed by recognizing the moral importance of good sanitation or of developing healthful habits. Even in mathematics the student can learn the value of finding the best solution to a problem—the most precise answer or the most efficient method.

This conscious process will help to supply the models the adolescent so badly needs, for it will provide the social context in which the teacher is best prepared to exemplify the ideal behavior. Under the teacher's guidance the best exemplars among the peer group can serve as models for imitation. And with the teacher's skilled direction the social environment can encourage the value-oriented behavior around which concepts can develop.

The adolescent, psychologists agree, is peculiarly vulnerable to what philosophers identify as one of the plagues of our times—the confusion of norms with ideals. The school must help to identify the best in conduct and to distinguish it from what the normal "well-adjusted" person does. Adjustment must be rejected or redefined in terms of ideals. Developmental psychologists recognize that there is change and growth in ethical awareness as children move into and through adolescence, but Gesell, Ilg, and Ames write descriptions that show a mixture of gain and loss in value discrimination.[24] The thirteen-year-old has a clearly defined sense of right and wrong accompanied by too little understanding of motives and social forces. As he grows older his ethical sense becomes more flexible and stable, but as he gets more understanding of others and of the world, he often loses some of the distinction between levels of behavior. Much of this loss is undoubtedly because he has learned that so much is relative and has had too little experience in discovering the *ideals* behavior relates to. He has a need for clarification of the personal and social value structure, for establishing hierarchies and priorities, and for separating and relating means and ends.

If the adolescent is fortunate, his family and other influences have laid a foundation of rational moral training and will continue to help

[24] Arnold Gesell, Frances L. Ilg, and Louise Bates Ames, *Youth: The Years from Ten to Sixteen,* New York (Harper), 1956, pp. 170-71, 209-11, 246-47, 270-71.

him interpret ideals and shape behavior. But his enlarging horizons, psychological vulnerability, and the increased complexity of his value-involving adjustments make the role of his formal and informal school experiences a key one. Learning to employ intelligence to select his goals and shape his behavior is one of his greatest requirements.

Increasing Range and Depth of Values

Bringing meaning and intelligible order to the value system is only the beginning of the school's responsibility. Closely associated with this aspect of developing values is the necessity for enriching the personal value system. This can be intellectual too—more than intellectual. Enriching values has been understood as one of the purposes for the study of literature, art, and music.

> To do good we must first know good; to serve beauty we must first know beauty; to speak the truth we must first know the truth. We must know these things ourselves, be able to recognize them by ourselves, be able to describe, explain, and communicate them by ourselves, and wish to do so, when no one else is present to prompt us or to bargain with us.[25]

Such an imperative carries many implications for the high school. The chief criticism Whyte offers of the schools of Park Forest is not merely that they devote themselves to the "social ethic," but that they do so in the absence of any necessity, that they choose to reinforce what needs no reinforcement rather than supply experiences and appreciations lacking outside of school.[26] To the extent that a school does this it deserves criticism, for youth need to learn the satisfaction of accomplishment as well as the satisfaction of social approval. Havighurst and Taba distinguish two requirements for strong character: "First among these characteristics is an intelligent understanding of moral principles and the ability to apply them to problems of daily conduct. Second, and more important, is the conviction that moral principles are worth sacrifice—even the sacrifice of social acceptance and popularity.[27]

The task of the school is to place the student in contact with models who can demonstrate such ideals, directly in the school environment and indirectly in literature, drama, history, art, and music. Values can

[25] A. Whitney Griswold, *Liberal Education and the Democratic Ideal,* New Haven (Yale Univ. Press), 1959, p. 136.
[26] William H. Whyte, *op. cit.,* p. 429.
[27] Havighurst and Taba, *op. cit.,* p. 189.

be deepened and enlarged by the dedicatory power of the Gettysburg Address, the message of the redeeming power of love in *Silas Marner,* the soaring inspiration of Handel's *Messiah,* or the spontaneous gaiety of European folk dances.

Translating Ideals into Behavior

The most difficult aspect of learning values for the individual, as well as for the high school concerned with discharging its function, is in putting the ideal into practice. The opportunities in the school situation are unlimited, but each opportunity has its accompanying hazard. In athletics, for example, the school officially teaches ideals of sportsmanlike conduct. Unofficially it may or may not teach them, but from the admired and glamorous figures of professional sports the schoolboy athlete hears, "Nice guys finish last." High school spectators cannot secure beer at the school field, but they can watch on television as a spectator at a professional baseball game empties his foaming cup on the center fielder. Many high school principals dread the holiday basketball games when recent alumni bring their college spectator "folkways" home to the high school stands.

Most schools have made an effort to make laboratories of behavior of their student councils, all-school dances, special-interest clubs, and student cafeteria. Teaching the form of honesty represented by faithfully performing one's own work fits naturally into the academic classroom. Cheating is reported to be a growing problem—a dishonest art in which students seem to become more proficient while in college.[28] Such problems provide situations for practice of behavioral ideals. High schools as well as colleges have established honor systems, conducted editorial campaigns, and experimented with rewards and punishments.

The school can provide a model environment for practice of fair play—one unequaled elsewhere. Ideals of courtesy and impartial treatment can be exemplified in the cafeteria line, in the assignment of student lockers, and in the evaluation of student progress. The large numbers of people in close proximity in the high school provide good conditions for learning respect and consideration for the property and personal rights of others.

[28] Marvin L. Henricks, "Changing Mores Concerning Cheating on Examinations," *School and Society,* November 1958, pp. 413-14, and William Graham Cole, "Cheating Your Way Through College," *Nation,* May 14, 1960, pp. 416-18.

Above all, the school in a democratic society can demonstrate commitment to the ideal of allowing and encouraging maximum self-development and providing varied opportunities for realizing achievement in and dedication to worthwhile goals. Truth, justice, integrity, sacrifice, consideration for others, chastity, courage, independence, and self-discipline can become goals understood, desired, sought after, and achieved by at least some students in the well-ordered and stimulating environment of a value-oriented secondary school.

SELECTED REFERENCES

BRINTON, CRANE. *A History of Western Morals.* New York. Harcourt, Brace & World, Inc., 1959.

BURNS, EDWARD MCNALL. *The American Idea of Mission.* New Brunswick, N.J.: Rutgers Univ. Press, 1957.

GINSBERG, ELI. *Values and Ideals of American Youth.* New York: Columbia Univ. Press, 1961.

HUGHES, EVERETT CHERRINGTON. "Prestige." *Annals of the American Academy of Political and Social Science,* September 1959.

KINKEAD, EUGENE, AND ARTHUR V. SHEA. "The Making of Men." *America,* October 13, 1959.

THAYER, V. T. *The Role of the School in American Society.* New York: Dodd, Mead, 1960.

WADDINGTON, C. H. *The Ethical Animal.* London: Allen and Unwin, 1960.

WALSH, MICHAEL P. "Values in Education: Brilliance Alone Has Proven to be Not Enough." *Vital Speeches of the Day,* June 15, 1960.

PART III

Organization and Program

Lane Technical High School in Chicago,
one of the largest schools in the United
States, requires complex organization and
skilled administration.

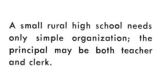

A small rural high school needs
only simple organization; the
principal may be both teacher
and clerk.

Organization of Secondary Schools

THE ORGANIZATION of a secondary school reflects the educational ambitions and philosophy of the faculty and community. It represents the conditions and working arrangements by means of which its functions are pursued. Once established, the organization helps to determine the efficiency and effectiveness of education itself. The nature of the organization and its responsiveness to the demands and requirements of particular educational programs depend upon such factors as the total setting in which schools operate, the theory of organization followed, the complexity of the school, and the part teachers play in shaping the organization to the educational program. It appears that recent experimentation in secondary schools is producing new trends in organization which may permit greater flexibility for the comprehensive high school and more responsiveness to the instructional plans of teachers.

SETTING FOR SCHOOL ORGANIZATION

Approximately 40,000 school districts, which employ over 1,400,000 professional staff members, spend in excess of $14½ billion each year to educate more than 36,000,000 children and youth.[1]

The uneven distribution of population and cultural and economic differences among communities, states, and regions cause organizational patterns and problems to vary from district to district. With growth, organization tends to become complex. Two qualities—complexity and variation—characterize the organization of secondary schools in the United States.

Decentralization a Principle—Centralization a Trend

Historically, the organization of public education in the United States is decentralized. Although the state is the legal unit for organization, each of the fifty state school systems is subdivided into numerous, almost autonomous, local districts. The result is a conglomerate of types and sizes of district organizations that defy precise classification. Unlike certain European countries whose school organizations are nationwide, the federal government exercises little influence on the manner in which education is organized. Only in states where federal schools for Indians and children of military personnel have been established does it affect organizational patterns. The local school district must be recognized as the typical organization for schools in the United States.

State systems—from weakness to strength. The legal structure of public education places control of education in the state government. Every state has its department of education headed by a chief state school officer. Some of these officers are elected; others are appointed. Forty-six states have their own boards of education that exercise control over elementary and secondary education. There is a growing tendency today to separate administrative and policy-making functions, the former being made the responsibility of the chief state school officer, with the latter being assigned to the board. Table 9-1 reveals the trend toward the use of state boards of education. Table 9-2 shows the changes which have been made in the method of selection of the chief state school officers.

Tables 9-3 and 9-4 serve to illustrate the differing organizational structures of state departments. In Illinois (Table 9-3) the superintendent of public instruction is selected by popular vote and no state board of education exists. In Maryland (Table 9-4) the state super-

[1] Figures derived from the Research Division of the National Education Association, *Research Bulletin*, February 1959, p. 3; and *Research Bulletin*, February 1960, p. 18.

Table 9-1. *Number of State Boards of Education*

COMPOSITION	1945	1950	1955	1960
Wholly or mostly ex-officio	8	4	3	3
Wholly or mostly appointed or elected	31	36	41	43
TOTAL	39	40	44	46

S O U R C E : The data given in Table 9-1 were obtained from Fred F. Beach, *The State and Education, Miscellaneous Bulletin No. 23*, Washington, D.C. (Office of Education), 1955, pp. 29-31, and the author's survey of certain state departments.

Table 9-2. *Method of Selection of the Chief State School Officer*

METHOD	1945	1950	1955	1960
Appointed by state board	8	13	18	20
Appointed by governor	7	6	4	4
Popular election	33	29	26	26
TOTAL	48	48	48	50[a]

[a] Includes Alaska and Hawaii.

S O U R C E : Same as Table 9-1.

intendent is chosen by a state board of education which is appointed by the governor. The fifty state departments employ in excess of 9,000 staff members, more than 3,600 of whom are professional employees. The state departments of education include superintendents or commissioners and their deputies; directors of divisions and chiefs of services and their staffs; and regional and district supervisors.

Since 1945 virtually every state has made major changes in its state department of education in order to provide greater leadership to local school districts. Prior to 1945, state departments, with rare exceptions, were compelled to concentrate their efforts on the administration of regulations and statutes. They were generally not provided resources necessary for research and instructional leadership. However, with chief state school officers taking the initiative, constitutional amendments, statutory revisions, and administrative improvements have been made—or are under way—in order to centralize and strengthen the leadership capabilities of each state education department.

A major reason behind the trend for centralization at the state level is the need to place the financial support of education upon a sound

Table 9-3. *Organization of the State of Illinois Department of Education*

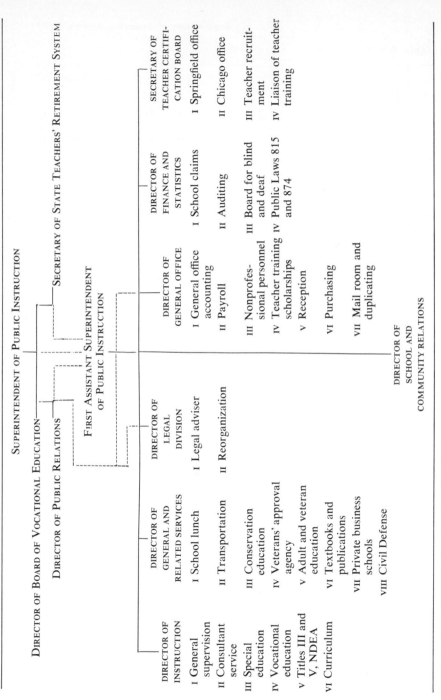

SUPERINTENDENT OF PUBLIC INSTRUCTION

DIRECTOR OF BOARD OF VOCATIONAL EDUCATION

SECRETARY OF STATE TEACHERS' RETIREMENT SYSTEM

DIRECTOR OF PUBLIC RELATIONS

FIRST ASSISTANT SUPERINTENDENT OF PUBLIC INSTRUCTION

DIRECTOR OF INSTRUCTION	DIRECTOR OF GENERAL AND RELATED SERVICES	DIRECTOR OF LEGAL DIVISION	DIRECTOR OF GENERAL OFFICE	DIRECTOR OF FINANCE AND STATISTICS	SECRETARY OF TEACHER CERTIFICATION BOARD
I General supervision	I School lunch	I Legal adviser	I General office accounting	I School claims	I Springfield office
II Consultant service	II Transportation	II Reorganization	II Payroll	II Auditing	II Chicago office
III Special education	III Conservation education		III Nonprofessional personnel	III Board for blind and deaf	III Teacher recruitment
IV Vocational education	IV Veterans' approval agency		IV Teacher training scholarships	IV Public Laws 815 and 874	IV Liaison of teacher training
V Titles III and V, NDEA	V Adult and veteran education		V Reception		
VI Curriculum	VI Textbooks and publications		VI Purchasing		
	VII Private business schools		VII Mail room and duplicating		
	VIII Civil Defense				

DIRECTOR OF SCHOOL AND COMMUNITY RELATIONS

SOURCE: George T. Wilkins, Superintendent of Public Instruction, State of Illinois, June 1960.

Table 9-4. *Organization of the Maryland State Department of Education*

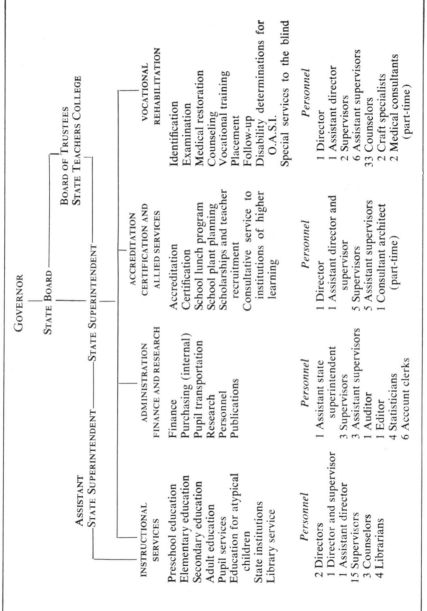

GOVERNOR

STATE BOARD ──────── BOARD OF TRUSTEES STATE TEACHERS COLLEGE

ASSISTANT STATE SUPERINTENDENT ──── STATE SUPERINTENDENT ──── STATE SUPERINTENDENT

INSTRUCTIONAL SERVICES	ADMINISTRATION FINANCE AND RESEARCH	ACCREDITATION CERTIFICATION AND ALLIED SERVICES	VOCATIONAL REHABILITATION
Preschool education	Finance	Accreditation	Identification
Elementary education	Purchasing (internal)	Certification	Examination
Secondary education	Pupil transportation	School lunch program	Medical restoration
Adult education	Research	School plant planning	Counseling
Pupil services	Personnel	Scholarships and teacher recruitment	Vocational training
Education for atypical children	Publications	Consultative service to institutions of higher learning	Placement
State institutions			Follow-up
Library service			Disability determinations for O.A.S.I.
			Special services to the blind

Personnel (Instructional Services)

2 Directors
1 Director and supervisor
1 Assistant director
15 Supervisors
3 Counselors
4 Librarians

Personnel (Administration Finance and Research)

1 Assistant state superintendent
3 Supervisors
3 Assistant supervisors
1 Auditor
1 Editor
4 Statisticians
6 Account clerks

Personnel (Accreditation Certification and Allied Services)

1 Director
1 Assistant director and supervisor
5 Supervisors
5 Assistant supervisors
1 Consultant architect (part-time)

Personnel (Vocational Rehabilitation)

1 Director
1 Assistant director
2 Supervisors
6 Assistant supervisors
33 Counselors
2 Craft specialists
2 Medical consultants (part-time)

SOURCE: Thomas G. Pullen, State Superintendent of Education, Maryland, June 1960.

and realistic basis. To achieve sound financial support the states are pursuing two courses of action. First, they have enacted legislation which serves to eliminate—or at least discourage—small, inefficient local districts. Second, they have provided sources of revenue at the state level to supplement overburdened local tax sources and to reduce the inequalities among local districts.

In addition to forces exerting pressure for centralization which are arising within the states, funds allotted by the federal government have contributed to this trend. Federal funds for educational purposes are channeled through the states. Under the National Defense Education Act, federal funds have been provided directly to state departments for their own use in research, in the purchase of electronic record-keeping and data-processing equipment, and for administration—at the state level—of federally financed programs.

Intermediate districts—asset or liability. Between the state and local districts all states, except Delaware, Hawaii, and Nevada, have organizational units called intermediate districts. The political boundaries of the county are the basis for these structures except in the six New England states and New York where there are intermediate districts, formed independently of existing political units, called supervisory districts. These supervisory districts have jurisdiction only over rural areas and villages; the larger communities and cities, called independent districts, are administered directly by the state. Certain very large cities such as Portland, Oregon, and Chicago, Illinois, have this independent status; consequently they do not function through an intermediary unit.

The intermediate district—as it is presently constituted—is now being questioned as a suitable organizational structure.[2] The chief intermediate officer is usually an elected political official, and the office operates primarily as an extension of the state office. Traditionally, the intermediate district functions to enforce state standards, to administer certain procedures prescribed by the state—such as teacher certification and financial accounting—and to offer educational leadership through teacher institutes, administrative meetings, and the like. Modern means of communication and transportation, improved administrative practices, and the reorganization of local schools into larger,

[2] See William P. McLure, *The Intermediate Administrative School District in the United States,* Urbana, Ill. (Bureau of Educational Research), February 1956; and Russell Gregg and George Watson, *The County Superintendency in Wisconsin, A Study of the Intermediate Unit of Educational Administration with Particular Reference to Wisconsin,* Madison (Univ. of Wisconsin), 1957.

more efficient districts—plus the involvement of the intermediate office in politics—are considerations which have caused many thoughtful citizens to question the value of retaining the intermediate district in its present form.

Local districts—diminishing in number and power. Local school districts are created by the state legislatures, who retain control over their boundaries, financial base, and scope of authority. Numerous patterns have been established for the organization of local districts. There are county-wide districts, township districts, community unit districts, city districts, separate high school districts, nonhigh-school districts, and others. Such factors as density of population, conditions of travel, and need for adequate tax base have prompted the states to permit this wide variety of patterns; no one type of unit appears adequate for all situations.

As long as the state governments contributed only a small proportion of the funds for support of education at the local level and chose to leave the determination of the educational program in local hands, they did not become too concerned about the organizational patterns that were followed. However, in recent years the states have found it necessary to increase sharply the amount of state funds for support of education. In 1960, the states directly contributed more than 40 per cent of the operating budgets of local districts. With the increase in the use of state funds came an understandable interest by the state in the efficiency of local districts and the adequacy of the educational programs being supported.

Action initiated at the state level resulted in the consolidation of small inefficient districts into larger ones better able to provide diversified educational programs of high quality. The number of school districts was reduced from 127,422 in 1931 to 40,605 in 1960. The modification of organizational patterns of local districts has usually been based upon studies of educational needs, and the change, although often resulting in the reduction of local autonomy, has been an improvement of public instruction.

Organization in Transition

The machinery of organizing public education represents the legal structure through which schools are operated. The various levels and units of school organization are legitimately constituted for the purpose of making teaching possible. Each level is invested with authority to develop policies, make decisions, and carry on activities appropriate to it. Changes in conditions, i.e., revisions and additions of programs, increases in size of organizational units, mounting costs, and the need for improved coordination and articulation between local districts, have operated to bring about organizational changes.

Although rapid change in school organization is apparent and efforts are constantly being made to improve organization, its major features are relatively stable. Seldom is a totally new organization created or an old one completely revised. Usually, segments of an organization are changed or new parts added and accommodated within the total pattern.

ELEMENTS OF ORGANIZATIONAL THEORY

The problem of understanding school organization can be made easier through knowledge of a few key concepts and principles of organization. Often the diversity and the decentralization of educational organization lead students to feel that American education is so atomized that knowledge of school organization can be gained only from school-by-school study. In fact, however, a great deal of knowledge exists about the elements and principles of organization that are common to all schools, and a body of useful theory is developing to aid in the study of school organization.

Necessary Conditions of Organization

The one-room elementary school requires the simplest form of organization: a teacher, a room, a county course of study, books and supplies. When enrollments justify it, a second unit is added and the grades are divided between the two. With the addition of a third teacher, the structure becomes more complex. Coordination is required to avoid duplication and to ensure continuity.

Even the smallest secondary school is more complex than the rural elementary school. Few secondary schools employ less than fifteen professional staff members; occasionally the number is in excess of two hundred. The ways in which the members of a staff are brought together and the systems of relationships which are developed to carry out the work of the school are referred to as the *structure* of the organization.

Formal structure—working relationships. In order to ensure that the purposes of a school organization are accomplished as efficiently and effectively as possible, the working relationships of the members are set down definitely and exactly. This systematic plan is called the formal structure and is usually pictured on a chart. Often job descriptions are written for each position so that every person clearly understands how he fits into the organization. Tables 9-5 and 9-6 show two actual organizational charts of high schools, one of a rather simple organization of small size, the other of a more complex and larger unit. These charts present graphically the *prescribed* working relationships of the professional staff members of schools. They reveal the lines of official communication, principal areas of responsibility and authority, and designated leaders. Considerable care should be taken in the use of charts, for they are a gross oversimplification even of the formal structure. In school B, for example, teachers have occasion to confer directly with the principal, and he with them, although this relationship is not indicated on the chart.

Designated leadership—status leaders. Designated leadership positions seem to be a universal element in organizations. (See Chapter 14 for an extended discussion of leadership in the secondary school.) To these positions are assigned the responsibility and the authority for the operation of the unit involved. Those who occupy such positions are referred to by social scientists as status leaders. The distinction between the status leader as a person and the position he holds is an important one, for authority accorded to the position is not the personal possession of the person who occupies it.

Table 9-5. *Organization of a Small High School*

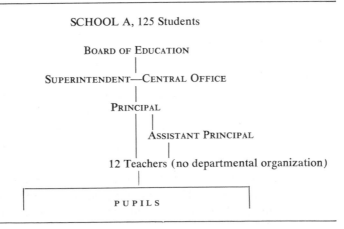

SCHOOL A, 125 Students

BOARD OF EDUCATION

SUPERINTENDENT—CENTRAL OFFICE

PRINCIPAL

ASSISTANT PRINCIPAL

12 Teachers (no departmental organization)

PUPILS

Table 9-6. *Organization of a Large High School*

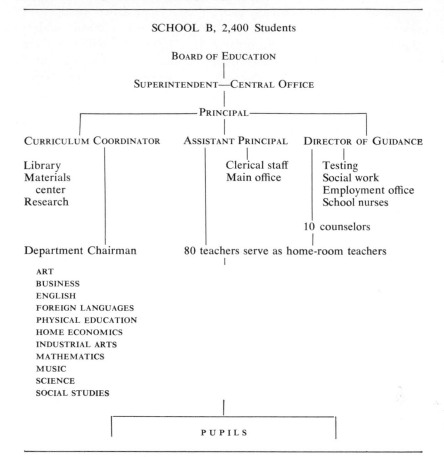

SCHOOL B, 2,400 Students

BOARD OF EDUCATION

SUPERINTENDENT—CENTRAL OFFICE

PRINCIPAL

CURRICULUM COORDINATOR   ASSISTANT PRINCIPAL   DIRECTOR OF GUIDANCE

Library   Clerical staff   Testing
Materials   Main office   Social work
  center   Employment office
Research   School nurses

10 counselors

Department Chairman   80 teachers serve as home-room teachers

ART
BUSINESS
ENGLISH
FOREIGN LANGUAGES
PHYSICAL EDUCATION
HOME ECONOMICS
INDUSTRIAL ARTS
MATHEMATICS
MUSIC
SCIENCE
SOCIAL STUDIES

PUPILS

The principal function of the status leader is to get people to work together with maximum effectiveness. Status leaders, as illustrated in the organizational charts, are placed in key positions to direct the work of others. They are responsible for the administrative tasks necessary to decision-making for their units, and, in well-planned organizations, they are permitted to exercise authority appropriate to the decisions reached.

Schools have a need for status leaders as do other organizations. Within the classroom itself certain of the functions performed by school administrators must also be carried out by teachers. In this sense, the teacher is also a status leader as he plans and directs the work of the classroom. Schools employ various kinds of status leaders: department chairmen, deans, directors, administrative assistants, assistant principals, and principals are all designations for positions commonly found in secondary schools. The specific responsibilities assigned to each position vary with the particular school and are determined, in the main, by such factors as the size of the school, the special problems of the school, and the personnel available.

Division of responsibilities—specialization. As purposes multiply and units increase in size, specialization of function occurs. This division of responsibility is a universal phenomenon in all types of organizations. Within public schools, specialization has occurred along two lines—by maturity of pupils and by function performed. Teachers in the junior and senior high schools generally teach only one or two subjects and confine themselves to one or two grade levels. In addition to subject-matter specialization, specialists have been added in remedial reading, speech correction, guidance, testing and evaluation, and teaching the handicapped.

Although specialization is an apparent necessity, it poses problems for secondary schools. Each specialist has a principal interest in his own field, and he tends to view his work as the most important function in the organization. This narrowness complicates communication and coordination and makes difficult the maintenance of a balanced and integrated program of instruction and service.

Formal organization and the teacher. The formal organization provides a structure for planning, for decision-making, and for coordinating the efforts of individuals. The formal organization, at least as far as public schools are concerned, does not control to any great extent the detailed actions of the teacher. The specifics of teaching, unlike the work on an assembly line, are almost impossible to control through administrative inspection and edict. The formal organization of a school works best when it provides conditions favorable for teaching. School administrators are well aware of this fact, and they generally encourage teachers to participate in planning and deciding those matters that directly affect their work.

Patterns of Organization

An organization is composed of suborganizations or units. When an enterprise is small and has but one purpose to carry out, only one unit is necessary. As size increases, identical units are added until a point is reached at which coordination becomes difficult. Then a new kind of unit, that of administration, must be added. Finally, if more purposes are added or if efficiency demands it, each unit is assigned only one part of the task and specialization enters to complicate organization. In the case of secondary schools, all of these processes are operating.

As the units of an organization accumulate, by subdividing some and adding others, continuity is maintained through the development of a pattern by which the subunits are integrated into the whole. Social scientists have identified four bases of organization, each of which is present in the organization of secondary schools. These are purpose, process, clientele, and place.[3] The pattern employed in a particular secondary school depends upon which of these four bases predominates.

Place as a basis of organization. Place has influenced the organization of secondary schools in two respects. First, schools must be located where concentrations of population create the need for them. The trend toward the reorganization of local school districts is largely explained by the consideration of place as significant to adequate organization. Second, the nature of the school is determined to some extent by its location. Apart from size, schools do vary from place to place. The type of community—city, suburban, rural, or industrial— as well as the section of the nation, conditions the organization of schools located in it.

Purpose and clientele: dominating bases of organization. Since the purpose of a school is defined in such a way as to emphasize the acquisition of knowledge from discrete subject fields, the organization of instruction is by separate subjects. Concern for clientele (pupils) caused schools to subdivide into grades based upon age. Both of these bases—purpose and clientele—dominate the organization of secondary schools.

1. *Subject organization: departmental structures.* In small schools the organization by subjects is relatively informal. Teachers of a single subject area can meet as a committee for planning purposes, and a permanent department chairman is usually unnecessary. When size causes supervision and coordination to become a problem, a formal departmental structure is employed. Departments are either created

---

[3] Luther H. Gulick first formulated this conception of organization in "Notes on the Theory of Organization," *Papers on the Science of Organization,* Luther H. Gulick and Lyndall Urwick (eds.), New York (Institute of Public Administration, Columbia Univ.), 1937, pp. 21-30.

for each subject area, i.e., English, physics, history; or for broad areas, i.e., language arts, science, social studies. Usually, permanent department chairmen are appointed and definite administrative functions are assigned to them.

2. *Grade patterns.* The traditional grade pattern used to be the eight-four plan: eight-year elementary school, four-year senior high school. Recognition of special problems of early adolescent years caused the development of the junior high school. Pupils are now grouped into the six-three-three, six-two-four, five-three-four, and six-two-two-two grade patterns, with the six-three-three plan the most widespread. Administrative functions, guidance and counseling services, and activity programs are organized upon the grade pattern from a "clientele-oriented" base.

3. *Shortcomings of traditional organizational structures.* Within the teaching profession there is dissatisfaction with traditional organizational arrangements. Confusion between instructional and activity programs in the curriculum is described in Chapter 10. Organizational conflicts also develop between departments, between "academic" and "nonacademic" areas, and between guidance and instructional divisions. Danger of friction is always present between organizational subdivisions especially at points where they overlap. In secondary schools this danger exists to a marked degree.[4]

Process: basis of experimental trend. Several experimental approaches now in use in secondary schools have rejected using separate subjects and rigid grade patterns as bases of organization. The experimental patterns attempt to establish structures of operation based upon process. Table 9-7 represents one such attempt now in use in a large secondary school. Here grade levels are eliminated as organizational building blocks—students must follow certain course sequences, but the students are not identified as being of a certain year or grade. Students are assigned at random, as they enter the school, to one of four divisions. The instructional program is planned around broad areas within each division, and teachers are assigned both to a particular division and to an area of instruction.

The plan just described has much to recommend it. The structure tends to focus a complete staff upon the education of a particular group of students. Each division principal is free to organize teams of

---

[4] The problem of organizational conflict in secondary schools is treated in *The High School in a Changing World,* Thirty-sixth Yearbook, Washington, D.C. (American Association of School Administrators), 1958, pp. 188-96.

teachers, counselors, and groups of students in the most productive patterns. Large and small group work, solitary independent study, television, and team teaching are all possible. A feature of the plan, commonly referred to as "schools-within-a-school," permits the use of staff and facilities of a very large school while retaining the intimate personal relationships of the small school. This one innovation (schools-within-schools) is being employed by more and more large schools, though without the curricular changes implied in the plan shown in

Table 9-7. *Organization of a Large Secondary School*
(process dominates as basis)

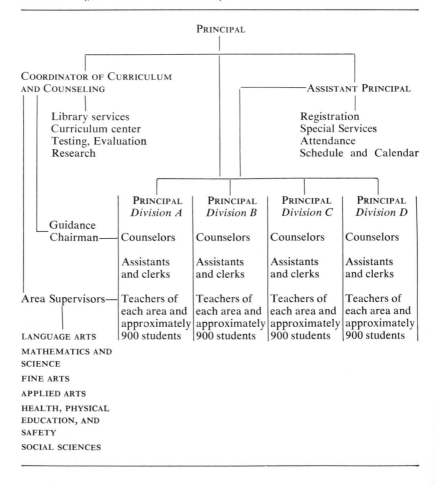

	PRINCIPAL *Division A*	PRINCIPAL *Division B*	PRINCIPAL *Division C*	PRINCIPAL *Division D*
	Counselors	Counselors	Counselors	Counselors
	Assistants and clerks	Assistants and clerks	Assistants and clerks	Assistants and clerks
	Teachers of each area and approximately 900 students	Teachers of each area and approximately 900 students	Teachers of each area and approximately 900 students	Teachers of each area and approximately 900 students

PRINCIPAL

COORDINATOR OF CURRICULUM AND COUNSELING

ASSISTANT PRINCIPAL

Library services
Curriculum center
Testing, Evaluation
Research

Registration
Special Services
Attendance
Schedule and Calendar

Guidance Chairman

Area Supervisors

LANGUAGE ARTS
MATHEMATICS AND SCIENCE
FINE ARTS
APPLIED ARTS
HEALTH, PHYSICAL EDUCATION, AND SAFETY
SOCIAL SCIENCES

Table 9-7. Other forms of the schools-within-schools plan are also possible. For example, Syosset Junior-Senior High School, Long Island, groups 250 students in ten classrooms in what are called "project areas" for general education, counseling, and activities. Random Falls, New York, and Fairfield, Connecticut, are among those school systems that lead in experimentation with variations of this newer form of organization.

GROWING COMPLEXITY OF ORGANIZATION

In almost every community the secondary school is the largest public enterprise, and it represents the largest single public expense. Size, scope of responsibilities, and other factors result in intricate organization. With appropriate organization, complexity and size can become assets because they make possible increased educational opportunities.

School Size

Increased enrollments and the reorganization of school districts have caused the elimination of small high schools and have tended to increase the size of individual attendance units.[5] Size affects organization by bringing into it larger numbers of professional, clerical, and custodial employees. The teacher in a large high school is farther removed from the principal and other supervisory staff members than is the teacher in the small school. In the larger schools the teacher usually does not know many of his colleagues well. Many more formal procedures for record-keeping, reporting, and other communication are required. On the positive side, increased size permits variety in the staff and facilities, which leads to a richer program for youth. Newer forms of organization tend to minimize the ill effects of large size, yet capitalize upon its advantages.

Expanded Services

Expanded services usually involve bringing additional specialists into the staff. As the purposes of secondary schools have multiplied and services have increased, many changes have been required in the ways in which teachers work together. New programs and services cannot just be tacked onto an organization. Responsibilities must be shared

[5] For a statistical appraisal see Walter H. Gaumnitz, "Small Schools Are Growing Larger," Washington, D.C. (U.S. Office of Education, Department of Health, Education and Welfare), Circular No. 601, September 1959.

and established; the professional staff must learn to use the new services and to coordinate its work with the work of the new personnel.

Professional counselors, social workers, juvenile officers, and teacher-aides are examples of specialized personnel who have been added to many schools in recent years. Evening classes for adults, junior college departments, and summer schools for regularly enrolled high school students are examples of rapidly developing programs in secondary schools. These programs and personnel additions offer possibilities for improving the effectiveness of the school. However, the actual contribution which additional services and programs can make to a school depends largely upon whether each teacher understands his purpose in the school and his relationship to the rest of the school.

Impact of Technology on Instruction

Television, the overhead projector, the various teaching machines, and the language laboratory are examples of the technological devices which have made an impact upon instruction. Even more revolutionary innovations are likely to appear in the near future. When properly employed, these devices are dramatic and powerful mediums for teaching. Each of the devices mentioned, and others certain to come, are not effective instruments for use by an individual teacher. Specialists on the staff are usually employed to aid teachers with their use. In addition, some major changes in teaching procedures and the grouping of students, usually involving cooperative teaching with several staff members working together, are required. Closed-circuit television, for example, is not economical unless it is used frequently enough to employ an engineer and a production director, and it is not practical unless several classes view it at a time. Thus, the nature of the device and the economics of using it require a break from the traditional organizational patterns of grouping students. Each of the other technological devices also presents its peculiar problems for organizing and scheduling.

Changes in Organization Through Research

Traditional organizational practices grew out of practical experience and were adopted largely because they worked. In the common parlance, they just grew. The organizational practice of bringing pupils and teachers together for a certain number of minutes five days per week in a ratio of about twenty-five pupils per teacher is an example of a traditional practice, which has no discernible rationale behind it.

On a rational basis, the assignment of groups of twenty-five to thirty students to a single teacher to meet for a short period daily, regardless of the capabilities of the teacher or the nature of the instruction, is questionable. Considerable interest is now developing in an attempt to apply research procedures to the problem of organizing teachers and students in more productive ways.

This new research on organization takes two approaches. One approach is an attempt to discover the factors which determine the most "teachable groups," regardless of class size or other traditional conditions.[6] The concern in this series of studies is with the needs of the learners, the climate of the group, and certain characteristics of the teacher. The second approach attempts to break the strait jacket of class size and timed periods and to use teachers more effectively.[7] The emphasis in this series of studies is on finding imaginative ways to create groupings and to use technological devices appropriate to the kind of instruction needed and to the best learning conditions for students.

TEACHERS AND ORGANIZATION

The single attendance unit—a secondary school with its students, its nonprofessional employees, its professional staff of teachers, counselors, administrators, and supervisors—is the immediate working environment of the teacher. The teacher needs to know more about more things and needs to be able to work in a greater variety of situations than formerly if he is to make an adequate contribution to education in the modern secondary school.

Perceptions of Teaching

The assigned tasks associated with teaching, the opportunities teachers take to experiment with creative ideas, and the degree to which teachers influence their own working conditions—all are changing under the impact of many of the same forces which have influenced school organization.

[6] This series of studies, directed by Herbert Thelan of the University of Chicago, is now under way in a group of high schools. See Herbert A. Thelan, *Education and the Human Quest,* New York (Harper), 1960.

[7] Sponsored by the National Association of Secondary School Principals and directed by J. Lloyd Trump, this series of studies—called the Staff Utilization Project—is under way in a number of schools throughout the country. The project is more fully described in a later section of this chapter.

Traditional teaching. In the secondary school the teacher typically is assigned one or two courses to be taught four or five periods per day. In addition some extra duties, such as supervising a study hall and the sponsorship of an activity, usually comprise part of the scheduled work load. Committee assignments, departmental and faculty meetings, individual aid to a student, or consultation with a parent are other tasks the teacher is expected to assume when necessary. The burdens of course preparations, clerical and policing chores, and extra duties cut heavily into teacher time. A survey taken in March 1956 revealed that secondary school teachers in the United States worked an average of 10.1 hours per day.[8]

Overscheduled and overorganized. The teacher's job is overscheduled and overorganized. After observing the practices of organizing and scheduling of schools, one might conclude that the teacher is able only to parcel out bits of knowledge and train students in a few limited skills. That teachers generally have concerned themselves with the deeper insights of their subjects and with the character and personal development of their students is a tribute to their ability and dedication. However, the point remains that overscheduling and overorganization prevent teachers from participating fully in those professional responsibilities that lie beyond their assigned tasks.

Teacher Contributions to Organization

Proved ability in the classroom and the contribution of worthwhile ideas to professional problems have won for teachers a wider, more interesting role in school affairs. One of the first major break-throughs from the status of dependent workers to that of self-directing professional people occurred for teachers with a changing concept of supervision. Until about three decades ago, the supervision of teachers was largely inspectorial in nature. Detailed courses of study were prepared by administrators and supervisors, and teachers were required to follow them. Supervisors, who knew "the correct way" to teach, instructed the teachers and inspected the classrooms. As teachers displayed the competence to judge the best procedures to follow under the conditions of a particular classroom, the role of the supervisor was changed from that of an inspector to that of a helper and source for ideas. The first large city system to employ this approach, Detroit, Michigan,

---

[8] National Education Association, *Research Bulletin,* Washington, D.C., February 1957.

ordered supervisors to remain in their offices until they were called upon by the teachers for help.

The recognition of the teacher as a competent, broadly educated, and sophisticated person led to more freedom for teachers in their own classrooms. Next, teachers were encouraged to cooperate with others in teaching projects and in the reshaping of the curriculum. Finally, teachers were encouraged to participate in planning and deciding professional matters beyond their special field of training. Education is now at a stage in which an alteration of the overorganized teacher's day could lead to gains in more effective instruction.

Beginning Teachers and the Organization

The beginning teacher must, in some regards, "earn his place on the team." While he will likely find that some of the principles enumerated thus far will be of help in understanding the broader picture of organization, the beginning teacher is primarily concerned with immediate situations.

Familiarity with organization theory and patterns. If the prospective teacher is to make the most of himself in the profession of public education, he will do well to gain as much understanding as possible of the theories of school organization and their application in schools. Organization has a considerable effect upon the task of teaching. It can limit a teacher or, if properly understood, can greatly increase his influence.

Early knowledge will provide the prospective teacher with a more appropriate frame of reference with which to view his own professional preparation and appraise later job opportunities. Once a position is accepted, the teacher must make his way in an environment created largely by the existing school organization.

Getting oriented. The administration usually provides some meetings and social activities which are valuable to the new teacher as a means of learning both the required procedures of the school and of building informal contacts with fellow teachers. Through such contacts and activities the new member can learn the expectations associated with both his new position and himself as a person.

Gaining a full partnership. The observant newcomer will note that many of the specifics of how the "system" operates are determined by the tradition of the particular school, by the habits of the staff, and by the point of view of the administrator. The wise newcomer will reserve judgment and avoid making issues until he is able to size up the situation in which he finds himself. The first task of the new teacher is to learn as much as possible about how the school operates and why it operates as it does. Often the most influential teacher is the one who is sufficiently well versed in the background of a particular situation to offer helpful suggestions when the time seems appropriate.

EMERGING TRENDS IN ORGANIZATION

To the many factors operating to cause change in school organization can be added increased enrollments and shortages of funds, space, and staff. These factors add urgency to the changes and, in some cases, may lead to hasty action and wasted effort. The more stable and sound influences—increased teacher competence, technological change, added purposes, and firmer knowledge of the theory of organization—have brought about new and interesting approaches to the problem of organizing and operating schools.

Widening Student-Staff Participation in Administration

Perhaps the best established trend in modern organization, but one receiving continuing and expanding attention, is the shift from the highly centralized direction of the school to that of shared participation in planning and decision-making. Many reasons are advanced for the need to involve students and teachers in planning and deciding policy matters relating to the operation of the school:

(a) Sharing permits an understanding of wider problems and develops a feeling of responsibility for making decisions work

(b) It permits the use by the staff of talent and leadership ability wherever it may be

(c) It stimulates students and teachers to seek to improve and to accept change

(d) It improves morale by instilling the feeling in teachers and students of having a real part in the operation of the school

(e) It is democratic in that those who are affected by a decision have a voice in its development

Limitations to sharing administrative responsibilities. There is no question that the decision-making, planning, and executive functions are within the province of the school administrator. The board of education both develops policies which charge the superintendent with the responsibility for making administrative decisions and gives him the authority to do so. To deny this would deny the existence of the administrative function. From this point of view, students and staff *participate* in the planning that precedes decision but do not make the decisions. The extent to which they participate depends upon the administrator.

Participation: effect on an organization. In a study of actual school operations, Francis Cornell investigated the question of staff participation and concluded that teachers who were above average in professional training had considerably higher morale in "teacher-centered" schools than had a similar group of teachers in "administrator-centered" schools. More important, he found that the higher the "morale factor," the better were teachers rated on their quality of performance in the classroom. He concluded that classroom performance depends upon:

(a) The extent to which teachers expect the administration to share
(b) The extent to which teachers feel they are given responsibility for sharing when they do participate in decision-making
(c) The extent to which teachers feel their participation is of genuine influence in making a final decision[9]

The administrator must decide what aspects of the operation of the school may best be shared with the staff and the best means to organize students and staff for this purpose. At times he may decide that the participation of staff will produce beneficial results; at other times he may decide that it is not the thing to do.

Teachers do participate. Concern about whether teachers actually wish to participate in administrative matters (and have the occasion to do so) led to a survey of teachers reported by the Commission on Staff Relations of the American Association of School Administrators. This survey, summarized in Table 9-8, suggests an affirmative answer to both questions and leads to the conclusion that teachers wish to participate to a greater extent than they are presently permitted.

Responsible Participation—Key to Democratic Organization

Democratic operations in school organization, just as in political organization, rest upon the responsible, enlightened conduct of its members. Teachers can broaden their influence and control over their own activities to the extent that they accept the responsibility for their own conduct. In this sense, the values and personal rewards of freedom

[9] Francis Cornell, "When Should Teachers Share in Making Administrative Decisions?" *Nation's Schools,* May 1954.

Table 9–8. *Results of Survey on Teacher Participation in Decision-Making*

PRACTICE	PERCENTAGE WHO HAVE SEEN TEACHER PARTICIPATION OPERATE SUCCESSFULLY	PERCENTAGE WHO BELIEVE TEACHERS SHOULD PARTICIPATE
Planning for new equipment	82	97
Planning for equipment replacement	81	98
Promoting cooperation among teachers	81	98
Determining playground supervision practices	80	93
Selecting equipment	79	95
Scheduling extracurricular activities	75	91
Arranging for extension courses	72	92
Enforcing rules and regulations	72	94
Constructing a list of general educational objectives	71	95
Conducting institutes	71	95
Planning specifications for equipment	71	89
Preparing school rules and regulations	71	92
Cooperative planning with civic officials	70	93
Making school population study	65	88
Encouraging teachers to experiment	63	90
Planning new building	62	93
Studying financial problems	59	82
Reorganization of schools	58	85
Studying the financial support of schools	56	83
Attending local administrative meetings	54	75
Studying school costs	50	82
Recommending type of new building	48	85
Checking architects' plans	46	77
Studying board policies	45	82
Organization of new schools	43	84
Making extracurricular assignments to faculty	43	66
Scoring existing school buildings	43	88
Budget planning	39	72
Distributing teacher load	37	63

SOURCE: Commission on Staff Relations in School Administration of the American Association of School Administrators, *Staff Relations in School Administration: the 1955 Yearbook,* Washington, D.C., 1955, p. 144.

and self-direction depend upon the competence of the participants, their ability to reach agreement upon goals, and to cooperate in the achievement of them. In the organization oriented toward sharing responsibility authority is not eliminated; it is merely held in reserve. Authority holds the organization together, but it is the authority of ideas and tactful guidance rather than the authority of orders issued by the status leaders.

SELECTED REFERENCES

National Association of Secondary School Principals. "Progressing Toward Better Schools: Third Report on Staff Utilization Studies." *Bulletin,* January 1960.

BENNIS, WARREN G. "Leadership Theory and Administrative Behavior." *Administrative Science Quarterly,* December 1959.

CAMPBELL, RONALD F., AND RUSSELL T. GREGG, eds. *Administrative Behavior in Education.* New York: Harper, 1957.

CHAMBERLAIN, LEO M., AND LESLIE W. KINDRED. *The Teacher and School Organization.* Englewood Cliffs, N.J.: Prentice-Hall, 1958.

DAVIES, DANIEL R., AND LAWRENCE JANNOCCONE. "Ferment in the Study of Organization." *Teachers College Record,* November 1958.

MILLET, JOHN D. *Government and Public Administration.* New York: McGraw-Hill, 1959.

PRESTWOOD, ELWOOD L. *The High School Principal and Staff Work Together.* New York: Bureau of Publications, Teachers College, Columbia Univ., 1958.

SIMPSON, RICHARD L. "Vertical and Horizontal Communication in Organizations." *Administrative Science Quarterly,* September 1959.

STODDARD, ALEXANDER. *Schools for Tomorrow: An Educator's Blueprint.* New York: Fund for the Advancement of Education, 1957.

TEAD, ORDWAY. *Administration: Its Purpose and Performance.* New York: Harper, 1959.

Comprehensive high school provides curriculum adapted to differences in students—all within one building.

CHAPTER 10

Planning and Development of the Curriculum

EDUCATION is the process through which the immature acquire the cumulated, organized, and systematic experience of their culture—including the attainment of knowledge, the development of skills, and the formation of values. The secondary school, as a specialized institution, has as its central purpose the transmission of certain vital parts of this cumulated experience to the youth of each new generation.

The relationship between the school and the mature world is an important one. As social changes occur, the teaching profession must not continue to teach outmoded ideas and skills. Attention must constantly be given to curriculum planning and development in order that schools stay abreast of the times.

The problem, however, is not merely a matter of updating the curriculum. Social stresses often rebound upon the school—as the segregation issue has done. New technological developments bring demands that the schools add new elements of instruction, such as driver training or advanced courses in physical science, to already crowded programs. When crises develop in the adult world, groups and individuals urge schools to alter the amount and kind of instruction in certain fields—as is presently being done in science and mathematics. These examples indicate that unless sound principles are followed, curriculum development can easily become a matter of "bending with the wind."

Although considerable evidence can be mustered to support the contention that secondary education has improved greatly over the past few decades, it nevertheless presents today a bewildering variety of unrelated courses and programs. A pressing problem of secondary education is to bring order and clarity to the development of its curriculum.

MEANING OF CURRICULUM

Critical appraisal of public education, especially of the secondary schools, has been almost continuous since the beginning of the century. The criticism, emanating from sources representing differing educational points of view, has produced several versions of what the curriculum should be; it has even blurred the meaning of the term.

Omnibus Term

Schools, seeking a clear mandate upon which to organize instruction, have found instead conflicting conceptions of what should be taught. Curriculum has come to be defined in several ways and to be broadened to include instruction, activities, services, and operational functions. Thus, the curriculum could be the content of the books used to instruct classes, the interests of the learners, or "life itself." The omnibus quality applied to the meaning of curriculum has served to confuse rather than to help those who must organize and conduct instruction.

Traditional definition. Two distinct scholarly traditions produced in the secondary schools a curriculum of prescribed subject matter. One, derived from the classical tradition, stresses the study of literature, grammar, rhetoric, languages, and mathematics; the other, based upon the great research disciplines, stresses the mastery of knowledge as contained in the subject fields of the research scholars. Each defines the curriculum as the content of certain fields of knowledge. Knowledge and concomitant intellectual skills are taught within the formally organized subject fields.

Reaction to traditional definitions. Attempts to remove the curriculum from the "prescribed content as disciplinary subjects" base has been almost continuous in the United States since Franklin published his plan for the academy. After 1900, the pragmatic philosophy of John Dewey, reinforced by findings derived from psychological and sociological research, led to the formulation of curriculums based upon two new conceptions. One approach contends that the curriculum should be defined by the needs and interests of the learners; the other, that it should be defined by significant social problems and trends.

Curriculum defined as every activity planned by the school. No single conception of the curriculum proved adequate for the secondary schools; often, even within the same school, several meanings are employed (depending upon the portion of the program considered). In order to attain some consistency, as well as to include the many new phases of the educational program, schools began to define the curriculum as every activity planned and provided by the school. Unfortunately, this conception created more problems than it solved.

According to the "learning experiences" definition, the curriculum is composed of classroom, out-of-class, and guidance activities, school-related work experiences, community services, and school services such as health, library, and recreation. Activities of these kinds may have educational values and they may be planned and conducted in ways which meet the purposes the school is to serve; but they are instructional devices—not the curriculum itself.[1]

Curricular Conflicts

Reacting to technological and social changes, and without an adequate conception of curriculum, schools added new courses in a piecemeal fashion. Some reorganized instructional programs wholly or in part upon one of the various new theories; others maintained a "prescribed content" approach and tacked new subjects to the established structure. As early as 1936, John Dewey recognized this jumble. He wrote, "The problem as to the direction in which we shall seek for order and clarity in education has now become the most important question facing education and educators today.[2] During the past decade criticism of public secondary schools, however ill-informed and misdirected and whether advanced by laymen, scholars, or professional educators, has centered upon the curriculum.

[1] Lindley J. Stiles examines the confusion of instruction with curriculum in the chapter "Instruction" of the *Encyclopedia of Educational Research,* Chester W. Harris (ed.), New York (Macmillan), 1960, pp. 710-14.

[2] John Dewey, "Rationality in Education," *The Social Frontier,* December 1936.

Charge of dilution. The inclusion of student activities and so-called "nonintellectual" subjects in the curriculum has precipitated the charge that the curriculum has become "diluted." In some instances colleges have criticized the public schools for the performance of entering freshmen in the areas of composition and mathematics. Evidence of weak preparation, damaging and deplorable as it is, must be carefully analyzed if it is to be properly corrected. Such evidence may not be the fault of the curriculum but may be due to the poor quality of instruction, to the inadequate scholastic capacity of students colleges are willing to admit, or to the inept guidance of the college-bound student. Thus, the confusion of instruction and guidance with the curriculum may cause the condemnation of such essential nonacademic programs as vocational training, fine arts, or home economics instead of revealing the true nature of the difficulty.

Dissolution of priorities. As subjects have been added haphazardly, little effort has been made to maintain priorities. The amassing of a certain number of credits, with a minimum of required subjects, is usually sufficient for graduation. Carnegie units, the coin of the educational realm, accord equal value to each course in the eyes of the student and, frequently, of the professional staff as well. The high school curriculum often resembles an educational supermarket in which the student may be permitted to pick the attractive courses rather than the ones he needs most.

Competing designs. A pattern based on subjects is the oldest and most widely used form of curriculum organization. Subjects are highly compartmentalized, and the content and internal organization of the subject field is retained. History, for example, is taught separately from economics and geography, and chronological sequence is followed. As the secondary schools have attempted to employ the subject pattern as a means of providing general education, the relationships of facts, concepts, and theories of one field to another and their applications to practical affairs have taken precedence over the need to maintain subject matter as the precise, logically ordered propositions employed by the specialized scholar and researcher. Thus, two or more subjects often are reordered into correlated, fused, or completely integrated patterns.

The activity pattern, based upon student interests and needs, is not used in secondary schools except peripherally in conjunction with some other pattern. In art, shop, or science students who develop special interests are sometimes grouped in order to pursue projects and activities for extended periods of time. No planned or prescribed subject matter is taught, but the instructor is available to help the student plan, conduct, and evaluate what he wishes to do. Seminar or independent study credit is usually given toward graduation.

The core pattern of curriculum is a direct attempt to base instruction upon social living or broad social problems. In one form of core teaching all the required portions of the school program are interrelated in one broad, unified core-of-studies. One branch of study, i.e., the natural sciences or the social studies, becomes the core around which all other studies are related. In a second form, rather than subject or interest categories, study is organized into social categories or major areas of life problems, such as civic responsibilities, earning a living, or family life. This version of the core is based upon the premise that education should be intimately concerned with the needs, the problems, and the future of the society.

Curriculum Defined as the Educational Emphasis Society Requires

To design or to modify a program of instruction the professional staff requires a clear mandate regarding *what* the school is to accomplish. In the United States the purposes which the schools are to serve and the order of emphasis to be given them are determined by society. Public education is maintained to preserve and to promote the interest of a particular people. The curriculum, then, must be defined as what society requires to be taught, including intellectual skills, knowledges, attitudes, and values.

Considerable attention has been given during the past decade to spelling out in clear terms the nature of the secondary education required by society and the specific objectives to be attained by it. This effort shows promise of bringing order to the curriculum. Surveying the work that had been accomplished by 1954, Dressel and Mayhew found a high degree of consensus among the groups who worked upon this problem: "There is less disagreement about general education objectives than the means of achieving them. . . . The objectives found in *A Design for General Education, General Education in Action, and the Report of the President's Commission* are illustrative of the better and most commonly accepted statements."

In 1957, Will French led a national group that attempted to state the goals expected of the public secondary schools.[3] These statements

---

[3] Will French, et al., *Behavior Goals of General Education in the Public Schools,* New York (Russell Sage Foundation), 1957.

can serve as a basis for discussion as citizens and educators attempt to reach a consensus regarding issues relating to the school's curriculum.

Statements of goals, when properly constructed, indicate for schools the purposes to be accomplished and the nature and scope of the outcomes desired. Authorities agree that such statements are most useful when given in behavioral terms and when focused clearly upon knowledge and skills, attitudes and values, relationships and social competencies.[4] Benjamin Bloom has led a small group of educational scholars to design a taxonomy of educational goals. This group has thus far published one part of a proposed three-part taxonomy.[5] Part I deals with the cognitive domain and provides a useful means of classifying and studying educational objectives.

CURRICULUM STRUCTURE

The purposes, scope, and emphases of the curriculum determined for schools, the controls established over it, the means employed to order it so that instruction can take place—all operate to give structure to the curriculum.

Bases

The bases of the curriculum are the individual needs of students, the goals of the social organization, and the structure of knowledge itself (see Fig. 10-1). Of the first two elements, neither may be elevated above, or given priority over, the other, for both are intimately interrelated. The third, the structure of knowledge, provides the substance out of which the needs of individuals and of society are satisfied.

In a democratic political structure, the whole social machinery, particularly public education, is committed to safeguard and promote the fullest development of every individual. Only in a democracy, in fact, are the dual goals of self-realization and social responsibility recognized as the most certain means of improving group life as well as promoting individual welfare.

Knowledge, its structure and utilization, is a historic and universal curriculum foundation. However the school program may be organized in response to the needs of youth and the emphases required by society, its content must be drawn from the accumulated facts, intellectual skills, and wisdom of the race.

---

[4] *Ibid.*, pp. 21-46.

[5] Benjamin S. Bloom (ed.), *Taxonomy of Educational Objectives,* New York (Longmans, Green), 1956.

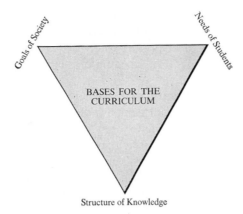

Fig. 10–1. *Bases for the Curriculum*

Individual needs. Some psychologists now believe that the first law of life is not self-preservation but self-realization. Gordon Allport represents this point of view by proposing that, for man, the motive in life is "the maintaining, actualizing and enhancing of the capacities of the individual organism."[6] The drive to *become* represents itself in physical needs, as biological functions, and in social needs, as the individual internalizes society's demands and expectations. Havighurst calls the social needs developmental tasks; he recognizes ten such tasks for the adolescent:

1. Achieving new and more mature relation with age-mates of both sexes
2. Achieving a masculine or feminine social role
3. Accepting one's physique and using the body effectively
4. Achieving emotional independence of parents and other adults
5. Achieving assurance of economic independence
6. Selecting and preparing for an occupation
7. Preparing for marriage and family life
8. Developing intellectual skills and concepts necessary for civic competence
9. Desiring and achieving socially responsible behavior
10. Acquiring a set of values and an ethical system as a guide to behavior[7]

[6] Gordon W. Allport, *Becoming: Basic Considerations of a Psychology of Personality,* New Haven (Yale Univ. Press), 1955, p. 16.

[7] Robert Havighurst, *Human Development and Education,* New York (Longmans, Green), 1953, p. 111.

Satisfaction of all of such needs, of course, is not the exclusive responsibility of the secondary school. Nevertheless, the curriculum must include opportunities to help each youth to realize his fullest potential for mental, social-civic, economic, physical, and vocational development.

Societal goals. Coordinated with the purposes centering upon self-realization are those of social responsibility or citizenship. Since the ability to think is so essential to both categories of purposes, individual and social, intellectual development is the central task of the high school. The specific social objectives and emphases placed into the curriculum because of the demands of organized group life arise out of the social realities of an evolving, dynamic culture. These designate the democratic values to be promoted and indicate the problem-solving abilities, knowledges, and skills which, brought into proper relationship in a planned curriculum, can attain the over-all goal of intellectual development.

Structure of knowledge. Education cannot take place in a knowledge vacuum. The needs of students are met by the mastery of intellectual skills and of knowledge. In turn, attitudes, values, and wisdom are derived from these. Behavior, a trait mentioned frequently in statements of students' needs, is an outcome achieved when intellectual skills, knowledge, attitudes, values, and wisdom are integrated into courses of action. Similarly, the goals of society require the application by the individual of his intellectual skills and knowledge to community, state, and national problems.

Some curricular emphases will deal with knowledge for specialized objectives. In such cases the relationship to the problems of society may appear remote; nevertheless, they may make contributions to particular, and highly unique, needs of individual students. A characteristic of liberal education, for which secondary schools lay the foundation, is the value it places on intellectual development and the mastery of established knowledge no matter how remote the utility may seem at the time.

Controls

The curriculum is controlled in certain ways by legal authority, professional requirements and decisions, pupil choices, and administrative arrangements.

Legal controls. State legislatures have left considerable autonomy to the local districts regarding the exercise of control over the curriculum. However, all legislatures have established some legal controls upon curriculums. Thirty-one of the states have enacted legislation characterized as general in scope. In Oklahoma, for example, the legislature has given the responsibility for the tax-supported schools to the Oklahoma State Department in the following act:

> The State Department has general control of the educational interests of the State.
>
> The State Department is responsible for determining the policy and directing the administration and supervision when they are free schools supported by public taxation.[8]

When general responsibilities are established by the legislature, it usually refrains from enacting any specific curriculum requirements. The state board, or the state department acting under the general directive of the legislature, provides supervision, prepares curriculum guides, approves courses of study and textbooks, and enforces minimum standards for accreditation and graduation.

In nineteen states, the general responsibilities are defined by legislative statute, but in addition, the legislatures have enacted specific legal requirements. These include the provision of courses or units of instruction in United States history; national, state, and local government; effects of alcohol and narcotics; driver education; physical education; safety, fire prevention; and first aid. This Virginia statute is typical of specific legislation:

> In preparing the course of study in civics and history in both the elementary and high school grades, the State board shall give careful directions for, and shall require the teaching of the Declaration of Independence, the Virginia Statute of Religious Freedom, The Virginia Bill of Rights and section 58 of the Constitution of Virginia, which subject shall be carefully read and studied, thoroughly explained and taught by teachers to all pupils in accordance with the State course of study. An outline shall be likewise given of the Constitution of the United States and general principles of the Constitution shall be carefully explained.

Massachusetts is the only state which, at this writing, has no statutory requirement for any subject. The state of Wisconsin requires only physical education by state statute. Table 10-1 gives the subject requirements of ten selected states.

[8] State legal requirements may be found in the section of state laws for each state called the School Code.

Table 10-1. *Subjects Required for Graduation*

Numbers represent Carnegie units;* X = number of units not specified. Letters indicate authority of requirement: B = state board of education; C = state constitution; D = state department of education; L = state legislation.

STATE†	ENGLISH	AMERICAN HISTORY	STATE HISTORY	CIVICS	SOCIAL STUDIES (UNSPECIFIED)	1 YEAR MATH	GENERAL SCIENCE	BIOLOGY	OTHER SCIENCE	OTHERS
ALABAMA	4 B	1 B	1 B	½ B	½ B	1 B	1 B	–	–	Health; Physical education; Conservation education
ALASKA	3 B	X B	–	X B	–	X B	X B	–	1 B	Physical education
CALIFORNIA	–	1½ LED	–	1½ LED	–	–	–	–	–	Health; Physical education; Driver education
IDAHO	3	1	–	½	–	1	–	–	1	Health; Physical education
INDIANA	3 L	1 L	–	1 L	–	1 B	–	–	1 B	Health; Physical education
KENTUCKY	3 B	1 B	X B	1 B	1 B	1 B	1 B	1 B	1 B	Health; Physical education
MINNESOTA	3 B	1 B	X B	–	1 B	1 B	1 B	–	–	Health; Physical education; Industrial arts; Home economics; Art; Music
NEW YORK	4	1	–	–	2	–	1	–	–	Health; Physical education
TEXAS	3	1	½	½	–	2	–	–	1	Health; Driver education
VERMONT	4	1	–	–	–	–	–	–	–	Health; Physical education; Industrial arts; Home economics
WASHINGTON	3 B	1 L	½ L	–	1 B	1 B	–	–	1 B	Health; Physical education; Industrial arts; Home economics

* A Carnegie unit stands for a class meeting 45-50 minutes per day, 5 days per week, for one school year.

† States shown in this chart were chosen only to give a geographical representation.

SOURCE: Howard H. Cummings and Helen K. Mackintosh, *Curriculum Responsibilities of State Departments of Education;* Miscellaneous Bulletin No. 30, Washington, D.C.: U.S. Department of Health, Education and Welfare, 1958, pp. 11-12.

School board regulations. Local boards of education have the legal authority to make rules and regulations. If these rules are in accord with the laws of the state, they have the effect of law. The local board may review all texts and materials and prescribe that certain matters shall or shall not be taught.

Before any curricular changes are made the provisions of the state and local legal authorities should be studied. Legal acts may prescribe in detail what must be taught, and in some cases the means to teach it, may explicitly deny the right to teach certain matters, or may merely indicate the general nature of education expected.

Professional controls. Apart from legal authority, the educational profession exercises a moral authority over educational matters. The profession claims a body of principles relating to its moral obligations to teach the young. The profession is bound to uphold right and truth and to make known legal (or other) transgressions upon its authority in these matters. Out of its claim to knowledge and from its moral authority, the profession exercises certain controls over the curriculum.

Three kinds of professional groups operate in various ways to influence what is taught: school faculties, professional organizations, and accrediting agencies. School faculties are involved at the local level where they conduct studies, make recommendations, and adapt stated purposes to local conditions. Boards of education are relying increasingly upon the local administration and staff to recommend curriculum policies. State and national professional organizations spend considerable time, money, and effort to influence legislation and to inform the public concerning educational problems.[9] The accrediting agencies, established cooperatively between colleges and secondary schools, evaluate the high school program and accredit member schools.[10] Accreditation includes an evaluation of graduation requirements, preparation of teachers, library, program of studies, and other aspects of the program—all of which have implications for the curriculum.

Pupil choices. Ultimately the program of the school is shaped by the needs and interests of its students. The nature of the curriculum is affected, to some extent, by pupil choices: as long as an elective system

---

[9] National professional organizations have provided a steady stream of studies, publications, and recommendations concerning curriculum. Some of these have achieved the status of classics in their field.

[10] There are five regional accrediting agencies: The North Central Association of Colleges and Secondary Schools, The Southern Association, The Northwest Association, the Middle States Association, and the New England Association.

is maintained, pupil choices will swell the enrollments of certain subject areas and deplete or completely eliminate others. A continuous study of pupil needs and a sound and realistic system of guidance is an essential feature of the modern secondary school, for pupil choices will continue, in some degree at least, to influence the structure of the curriculum.

Administrative patterns. Administrative procedures often serve as a system of controls upon the curriculum. Administrative patterns are sometimes adopted without concern for their effect upon the curriculum. Greater still is the danger that patterns, effective in serving particular curriculum needs, restrict necessary curriculum revisions at a later date. Marking symbols (A, B, C, D), procedures (use of normal distribution curve), credit accounting in Carnegie units (16 credits for graduation), and grouping by age into grade levels are a few examples of administrative controls upon the structure of the curriculum.

PLANNING THE CURRICULUM

Through certain procedures established within each school district, and taking into account the factors of control noted above, the guidelines of the curriculum for a particular school are established. A number of important decisions remain before instruction can take place.

Responsibility

The planning and organization which is required to bring the curriculum to reality in terms of instruction is largely a professional task. As curriculum development moves in stages from the determination of purposes and the selection of content to actual instruction, the professional staff should become progressively more involved until the point is reached where teachers assume direct responsibility for teaching.

Teacher's role in planning. Teachers possess valuable skills and knowledge which are needed in all phases of curriculum development. Representatives of the profession, teachers, supervisors, and administrators are frequently consulted, even at the stage of determining the broad purposes to be achieved. Teachers, for example, played a prominent role in the White House Conference that produced the document, *What Should the Schools Accomplish?* They often testify before committees of state legislatures. The State School Problem's Commission of Illinois, for example, regularly invites teachers to express their views. Some teachers are made special consultants to state departments of education.

Values of teacher participation. The interaction of representatives of all levels of the professional staff makes possible a continuous communication and understanding, as well as smooth review and criticism of plans in light of a realistic appraisal of the teaching task. Democratic values, which can only be taught through their application within the school, require that a cooperative atmosphere permeate the activities of the professional staff in such matters as curriculum planning.

Stages

As purposes and emphases become formulated, schools must organize in order that purposes can be implemented and realized.

Definition and assignment of objectives. Unless a particular curriculum design is already in operation and does not require modification, one will have to be adopted in the early stages of local planning. What the school is to teach and the scope and emphasis of the program become the basis for detailed formulation and assignment of objectives. At this stage the quality of local professional leadership is a crucial factor. The principal and the supervisory staff may decide themselves to interpret school purposes in terms of an outline of content organized by subject area and grade level which is presented directly to teachers as a guide for making daily lesson plans. On the other hand, they may obtain the cooperation of the staff in making such important decisions as will significantly influence the nature of the curriculum and the quality of the education provided.

Organization of coordinated programs. As the responsibilities for certain objectives are assigned, the professional staff can determine the nature of instruction to be provided and can decide upon its scope and sequence. It is at this stage that detailed guides for instruction are made out. Courses of study, course guides, scope and sequence charts, and other tools are often used to specify how the objectives are to be structured for the guidance of instruction. These materials are usually planned and written by the teachers who are responsible for the instruction. They are then reviewed by some group concerned with the coordination of the total program of the school.

Pritzkow, after a study of school practice, notes the diversity of procedures used:

In one school system this program may be a rather rigid prescription of learning experiences through which it is hoped that children will grow in competencies for effective living. In another school system, the program may be based on a statement of objectives and general procedures sometimes called a 'guide to learning experiences.' . . . Still other systems may have suggested resources and excerpts of experiences designed to promote a continual study and examination of ideas toward expanded meanings and understandings. In some school systems rather complete bulletins or courses of study have been developed.[11]

Implementation. To carry out a program, once planned and specified in some detail, instructional materials must be selected or created, pupils grouped for instruction, and the groundwork for instruction prepared through teacher-pupil interaction in the classroom.

Instructional materials. The curriculum guides usually indicate the content and project activities which the teacher must include. Samples of prepared materials can be studied and the ones selected reserved for use. These include texts and manuals, maps and charts, films, slides and tapes, printed library materials, and special apparatus. Certain needed materials may also be prepared—including teaching and resource units, bibliographies, outlines, study guides, assignment sheets and exercises; even manuals, texts, kinescopes, films, slides, and tapes are prepared for specific purposes in many schools.

The teaching unit has become a common means of ordering logical segments of instruction and bringing the various instructional materials into a plan which can be followed by the teacher to conduct instruction. It includes the content outline, activities, use of texts and materials, and evaluation procedures all written in the sequence to be followed with the class. Some teachers prepare the unit so that it can be placed in the hands of students and used with them as a basis for planning. Other teachers do not use the unit as a daily teaching guide. Instead, they adapt the unit for their own use as a source of ideas and references, exercises, and project possibilities.

Grouping pupils. Since most education is cumulative and since ability, maturity, and past achievement of pupils influence learning, pupils must be grouped to attain some semblance of homogeneity for instructional purposes. Grouping practices are based primarily upon age but with slight modifications. A few schools are attempting other

[11] Philo T. Pritzkow, *Dynamics of Curriculum Improvement,* Englewood Cliffs, N.J. (Prentice-Hall), 1959, p. 1.

plans for grouping pupils; at present, however, traditional practices are almost universally followed. Planning of instruction and pupil grouping are intimately related, inasmuch as time allotments, sequence of instruction, and level of abstraction of materials depend upon grouping procedures.

Planning by teachers and students. Student participation in planning varies widely. It depends largely upon the teacher's competence and preference (often conditioned by the broader curriculum plan), upon the kind of instruction, and upon the maturity of the students. Instruction in attitudes, values, and knowledge—in social studies, for example —offers more opportunities for pupil planning than does instruction in skills such as those used in art or typing. Cooperative planning with students can be of value to the teacher as an aid to the establishment of a proper climate for learning, to individualization of instruction, and as a means of teaching democratic values. There is research evidence to indicate that learning is usually improved when students help to plan some details of their work.[12]

Measuring effectiveness. As instruction progresses, the curriculum should be evaluated to determine whether the school's original purposes are being met. It is not likely that one particular kind of evaluation will be adequate nor that an evaluation will be effective unless it is a regular part of the school's activity. Often schools publicize the number of graduates who gain admission to college or the number of students who score well on national examinations as evidence of a sound curriculum. These kinds of evidence are valuable, but they represent only one dimension upon which an evaluation should be based. The primary problem in evaluation is to determine how well the stated objectives of instruction have been met.

National examinations: new trend. Within the past decade national testing, as a basis of scholarships and college admissions, has increased to the point that the National Association of Secondary School Principals has formed a commission to study its effects upon the curriculum and to make recommendations on the control of the amount and kinds of testing. National testing groups, however, are concentrating upon the development of tests which center upon what students can *do* rather than the factual content of what they learn. According to the College Entrance Examination Board, Educational Testing Service, Princeton, New Jersey:

[12] Lindley J. Stiles and Mattie F. Dorsey, *Democratic Teaching in Secondary Schools,* New York (Lippincott), 1950.

The present College Board Mathematics Achievement tests are designed to test (1) manipulative skills and abilities, (2) knowledge and understanding of formulas, theorems, and mathematical terms, (3) ability to interpret algebraic or graphic form and conversely, the ability to interpret algebraic or graphic representation, (4) ability to draw conclusions from data given, (5) ability to recognize which facts or processes are necessary for the solution of a problem and to use these accurately in the solution, and (6) ability to visualize forms and relationships in three dimensional space and to apply knowledge of algebra, plane geometry or trigonometry, as well as solid geometry to problems involving them.[13]

Evaluation: basis of replanning. A planned program of evaluation will include a number of types of devices and a number of kinds of evaluation. The mastery of knowledges and skills can usually be evaluated through examination, but the total effect of the school, especially training in values and attitudes, must be measured after graduation in follow-up studies. Often the school curriculum committees, sometimes with outside consultant help, have conducted extensive evaluations. Evaluation in relation to the school's objectives thus completes the cycle to become the basis of curriculum replanning.

STATUS OF CURRICULUM OFFERINGS

Two kinds of information are of particular importance to those who are interested in curriculum developments at the national level: the offerings of the nation's schools in terms of the subjects and the various curriculum designs in use and the numbers of students actually receiving various kinds of instruction in the public secondary schools.

Academic Offering

The five subject areas commonly referred to as the academic offering are English, foreign languages, mathematics, science, and history or the social studies. Those who charge that the public school curriculum has become diluted usually refer to the proportion of the offering in these subjects to that of the remainder of the curriculum; as evidence they site that large numbers of students no longer enroll in these subjects. Unfortunately, these critics usually fail to investigate the facts behind their charges or else carefully select those which serve their purposes.

[13] From a letter received from John A. Volley, Program Director of Educational Testing Service.

Academic offering: the fifty-year picture. One view of the status of the academic offering may be obtained by an analysis of enrollments in these subjects in 1900 (Table 10-2) and again in 1950 (Table 10-3). Two important conditions must be kept in mind in the study of these data. First, they represent a picture of enrollments *only for one year* although students remain in high school for four years. Second, the ratio of the total number of youth in school to the number of youth of high school age, given at the bottom of each illustration, must be taken into account.

These data reveal the phenomenal growth in gross numbers in each subject as well as in the total enrollment. The limited service of the secondary schools in 1900 is apparent from the fact that only 8 per cent of the youth of high school age were in attendance. Too often the percentage figures taken from the center column, representing the percentage of the number of students in actual enrollment, are given, without explanation and without other data, as evidence that enrollments in certain subjects are declining. This is not the case.

Primary attention should be given to the percentage of the *total* number of high school-age youth in the country who *actually* enrolled in these academic subjects—the last column of the tables. In a representative group of one hundred students, English enrollments improved

Table 10-2. *Enrollments in Academic Subjects in 1900*

SUBJECT	ENROLLMENT	PERCENTAGE OF ENROLLMENT	PERCENTAGE OF TOTAL YOUTH OF HIGH SCHOOL AGE
ENGLISH	199,803	38.5	3.3
FOREIGN LANGUAGES	377,570	72.7	6.2
MATHEMATICS	444,437	85.6	7.2
SCIENCE	435,844	83.9	7.1
SOCIAL STUDIES	322,958	62.3	5.2

Total enrollment in high schools: 519,251

Percentage of high school age population: 8

Total number of youth of high school age: 6,162,231

SOURCE : *Biennial Survey of Education in the United States, 1948-50,* Washington, D.C.: U.S. Office of Education, Chapter 5.

at a ratio of 20 to 1; foreign languages (the smallest), at a ratio of 2 to 1. The foreign-language figures are of interest because exactly two-thirds of the enrollment in the foreign languages in 1900 was in Latin, one-third in modern languages. In 1950, Latin represented 30 per cent of the language enrollment, and modern languages 70 per cent. This reversal in enrollments reflects the historical transition from ancient to modern languages. At an earlier time a similar transition occurred from Greek to Latin.

Enrollments in academic subjects do not reflect completely the quality of education at a given time. An increase in enrollment in algebra, for example, if excessive numbers of students of lower ability were added, might lower academic standards. Nor can it be assumed that quality of education was high in 1900 and the present need is only to keep abreast of that standard. Enrollment figures of the type described here can prove only that secondary schools are guiding certain proportions of their student populations into the study of basic subjects.

Academic offering: the four-year picture. The data presented above do not reveal the pattern of enrollments in academic subjects taken by students during their four years in high school. Examination of the chart showing the percentage of enrollment in science as 53.8 (Table 10-3) might lead to the conclusion that the remaining 46.2 per cent did not have the opportunity to study science. (One college professor arrived at this conclusion and published it as a criticism of

Table 10-3. *Enrollments in Academic Subjects in 1950*

SUBJECT	ENROLLMENT	PERCENTAGE OF ENROLLMENT	PERCENTAGE OF TOTAL YOUTH OF HIGH SCHOOL AGE
ENGLISH	5,121,916	94.9	60.9
FOREIGN LANGUAGES	1,080,585	21.8	12.8
MATHEMATICS	2,955,539	54.7	33.5
SCIENCE	2,908,682	53.8	33.4
SOCIAL STUDIES	3,648,980	67.5	43.5

Total enrollment in high schools: 5,399,452

Percentage of high school-age population: 64

Total number of youth of high school age: 8,404,757

SOURCE: Same as Table 10-2.

Table 10-4. *Total Semesters of Study in Academic Subjects Taken During Four Years of High School by Students in a Sample of Illinois Schools (work shown as percentage of total sample of 1,557 boys, 1,618 girls)*

| | | | | SCIENCE: | |
SEMESTERS	ENGLISH	FOREIGN LANGUAGE	MATHE-MATICS	NONCOLLEGE	COLLEGE
None	0.03	not given	7.2	23.9	3.1
2	0.20		30.5	72.8	30.8
4	0.20	25.9	32.9	3.3	32.9
6	19.90		16.4	—	22.8
8	66.80	5.6	12.7	—	9.9
More than 8	12.87		0.3	—	0.5
TOTAL PERCENTAGE	100		100	100	100

SOURCE: This table was constructed from original documents of the study referred to in text footnote 14. This study is available from the Superintendent of Public Instruction, State of Illinois, Springfield, Illinois.

secondary schools in an article in a popular national magazine.) A study of a representative cross section of students was conducted to determine their four-year course enrollments.[14] These data presented in Tables 10-4, 10-5, and 10-6 tend to amplify the picture of the national situation presented in Table 10-3. As shown in Table 10-4, four or more semesters of a foreign language were completed by 26 per cent of the students; in mathematics, by over 60 per cent; and in college-preparatory science, by over 65 per cent. Nearly 80 per cent of the students completed eight or more semesters of English. Table 10-5 reveals the semesters of academic study (English, languages, mathematics, science, and social studies) completed by *all* of the students attending the schools included in the sample. Only 7 per cent of the students completed less than sixteen semesters; almost one-half completed between sixteen and twenty-three semesters; nearly 45 per

[14] Conducted in Illinois in 1960, the study included the records of *all* students of a carefully constructed, stratified sampling of high schools of the state, exclusive of Chicago. The study was directed by Harold Hand, Professor of Education, University of Illinois, for the State Department of Education.

Table 10-5. *Semesters of Academic Subjects Taken During Four Years of High School by Students in a Sample of Illinois Schools*

SEMESTERS OF ACADEMIC WORK	PERCENTAGE OF STUDENTS IN SAMPLE
Less than 12	0.8
12—13	2.0
14—15	4.2
16—23	49.0
24—26	18.6
27—29	11.5
30—32	12.0
More than 32	2.3

S O U R C E : Same as Table 10-4.

cent completed twenty-four or more semesters of these subjects. Table 10-6 shows a breakdown of specific courses taken within the area of the social studies. An analysis of the mathematics and science offerings and enrollments is presented in the next section of this chapter.

Study of three subject areas, not shown in the charts, reveals that over 40 per cent of all students had no art or music training, and almost 30 per cent of the girls received no training in home economics. It appears that these subjects have not received the attention which they are sometimes purported to have.

Mathematics and science. The concern for the teaching of mathematics and science has increased sharply since October 1958. Table 10-7 shows the extent of the offerings of college-preparatory mathematics and science in cities of various sizes. Tables 10-2 and 10-3 above indicate the growth of enrollments in these two subject fields, and Table 10-4 shows the current situation regarding the amount of mathematics and science being taken by students. Table 10-7 relates the size of city to the offerings of science and mathematics. Table 10-8 from Hand's study for the state of Illinois shows the percentages of students who completed specific courses in mathematics and science during four years of high school.

Table 10-6. *Percentages of Students Completing Courses in Social Studies During Four Years of High School in a Sample of Illinois Schools*

SOCIAL STUDIES COURSE	PERCENTAGE OF STUDENTS WHO COMPLETED COURSE
AMERICAN HISTORY	99.5
WORLD HISTORY	44.4
CIVICS	38.9
SOCIOLOGY or PROBLEMS OF AMERICAN DEMOCRACY	35.9
ECONOMICS	19.3
GEOGRAPHY	10.8
MODERN HISTORY	4.7
ANCIENT HISTORY	.6
OTHER	37.1
NONE	1.1

SOURCE: Same as Table 10-4.

Table 10-7. *Science and Mathematics Offering*

COURSE	POPULATION			
	100,000 OR MORE	25,000-99,999	10,000-24,999	ALL CITIES
ADVANCED GENERAL SCIENCE	46.2	54.5	49.1	44.1
BIOLOGY	97.3	100.0	100.0	95.5
CHEMISTRY	97.6	100.0	100.0	97.6
PHYSICS	98.2	100.0	100.0	96.0
INTERMEDIATE ALGEBRA	90.0	100.0	100.0	87.6
ADVANCED ALGEBRA	82.4	90.9	81.9	82.2
SOLID GEOMETRY	95.1	100.0	95.7	94.6
TRIGONOMETRY	93.3	81.8	95.7	92.6

SOURCE: *Biennial Survey of Education in the United States, 1957-58.* Washington, D.C.: U.S. Office of Education, Chapter 1, p. 54.

Table 10-8. *Percentages of Students from a Sample of Illinois Schools Who Completed Specific Mathematics and Science Courses During High School*

MATHEMATICS		SCIENCE	
Course	*Percentage*	*Course*	*Percentage*
ALGEBRA	76.3	GENERAL SCIENCE	73.6
GENERAL MATHEMATICS	27.2	BIOLOGICAL SCIENCE	66.9
PLANE GEOMETRY	51.4	CHEMISTRY	34.9
INTERMEDIATE ALGEBRA	24.8	PHYSICS	21.6
SOLID GEOMETRY	16.7	OTHER	8.4
TRIGONOMETRY	12.7	NONE	3.1
CALCULUS	0.03		
OTHER	11.5		
NONE	7.2		

SOURCE: Same as Table 10-4.

Patterning of Curricular Offerings

The curriculum patterns of the nation are surprisingly uniform. Authorities generally agree that the minimum requirements for high school graduation imposed for accreditation by state legislatures and accrediting agencies are largely responsible for this condition. The required program is commonly referred to as the program of general education, while the elective portion is called the specialized program. Programs of instruction are patterned within this concept of general and special education.

Separate subjects. The separate subject (following the Carnegie definition of a class as meeting 45-50 minutes per day, five days per week, for one school year) is the dominant pattern of curriculum organization. Although a survey of all secondary schools of the country has not been attempted to ascertain the frequency of various patterns, evidence from a number of studies of samples of school districts can be used to produce estimates.[15] Approximately 90 per cent of the senior high schools and 70 per cent of the junior high schools of the nation use separate subjects as the building blocks of their curriculums. Various adaptations of the separate subject approach have been carried out in secondary schools.

The standard curriculum pattern for small schools is called the required-elective, or constant-variable, plan. In effect, this is a "single" curriculum with all students required to enroll in the same basic subjects with a minimum number of elective courses. In larger schools, the multiple-track curriculum which provides parallel groupings of subjects, both required and elective, is popular. College preparatory, business, vocational, and general are the labels usually given to such separate programs. Some large schools have moved away from the multitrack plan to a pattern of general education, required of all and supplemented by a wide range of elective courses for specialization purposes. In this type of plan, when it exists in a large school, it is possible to provide each student with a program of courses tailored to his needs. Some secondary schools have also planned curricular arrangements that permit relating the instruction of two or more subjects. This development produced (within the subject curriculum) fused, correlated, and broad field patterns.

Block-time patterns. As a result of widespread curriculum experimentation prior to World War II, a number of secondary schools (with junior high schools leading the way) organized subject instruction into block-time patterns. This departure permitted one teacher to teach fewer students for longer daily periods—usually two or three regular length periods. In addition, the teacher planned the work of two or more subjects within the block of time. In a recent study, 34 per cent of the schools included used a block-time pattern.[16]

1. *Subject-centered block-time patterns.* The majority of schools using block-time patterns retain subject-centered instruction. Usually two subjects, sometimes three, are in the same block and taught by one teacher. The English-social studies combination is found far more frequently than any other, with science-mathematics next in popu-

[15] Refer to: Nelson Bossing, "Developments of the Core Curriculum in the Senior High School," *School Review,* May 1956; J. Minor Gwynn, *Curriculum Principles and Social Trends,* New York (Macmillan), 1960, pp. 406-16; and Grace S. Wright, *Block Time Classes and the Core Program,* Washington, D.C. (U.S. Office of Education), 1958.

[16] Grace S. Wright, *op. cit.,* p. 4.

Table 10-9. *Comparison of Two Surveys of Schools Using Block-Time Patterns of Instruction (per cent)*

	1952	1957
Correlated or separate subjects within blocks of time	41	68
Subject-centered core or unified studies	23	20
Experience type core	24	12

NOTE: Percentages do not add to 100 in every case because schools were not tabulated unless they indicated the pattern as used exclusively or as "most used."

SOURCE: Grace S. Wright, *Block Time Classes and the Core Program,* Washington, D.C.: U.S. Office of Education, 1958, p. 20.

larity. More than two-thirds of all schools using block-time patterns retain a subject-centered approach (Table 10-9), but of this group more than 80 per cent attempt to interrelate the content of the subjects taught.[17]

2. *Subject-centered core or unified studies.* Within the block-time pattern some schools have retained the subject content but have eliminated the "natural" structure of the subjects involved. History, for example, in conventional practice is taught in chronological sequence; literature, by periods or themes; and geography, by areas. Under the unified studies plan, the unit method is employed. In English-social studies instruction, units in social studies are planned with language arts as the vehicle of instruction. A unit on "international relations," for example, would require the selection of content throughout the whole period of United States history and would entail the study of literature, historical documents, report writing, library research, and oral reports. The advantages of such an approach are apparent, for if the teacher is adept in this method, the normal academic skills can be taught directly as they are used, thereby making a problem-centered type of instruction possible.

3. *Experience-centered core.* As shown in Table 10-9, approximately 12 per cent of the schools using block-time patterns may be expected to employ the experience-centered core program. This type of instruction is also frequently referred to as the activity curriculum. The term "core" usually denotes the fact that only personal-social problems make up its content and that other studies in the remainder

[17] *Ibid.,* p. 10.

of the daily schedule are organized as separate subjects. Two types of experience-centered core programs are in use. One type is the "structured" core which is taught by the use of resource units predetermined by the teacher or the school. The second type is the "unstructured" core which is developed by the teacher with the class through pupil-teacher planning techniques. The content of both types of core programs is determined by the personal needs of the particular group of students in terms of existing social problems. An attempt is made to maintain a strictly problem-centered approach and, when possible, the class undertakes the study of current social problems or issues. From the studies noted in footnote 15, there is evidence that the block-time pattern is increasing in popularity; whereas the experience-centered core, as indicated in Table 10-9, is decreasing in use.

OVER-ALL DESIGN OF THE SECONDARY SCHOOL PROGRAM

To justify any program of secondary education one must be able to show that it is designed to achieve the goals expected of it. Two ultimate and pervading aims held for secondary education underlie its design and point to the standards by which it can be evaluated. These aims are to educate *all* of American youth to participate effectively in society while, at the same time, aiding each student to develop his individual interests and abilities to his maximum.

Balance

American secondary education seeks to provide, within one unified program, an education for both social unity and individual diversity. A balanced offering of general and special education is essential to any design which purports to satisfy these two conditions. General education, that portion of the program taken by all students, provides the foundation for specialization. Specialized education, that portion of the program not required of all students, should increase until it becomes a major part of the program of the final two years.

Flexibility

In the sense that the school has adequate provisions to determine each student's maturity and the nature and immediacy of his educational and vocational goals, a unique program of studies is provided for each student. To achieve this condition the design of the curriculum must be flexible enough that students are not prematurely committed to a course of study which precludes change.

Variety

The curriculum should provide enough variety to meet the educational needs of all the students who comprise the school. Although the extent of offerings has increased considerably in recent decades as secondary education has become available to all, there is evidence that the curriculums in many schools are still designed to serve only a particular portion of the youth who enroll. Studies of the students with high ability who have dropped out of school indicate that large numbers of school curriculums hold no challenge for them.

Challenge

The quality of the programs is perhaps the most serious weakness of secondary education. The pressing problems of increasing secondary school enrollments (from about 500,000 in 1900 to almost 8,000,000 today) have tended to deflect attention from the quality of the education offered. An effort equal to that of making education available to all must now be given to making education challenging to all. Ability grouping, independent study, new teaching devices, and improved teacher education are some of the means by which the quality of education is being improved. The design of secondary school programs should allow for controlled experimentation and for adaptation of proved methods to increase the quality of instruction.

SELECTED REFERENCES

ALCORN, MARVIN, AND JAMES M. LINLEY. *Issues in Curriculum Development: A Book of Readings.* Tarrytown, N.Y.: World Book Co., 1959.

BLOOM, BENJAMIN S., ed. *Taxonomy of Educational Objectives.* New York: Longmans, Green, 1956.

FRENCH, WILL, ET AL. *Behavioral Goals of a General Education in High School.* New York: Russell Sage Foundation, 1957.

GWYNN, JOHN M. *Curriculum Principles and Social Trends.* New York: Macmillan, 1960.

HOPPY, ARTHUR A. *The Core in Junior High School.* Bloomington: Univ. of Indiana Press, 1957.

KING, EDMUND J. *Other Schools and Ours.* New York: Rinehart, 1958.

KRUG, EDWARD A. *The Secondary School Curriculum,* New York: Harper, 1960.

MOWRER, HOBART O. *Learning Theory and Behavior.* New York: John Wiley, 1960.

NOVAK, BENJAMIN J. "98 Curriculum Definitions." *Clearing House,* February 1960.

PRITZKOW, PHILO. *Dynamics of Curriculum Improvement.* Englewood Cliffs, N.J.: Prentice-Hall, 1959.

Telemation laboratory at the University of Wisconsin automatically provides slides, motion picture films, video tape and other audio-visual aids. These are shown simultaneously on three different screens to augment professor's lecture to large group.

Students at West Lafayette (Indiana) High School view television lessons beamed from a flying studio plane in the Midwest Airborne television program. The program is available to two million students in the Chicago area.

CHAPTER II

Instruction in Secondary Schools

EDUCATIONAL excellence requires good teaching. A growing awareness of this fact by the people of the United States has stimulated widespread interest in the quality of instruction in secondary schools. Over the next fifteen to twenty years the demands for better and more efficient teaching may alter the nature and organization of secondary school instruction even more than its buildings have changed in the last fifty.

One factor that promises to limit the selection, organization, and utilization of instructional competencies and resources is the general manpower shortage, a condition which will prevail for some years to come. Partially for this reason modern electronic techniques and devices of communication are being introduced into schools. Many of these new developments first proved valuable in the educational programs of business, industry, and the armed forces. Traditional methods of secondary school teaching are being critically examined with the end in mind being the improvement of both the quality and efficiency of instruction. Consequently, there is a greater emphasis today on evaluating particular approaches and aspects of teaching procedures. In addition, it is coming to be recognized that quality teaching should be rewarded.

ORGANIZATION OF INSTRUCTIONAL RESOURCES[1]

In contrast to the elementary school, secondary education has always required greater subject specialization by staff members. Even so, the tradition of assigning high school teachers to teach in two or more fields has prevented many of them from attaining the depth of concentration in their pre-service preparation and in-service study that is essential to good teaching.

The rapid expansion of knowledge in all fields, but particularly in the sciences, coupled with the drive for excellence in education, highlights the necessity of organizing instruction in secondary schools in such fashion that teachers can become, and continue to be, competent scholars in the subject they teach. There is growing awareness, also, that some subject fields recognized in the past (such as science) are too broad to enable one person to keep abreast of the expanding scholarship in his field. As a consequence, attention is being directed toward redefining fields of specialization for teachers that will permit more concentrated study and greater efficiency in teaching.[2] For example, it is proposed that a teacher should prepare to teach mathematics and physics, or mathematics and chemistry, instead of attempting to become proficient in all the branches of science included in the secondary school program. It is recognized that some teachers of English are unusually skilled at teaching creative writing and composition while others do better when teaching poetry and literature.

Differentiated Use of Staff

Instruction is often weakened by requiring classroom teachers to perform many duties that require no special professional competence, such as noting attendance, keeping routine records, supervising study halls, lunchrooms, and social events, or sponsoring student activities. Experiments have demonstrated that even such tasks as criticizing student themes and marking mathematics assignments can be performed with competence by noncertified college graduates who are carefully selected and provided with brief training programs.[3]

[1] Experimentation with new ways to organize instructional resources is now going forward in centers throughout the country. They are described here for purposes of information, rather than advocation.

[2] J. Lloyd Trump, "New Horizons for Secondary School Teachers," *Bulletin of the National Association of Secondary School Principals,* undated.

[3] Mathew F. Noall and Parry Wilson, "Paraprofessional Helpers in a Language Arts Program at the Logan City High School, Utah," *Bulletin of the National Association of Secondary School Principals,* January 1960.

The object of moving toward a greater differentiated use of the high school staff is to provide students of various ability levels with teachers who possess both scholarly competence in the content to be taught and skill in presenting that content. At the same time, secondary school teachers should enjoy professional conditions that permit them to develop as teacher-scholars in their fields of interest. Different levels of professional rank would allow teachers to advance from one stage of professional practice and responsibility to another as they grow in skill and knowledge.

Such fields as medicine and engineering have shown by the way they are organized that a profession can permit and encourage specialization to the benefit of the client and to the satisfaction and advantage of the professional practitioner. These fields have shown, too, that by scheduling professional practice in terms of kinds and levels of competence, as well as responsibility, the time of highly skilled specialists will not be wasted on nonessentials.

Instructional Teams[4]

The most recent efforts to improve the organization and use of resources of instruction at the secondary school level involve the development of various types of instructional teams.[5] The instructional team organization for teaching is accomplished by assigning several teachers who possess complementary strengths, along with certain noncertified personnel, and frequently one or more interns or probationary teachers. As a team, they instruct as many as 150 or more students in a broad field such as history, English, or science. The team works together to organize the instruction in such fashion that students will study in the optimum size groups for each phase of work. At each step the instruction or supervision is supplied by the member of the team most capable of providing it. The benefits of a wide variety of audio-visual resources for learning are also available. This arrangement gives students individual help when needed as well as freedom to work independently and to progress as rapidly as maturity and ability permit. Teams may be organized to instruct five or six sections of a course, such as American history, with members working together, rather than in the traditional isolation. They have been used to provide instruction in a field such as English for students at different year

4 See Lindley J. Stiles, "Education in Orbit," *Nation's Schools*, June 1959.
5 Henry S. Bissex, "Newton Plan Challenges Traditions of Class Size," *Nation's Schools*, March 1960, pp. 61-64.

levels, e.g., freshmen, sophomores, and juniors, whose abilities in particular skills are more alike than different.

Composition of teams. A sample team to instruct 150 high school pupils might consist of the following personnel:

1. PROFESSIONAL MEMBERS:

   TEAM LEADER: This is a highly competent teacher in the subject field who possesses not only the special strengths of scholarship and pedagogy needed but also is able to organize the team into a smooth, functioning unit.

   CAREER TEACHERS: A team to instruct 150 pupils would probably have two career teachers. Such individuals, like the team leader, are experienced and capable teachers who have specialized in phases of the work and have skill to supervise interns in training.

   INTERNS: Two such individuals work as full-time team members, as apprentice teachers, performing various functions— both to develop their own professional skills and to assist the work of the group.

2. NONCERTIFIED PERSONNEL:

   LAY READERS: These team members usually work on a part-time basis, reading papers or grading examinations. They typically are outstanding college graduates who, with brief periods of training, are able to relieve professional team members of the heavy burdens of paperwork that are essential to good instruction.

   TECHNICIAN: The technician assists with audio-visual equipment, keeping it in working order. Such personnel may serve several teams and individual teachers at once.

   INSTRUCTIONAL SECRETARY: This team position is filled by an individual who possesses secretarial skills but is trained also to collect and record information about pupils, to make reports, and to administer and score standardized examinations.

The number of individuals included in a team will depend, of course, on the size of the total group to be taught. In addition to those listed above, teams may have help from principals and central-office curriculum and specialized personnel. The work of the team may also be supplemented by educational television in schools that have either closed-circuit resources, direct programs, or telefilm lessons.

Nature of team teaching. In the typical secondary school, one teacher provides all the instruction in a course, including the selection and preparation of materials, the construction and grading of examinations, the keeping of records, and the coaching of both bright and slow pupils. Within the same school several other teachers may be going through similar procedures for other sections of the same course.

Team teaching, in its simplest form, arranges for two or three teachers to work together to perform all these functions, with each making his contribution in the area of his greatest strength and interest. For example, if one is unusually successful in stimulating academically talented students, the work of the group can be so scheduled that his ability can be made available to all such students. Another may possess skill in presenting large-group demonstrations, while a third may prefer coaching skill practice in small groups. In effect, teachers carry out, in an organized and planned fashion, what many have termed the "trading" of teaching functions.

A key characteristic of team teaching is its flexibility. It permits the adaptation of instruction both to the nature of the skills or material to be taught, as well as to the individual differences in ability of pupils. Some lessons, such as the dramatization or film presentation of a Shakespearean play to an English class, can actually be presented better, and with greater economy, to a larger audience. For this type of instruction the entire large group of students can be assembled under the direction of one member of the team. Other types of work, such as the perfection of writing skills, often demand tutoring in small groups of not more than six to ten members. By arranging for one team member to teach a large section, others are freed to work with small groups on highly individualistic problems or in special phases of the study that would be appropriate for selected students. Instruction in large groups, in effect, allows for even smaller groups and more individual attention than is possible when one teacher is responsible for the total program.

Television and Other Audio-Visual Resources

Good teachers have always known that more could be taught, with greater efficiency, by the use of multiple visual and auditory resources. Within the past twenty-five years, experiences with still and motion pictures and sound films, as well as with the variety of teaching devices such as mock-ups, tape recordings, records, charts, and maps, have demonstrated that quality of instruction is materially improved when teachers make proper use of audio-visual aids.[6] The recent development of television lessons, via either closed-circuit, telefilm, or direct broadcast makes available to teachers an up-to-date source of instruction.

More research is needed to define the best uses of television in education. Procedures already are being adapted to make this resource available in appropriate ways to teachers and pupils. There is a good chance that educational television will be depended upon heavily in future years. Carefully controlled research by Wittich and others[7] in Wisconsin has demonstrated, for example, that students taught exclusively by the White "telefilms" learned as much of the content of high school physics as did control groups in regular classes. Students in small high schools which did not have competent physics teachers were able to learn as much physics through a combination correspondence and television course, which was taken without a teacher, as did those in larger high schools with fully equipped laboratories and well-trained teachers.

Experiments with teaching machines have furnished insights into ways in which high school students may learn on their own without close, continuous supervision and direction from teachers.[8] Telemation, which supplements teachers' presentations with multidimensional and proportional visual illustrations and other audio-visual devices, has been used in instructional programs of the armed forces to increase the amount of learning by as much as 9 per cent while reducing the time required by as much as 30 per cent.

These and other developments in the field of educational television, and other aspects of audio-visual resources for teaching, may well exert potent influences on instruction in secondary schools in the years ahead. Not only may they change the nature of teaching itself; their use will require changes in courses of study and curriculums, as well as in the plans and designs of educational buildings and facilities.

[6] William H. Allen, "Audio-Visual Communication," *Encyclopedia of Educational Research,* Chester W. Harris (ed.), New York (Macmillan), 1960. Audio-visual, p. 118; television, pp. 119-22; radio, recordings, filmstrips, slides, pictorial illustrations, pp. 116-22.

[7] Walter A. Wittich and others, *The Wisconsin Physics Film Evaluation Project,* research report, Madison (Univ. of Wisconsin), 1959.

[8] B. F. Skinner, "Teaching Machines," reprinted in A. A. Lumsdaine and R. Glazer, *Teaching Machines and Programmed Learning,* sourcebook, Washington, D.C. (Department of Audio-Visual Instruction, National Education Association), 1960.

Adaptation to Individual Differences

As the population of the secondary school has become more heterogeneous, the need to adapt instruction to individual differences in pupil abilities has become more pronounced. Although some schools have attempted to accomplish this objective by homogeneous grouping, most have depended entirely upon the nature of the course as the basis for differentiation in level and quality of instruction. The results in either case have not kept pace with the increasing ranges of differences present in a typical high school student body.

Emphasis on quality in education demands that instruction be so organized as to permit each pupil to make maximum progress in terms of individual capacities and educational objectives. Apart from the new possibilities for adapting instruction to individual differences that the instructional team organization provides, secondary schools are today exploring new ways to group students, organize courses, and accelerate able students. More attention is being given to measuring achievement by amount learned, rather than time spent in class, with students being encouraged to study independently in order to advance more rapidly. In the past, emphasis has been placed on keeping pupils in high school, that is, reducing the number of dropouts. The future may well bring a parallel concern for getting gifted students out of high school, and into college, sooner. The organization and instructional resources of a school will no doubt be called upon to respond to this trend.

INSTRUCTIONAL PROCEDURES

Although basic principles of learning and teaching are generally applicable to different ages of pupils, certain applications are more successful at one level than another. Educational theory and research in instruction have been concerned with the instructional procedures best adapted to youth of secondary school years as well as with the relative effectiveness of different methods of teaching.[9]

General Characteristics of Teaching Procedures for Secondary Schools

The characteristics of teaching procedures that work best in secondary schools are determined both by the nature of the content to be taught and the ranges in maturity levels of high school pupils. Methods

[9] Lindley J. Stiles, "Instruction," *Encyclopedia of Educational Research,* Chester W. Harris (ed.), New York (Macmillan), 1960, pp. 710-15.

are influenced, also, by the nature of life in the United States and the type of citizenship behavior and responsibilities that education is expected to promote. As is true with all instruction, the personal qualities of individual teachers and their skill in the art of teaching play an important part in the success of any procedure. Among the more important general characteristics of instructional procedures are the following:

1. Instructional procedures for secondary schools must be adapted to the wide range of maturity levels represented by youth passing through adolescence. Some pupils require close, continuous direction; others exhibit considerable initiative and ability to study independently; all may be expected to fluctuate, more or less, from one extreme to the other in ways that are often almost unpredictable.

2. Methods of teaching that involve students in the processes of identifying goals of instruction, planning and carrying out individual and group learning activities, as well as in evaluating outcomes, have high motivational potential at the high school level and tend to promote growth toward self-direction in learning.

3. The transition from firsthand to vicarious learning that takes place on a broad scale at the secondary school level is enhanced by the use of a variety of audio-visual resources to bridge the gap from the real to the envisioned—from experience to verbalization.

4. Inasmuch as the force of the group is strongest during adolescent years, patterns of instruction that utilize to advantage the control and motivational impacts of group rapport achieve the best results at the secondary school level.

5. Methods of instruction for secondary schools should give attention to strengthening the basic skills of learning and communication; at the same time they are expected to lay a foundation for sound scholarship in the major fields of knowledge.

6. Teaching procedures should cater to the natural drives of high school students for independence, new experiences, recognition, and success, as well as acceptance as young adults.

Laboratory Methods of Teaching

The introduction of science into the secondary school prompted the development of what has been called the laboratory method of teaching.[10] As distinct from the older procedures of the lecture and recita-

[10] Thomas H. Briggs and others, *Laboratory Techniques of Teaching,* New York (Teachers College, Columbia Univ.), 1938.

tion, in which the emphasis was on the transmittal and testing of correct knowledge by the teacher, the laboratory process focused attention on the solution of problems by students under teacher guidance.

Variations of laboratory methods have been adapted to such fields as the social studies and the humanities, as well as to the natural and physical sciences. They have brought different content organizations to the secondary schools as subject matter and skill mastery have been arranged into units covering several weeks' study—as contrasted to the lesson-a-day assignments characteristic of the lecture and the recitation.

Different titles given to the laboratory method include: problem solving, the contract, The Winnetka Plan, The Dalton Plan, the project method, and the unit plan.[11] The method, whatever its name, provides opportunities for students to pursue learning creatively. The student is actively involved in the identification of problems; he must use both inductive and deductive reasoning; he is trained to assemble facts and information, to test hypotheses, to draw conclusions, and to appraise success. The objective of the laboratory approach is to encourage the learner to follow procedures that lead to independence in learning, rather than to dependence upon the teacher.

Laboratory methods of teaching, including the relatively long unit of study, may be said to be the major advancement in patterns of teaching at the secondary school level during the past half-century. These methods brought to adolescents instructional procedures that made them active participants in the learning venture, challenged their curiosities, and freed their minds to explore, speculate, create, and appraise. They also changed the role of the teacher from that of taskmaster to guide.

Teacher-Student Planning

Another advance in the theory and practice of instruction for secondary schools that has influenced practice during the past thirty years is teacher-student planning.[12] Students, with teachers as guides, engage in the cooperative planning and execution of learning experiences. The objective is to stimulate in students the development of such qualities as initiative, self-direction, self-discipline, creativity, and habits of independent scholarship, as well as skill in cooperation.

[11] G. Max Wingo, "Methods of Teaching," *Encyclopedia of Educational Research,* Chester W. Harris (ed.), New York (Macmillan), 1960, pp. 851-52.

[12] Alice Meil and others, *Cooperative Procedure in Learning,* New York (Teachers College, Columbia Univ.), 1952.

Results of experiments with teacher-student planning have demonstrated its superiority over the lecture and recitation, especially when the procedure is judged in terms of the behavior it produces in learners, the mastery of skills, and the learning and retention of facts. The results of these experiments reveal that high school students, when taught by such procedures, are capable of high levels of mature scholarship, individual initiative, and self-discipline.[13]

Independent Scholarship

Few would disagree with the principle that all good education is self-education. Yet methods of teaching often seem to be based on the opposite assumption. It is possible for instruction to be so organized that students become increasingly dependent, docile, and unresponsive to intellectual stimulants that are not accompanied by teacher-controlled rewards or punishments. Mass instructional procedures in secondary schools have been particularly ill-adapted to promoting independence in scholarship. Assignments, exercises, and examinations, in spite of efforts by teachers to provide for individual differences, tend to promote conformity to routines and directions, rather than intellectual curiosity, creativity, or independent scholarship.

Academically talented students have suffered most under instructional procedures that discourage independent study. They have been forced to move with the pace of the group, unchallenged and frequently bored. Because progress has been measured in terms of assignments completed, time spent in class, and responses to teacher-constructed exams on assigned material, little incentive has been provided for outstanding students to plan and carry out their own programs of study.

ASPECTS OF INSTRUCTION

Whatever the method of instruction followed, certain aspects of the teaching function are always present. Characteristics of these will be familiar to all who have prepared for teaching. Such features, however, are currently being influenced significantly by the revolution in instruction that is under way in secondary schools.

Motivation

Efforts to improve the quality of secondary education center heavily

[13] Lindley J. Stiles and Mattie F. Dorsey, *Democratic Teaching in Secondary Schools,* New York (Lippincott), 1950.

upon the motivation of learning. Impetus comes in part from the fear that totalitarian nations are able to motivate their youth to greater academic efforts. In addition, awareness of the impact of community attitudes on intellectual accomplishments in school places the problem of motivation in a broader setting than the classroom itself. In fact, motivation, particularly of the academically talented students, is now seen as a matter urgently requiring the attention of national groups and the federal government.

It is now recognized that the individual teacher is not in complete control of all the forces that motivate or inhibit learning in high school classrooms. For this reason, teachers and school officials find that they must work together with representatives of their communities to create the kind of environment and opportunity that will encourage students to intellectual achievement. Systematic programs to identify gifted students, to guide them toward their maximum development while in high school, to provide advanced and honors courses in basic subjects that permit acceleration—all have been found to help change the school climate of opinion about academic attainments. Similarly, the establishment of national honors awards, the national science talent contests, the nation-wide program of merit scholarships have all helped focus attention on good scholarship.

The emphasis placed in some high schools on reckoning pupil achievement in terms of national norms rather than in terms of the highest possible scores has lulled many pupils and their parents into contentment with average progress. This, combined with the tendency of some teachers to give passing marks to all pupils, plus a general rejection of high marks as desirable goals by students themselves, have reduced motivation. To counteract such weaknesses, it is now being suggested that maximum achievement goals be established;[14] students are, in effect, being urged to "play over their heads" intellectually, as they do, physically, in athletics. It is believed, also, that as approval and recognition are given to students who excel in academic studies, intellectual attainments will be held in higher regard by both students and parents.

The growing emphasis on guidance is a part of the current effort to increase the motivation for intellectual achievement. One radical

[14] Lindley J. Stiles, "America's Dual Mandate: Universal and Quality Education," *Cook County Education Digest,* November 1959. This point was also made by Dr. James B. Conant in a speech to the National Association of Secondary School Principals in Portland, Oregon, in March 1960.

change in the philosophy of guidance is worthy of note. Early guidance doctrine tended to identify strengths and weaknesses in student abilities with the goal of encouraging students to build on their strong points. Recent thinking in this field suggests that students, particularly the academically talented, should be guided toward remedying their weaknesses in order to widen their potentialities, thus expanding their academic foundations for unforeseen opportunities in the future.

Classroom Management

Changes in the organization of teaching itself, such as the use of instructional teams, supplementation by television lessons or other electronic aids, complicate the problems of classroom management. The instructional team, for example, permits many of the tasks involved in the management of the classroom to be performed by nonprofessional personnel. In this type of organization, teacher aides may provide the resources and arrange the physical facilities of the classroom. They may also help with pupil control and with the scheduling of small- and large-group learning activities. The shifting of regulatory and organizational details from the professional teacher to a nonprofessional team member is one of the strong appeals of the instructional team arrangement.

The study and diagnosis of pupil adjustment and the maintenance of appropriate classroom conduct, a process traditionally called discipline, is likewise undergoing change in secondary schools. Where instructional teams are employed, specialist members of the team are available to help perform such functions. Those making decisions about individual pupils have the benefit of the pooled information and shared judgments of all the team members. Students who need individual attention can be assisted by guidance specialists. Even in schools that do not provide instructional teams, the practice of making available the services of specialists on a school-wide basis is becoming common. In such situations, teachers may refer students to specialists for help, thus reducing their own responsibilities for resolving behavior problems.

Planning Instruction

The reorganization of content of courses, the adaptation of instruction to differences of pupils, the multiplication of learning materials, the use of programmed material with and without learning machines— all complicate the high school teacher's task of planning instruction today. In practically all subject fields, teachers are pressed to keep abreast of rapidly expanding knowledge and often the relationship of that knowledge to national and world problems as well. As they update their academic foundations, teachers are obligated to adapt the results of their scholarship to the high school courses they teach. Unfortunately, little help is available to them from state courses of study since such resources are typically out of date. Even the textbooks available may be inadequate to the courses planned by scholar-teachers. Laboratory aids, maps and charts, audio-visual resources, as well as library reference books must be kept up to date with newer emphasis in course content.

The synchronization of closed-circuit and live television lessons with classwork represents another modern complication in the planning aspects of teaching. Where telefilms are available, these of course can be scheduled as are other films; but careful scheduling is essential when the teacher uses lessons that are televised live. Even the use of live television lessons during out-of-class time requires substantial planning and supervision to assure maximum benefits to students.

Increasingly, school systems are finding it profitable to support the study of teachers during summers in order that they will have time to plan their work for the ensuing year. In certain fields, such as science, mathematics, and foreign language, scholarships from the National Science Foundation have made it possible for teachers to return to college campuses to study new knowledge in these fields and to otherwise upgrade their competence for teaching. Scholarships have been available, also, in such areas as family finance and economic education to help teachers of social studies, mathematics, business education, and home economics remedy deficiences in their preparation. Another means of helping teachers improve their planning has been local workshops sponsored by school systems themselves. In these intensive summer work programs teachers have both the opportunity to come into contact with new knowledge and the time in which to translate this knowledge into resource and teaching units that will update their instruction.

A new trend is the development of recommended content for high school courses by national groups. This is already being done in the fields of mathematics, physics, and biology. Currently, the National Association of Teachers of English is urging that similar procedures be followed to develop a nation-wide reorganization of the program of secondary school English. Incorporated in such developments is the hotly debated question: Should there be a national curriculum for schools in the United States? However the debate goes, it seems evident that organized groups of specialists in various subject fields are already moving toward nation-wide course patterns.

Classroom Presentations

The laboratory method, group discussion techniques, the use of audio-visual resources and television lessons, as well as the emphasis on self-direction in learning have radically broadened conceptions of the teacher's role in classroom presentations. Although many teachers still rely heavily upon recitation and lecture techniques, greater numbers are experimenting with a variety of procedures. In fact, variety in approach to teaching is believed to be one secret to quality in instruction. Even the traditional lecture and recitation are undergoing refreshing innovations that provide variety and increase their efficiency as teaching procedures. Telemation, or automatic visual illustration, is being used to supplement and strengthen the lecture. This procedure, which was first tested on the college level at the University of Wisconsin in 1961, promises to increase the rate and amount of learning. The recitation, likewise, is undergoing changes as teachers experiment with the nondirective group discussion and Socratic questioning techniques.

The qualities needed for effective classroom presentations are not uniformly and generously distributed among all teachers. Many teachers are good scholars but are weak classroom performers. The individual who is able to stimulate learning in large classes may be inept when dealing with a small discussion group. The instructional team aims at utilizing the strengths of each member at his maximum efficiency. One may specialize in large group presentations, another may become a television instructor, others may concentrate on working with students individually or in small groups. However the work is divided, greater emphasis is placed upon the quality of classroom presentations.

Current concern for quality in classroom presentations extends to the goals sought as well as to the amount learned. A recent book by Hullfish and Smith examines the teacher's contribution to reflective thinking. These authors remind high school teachers that:

> The effective way of teaching, once decisions have been made as to which facts should be emphasized at each stage of growth, is the reflective way. It is effective because it is man's sole way of providing for a continuity of learning that will carry beyond the classroom into the continuing affairs of life. When coverage of

knowledge and the fostering of thought conflict, therefore, it is but elementary educational wisdom to give the right of way to thinking.[15]

Such admonitions strike at the heart of classroom presentations. They remind all who teach that the quality of instruction depends upon the teacher's commitment to goals as well as upon his grasp of subject matter, familiarity with available resources, and care in lesson preparation.

Appraisal of Learning

Efforts to improve the quality of secondary school instruction have led to a search for better ways to appraise learning. The most striking evidence of the increased concern for appraisal is found in the expanded use of standardized tests in high schools. These instruments not only supplement teacher-constructed examinations; they furnish a basis for predicting a student's success or failure in academic work in high school and college.

Other significant developments, some new, some old but in a different guise, in the appraisal of learning are the use of tape recorders to permit students to judge their own responses; the use of learning machines and programmed textbooks which incorporate appraisal operations with the steps of learning; the analysis of reasoning processes; greater use of essay responses to test ability to organize and to present ideas; and observation of student academic progress under laboratory conditions.

Appraisal of learning is being improved under experimental conditions in some high schools by accomplishing much of the tedious work involved in testing students with the assistance of instructional secretaries and automatic scoring machines. Such services to teachers make possible more frequent testing, the provision of written analyses of learning difficulties, and retesting to the level of perfection. Lay readers have improved appraisal procedures in fields such as English and history that depend upon essay examinations and term papers as means of checking student academic progress.

EVALUATION OF INSTRUCTION

Without systematic, comprehensive evaluation, quality in instruction is left to chance. Good teachers rigorously evaluate their work and

[15] H. Gordon Hullfish and Phillip G. Smith, *Reflective Thinking: The Method of Education*, New York (Dodd, Mead), 1961, pp. 228-29.

draw heavily upon supervisory and administrative personnel as well as on their pupils and colleagues for assistance. In far too many secondary schools, however, little effort is made to evaluate instruction. Such neglect is due as much to the false assumption that the work of professional people is not subject to evaluation as it is to the erroneous premise widely endorsed by certain teachers' associations that it is impossible to differentiate between good and poor teaching. Whatever the reasons for the reluctance to evaluate instruction in the past, they will be severely challenged in the future as the urgency of achieving excellence in education imposes demands for more careful appraisal of the quality of instruction.

Agents of Evaluation

In a literal sense, everyone evaluates instruction: pupils, parents, professional colleagues, supervisors, administrators, school board members, as well as the individual teacher. Post-high school agencies, both educational and industrial, pass judgments on the quality of instruction in particular schools and in given fields. Such evaluations are typically informal and subjective, although colleges often have fairly objective evidence regarding the quality of instruction in college-preparatory subjects in the secondary schools from which they accept students.

The official agents of evaluation in a school, including all who have legal and professional responsibility for judging the quality of instruction, are the teacher himself, his colleagues, school officials, and the board of education. Others may help to provide information pertinent to evaluation, but the official judgments about instruction must be made by these individuals.

Criteria for Evaluation

Opponents of efforts to evaluate the quality of instruction frequently point to the absence of standard, objective criteria that are nationally recognized as a basis for measuring the effectiveness of teaching.[16] Actually, the evaluation of instruction is more effective, and typically done with greater fairness to the individuals involved, when the criteria are developed by teachers and administrators on a cooperative basis, and on the level of the local school system. Criteria developed should be attuned to the characteristics and objectives of instruction of each field of the secondary school and to particular courses and levels, as

[16] C. Currien Smith, "Why Teachers Dislike Merit Rating," *Overview*, February 1960, pp. 41-44.

well as to the goals of the educational program as a whole. Only if teachers share in the formulation of criteria are the standards likely to measure qualities that are significant and the process be respected by professional people.

Criteria for evaluation of instruction typically relate to such aspects of it as the following:

1. Extent to which students achieve, in accordance with individual capacities, the goals of a course, e.g., the perfection of learning skills, mastery of subject content, development of understandings, or refinement of ability to solve problems that require reasoning and analyzing

2. Selection, organization, and presentation of the program of instruction

3. Choice of instructional procedures and skill in their use

4. Use of audio-visual and other resources, human and material, to facilitate learning

5. Student evaluation, both immediate and delayed, of instructional effectiveness, within the capacity of their maturity and the limits of their sincerity

Evaluation Procedures

Procedures employed in evaluating instruction will be related to the criteria that guide the process. They include both gathering reliable evidence and making a judgment based upon that evidence.

Methods of gathering evidence about instruction. Examples of ways in which evidence about the quality of instruction may be assembled include: analyses of assignments and examinations (including standardized tests); study of organization for teaching (including choice of plans and resources); observation of classroom performance; analysis of standards established (including the distribution of marks in relation to capacity of students); appraisal of pupil maturation, work habits, and deportment; follow-up of subsequent success of students in advanced study; review of procedures employed in instruction (including such aspects as classroom presentation, appraisal techniques, individual tutoring, and problems of classroom management); and pupil interviews.

Such methods as these may be employed by the teacher, his professional colleagues, and members of the supervisory and administrative staff. The degree of cooperation and permissiveness that prevails is often determined by the desire of the individual teacher to improve the quality of his instruction. Supervisory and administrative approaches play an important part also in creating a climate in which teachers willingly engage in the evaluation of instruction.

Judgment of evidence. The key person in the process of judging evidence relative to the quality of instruction is the teacher involved. Improvements in teaching, as is true in all types of work, depend upon awareness of weaknesses. A teacher who evades the process of collecting and judging evidence about his teaching is unworthy of the professional responsibility that is his.

Evaluation of evidence by colleagues and school officials is an important phase of instructional improvement and a necessary step toward fair appraisal of an individual's contribution to the work of an area of instruction as well as to the school as a whole. Such evaluation also provides the base on which recognitions of excellence in teaching may be founded. Generally speaking, the participation of a number of responsible professional people in the judgment of evidence about teaching is a safeguard against misinterpretations or unfair deductions about a teacher's work.

RECOGNITION OF QUALITY TEACHING

Teaching is perhaps the only profession that does not identify and reward quality. The outstanding doctor, lawyer, or engineer is recognized as such by his profession—and commands a higher fee for his services. The great teacher often goes unnoticed by his professional associates and unrewarded by his school system because of a group belief supported by various teacher guilds that quality in teaching cannot be identified. Such reluctance by the profession to stand forthright for excellence in teaching undermines public confidence and drives able and ambitious people to other fields. It also reduces the quality of professional practice in schools by surrounding teachers who desire to be outstanding with group attitudes that discourage attempts at excellence and with administrative routines that prevent the appraisal of individual performance.

Disregarding the dogma of many educational organizations, a few school systems have developed successful personnel programs that recognize and reward excellence in teaching.[17] In each example, teachers have worked cooperatively with officials to devise suitable criteria and procedures for evaluating the quality of instruction. Communities,

[17] David V. Tiedeman (ed.), *Teacher Competence and Its Relation to Salary,* Boston, Mass. (New England School Development Council), 1956.

too, have demonstrated a willingness to promote and accord higher pay to outstanding teachers. Morale of teachers in schools that recognize quality in instruction is not destroyed by the evaluation process as is often claimed by members of the teaching profession who oppose such plans.[18] Evidence exists that schools that reward excellence in teaching are able to attract and hold outstanding teachers. The trend today, according to the research reports of the National Education Association, is toward rewarding competence in teaching. Those school systems that have moved in this direction find that the objections to such procedures do not materialize as often as predicted.[19]

SELECTED REFERENCES

BROWN, EDWIN, AND A. T. PHELPS. *Managing the Classroom.* New York: Ronald Press, 1961.

CROSS, A. J., AND IRENE F. CYPHER. *Audio-Visual Education.* New York: Thomas Y. Crowell, 1961.

FORD FOUNDATION. *Teaching by Television.* New York: Fund for the Advancement of Education, 1959.

GOODLAD, JOHN I. "The Increasing Concern for Effective Teacher Utilization." *The High School in a New Era,* Chicago: Univ. of Chicago Press, 1958.

NAGLE, A. J. "Team Concept in Organizing a Secondary School Program." *Bulletin of the National Association of Secondary School Principals,* April 1959.

RYANS, DAVID G. *Characteristics of Teachers: Their Description, Comparison and Appraisal.* Washington, D.C.: American Council on Education, 1960.

STILES, LINDLEY J. "Instruction." *Encyclopedia of Educational Research,* Chester W. Harris, ed., New York: Macmillan, 1960.

TARLET, DONALD G. *Television and Our Schools.* New York: Ronald Press, 1961.

TRUMP, J. L. "A Look Ahead in Secondary Education." *Bulletin of the National Association of Secondary School Principals,* January 1958.

WINGO, G. MAX. "Methods of Teaching." *Encyclopedia of Educational Research,* Chester W. Harris, ed., New York: Macmillan, 1960.

WOODRING, PAUL. "Promising Experiments in Education." *High School Journal,* October 1958.

[18] B. J. Chandler and Claude Mathis, "The Effect of School Salary Policies on Teacher Morale," Evanston, Ill. (Northwestern Univ.). July 1957. (Mimeographed.)

[19] National Education Association, "Salary Provisions for Quality of Service," *Research Bulletin,* December 1959, pp. 106-10.

A high school student takes a Minnesota "Rate of Manipulation Test" under the professional supervision of Dr. John W. M. Rothney, co-director of the Research and Guidance Laboratory for Superior Students at the University of Wisconsin.

In a democracy where choices are permitted, guidance is essential.

Programs of Guidance

THE FIRST organized efforts to systematize guidance services developed during the first decade of this century, just as the expansion of high school enrollments and functions was becoming pronounced. Early programs were vocationally centered, with their activities focused upon helping individuals choose careers and find jobs. For thirty years or more, the term "guidance" was generally accompanied by the qualifying adjective "vocational." In 1939 an Occupational Information and Guidance Service was established by the U.S. Office of Education and placed, naturally enough, in the Vocational Division. The Office in 1955 consolidated this service with others which had served the Division of Higher Education and State and Local School Systems to form a Guidance and Student Personnel Section. In spite of nomenclature, however, the impetus for the expansion of guidance services has come from concern for the individual. His opportunities to exercise choice in schools making provision for individual differences, within a social and technological framework that makes wise decisions increasingly difficult, have created the demand for guidance programs.

GUIDANCE RATHER THAN COMPULSION

A tradition-governed society has little need for guidance; an authoritarian society, while it may need elaborate apparatus for the progressive selection of youth for training and for channeling them into jobs to meet requirements of the society, also can function without guidance services. On the other hand, a system that recognizes the individual's right to choose must provide services to help youth see and understand more about themselves, their opportunities, and how to make use of their potentialities. Faith in freedom of choice in human activity as a wellspring of good for both society and the individual has been a key element in the philosophical beliefs of people in the United States. For freedom of choice to have meaning, choices must be intelligently grounded; such grounding calls for help in self-understanding, the understanding of the environment, and the techniques of decision-making.

Increasing Emphasis on Guidance

Self-evident as the need for guidance appears, it is surprising to find so much agreement upon its present importance. Persons who can agree on little else in the field of education unite in calling for expansion of guidance efforts. Conant in his "first report to interested citizens" made the provision of guidance his first recommendation.[1] When federal activity to improve education was stepped up through passage of the National Defense Education Act of 1958, Title V of the Act was devoted to guidance. This has had the effect of associating guidance programs with instruction in foreign languages, mathematics, and science, as well as with the discovery of academically talented students, all areas where crash efforts are needed during the present, apparently indefinitely continuing period of national emergency.

The Rockefeller report[2] emphasized guidance services as one way to move toward excellence in secondary education. A state-wide study in Illinois in 1958 disclosed that principals, teachers, and students felt sure that boards of education, the public, and teaching staffs were prepared to support the expansion of guidance programs.[3] Principals were more optimistic in this respect than teachers and counselors.

[1] James Bryant Conant, *The American High School Today,* New York (McGraw-Hill), 1959, pp. 44-46.

[2] Devereux C. Josephs and others, *The Pursuit of Excellence: Education and the Future of America,* Garden City, N.Y. (Doubleday), 1958.

[3] *Counseling Services in the Secondary Schools of Illinois,* Urbana (Allerton House Conference on Education, Univ. of Illinois), 1958, p. 21.

The student of guidance quickly learns that though apparent agreement upon the necessity of guidance programs exists, the impact of such unanimity is limited. There are diverse opinions on the purposes of guidance activities and sharp disagreements as to the priorities that should be assigned to various phases of guidance. While the disagreements are of much importance to schools, extending as they do throughout various groups from the public through the ranks of school guidance workers, the increasing emphasis on guidance rests upon consensus derived from conclusions of social analysis that are hardly disputed. Parents and educators are agreed that students are confronted with a widening range of choices. At the same time, the nation is confronted by persistent and continuing shortages of trained manpower, the necessity of conserving mental resources, and the challenge of totalitarian systems. Guidance at its best can serve both the individual and his society despite disagreement on details.

Widening ranges of choices. One result of man's increasing control over his material environment has been the expansion of his opportunities to exercise choice. In the United States increased ability to manage the material environment has coincided with the development of individual social and political freedom.

As advances in material production have occurred, more and more youth have been able to continue their formal schooling for longer periods of time. At the same time, changes in educational theory have given increasing numbers of students the opportunity of deciding what to study in high school. Beyond high school are other choices—college or trade school, industry, or government-sponsored technical training such as that offered by branches of the military services. If college is decided upon, still other choices present themselves—large university or small college, urban or rural, public or private, denominational or nonsectarian, coeducational or not.

Occupational choices are constantly enlarging as new specialties and new fields within specialties open up. These options are accompanied by related ones as to place of employment or pre-entry training and the merits of one possible employer as opposed to another.

As the average age of marriage has moved downward, the average length of the educational period has increased. Young men and women are now faced with many important personal decisions at an earlier age than a generation ago. These choices complicate, and are complicated by, educational and vocational decisions. Greater opportunities for women, not only before marriage but also while or after carrying out responsibilities for homemaking and child-rearing, have opened up choices with which other generations were not concerned. Increasingly, new areas of choice are opening to minority groups who, for a variety of reasons, find that their opportunities are no longer so restricted as formerly.[4] The effect of these and other changes has been to present youth with situations marked by a necessity for choice and adjustment in an environment that never completely stabilizes.

Manpower shortage. Decisions cannot be made without reference to social responsibility. One of the social and moral characteristics of human beings is to seek rewarding outlets for their innate and developed capacities. While many astute observers feel that the rewards and incentives in American social and economic life tend to direct individual efforts into activities that would receive little attention in a culture with a truer, or clearer, system of values, responsible youth do not ignore the defined needs of their society. Figure 12-1 shows the change in numbers of jobs at various levels of complexity and skill as projected for 1970 in contrast with 1957. These anticipated shifts have various implications for guidance. They clearly indicate the expansion of needs for the highest levels of training and competence, the biggest growth being anticipated for professional workers. The need for skilled workers will continue to grow, while laborers will show no increase, and the numbers of farm laborers will continue to decline. Within the broad categories growing needs will increase. The need for health workers, teachers, and engineers is going to be greater than the supply, and among skilled workers, tool and die makers will present a similar problem.[5]

One of the older concerns of guidance programs is "realism" of vocational choice. Guidance experts know that families and the associates of young people sometimes encourage them to aspire to careers beyond their educational capacities. While this kind of unrealism remains a problem, schools are belatedly becoming concerned about students who are "unrealistic" in the other direction, those who fail to aspire to the kinds of work that would make best use of their abilities. A study of a carefully selected random sample of 508 high school graduates of the classes of 1954 and 1955 in Baltimore, Maryland, revealed that 37 per cent of the seniors were "undershooting" in voca-

[4] Robert Kiehl, "Opportunities for Negroes in Engineering," *Personnel and Guidance Journal*, November 1958, pp. 219-22.

[5] "Worldwide Shortage of Skilled Men," *Time*, July 18, 1960, p. 72.

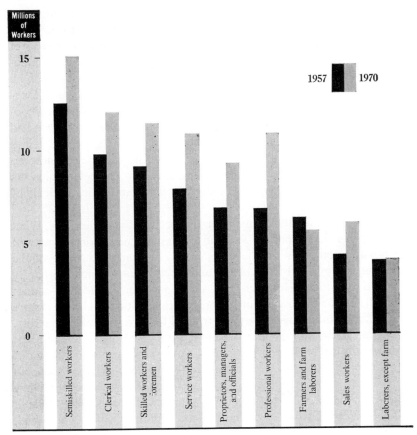

Fig. 12–1. *Employment in Major Occupational Groups, 1957, and Projected, 1970*

tional preference.[6] Only 5 per cent were attempting goals beyond their abilities as far as these can be predicted from student records. This study concluded that realistic vocational choice is an individual rather than a group phenomenon. Early attention to the individual is essential to the manpower requirements of a dynamic technology.

Necessity of conserving mental resources. Human resources are more nearly analogous to the water power provided by harnessing a flowing stream than to such resources as mineral deposits. They are incapable of being stored; they must be developed and released or they

[6] William V. Lockwood, "Realism of Vocational Preference," *Personnel and Guidance Journal,* October 1958, p. 105.

are wasted to the individual and his society. This is true at all talent levels; consequently, essential as it is to locate and develop the most gifted individuals, the cumulative effect of the neglect or misuse of abilities of average or below-average youth is also serious. A three-pronged challenge faces society: the future must be provided for by finding and educating tomorrow's creative leadership today; the changing shape of society must be met by developing the skills and competencies required to increase productivity and provide new services; and there must be found useful and satisfying roles for the people whose traditional function has been to supply the human power now so rapidly being replaced by mechanization. Many competent analysts consider the last as important as the first two, and more difficult of accomplishment.

No one can guarantee any man the security of tomorrow. What guidance can do is lead the student to prepare today for as many of the possible tomorrows as he can. Society is changing. Many of the jobs that millions will work at ten and twenty years hence are hardly dreamed of today. However, this does not mean guidance cannot point the student toward fruitful preparation. No time in the future will a trained mind, that is, a mind trained to train itself, be a liability. There can be no mistake in counseling youth to be ready with the best within them for whatever comes. Our society has problems. Some of its members by force of circumstance and injustice work at jobs beneath their worth, at least as many more do unworthy work because they were prepared to do no other. The ideal is simple in statement, difficult in application. If youth is guided to acquire human values youth will, by a multitude of individual choices, end up creating a human society.

Challenge of totalitarian systems. It has long been a truism that Western civilization is engaged in a lasting and serious rivalry with other cultures, particularly with those based upon Communist ideology. As a New York City school administrator has observed:

> If the United States had the manpower resources of the Soviet Union and its satellites (more than ten times that of the U.S.), this would still be a problem, but not nearly so serious. As it is, this country at present cannot afford the luxury of losing the services of its gifted manpower not now identified, motivated, or educated.[7]

Carrying responsibilities for its own citizens and for leadership of a way of life, the United States cannot afford waste and frustration of

[7] Morris Krugman, "Identification and Preservation of Talent," *Teachers College Record,* May 1960, p. 460.

youth on any ability level. To be sure many of the things that need to be done to keep the channels open for all youth to put their capacities for accomplishment and self-development to use are beyond the power of schools, but, nevertheless, school guidance departments have an important responsibility. When the National Defense Education Act provided support for fifty guidance workers for New York City, twenty of them were assigned to academic high schools. It was not without reason that thirteen of these schools, given the opportunity to assign these workers as they saw fit, chose to use them in work with underachievers.[8] There has been growing recognition that adolescents and their parents unaided cannot make the choices necessary in face of the complexities and stresses of modern times.

Where Choices Exist, Guidance Is Needed

From the beginning there has been in the United States an insistence on the individual's right to work out his own destiny. In the earliest days of the republic European visitors often commented with surprise on the tendency to extend freedom of choice to children and youth. Today's criticism of paternalism in government and business is based principally, not upon the autocracy of our institutions, but upon the tendency of some individuals to select the security of overorganized and overinstitutionalized positions rather than more independent ways of earning a living.[9]

Decline of paternalism: at home and in school. Whatever may be the situation in adult life—and it is being debated vigorously from many points of view—the position of secondary school youth has been increasingly less subjected to paternalistic direction from the home and the school. In the home that still exists in the memories of many adults it was possible for parents to teach many of the skills and functional roles needed by the children. As home duties have diminished and specialization and concentration have taken economic functions to locations remote from the home, relationships have changed. With the changes parents have lost the opportunity, the inclination, and the confidence for immediate direction of the lives of youth. Experienced teachers, counselors, and principals are quite aware of the large numbers of parents who are conscious of the lack of aims in the lives of their sons and daughters. Some of them are aware of the diffi-

---

[8] *Ibid.*, p. 461.

[9] See, for example, Alan Harrington, *Life in the Crystal Palace*, New York (Knopf), 1959.

culty of forming such goals and making the instrumental decisions. Most parents seem to feel as much uncertainty at this prospect as do their children.

The school has become as reluctant as parents to undertake the kindly ordering of the lives of its pupils. The complexity and kaleidoscopic alterations in the situations that impinge upon the lives of the young lead educators to hesitate. Many teachers simply observe that "a student has a right to make his own mistakes." Neither parents, teachers, nor pupils have confidence in the wisdom of adults to show students the way into the future, however unquestioned their sincere interest may be.

Elective system. Before guidance programs were formalized both colleges and high schools had firmly established elective systems. Competition for college admission, as well as public concern growing out of the threat of Soviet might and scientific progress, has brought some sharp looks at high school offerings. Some schools have reduced the number of elective courses. The broad spectrum of abilities in a comprehensive high school and the specialized requirements of modern society, however, require a curriculum composed to a large extent of differentiated elective courses. A typical large suburban high school offers more than 200 different semester courses, only about one-tenth of which are required of every student.[10] In this school a student who wishes to meet a college entrance requirement of two units of foreign language has a choice among six different languages. In smaller schools the problem of selecting elective courses is different in degree rather than in kind.

New career opportunities. A striking aspect of the rapid changes taking place is the large numbers of new careers being created. In 1956 white-collar exceeded blue-collar workers in the United States for the first time. With this shift has come a change in the nature of white-collar occupations, even at the highest levels. Individuals working independently are in less demand; the trained individual playing a specialized part on a team becomes more predominant each year.

New electronic inventions are rapidly revolutionizing office work, both as to kinds of skills required and the way they are performed. The elaborate new equipment is expensive and calls for consolidation. This encourages small concerns to farm out work on a fee basis and indirectly encourages larger enterprises.

[10] *Teachers Handbook,* Cicero, Ill. (J. Sterling Morton High School and Junior College), 1960.

Some fields are growing much more rapidly than others. Chemistry, for example, maintains a higher growth rate than the average industrial operation. New fields, such as rocket-fuel chemistry and chemurgy, add new opportunities. Physics also is producing new fields. Solid-state physics and physics as applied to medicine are examples of fields that have grown out of space research and the study of radioactivity.

Changes such as these have the cumulative effect of adding more and different career areas, but at the same time they may lead to the disappearance of some occupations. While many of the jobs that become obsolete are at the lower end of the scale of skills, more and more of the highly skilled and even professional specialties are becoming out of date. Armour and Company in 1960 began spending $500,000 to find out what happened to employees in the meat-packing industry who had been thrown out of work by automation.[11] The company's announcement followed the closing of its sixth plant in a period of a little more than a year.

Multitudes of choices, decline of paternalistic direction, the elective system in schools and colleges, the rise of new careers and the obsolescence of old constantly add to the need for guidance for secondary-school youth.

Types of Student Choices for Which Guidance Is Provided

While the need for guidance has expanded, a rough consensus has gradually developed concerning the kinds of choices for which schools can and should provide assistance. Areas of choice can be roughly centered about educational plans, career decisions, and personal adjustment.

Educational plans. While it is basic to the philosophy of guidance that the concerns of educational planning occur in a complex of personal, vocational, and other considerations, there are many problems that are primarily related to continuing education. A representative list includes: securing information about the school and its opportunities; selecting a curriculum or particular courses; making the goal decisions at the appropriate time as they affect education; selecting a college or other post-high school training institution; considering financial problems and opportunities related to education—including part-time and summer employment, building interest, study skills, and habits; and entering into extracurricular experiences. An important

[11] "Study Loss of Jobs by Meat Packers," Chicago *Daily News,* July 19, 1960, p. 31.

element of the choice situation is getting the student to confront his choices on a conscious level.

Career decisions. The effective choices a student must make concerning careers involve choosing an occupation, preparing for entry into it, securing a first job, and progressing in it. For more and more career fields part of these decisions must be deferred until several years after completing high school, but the base for these decisions must be laid in the high school and earlier. Choices made at the high school age nearly always have to be regarded as tentative, but they should gradually become both more specific and more nearly final. This process is filled with pitfalls. David Riesman has called attention to one of the major hazards:

> One danger in such a setting is that a young person will decide too soon what he is good at, and often he will decide in favor of what he is rewarded for doing. He will then be encouraged to concentrate on what have become defined as his strengths, which are also the strengths of the school in its competition for places in college and in the life of the eminent after college. . . . Before a young person has had a chance to explore his potentialities to the full, they captivate him by furnishing him with a premature but clear and visible image of his place in the intellectual or athletic firmament, and then rewarding him for fitting into that place.[12]

What is excellence in high school may be mediocrity in college and inadequacy in some of the "prestige" career fields. The remoteness of the attainment of professional competence makes the student's choices difficult and career guidance complicated, even when the student's fulfillment is kept foremost.

Personal adaptations to environment. It has become customary to consider personal adjustment as a phase of educational and vocational adjustment. People are often faced with personal problems; some of these have particular intensity or distinctive characteristics during adolescence. Some of the personal adjustments of particular importance during junior high and high school years deal with home and the family, physical health and development, emotional balance, finances, general social relationships, sex and courtship, and development of ideals and values. The fact that the framework and foundation in these areas of personal development are ordinarily laid earlier does not pre-

[12] David Riesman, "Education and Exploitation," *School Review,* Spring 1960, pp. 30-31.

vent the secondary school years from being a period of stress during which these adjustments are of crucial importance.

During adolescent years a person begins to understand himself and what is required of him, to recognize normal and rewarding behavior in problem situations, and to evaluate his experiences and previous decisions in order to shape his future behavior. Under careful, tactful guidance, the student can use his expanding perceptions of the human and physical factors of environment to help in making decisions about his future.

THE GUIDANCE PROGRAM IN SECONDARY SCHOOLS

It has become customary to consider personnel services in schools as encompassing *guidance, counseling,* and *therapy.* These terms carry obvious shades of meaning in terms of depth and intensity of activity and the qualifications of the personnel accepting responsibility for the activities. There continues a custom (followed in this book) of also using "guidance" as an inclusive term embracing the study of student personnel, informational services, group activities directed toward understanding oneself and the choices available, placement and follow-up, counseling, and therapy. Even the most richly provided school is, at present, unable to offer all of these services to the extent that would be ideal: to make available to each student the maximum resources for developing his capacity for wise choices.

Study of Student Personnel

The collection and evaluation of information about individuals and the groups of which they are members provide the foundation of the guidance program. To gather essential information, provision must be made for testing abilities, aptitudes, and achievements, obtaining records of previous schooling and recording pertinent data as they become available, organizing information pertaining to educational, vocational, and personal opportunities, carrying out case studies, and making follow-up studies of individuals and groups.

Testing. Testing in the modern sense dates from World War I when it obtained impetus from the need to classify great numbers of soldier-trainees. The movement built on pioneer work by E. L. Thorndike, Alfred Binet, and others. Then, as now, psychologists were interested in sampling a person's present ability in order to arrive at a dependable prediction of his future performance. One of the principal references on tests and testing is a book of huge proportions.[13] New testing instruments are constantly being developed and validated. The use of standardized tests increased from 1955 to 1959 by more than 10 million per year, until in 1959 more than 147 million tests were given to students at all levels.[14] By 1959 the American Association of School Administrators adopted a resolution approving tests but warned of their misuse as a "glaring danger to good educational programs."[15]

Six major purposes of tests are listed by one specialist.[16] They may be used to identify pupils with superior talents or low ability and to find the particular types of abilities each pupil possesses. Tests are useful for classification, grouping, and assignment of pupils. They are helpful in selection of students for college and for particular positions. They are useful in evaluating instruction and progress. Tests are used to supply basic data for planning, and they assist students in making adjustments. While the last two are more directly connected with other guidance services, all have their ramifications in the guidance program. The administration and interpretation of tests is a function of the school's guidance organization. Test results must be interpreted in various ways to parents, teachers, and school administrators as well as to pupils.

Provision of organized records. Cumulative records for use of faculty, counselors, and the student himself are essential to good education and sound guidance. The individual record reveals the rate and direction of the student's development—intellectual, physical, social, and moral. It provides a basis for appraisal of the progress of the individual and the effectiveness of the school. It records the school's efforts, successful and unsuccessful, to discover and develop the pupil's potentialities. The cumulative record preserves a comprehensive picture of a student's growth and is available to all those concerned. Availability is essential to utility; therefore the school's goal will be to increase the use of pertinent data while reserving to the few who need it all confidential material. Some information used only by the student and his counselor may well be separately maintained by the counselor. All records must, of course, be handled under professional conditions with respect for the student's privacy.

[13] Oscar K. Buros (ed.), *The Fifth Mental Measurements Yearbook,* Highland Park, N.J. (Gryphone Press), 1959.

[14] Arthur E. Traxler, "Educational Measurement: An Aid to School Administration," *School Review,* Summer 1960, pp. 196-209.

[15] *School Life,* September 1959, p. 5.

[16] Dolph Camp, "Uses of Tests," *School Life,* September 1959, pp. 14-15.

The student's record should show his educational, vocational, and personal interests as well as the salient features of his attempts to explore, refine, and develop them.

Good schools usually record autobiographical information, health history, test records, school marks, anecdotal information as collected from observations over the years, participation in cocurricular activities, work experience, and any other material that contributes to the understanding of the individual.

Conducting case studies. One often-neglected activity is intensive study of students who have behavior problems: who show symptoms of undermotivation or underachievement; who exhibit symptoms of tension, fatigue, or inability to participate; or who show insufficient accomplishment or progress toward worthwhile life goals. This is unfortunate, for common-sense experience and objective study confirm the judgment that well-planned individual analysis is usually profitable. Even when the information developed leads to no conclusions for action, the very expression of interest involved in the study of a particular person carries an assurance of his importance as a person that usually affects him favorably.

The process by which a person becomes a "case" for study is not dehumanizing; rather, it suggests a laboratory approach in which all resources are brought to bear objectively upon problems that intensely need solution.

Case conferences, at which those persons with the most information about an individual and those most strategically placed to help him meet to pool information and plan action, are much underused in high schools. No doubt this is because they are time-consuming and difficult to schedule. There are perhaps three chief reasons for recommending their more frequent use. By bringing together those with information and those in a position to act on that information, it becomes possible for each individual to be more effective by acting in concert with others. By avoiding many intermittent planning sessions between individuals or among a few of those concerned, time may actually be saved. The case conference can be a learning experience for all those participating, helping them in understanding not only the case under consideration but other cases as well.

Case studies and case conferences ordinarily include a counselor, the teachers of a student, and the principal or other person who makes administrative decisions regarding the pupil. In many instances they include also the parents and such persons as the school nurse or physician and, perhaps, a consulting psychologist or psychiatrist.

Follow-up of choices. Essential to the progressive improvement of guidance and other school services is a systematic follow-up of students after they leave school. In their follow-up the guidance workers concentrate upon the choices made by students. Has the school provided sufficient background for the choices the student had to make? Has the student had enough training in the technique of making choices? What satisfactory and unsatisfactory choices have students made? Have the assumptions the school, the parents, and the students have made about the nature of future problems and opportunities been correct? The reasons for follow-up are self-appraisal, self-criticism, self-judgment, and self-improvement. It is an extremely important part of the school's effort to evaluate and direct itself.

Individual Counseling

The term *counseling* is generally used to identify a face-to-face relationship between two individuals in which participation is mutual but the focus is upon self-clarification and self-decision by the counselee, or student. This aspect of guidance, however, has been fluid from its beginning and can be expected to continue to change as research brings new understanding of the individual and new theories to be tested. A newer term, "multiple counseling," is used to indicate a closeness of purpose to individual counseling and to distinguish it from group guidance or routine informational services.[17]

Objectives. There is more agreement about the goals of counseling than upon procedures, techniques, and training needed by counselors. In schools the chief objectives are to help students assemble pertinent data to aid in choices, to help students study themselves, and to guide them in interpreting facts and situations. The personal interview is the principal method used to attain these ends. The best experience more and more tends to indicate the need for versatile counseling techniques and arrangements: "In the school system, the link between the parents, teachers, and students is the counselor. Effective student behavior in the area of human relations may depend on an increased number of counselor arranged student-parent-teacher conferences."[18]

[17] E. Wayne Wright, "Multiple Counseling: Why? When? How?" *Personnel and Guidance Journal,* April 1959, pp. 551-57.
[18] William J. Mueller and J. W. M. Rothney, "Comparisons of Selected Descriptive and Predictive Statements of Superior Students, Their Parents, and Their Teachers," *Personnel and Guidance Journal,* April 1960, p. 625.

The counseling relationship is often founded upon the counselor's helpfulness in assembling information or suggesting informational sources to the student. He is expected to be well versed in occupational fields, educational and training opportunities, scholarships and financial aid, and the like. He is also expected to have information at hand about boy-girl relationships, family adjustments, teacher-student difficulties, school social organizations, and community problems. Students expect him to supply objective information or to direct them to informational sources in an objective manner. By such work with students the counselor makes it easier for the student to enlist the counselor's help in gaining better understanding of himself.

"Know thyself" is a major commandment of education at all levels. A well-trained counselor is in a key position to help in this phase of education. He can review with the student the student's school record, and his aptitude, achievement, interest, and personality tests. He can supply normative information to help the student put this knowledge about himself in perspective, and he can serve as a sounding board and adult confidant as the student grapples with his maturing self-knowledge. These activities help the student through valid factual information and sound self-understanding to arrive at reasonable decisions and make adequate choices.

Staff. The growing recognition of the importance of guidance, coming at a time of scarcity of all educational workers, has resulted in a situation where adequately trained guidance workers have been far too few to meet the need in schools. A goal of one full-time counselor for every 300-500 students, a ratio semi-officially promoted by the United States Office of Education and state departments of education, has been difficult of attainment. A more desirable standard is considered to be one full-time counselor for every 200-300 students. Even then it would be difficult for the counselor to know all his students well.

When the National Defense Education Act was passed in 1958, the ratio of counselors to high school students for the nation as a whole was only 1 to 750 and more than half of these were in only seven states.[19] The shortage of counselors was estimated at 15,000. While the special inducements of the Act brought some immediate results, growing enrollments reduced their effect.

The importance of good relationships among counselors and teachers have led many schools to restrict counselor appointments to staff

[19] "Guidance, Counseling, and Testing," *School Life,* October-November 1958, p. 15.

members who have already established cooperative relationships on the school's faculty. Such a practice has an obvious effect on the rapidity with which guidance staffs can be increased.

Some schools have formulated a policy requiring counselors to teach also. Teacher-counselors may have only one period free from teaching for guidance work; they may divide their time equally between the two kinds of work or spend only a token amount of time in the classroom. Many of the schools that pioneered in counseling have clung to teaching responsibilities for counselors out of a conviction that this practice contributes to teamwork and mutual understanding on the staff. While the advantages of requiring teaching experience in the school are obvious, it may help to explain why an Illinois study found that only about one in four persons assigned to counseling had even minimum training.[20] It may have contributed to the situation in Ohio where a study found that only 6 per cent of the schools were providing as desirable a ratio as one full-time counselor to 500 pupils.[21]

As the counseling field becomes both better defined and better established, career counselors with well-defined preparation requirements will become a much bigger part of the picture. Classroom teaching experience may or may not become an essential part of the training. Practice in those states which have preparation standards, either required or recommended, as well as university training programs, now differ on this point.[22] There can be no doubt that the work of the counselor necessitates rigorous standards of training and personal qualifications. Some of the knowledge and personality characteristics are quite distinct from those needed for working with groups in a classroom.

Director of guidance. Large schools need to provide for the planning and coordination of pupil personnel services as for any other major service to students. The provision of a well-trained guidance worker to head these efforts does much to foster the program. A small school may place these functions in the hands of its only teacher-counselor, but provision for planned communication and improvement and evaluation of services is essential.

It has been found to be good practice in schools of all sizes to

[20] *Counseling Services in the Secondary Schools of Illinois,* p. 22.

[21] Gail F. Farwell and Anne M. Vekich, "Status and Certification of Counselors in Ohio High Schools," *Personnel and Guidance Journal,* December 1959, p. 289.

[22] *Guidance Workers Certification Requirements,* Washington, D.C. (U.S. Government Printing Office), 1960.

establish a guidance committee to ensure liaison among teachers, counselors, school administrators, parents, and pupils. Parents, and sometimes pupils, have been successfully included on such committees.

Group Guidance

There are high school situations in which a guidance worker meets with a group of students to provide guidance services. "Group guidance" is a term for designating these activities. Group procedures are often used for such things as orienting a student to a new school or the guidance services themselves, testing and general interpretation of test results, presenting educational and occupational information, and discussing common problems of the group. Such activities are efficient in the use of time and make it possible for a student to have more frequent contact with guidance workers. It provides opportunity for group discussion which has been shown to provide favorable conditions for changing attitudes and behavior. It can open questions for later consideration in counseling interviews.

There has been an unfortunate tendency of guidance workers and teachers to depreciate group guidance by comparing it with the one-to-one relationship of counseling and by equating it with the many semiclerical and semiadministrative activities that must be done in groups to ensure the smooth functioning of a school. Simply collecting data on each student should not be construed to be guidance. The collection is routine and should be kept to a minimum in sessions that are devoted to guidance.

The many situations for group guidance include home rooms, student activities, assemblies, and the occasional opportunities of formal courses. In many schools the most important of these is the home room. The Association for Supervision and Curriculum Development, in attempting to describe high schools adequate to today's needs, included a home base group in which a student has a continuing relationship as one important characteristic of the adequate school.[23]

Such an organization requires the participation of most teachers in the school and provides an opportunity for many distinct contributions to the guidance program. A valuable attribute is the probability of students' continuing discussion, beginning in the home room, with informal groups of their peers. This provides for wider dissemination of learnings and their reinforcement.

[23] Kimball Wiles and Franklin Patterson, *The High School We Need,* Washington, D.C. (Association for Supervision and Curriculum Development, National Education Association), 1959, p. 13.

RELATIONSHIP OF GUIDANCE TO INSTRUCTION

Both the teacher and the guidance worker seek to help the student develop himself as a person. Both draw upon the same resources of knowledge about people and the learning process. It is inevitable and desirable that there be overlapping of procedures and services and that teacher and guidance worker accept common obligations. At the same time, growing knowledge and increasing complexity and specialization require differentiated functions for the teacher and the guidance specialist.

Overlapping Procedures and Services

The teacher is primarily concerned with promoting learning, while the purpose toward which that learning is aimed involves guidance. The counselor is interested in helping the student formulate his goals, understand himself, and make wise choices. The teacher is interested in having the student gain specific knowledge that will make the desired goal a reality.

Teaching accepts the guidance point of view. Teachers cannot overlook the needs, problems, and interests of pupils who make up their classes. Good teaching aims to strengthen self-confidence, reduce frustration, and add meaning to the student's environment and his understanding of himself. The individual learns with his whole organism; he cannot be one pupil in algebra, another in English, and yet a third in the science laboratory, although the degree of capacity and interest he displays may differ in each of these studies. What the learner does rather than what the teacher does is the meaningful part of the learning situation.

Guidance relies upon the learning process. The student's benefiting from the guidance program is as dependent upon the principles of learning as is his development in the classroom. Students are sometimes disappointed when counselors display no new magic; teachers, too, sometimes expect too much of counselors to whom they make referrals. The student's capacity for learning is largely inherited and is as subject to his earlier experiences when he works with a counselor as when he works with a teacher. The counselor is therefore forced to depend upon his ability to establish with the student opportunities and conditions favorable to learning. The opportunities and conditions for learning may be different, but they are parallel to those toward which the teacher must work. Motivation is essential to learning in both sets of circumstances.

Everyone is familiar with the frequency with which teachers, parents, and others say, in regard to the problems of a student, "He needs guidance." Only those intimately involved in a school situation know how frequently the counselor says, "If only there were some positive element with which to work." Freely translated this means, "If only some teacher were interested in this youngster, or had his interest and a firmly established, sympathetic relationship."

Common Obligations of Guidance and Instruction

Both counselors and teachers study youth, and by the same methods. Both establish counseling relationships with individual pupils, although there is an unfortunate tendency in guidance literature to hold that counseling is something that occurs with a guidance specialist rather than an activity characterized by the nature of the process. Both guidance and instruction promote self-evaluation and self-direction.

Studying youth. Teacher and guidance worker study individuals through both formal and informal methods. They have the opportunity to exchange the fruits of their study for mutual help in the pupil's development. Information the teacher collects is likely to be more direct and informal by the nature of his contacts. The counselor's information may be more scientific, and at the same time more detached, except in those cases where frequent interviewing permits closer relationships.

The teacher sees the student in many situations. He sees examples of accomplishment or lack of it. He sees the young person interact with his age-mates. He has the opportunity to learn the pupil's interests and hobbies.

Frequently the teacher is able to translate the information in the cumulative record into more meaningful terms by the daily opportunity he has to observe and interact with the pupil. For this reason the teachers who have worked with a pupil are valuable sources of information for the counselor.

Counseling individuals. Teachers must recognize the limitations of their ability to work with personality disorders—as indeed must counselors. Nevertheless, the teacher has many opportunities to offer assistance in self-understanding and control of and adjustment to the environment. Teachers who meet 125 to 150 or more students daily cannot expect to counsel all of them effectively. However, they meet their classes 180 or more times a year in many schools and can establish productive individual relationships with numbers of their pupils.

These relationships may center around some aspect of the curriculum, but they need not stop there. In the study of counseling in Illinois schools previously referred to, 1,200 students were asked to whom on their school staff would they turn for help with a problem. Two hundred seventy-four said the teacher of a particular subject, 212 said the home-room teacher; and 181, a counselor.[24] Even remembering the low level of counselor training shown by this study, these figures are significant.

Promoting self-direction and self-evaluation. The teacher's position to help the student evaluate himself and his progress is so strategic as to need little amplification. This is a place where counselor-teacher planning and cooperation can accomplish a great deal. The teacher who is most successful with a particular student may not be sensitive to his lack of progress in other areas even though he is so well placed as to help him take stock and correct any such lack. Here a common approach to a common obligation can bring faster and more lasting progress for the pupil.

PROBLEMS CONFRONTING GUIDANCE PROGRAMS

There are a number of problems peculiar to guidance programs that seem likely to persist in modified form; there are also new problems growing out of changes in high schools and the society they serve.

Guidance and Discipline

One of the perennial problems has been the relationship between guidance and discipline. By their nature guidance programs have a permissiveness not characteristic of schools in general. The desire by guidance personnel to remove barriers inhibiting pupils has made it imperative to separate the guidance function from the school apparatus for dealing with symptoms of poor adjustment, such as tardiness, truancy, resistance to authority, or conflict with classmates.

The disciplinary organization is usually quite willing to understand and sympathize but unwilling to make exceptions to the orderly rules necessary for group activity. The guidance organization recognizes the student's necessity for meeting the school's conditions, but it sees these difficulties as manifestations of deeper problems. The different approaches lead to conflict or uneasy compromises within

[24] *Counseling Services in the Secondary Schools of Illinois,* p. 44.

the school's professional staff. They place an additional burden on the guidance personnel to resolve any apparent inconsistency in the institutional situation for a student who may be harmed by it.

This is only an illustration of a gap likely to exist between an area of school concern predominantly focused on individuals and areas where group responsibilities and socially oriented responsibilities are the focus.

Synchronizing Contributions of Various Staff Members

Teamwork within the school is important in all areas. In the guidance program it is particularly vital, and the nature of guidance makes contributions difficult to mesh. One of the reasons for this is the way in which most valuable contributions to guidance are likely to come from the individual personalities of staff members. Effective guidance is made up of scientific knowledge and objectivity combined with human warmth and understanding in unusual ways. In organization this calls for careful planning and step-by-step procedures which, however, must leave plenty of freedom for students and staff members to individualize their own needs and abilities.

Providing Adequate Personnel

There is hardly a school that can claim its guidance program has been adequately staffed to carry the interview load essential to the accomplishment of guidance goals. Some of the reasons for this have already been reviewed. There are two additional reasons why there will be a continued shortage of counselors. The first of these is principally material. The individual and small-group activities of the guidance program are costly. In a time of general financial pressure on school budgets, rapidly expanding enrollments, and broad-based efforts to improve the quality of secondary education, guidance is in sharp competition with other demands on the budget dollar. Studies continue to demonstrate that both the public and school personnel strongly support guidance expansion, but repeated efforts have failed to bring forward concrete evidence of contributions of guidance to the lives of students.

The second factor which makes it difficult to find personnel for the guidance staff is the real shortage of people with the qualifications for such delicate and complex work. This is partly, but not entirely, a lack of trained personnel. The major efforts, begun in 1958, to make better provision and offer special inducements for training must struggle against the shortage of people able to complete and utilize such training. Added to this shortage is not only the competition for able people from the expanding personnel services in colleges, government, and industry but also competition from closely related personnel fields which require similar kinds of qualifications and sometimes provide greater tangible rewards.

The profuse literature of guidance indicates both directly and indirectly how far schools are from the quality of staffs needed. One of the strong indirect indicators is the complaint about clerical and administrative details that runs like a refrain through the writings of guidance workers. This may indicate a lack of understanding by administrators, as is often charged, but it also indicates a tendency of partly trained people to find refuge in routine rather than cope with the difficult and personally threatening challenges of the face-to-face interview.

Keeping Informational Resources Current

The swift changes in the educational and employment scene pose serious difficulties for the guidance program, making many materials obsolete before they are off the press and confronting guidance workers with tasks that would defeat encyclopedia editors. In this situation even the use of all faculty resources and the help of the school library and community resources of all kinds can hardly suffice to meet the student's needs for information.

The only reasonably adequate solution will require guidance workers to be skilled in the librarian's techniques of locating and screening materials and skilled in mobilizing all the human resources for information within the school and the community.

Adapting to Newer Organizational Arrangements

The changes in school organization, so evident in secondary schools, must, of course, have their effect on guidance programs. As a matter of fact, improved student guidance is prominent among the reasons given for the newer arrangements.

Schools within schools. One of the earliest attempts to break a large school into smaller units to serve guidance purposes was at Evanston Township High School, Evanston, Illinois, where huge study hall-home rooms had long been used. By 1959 this school had been reorganized into four divisions or smaller schools within the school. Each division has about 900 pupils, headed by a division principal, contains four home rooms each with a division assistant, and has a group of counselors responsible for the administrative and guidance programs.

The West unit of Maine Township High School in Des Plaines, Illinois, was designed especially to house a small-school organization based on the closely related principles of greater intimacy between pupils and teachers and better opportunities for guidance. It opened in 1959 with facilities for an eventual 3,000 pupils.

These are typical of pioneering efforts to integrate guidance into newer and more functional organizational arrangements.

Guidance as part of instructional teams. While much of the first experimentation with teaching teams in elementary schools was based on more effective use of different levels of professional training and proficiency, the first teaching teams in high schools were more concerned with integrating guidance with instruction.

For example, J. Lloyd Trump has recommended that schools "employ one staff specialist in pupil personnel services for each five teachers, the specialists working part of the time as members of teaching teams."[25]

In a high school opened in Wayland, Massachusetts, in 1960, the learning program is organized around teaching teams with pupils grouped in learning centers. As a part of this approach, approximately twenty students are assigned as advisees to each team member. This adviser takes charge not only of many traditional guidance functions, but also new functions of guiding and coordinating the day-to-day learning experiences.[26]

Grouping. Emphasis upon quality education with differentiation for all kinds of students has revitalized the study of grouping. Guidance programs must be expected to provide leadership for developing new kinds of grouping, for improving grouping practices, for evaluating grouping methods, and for emphasizing the importance of the individual in the group.

Guidance personnel will find many of their problems concerned with

---

[25] J. Lloyd Trump, *New Directions to Quality Education,* Washington, D.C. (National Association of Secondary School Principals), 1960, p. 12.

[26] Edward Anderson and John C. Harkness, "Planned Variability," *Nation's Schools,* April 1960, pp. 83-91.

helping students and teachers cope with group situations of all kinds.

Interpretation of the role of guidance. As the concepts of guidance continue to shift to meet conditions that change as understanding of young people improves, the definition and redefinition of the role of guidance will remain important. Guidance workers have sought to define their role from the beginning and continue to differ on this score.[27] The guidance movement has contained too much that smacks of cults and mysticism to satisfy many educators. Different theories, (e.g., trait-and-factor-centered, communications, self or nondirective, psychoanalytic, and neobehavioral), have confused teachers and administrators. Similarly, emphasis on a variety of goals and purposes, combined with overconcern for professional status by guidance specialists, have served to confuse rather than to clarify the role of guidance.

The controversy in the guidance field and the evident desire for improved methods may be expected to stimulate a great deal more research. Some of this, perhaps a greater proportion than in the past, may take place directly in the high schools. The nearly unanimous agreement on the value of guidance should lead to greater clarification of its role and constant improvement of its functioning.

SELECTED REFERENCES

BERNARD, JESSIE, ed. "Teen-age Culture." *Annals of the American Academy of Political and Social Science,* November 1961.

CALDWELL, EDSON. *Group Techniques for the Classroom Teacher.* Chicago: Science Research Associates, 1960.

DAMRIN, DORA E., AND PHILIP J. RUNKEL. *Practices and Attitudes Concerning Guidance and Counseling in Illinois High Schools in 1959.* Urbana: Bureau of Educational Research, Univ. of Illinois, 1960.

Guidance Workers Certification Requirements. Washington, D.C.: U.S. Government Printing Office, 1960.

HENRY, NELSON B., ed. *Personnel Services in Education: The Fifty-Eighth Yearbook of the National Society for the Study of Education.* Chicago: Univ. of Chicago Press, 1959. Part II.

JOHNSON, EDGAR G., AND OTHERS. *The Role of the Teacher in Guidance.* Englewood Cliffs, N.J.: Prentice-Hall, 1959.

[27] See, for example, Donald E. Walker and Herbert C. Peiffer, Jr., "The Goals of Counseling," *Journal of Counseling Psychology,* Fall 1957, pp. 204-209.

JOHNSON, MAURITZ, JR., WILLIAM E. BRSACKER, AND FRED Q. BOWMAN, JR. *Junior High School Guidance.* New York: Harper, 1961.

KRUG, EDWARD A., AND OTHERS. *The College-Preparatory Function in Wisconsin High Schools.* Madison: Univ. of Wisconsin, 1959.

MILLER, CARROLL, H. *Foundations of Guidance.* New York: Harper, 1961.

ROGERS, CARL R. "The Characteristics of a Helping Relationship." *Personnel and Guidance Journal,* September 1958.

STEWART, C. C: "A Bill of Rights for School Counselors." *Personnel and Guidance Journal,* March 1959.

Play rehearsal provides educational benefits to high school students.

High school club members explore architecture by building models of houses they have designed.

A state high school basketball tournament illustrates the most highly developed extracurricular activity of the secondary school—interscholastic athletics.

CHAPTER 13

Student Activities

STUDENT activities are unique to secondary education in the United States. No other country attaches to its program of schooling for youth of adolescent years such an array of informal educational, social, recreational, competitive, and entertainment functions. No other feature of junior and senior high school programs has attracted so much student and community attention, or stimulated such a wide range of opinion as to its worth.

That student activities are integral to the character of secondary education in this country, there can be no doubt. Depending upon how they are organized and managed in a given school, they can and do contribute to the basic goals of education and to individual student development in extremely wholesome ways. Their influence, under favorable conditions, on student morale and allegiance to the school is often extraordinary. Yet when programs of activities become overemphasized—detached from the basic goals of education—or when they are mismanaged, their effect upon educational functions of the school can be devastating.

NATURE OF STUDENT ACTIVITIES

What may fit the definition of student activity in one institution resembles a regular aspect of the formal curriculum in another. It is possible, however, to formulate a general definition of activities, to describe their typical characteristics, and to identify the types into which most student activities may be classified.

Definition

Student activities may be defined as programs or events that carry no, or only partial, academic credit and that are sponsored or formed by student organizations or by the school. They are designed primarily to entertain, to provide exercise of interest and ability, and to develop personal traits or talents other than intellectual qualities. In all cases they are subject to some measure of control by the school.[1]

The term "student activities" is more appropriate than others—such as extracurricular, cocurricular, or extraclass—since it permits a degree of inclusiveness that is necessary in the face of the variety of practice in secondary schools. In some institutions, for example, student activities carry no academic credit, are conducted outside the regular daily class schedule, and are not supported by the school budget. In others, certain functions, e.g., journalism, debate, orchestra, and chorus, carry partial academic credit toward graduation, are scheduled as regular high school courses, must be taught by fully certified teachers, and are supported by school funds. Quite clearly, some student activities have already become curricular; consequently, the term "extracurricular" is inadequate to designate them. Some educators predict that the distinction between curricular and non-curricular, the rigid class schedule of the high school, and even the Carnegie unit system of measuring progress, are all due for further modification.[2] It becomes necessary, therefore, to employ a term with a connotation sufficiently broad to include all activities, even though their organization, administration, and relationship to the basic program of the school varies and changes from school to school and over periods of time.

Characteristics of Student Activities

The primary characteristic of student activities is the emphasis placed upon pupil functions, either formal or informal, which high-

[1] Carter V. Good, *Dictionary of Education*, New York (McGraw-Hill), 1960.

[2] Alexander Stoddard, *Schools for Tomorrow: An Educator's Blueprint*, New York (Fund for the Advancement of Education), 1957; and J. Lloyd Trump, *New Horizons for Secondary School Teachers*, Washington, D.C. (National Association of Secondary School Principals), 1959.

light each activity. These may be designed to entertain, to develop physical, social, or aesthetic talents, or to promote leadership abilities. Participation by students is voluntary. The planning and direction of the activity, if formally organized, is usually assumed largely by students or else shared by faculty members and elected representatives of the student body.

Although the contributions of student activities often supplement the educational values of the formal school program, as would probably be true of club work in fields such as science, drama, or art, they are not indispensable functions as far as the achievement of the basic goals of education is concerned. This evaluation, although not accepted by all advocates of student activities, is supported by the fact that the particular student activities offered by different secondary schools vary considerably.

A third characteristic of student activities is the responsibility assumed by pupils for their management. Teachers typically act only as sponsors or advisers. Plans and programs are formulated and carried out by student members. Likewise, regulations regarding standards for admission to participation in a particular activity and for conduct as a member of the group are usually drawn up by students, with assistance from sponsors as needed. The function of the teacher-sponsor often is one of protecting the interest of the school by helping students arrive at decisions that will not reflect discredit on them or the institution.

Many student activities emphasize performance before an audience, as in athletics, band, or dramatics; other activities focus on individual interests or hobbies, as in certain club programs. No defined course of study is employed to give structure to the work. Instead members of a group are relatively free to plan each phase of an activity in terms of events and interests that may be present at a given time. In activities such as choir, band, orchestra, dramatics, journalism, student council, and interscholastic athletics, teacher-sponsors take considerable responsibility for training pupils in the skills required for public acceptance of the production of pupils. Often these activities become centered in the personality and professional career of the teacher-sponsor. When this occurs, student members serve to carry out programs of activities that are operated for already defined purposes—such as community entertainment or service to the school. In such situations planning and direction are usually in the hands of the faculty staff member.

Another characteristic of some programs of student activities that has become apparent in the past twenty-five years is a trend toward sectional, state, regional, and even national organizations of activity groups. Such associations function with either tacit or open approval of school authorities. They exist for the express objective of extending the participation of students in particular activities and to help students interested in the activity to feel a common identification with others with similar concerns in other parts of the state or nation. The complexity of activity functions and schedules, with the demands they often make on student time and energy, has forced the establishment of a complex system of control.

The National Association of Secondary School Principals has established a national committee to approve school contests. This committee recommends a list of approved activities to each regional accrediting agency. In the central portion of the United States, for example, the North Central Association of Schools and Colleges automatically accepts this recommendation and limits the member schools throughout the nineteen states to the activities approved. This national committee in 1960 refused to give its approval to any essay contests and the North Central Association immediately banned such contests in member schools. All state and local interschool music, speech, drama, foreign language, and athletic competitions are affected by these controls.

Types of Student Activities

Any classification assumes an arbitrary cataloguing of activities in terms of specific criteria. The classification below might be called functional because it is based upon what appear to be the chief purposes of student activities. Any such general classification is bound to be inaccurate in certain particular situations. Nevertheless, it indicates the general public image that student activities have created across the nation.

Public entertainment. Certain student activities associated with secondary schools have taken as their primary objective the provision of public entertainment, both for members of the student body and for the general community. This category typically includes interscholastic sports programs, e.g., football, basketball, baseball, track, swimming, tennis, wrestling, and in some schools, gymnastics, soccer, and boxing. Marching bands and dramatics groups that produce plays for public viewing, as well as competitive speech and debate societies, also often deserve this classification. Certain dance and swimming groups—

usually composed of girls—whose major interest is providing demonstrations and programs, also function primarily to entertain.

The test of whether a student activity should properly be placed in this classification is a simple one. If the program would not otherwise exist, or if its nature and character would be substantially modified, should its function of public entertainment be discontinued, then it clearly deserves to be called a public-entertainment activity.

So to classify an activity does not necessarily mean that it may not contribute significantly to the development of individuals who participate. Often the public performance, itself, represents an important developmental experience for a boy or girl. Such activities, if properly controlled and supervised, may contribute also to the general *esprit de corps* of the school. They have often served to rally community support for the total school. Some communities, for example, have been known to vote favorably on school bond issues largely because of interest in obtaining a larger gymnasium or auditorium to house the school's entertainments.

School service activities. Secondary schools have developed numerous activities that are designed primarily to carry out services that have become essential to the educational program and control of student behavior and activities. These include student government, home-room organizations, school publications, usher and escort service groups, as well as various special assignments for individual students that relate to student participation in running the school.

Other types of services performed by students, voluntarily and without remuneration, include serving as library assistants, managing the stage for assembly and other auditorium programs, managing film and television equipment, and acting as aides in the various offices of the school and for individual teachers. Students may also assist the school nurse, work in the commercial department, or run errands.

The importance of school service activities is reflected by the practice of some schools' giving awards, such as achievement points or school letters, to students whose service records—often counted in terms of number of hours of work—reach defined goals. Service responsibilities are typically recognized as honors that go to the individuals who have demonstrated high scholastic achievement, maturity, exemplary deportment, and interest and loyalty to the school.

Recreational activities. Some activities in high school are purely recreational in purpose and character. They provide wholesome outlets for pupil interests and energies, they exert an influence against the antisocial pursuits of young people, and they promote good mental and physical health. These activities include intramural programs, informal participation in sports such as swimming, skiing, skating, hiking, bowling, or golf. Music, arts and crafts, and some club groups may be primarily recreational.

Social activities. Some high schools provide almost the entire social life of members of their student bodies. Student groups sponsor parties, dances, teas, receptions, reunions, carnivals, picnics, and other primarily social types of gatherings.

Social fraternities and societies, though not widely approved by faculties and boards of education, exist in some schools. Many states ban organizations of students who vote upon the admission of members, conduct hazing-type initiations, and use clothing or insignia which set them apart from the student body. Oregon has passed strong legislation forbidding such practices and schools of the state have conscientiously enforced it.

Educational and cultural activities. Another category of activities includes those whose immediate objectives are to extend the educational and cultural influences of the formal educational program of the school. Such functions may include honor societies, hobby clubs that grow out of formal courses, art and music-appreciation groups, and various informal conferences, meetings, and lectures arranged to enrich the program of the school. Some schools present assembly programs by outside performers or members of the student body. The central objective is to provide group educational and cultural experiences to the entire student body.

Often student activities aimed at educational and cultural goals serve to supplement the formal program provided in the established curriculum. Academically talented students are afforded opportunities to specialize in certain phases of their studies, with the help of competent teachers or laymen in the community. These developments have been encouraged by the nation-wide talent-search contests sponsored by the National Science Foundation and by other types of recognition of academic specialization in foreign languages, commercial subjects, art, music, English, and citizenship.

DEVELOPMENT OF STUDENT ACTIVITIES

Student activities, a recent development in the United States, have come into prominence substantially within the past forty years. Until

1920, such functions were viewed generally as extra features of the school program more likely to be detrimental than beneficial. Principals and teachers often opposed their existence. In fact, official sanction ultimately came largely because schools found themselves responsible for the manner in which activities functioned. Realizing that they would be held accountable for the conduct of activities that were carried on unofficially in the name of the school, faculties had no alternative but to provide supervision and tacit approval.

Early Attitudes Toward Activities

Teachers and school officials first viewed student activities as competing with the established curriculum. Reactions ranged from outright opposition and censorship to disclaimers of responsibility or reluctant tolerance. In the face of such resistance students often turned to parents or other adults in the community for sponsorship and assistance. Many early athletic teams were coached by interested laymen who volunteered their services. In some communities plays were directed by interested, experienced citizens. Such developments actually represented a type of community activity for young people; but because they used school facilities and drew their clientele from high school student bodies, they soon became identified as school groups.

Stages in the Development of Student Activities

Although each student activity has developed uniquely in terms of its own nature and student and community support, certain characteristics are sufficiently common to the growth of all to suggest four general stages through which activities in secondary schools have passed.[3]

Recognition refused. Initially student activities were largely ignored by the professional staff of secondary schools. Such attitudes were rooted in the educational theory that school learning should be a passive affair with the impartation and mastery of knowledge in selected traditional fields as the only function of the organized school. Teachers were expected to teach their planned lessons, examine achievement, and, perhaps, to tutor those in need of help. They recognized and accepted no responsibility for aiding the development of students in other ways.

[3] Such generalizations are arbitrary inasmuch as no clear-cut uniform transitions were common to all high schools. Three classifications were used to identify the evolutionary development of school activities in Harry C. McKown, *Extra Curricular Activities,* New York (Macmillan), third ed., 1952.

As young people organized games and social affairs outside the school, they naturally used the school as a place for planning, meeting, and conducting some activities. A few teachers and administrators took interest in, and even assisted with, certain activities, but they were not accorded official status or recognition by the school.

Condemnation and prohibition. As enterprising students developed highly organized forms of activity, parents and school officials were confronted with the dangers that are ever present when youth conduct their own unsupervised functions. Almost every secondary school had unfortunate experiences and endured criticism as a result of student-organized athletic events, dances, parties, or trips that had no adult supervision. Since some events involved the obligation of substantial sums of money and the extensive use of school facilities and equipment, they demanded careful planning and organization for their success. During this phase of the development of student activities, the unsupervised functions of young people were considered as undesirable ventures for them, as well as disruptive influences on the school. Because they could no longer be ignored, and inasmuch as school authorities were often challenged by parents to intercede, the practice of condemning and prohibiting student activities became prevalent.

Control and supervision. In most communities it ultimately became apparent that as soon as certain activities were censored or prohibited, students found means of organizing others. Criticisms of lack of supervision were often met by students by enlisting the help of parents or other laymen to sponsor the events. Frequently, such adults, inexperienced as they often were in dealing with large groups of youth, were ineffective in eliminating the undesirable aspects of student functions. As more and more parents became involved with high schools through expanding enrollments, the demand for help from school authorities grew. Consequently, schools were eventually compelled to undertake the official control and supervision of student social and sports events.

As control and supervision were assumed, the attitude of teachers and principals was largely one of compliance with student and community demands. The action was rationalized on the ground that student activities could have some value as devices for controlling student behavior and, perhaps, would encourage some students to remain in school and to pursue the formal academic programs. Although the contribution of activities to the goals of education was often admitted by teachers, no great dependence was placed on such functions as a means of achieving defined educational objectives.

Practically every type of student activity has passed through, or still remains in, this stage of acceptance and recognition. As late as the early 1950's, a new wave of undesirable activities by secret clubs and societies arose in secondary schools in major cities across the country. Established precedents for approving, recognizing, and supervising student activities permitted high schools to react quickly to this new type of activity.[4]

In this phase of their acceptance, student activities have been exploited generally by schools for their value to the institution, rather than for their contribution to the development of individual pupils. Interscholastic athletics, marching bands, and dramatic groups have been encouraged in many schools primarily as a means to improve public relations between the school and community and as a means of boosting student body morale.

Assimilation into school programs. The fourth stage in the advancement of student activities is one that involves serious efforts by faculty groups to assimilate these functions into the total program of the school. In so doing, the emphasis is on discovering the unique contributions that each activity may make to the educational objectives of the school and on determining the priorities, place, and time that should be accorded to it. Enthusiastic teachers, working with pupils whose interests are motivated by activity participation, are demonstrating the contributions that such programs can make to effective learning experiences for high school youth. As the values that can be derived from student activities are identified, the differentiation between curricular and extracurricular offerings tends to be subordinated.

The assimilation of student activities into the school curriculum has produced serious conflicts with the established courses. Schools have been sharply criticized for overemphasis on what some call "frill" subjects, while one national organization is waging a campaign to return to "basic education" for all high school students.[5]

Underlying Forces

Change in attitudes toward, and endorsement of, student activities has been brought about by a number of social and psychological forces. Sweeping changes in the home and family life have thrust on secondary schools more responsibility for moral and vocational training. The

[4] Lloyd E. McCleary, "Controlling the Student Club Program," *Clearing House,* March 1951.

[5] The Council for Basic Education, Washington, D.C.

urbanization of the nation has increased demands for organized recreation; these, too, have pointed to schools.

A further factor has been the expansion of the conception of function assigned to secondary schools, as reflected in the 1918 report of the Commission on the Reorganization of Secondary Education.[6] The emphasis placed on such goals as personal development, vocational efficiency, family membership, use of leisure time, and economic understandings—all citizenship goals—made the kind of learning experiences afforded by many student activities more attractive to curriculum planners.

During the same time, interest in developmental aspects of human growth, as compared to simple mind training, was leading educators to study learning in a broader setting. The role of firsthand learning through experience in publishing newspapers, producing plays, organizing discussion groups, and developing hobbies caused a higher value to be placed on certain student activities. Teachers began to think of learning as an active, rather than passive, process. They began to see in wholesome activities not only a source of motivation but a procedure by which desired educational goals could be accomplished with greater attainment and retention.

At the same time, it must be admitted that one of the primary forces that has promoted student activities is the teachers' own ambitions. Teachers, who are often employed more for their abilities to direct specific student activities than for their competence at instruction in basic subject fields, quite naturally develop vested interests in the activities they direct. Their professional stake in the success of the activities, plus the publicity they get in the general community, creates a teacher lobby for student activities that is difficult to counteract.

ORGANIZATION OF PROGRAM OF ACTIVITIES

The question facing most secondary schools today is not whether student activities will be recognized, but rather, how programs shall be organized to obtain maximum benefit for students without undermining the educational program. Underlying this question, of course, is the struggle for balance that is going on in high schools. To establish priorities for student activities, each school faces the continuing obliga-

---

[6] National Education Association, Commission on the Reorganization of Secondary Education, *Cardinal Principles of Secondary Education,* Bulletin 1918, No. 35, Washington, D.C. (Government Printing Office), 1918.

tion of assessing the interests and needs of students. Such an assessment can provide valid criteria for appraising the worth of activities. The task of coordinating established activities with the basic educational program of the school is one that demands complete faculty-student cooperation.

Struggle for Balance

Maintaining balance in high school programs, in the face of the mushrooming of student activities that has taken place in the past thirty years, is, perhaps, one important key to the attainment of excellence in secondary education. First of all, it is imperative that student activities not be permitted to crowd out basic courses in the school curriculum. This can easily happen when elective systems permit pupils to substitute activity-type courses for others, e.g., dramatics or journalism for a course in English. Graduation requirements may permit the inclusion of credit from student activities in a way that tempts students to neglect work in academic fields.

Another problem is balance among the various activities themselves, whether or not they carry credit within the curriculum or exist as noncredit functions. A community that is enthusiastic about sports may favor such activities and directly, or indirectly, push student interest in this direction—to the exclusion of cultural or other types of programs. The overemphasis may even be on only one sports activity. Some high schools have let themselves become so involved with interscholastic football that their entire program of student activities, and often aspects of the academic program, are planned to favor this sport. Excessive expenditures for stadiums—their use being almost exclusively for football contests—and salaries for coaches exceeding those for other teachers of equal competence are only the outward signs of such imbalances.

The overparticipation of individual students may create a problem of balance also. In small high schools, particularly, capable young people are urged to engage in numerous student activities at the same time—for the good of the school. A capable boy, for example, may play on the football team, sing in the choir, serve as editor of the school paper, and hold an office in the student government, as well as work on various other social programs. Even in large schools where talent is more plentiful, students are impelled to enter numerous activities partly through natural desire to participate and partly through such practices as listing the activities of students with their pictures in school annuals. Often boys and girls commit themselves to participate in so many activities that they have little time or energy left for serious study. It is not uncommon, for instance, for football participation—including time for practice and games, as well as the study of team plays and opponent formations—to require 14-18 hours per week.[7] When this time is added to the 25-30 hours the student is scheduled in classes, it becomes apparent that study must be on an "overtime" basis.

An assessment of the actual extent of individual participation and the range of activities currently provided in secondary schools is difficult to make with precision. A recent survey of a stratified sampling of secondary schools in one state (see Table 13-1) provides reasonably reliable information. These data reveal the differences in extent of participation between boys and girls as well as the percentage of participation in each type of activity by all the students comprising the sample. It is interesting to note that approximately one-fourth of the students participated in interscholastic athletics, one-fourth in debate-speech-drama activities, and one-fourth in subject-centered clubs. The largest percentage of total participation was in music activities with more than one-third of all students participating. The amount of participation by each student and the differences between schools of various sizes are not shown. These and similar conditions should be examined regularly within each school.

Assessment of Needs and Interest

The maintenance of balance in activity programs requires the continuous assessment of needs and interests of students, in terms of individual potentialities and community values, as well as educational objectives. The experiences of schools have identified a number of procedures that can be followed at regular intervals to provide up-to-date information on activity programs.

A basic process that has been found invaluable is that of maintaining a continuing study of the amount and nature of pupil participation in activities. This involves ascertaining for each pupil the number and type of groups to which he belongs. Often the amount of time devoted weekly to each activity is also noted. Such information usually is included in the cumulative record for the individual. Additional aspects of this type of checking include determining the nature of

---

[7] This information was obtained by one of the authors from an informal survey of seventeen coaches in northern Illinois.

Table 13-1. *Percentages of All Graduates Who Participated in School Activities in a Sample of Illinois High Schools*

ACTIVITY	BOYS (N = 1,557)	GIRLS (N = 1,618)	TOTAL (N = 3,175)
Academic	8.2 (2.7)[a]	14.7 (0.4)	11.5 (3.2)
Art	1.4 (0.4)	3.8 (0.4)	2.6 (0.4)
Assembly	2.1 (0.2)	4.9 (0.3)	3.5 (0.3)
Interscholastic athletics	50.2 (9.6)	4.0 (0.4)	26.6 (4.9)
Intramural athletics	13.7 (1.1)	36.0 (4.8)	25.1 (3.0)
Class organization	13.4 (9.0)	18.9 (9.6)	16.2 (9.3)
Subject clubs	22.2 (3.9)	31.5 (4.5)	26.9 (4.2)
Hobby clubs	10.0 (0.7)	9.5 (1.4)	9.6 (1.0)
Debate, drama, speech	18.6 (1.5)	31.5 (5.3)	25.2 (2.7)
Music	24.1 (3.1)	35.2 (3.9)	34.9 (4.3)
Publications	15.3 (2.6)	27.9 (6.9)	21.7 (4.8)
Character building	3.9 (0.6)	9.8 (2.5)	6.9 (1.6)
Community service	9.2 (1.5)	21.6 (2.3)	15.6 (1.9)
School service	20.5 (2.5)	44.4 (9.3)	32.7 (6.0)
Social	6.3 (0.8)	20.0 (3.1)	13.3 (2.0)
Student government	11.9 (3.3)	14.0 (4.5)	12.9 (3.9)
Other activities	15.9 (5.1)	31.9 (8.0)	24.0 (6.6)
No activities	8.7	3.2	5.9
No information	8.5	5.3	6.8

[a] Percentage given in parentheses indicates leadership positions were held by that ratio of the students.

SOURCE: A study conducted by Professor Harold Hand for the State of Illinois Department of Public Instruction. The study may be obtained from the Superintendent of Public Instruction.

student participation at each grade level of the secondary school. The number of students engaged in activities, the range of participation with respect to number of functions and time devoted, and the number of nonparticipators are factors considered in such tabulations.

Other devices that have been employed to evaluate needs for and programs of activities include:

(a) Participation studies for individual activities

(b) Surveys of school and community facilities
(c) Surveys of leadership talent
(d) Inventories of pupil interests
(e) Estimation of the values to which activities contribute
(f) Studies of cost of activities
(g) Appraisal of sponsor contributions to activities

Such studies are often conducted by committees consisting of pupils, parents, and teachers. They can, when carefully controlled, yield information on which sound decisions may be based.

Criteria for Appraising Activities

Evaluations of student activities typically involve the judgments of both faculty and student representatives. Because circumstances differ from school to school, the worth of particular programs often varies. To guide such judgments, nevertheless, certain rather well-established principles have come into common use.

1. *Activities should grow out of and augment the established instructional program of the school.* Assemblies, clubs, hobby and discussion groups, and various other educational and cultural, as well as some recreational projects, will be of the greatest value if they develop as extensions of the regular curriculum. When such is the case, activities benefit from the training students receive in established courses; similarly, the formal work of the school is motivated and enhanced by the extension provided through activity participation.

2. *Activities should provide students opportunities to develop and practice the skills, values, and attitudes that are recognized as goals of the total educational program.* Such objectives as learning the responsibilities of citizenship, acquiring knowledge and understanding in any subject, and learning socially desirable behaviors can be given support by various student activities. Social skills, sound mental and physical health, and wholesome recreational pursuits are other examples of goals to which certain activities contribute.

3. *Activities should contribute to providing a balanced offering to students.* Often student organizations can supply educational features that have not yet been established as a regular part of the curriculum. Also, a student may gain opportunities for development through activity participation that might not be open to him through regular courses. A good example is the training in leadership, family finance, and business management that is provided boys through Future Farmers of America clubs. Frequently students interested in academic majors,

such as science, find opportunities to develop talents and appreciations through participation in nonacademic school activities such as art, music, or drama.

Coordination with Educational Program

The problem of coordinating student activities with the rest of the educational program involves the time of both students and teachers. Inasmuch as such enterprises were originally "extra," they were added to the school day (as noncredit functions) in the after-school time of both the pupils and faculty who participated. The practice of scheduling many of these programs—music, journalism, dramatics, student government meetings, and some club activities—during the regular school day has made it necessary for schools either to lengthen the scheduled day, shorten the periods for the academic subjects, or curtail the out-of-class work of such subjects.

For teachers the sponsorship of activities often demands so much time and energy that they are forced to slight other teaching duties. This is particularly true when the direction of an activity is added to a full instructional load. If the function meets after school or in the evening, if its programs involve travel to other communities, the amount of responsibility accruing to the sponsor may be substantial. Nevertheless, the tendency of communities and school officials to give heavy weight to activity direction in the selection and advancement of personnel makes it difficult for individual teachers to decline to serve. Also, the practice of according extra pay for supervising certain activities forces some (usually those with families to support) to accept the extra work.

A third problem of coordination relates to the tendency of many high schools to give priority to activity functions over regular academic classes. Leniency in excusing pupils from classes to permit them to carry on preparations for special occasions, and the wholesale dismissal of school for games, concerts, and other types of public performances, can so disrupt class groups that valuable instructional time is lost for all pupils. This problem has grown so acute that secondary school principals in some states are taking steps to correct it.

Faculty-Student Cooperation

Programs of student activities lose much of their value when they become teacher-dominated; nevertheless, they need guidance and assistance from interested adults. When a function becomes oriented to community entertainment or the performance of established duties for the school, it typically assumes the character of a faculty-directed, rather than a student-directed, activity. When this happens, activities may serve to advance the professional interests of such teacher-sponsors as athletic coaches or band and play directors who find their careers intertwined with the success of the functions they direct. Thus, the needs and interests of students may become subservient to the professional ambitions of teachers.

No better illustration can be found of the transition that can take place from student- to faculty-centered activities than that existing in college athletics. In the early days of intercollegiate athletics, students commonly would appeal to the president of their college to employ a coach so that they might have a football team. Today, the situation is reversed. The coach, supported by the alumni, often seeks to find acceptable ways by which he can employ players to achieve the same objective. It is not necessary, however, to point to the colleges for undesirable examples of the manner in which teachers have wrested complete control of activities from students. High school bands, choirs, dramatic groups, publications, and sometimes certain clubs, are frequently identified with their teacher-coaches rather than with the students for whom the activity exists. Such highly organized teacher-centered activities are even now becoming established in junior high schools as low as the seventh grade.[8]

Another problem related to the control of activities is the tendency of students from higher socioeconomic groups to dominate both the membership and the leadership of various functions.[9] Economic and prestige factors may make it difficult for large numbers of young people to participate in particular student activities.

Such factors illustrate the importance of faculty-student cooperation in the organization, administration, and management of student activities. Most large high schools have found it beneficial to maintain central coordination, both to evaluate the total impact of activity programs and to synchronize their schedules of meetings and functions. The use of a school-wide policy committee, composed of both teachers and students, has proved to be a useful device for influencing the policies and actions of various student agencies. This body estab-

[8] James B. Conant, "A Preliminary Report on the Junior High School," *The Gist*, February 17, 1960, p. 1.
[9] August B. Hollingshead, *Elmtown's Youth*, New York (Wiley), 1949, pp. 168-70, 171-72, 201-203.

lishes policies for such functions as fund-raising, dances, trips, membership drives, public performances, and duplication of membership. To function effectively, the activity council must be able to call upon an administrative official for detailed help in scheduling the use of facilities, assigning sponsors, accounting for funds, and the purchase of supplies. These administrative functions may be carried by members of the staff, but the final responsibility for them resides with the principal.

VALUES PROMOTED BY STUDENT ACTIVITIES

The values that student activities are purported to promote encompass the total range of the goals of education. In most instances these claims are based upon the personal experience of individuals who feel that the training received through participation in particular activities played an important part in determining their success in life.

The number of objective studies of the outcomes of activity participation is small. Earlier approaches to evaluation involved attempts to compare success in activities with achievement in academic courses. Efforts were made in some studies, also, to measure by tests, case studies, and controlled experiments, the degree to which values claimed for particular activities were achieved by participants.[10] The trend in recent years has been to broaden the basis of evaluation to the extent of measuring the contribution of activities to the total objectives of the secondary school. The Evaluative Criteria, developed by the Cooperative Study of Secondary School Standards as a guide for the evaluation of high schools, includes a section dealing with student activities.[11]

Despite the absence of research evidence to defend the values claimed for student activities, it is possible to classify the primary outcomes that have won such widespread endorsement by students, parents, and teachers. These include values that are personal-social in nature, ones that may not be stressed by the academic program of the school. They include also the contributions that activities make to the atmosphere of the high school, contributions to the career

[10] Ronald C. Faunce, "Extracurricular Activities," *Encyclopedia of Educational Research*, Chester W. Harris (ed.), New York (Macmillan), 1960, p. 510.

[11] Cooperative Study of Secondary School Standards, "Pupil Activities," *Evaluative Criteria*, Washington, D.C. (The General Committee), 1950, pp. 191-207.

orientations of pupils, and extensions of the formal learnings of the academic curriculum.

Personal-Social Development

The growth of student activities has paralleled the spread of concern for the personal-social development of students that is now found in schools at all levels. Like personal-social development, it made its greatest advances during the period from World War I through the depression of the 1930's when emphasis was more on personal development than on academic attainments. A harsher judgment might be that the growth of student activities was fostered by the general anti-intellectualism that prevailed during this period.

Whatever the forces that supported student activities, general agreement now prevails that certain desirable outcomes can be achieved through participation in such programs. These include (a) improvement of skill in human relations, including the ability to give and take, to respect the other person's contribution, and the general acceptance of others; (b) improvement in such skills as oral expression, group discussion, and parliamentary procedure, as well as in personality generally; (c) development of recreational and social skills; and (d) development of leadership competence, involving both skills of judgment and persuasion, organizational ability, responsibility for others as well as self, and creative insights into problems confronted by a group.

Atmosphere of the School

It might be said that administrators and teachers in secondary schools have developed almost a passion for making school a pleasant experience for young people. The goal seems to be to refute the age-old insults and condemnations that students and alumni have aimed at schools as dreary, dreadful places of drudgery. The growth of student activities has provided a valuable aid to the modern crusade for a pleasant atmosphere in the school.

Without doubt, the program of student activities has given the secondary school an atmosphere that students enjoy. Such functions add to the interest of being in school. When properly managed, they contribute to group morale—student spirit as it is often called—in ways to increase pride in the total educational operation and high standards of student conduct. The existence of a broad range of student activities is credited with helping to increase the holding power of high schools.

Students who find the academic courses dull or difficult often remain in school because of the satisfactions they receive from participation in certain activities.

Programs of activities contribute to the atmosphere of high schools, also, by providing a common meeting ground for the interests of pupils, parents, and teachers. No other phase of the high school program has contributed so much to uniting communities behind the work of schools. Evidence of this fact is found in the effect of student activities in newly consolidated high schools. In New York and other states school administrators have found that resistance to reorganized large high schools diminishes as soon as students begin enjoying large group activities—such as band, choir, and athletics—that were not possible in the smaller schools.

Career Orientation

Until recent years, career orientation was provided by the home. However, the complexities of economic, industrial, and business developments have made the successful continuation of this practice impossible. The introduction of vocational guidance into high schools has come largely through the facilities of programs of student activities. Clubs have provided exploratory experiences to orient students to various career possibilities and to help them test their own aptitudes for different types of work. Home-room programs have recently made possible more extensive group guidance, testing, and counseling procedures.

In addition, experiences students gain through such activities as publications, dramatics, science experimentation groups, athletics, and music, often promote the development of personal marketable skills that ultimately contribute to career success. Perhaps some of the best examples of the manner in which activities aid career orientation is found in the work of Future Farmer groups, 4-H organizations, and homemaking clubs. These activities deal directly with the skills and knowledges that are essential for success in the fields of agriculture and home management.

Extension of Formal Learnings

In some student activities, the determination of where the formal program of studies stops and the activity begins is impossible to make. This is true, for example, of a chemistry research club that extends the student's scientific knowledge and laboratory techniques. Usually such groups function under the sponsorship of the regular teacher who is able to help students project their scientific research well beyond the regular courses.

Other activities, such as foreign language, creative writing, drama, and historical or political science clubs, contribute significantly to the strengthening of intellectual skills and the extension of knowledge and cultural values that formal courses attempt to promote. Similarly, activities in art, music, and health study may represent wholesome extensions of the formal learnings that the school is committed to promote.

THE TEACHER AND STUDENT ACTIVITIES

Student activities have become so much a part of the program of the school, and so complicated in their organization and operation, that their success requires mature, trained leadership from teachers or other adults. Although the sponsorship of activities typically has been added to the heavy teaching duties of staff members, gains to the instructional program have resulted. On the whole, however, the growth of activities has created certain dilemmas that plague teachers and reduce their total effectiveness.

Impact of Activities on Teaching Procedures

The direction, or sponsorship, of activities imposes on teachers a more complex type of instructional leadership than is necessary in traditional courses. It requires, first of all, that the teacher serve as a guide, a consultant, as one who shares in the planning with students, instead of the taskmaster who is in complete control and whose plan must be followed. Such relationships force teachers to view students more as co-workers, to respect their ideas and contributions, and to find ways of promoting student leadership.

The type of teaching and control required of sponsors of activities places greater emphasis upon adapting projects to the interests of students. It necessitates the acceptance of levels of performance by pupils that are more characteristic of their maturity than those often prescribed for classroom work. Most of all, it demands a kind of nondirectiveness on the part of the teacher that places the spotlight upon the students, their activities, agreements, goals, and values.

As teachers learn to work with students effectively in activity situations, it is inevitable that their new leadership skills and procedures will be translated into the more formal classroom work. As a result, pupil-centered and laboratory methods of instruction have been expanded. Teacher-student planning is another type of teaching that no doubt has received considerable impetus from the experiences of teachers in working with young people in activity situations. As teachers discover how effective their informal, nondirective leadership in student activities is, they seek ways of utilizing the same techniques to promote and improve their instruction in the classroom.

Preparation for Activity Direction

Officials typically seek to employ teachers who can direct specific student activities as well as teach formal courses. Such demands have encouraged institutions that prepare teachers to place greater stress on the prospective teacher's own participation in student activities, in both high school and college, and on programs of training that emphasize techniques for directing activities.

One of the major arguments for the new plans for student teaching and the internship, which permit prospective teachers to spend full time in a school for two to four months, is the opportunities such arrangements permit for training in leadership of student activities. Typically, student teachers learn to assist with the sponsorship of such functions just as they learn to teach classes.

Newer experiments with the instructional team, in which interns in training are included as members of the group responsible for instruction, offer even greater advantages to the prospective teacher who is learning to direct activities as well as handle formal situations. The intern often has opportunities to work with small subgroups of students in informal situations that demand nondirective leadership skills. In addition, he has opportunities to observe highly competent professional teachers demonstrate their skill in working with such situations.

Dilemmas of Conducting Activities

The nature of student activities, and the careful management required when students take responsibility for their programs, imposes special problems on teachers. Aside from the strictly managerial problems, difficulties arise because the educational requirements of the school must be applied also to activity programs. The resulting dilemmas torment both teachers and school officials; often they lay the basis for community dissatisfactions with the secondary school.

Lack of adequate and suitable supplies and equipment. Many student activities must support themselves, either by membership dues or fund-raising ventures. When provided for in the school budget, the allocations are often meager. Even when funds are available, the extemporaneous nature of some plans makes acquiring suitable supplies and equipment a problem.

Competition for the time of students. The talents and interests of students often involve them in several activities if restrictions on multiple participation do not exist. Inevitably, competition develops for those most talented.

Educational values versus public performance. Activities committed to public performance frequently produce conflicts between sound educational values and procedures necessary to satisfy the public. Competitive athletics, musical activities, and dramatic productions require long periods of intensive training to achieve creditable public presentations. Often compromises between the welfare of pupils and the quality of the product are made. In addition, practice may be continued far beyond its educational value for the sake of the ultimate public appearance.

Achievement of peak-level performance while promoting individual initiative and creativity. One desirable characteristic of student activities is the freedom permitted for individual initiative and creativity. When peak-level performance is prized as a goal, by either the sponsor, the student body, or the public in general, such objectives will often be in conflict.

Experimentation as opposed to tradition. In theory, student activities offer rich opportunities for experimentation; nevertheless, traditions soon develop that require conformity to previously established patterns. The importance of the activity becomes reduced, therefore, since it often does not permit new groups of students to pursue their interests or to test their ideas.

Conflict between teaching duties and activity sponsorship. Successful teaching, like competent activity direction, makes increasing demands upon the individual teacher. The problem of maintaining a balance between these two obligations, when, as is often the case, the teacher is good at both, is almost insurmountable.

There are no clear solutions to these dilemmas, but the teacher of an activity can at least anticipate some of the problems he will face. Teachers should expect to encounter difficulties and not become overwhelmed by them. Teachers should not attempt an activity if it must be conducted under unreasonable conditions. However, the greatest teachers are those who can alter conditions under which they operate and who refuse to let obstacles force them to give up desirable educational opportunities for youth.

FUTURE OF STUDENT ACTIVITIES

The trend in student activities in secondary schools is toward a closer integration of these functions within the traditional school day and curriculum. At the same time, a growing uneasiness exists about the possibility of educationally unhealthy imbalances developing between activities and basic studies.

The criticism that activities are being overemphasized is forcing school faculties to appraise more carefully the quality and values of specific activities, as well as the priorities that should be accorded to academic studies as opposed to activity participation, in the requirements established for high school graduation. As a result, it may be anticipated that certain less valuable activities will be discarded. That the number of such programs will be reduced, however, does not yet seem likely. Actually, a trend to create more activities seems to be developing as teachers promote student groups related to academic subject fields, such as science, foreign language, history, and mathematics.

Schools are now accepting student activities as integral to their total educational programs. Budgetary support is being provided (and in more adequate denominations), events are being scheduled so as to reduce conflicts, and staff-student cooperation in the establishment of policies and appraisal of results is being achieved. Some large high schools have appointed staff members to administer their activity programs under the general direction of the principal. Teachers generally are expected to take responsibility for the sponsorship of activities along with their formal teaching duties.

The trend toward promotion and regulation of specific activities by state and national associations promises to define the role of these functions more clearly. It may be expected, also, to contribute to the continuation of activities and to their extension to other schools because of the vested interests of personnel at both state and local levels. One healthy sign is that steps are being initiated, in some states, to reduce the infringement of student activities on the basic instructional program. The success of this movement, however, will depend upon the willingness of many different, and strong, groups—including many that thrive in colleges and universities—to submerge their dedication to special interests in favor of allegiance to the total educational program of secondary schools.

As their quality is improved and as more discriminating attention is given to the development of activities, there will be a greater recognition of their values to the maximum growth of youth. Guidance workers will aid pupils to choose their activities more wisely so that some students will limit their participation; others will increase it. School records will not only note activities of pupils but will include the amount and kind of their participation and attendance. Finally, schools will rely more heavily upon nonprofessional adult leadership and will consider more wisely community facilities and services in their planning for student activities.

SELECTED REFERENCES

BYDSLEK, GRACE. *Extra-class Activities in the Junior High School Grades.* Springfield: The Junior High School Association of Illinois, 1957.

GRAHAM, G. "Sponsor Leadership Makes a Difference." *School Activities,* February 1958.

HAMILTON, HOMER. "Educational Values of Extracurriculum." *Bulletin of the National Association of Secondary School Principals,* December 1959.

KILZER, LOUIS R., HAROLD H. STEPHENSON, AND H. ORVILLE NORDBERG. *Allied Activities in the Secondary School.* New York: Harper, 1956.

National Association of Secondary School Principals. "Music—A Vital Force in Today's Secondary Schools." *Bulletin,* March 1959.

SINGLETON, M. D. "Public Relations Via Student Activities." *School Activities,* February 1959.

WELTY, M. L. "Does Activity Participation Impair Academic Achievement in High School?" *California Journal of Secondary Education,* May 1958.

ZIRBES, LAURA. *Spurs to Creative Teaching.* New York: Putnam, 1959.

PART IV

Human and Physical Facilities

Interviewing prospective teachers is one of the important tasks the principal performs.

Meetings such as the Annual Convention of the National Association of Secondary School Principals (45th convention, February 1961) bring together principals who represent every conceivable type of educational leadership.

Leadership for the Secondary School

EFFECTIVE educational leadership is a prerequisite to good secondary schools. Although this premise is generally accepted, it has not always been followed in the selection of high school administrators. Such factors as family and political ties, seniority of tenure, sex, ability to control youth in informal and extracurricular activities, organizational ability, or personal popularity have too frequently been accorded disproportionate weights in the selection of secondary school administrators. Furthermore, until recent years, leadership at the secondary school level has not been envisioned as a career; it has served, rather, as a steppingstone to general administration, college teaching, or to business opportunities. The result has been, all too frequently, that the able administrators move on to other types of work, while those who continue are less than adequate.

Every school, of course, has leadership—of one type or another. It may come from the status, or legally appointed, leaders: the principal, supervisors, department heads, or chairmen of standing committees. It may be provided by individual faculty members, or cohesive groups of teachers, whose influence exceeds that of status leaders. At times, it may come from members of the student body or from parents. Whenever appointed leaders are weak or ineffective in a school, competition for leadership usually develops, with responsibility being assumed by the individuals who win broadest support. Such situations are more likely to occur when the role and responsibilities of leadership are poorly defined and not well understood.

NATURE OF LEADERSHIP

Research on the nature of leadership has been going forward in recent years in practically all fields: political science, business management, social psychology, military science, as well as school administration. Such investigations usually approach the study of leadership from the point of view of the special responsibilities of a field, or its subdivisions, without reference to the characteristics of leadership in other areas. These diverse approaches, however, reveal the existence of a variety of concepts of leadership; they help, also, to identify areas of agreement about the nature of leadership in general.

Leadership may be identified in terms of its source of authority, its functions, the means of its execution, or its impact on a group or an institution. A composite picture of the leadership of a secondary school would indicate its character in relationship to each of these aspects.

Source of Authority

The source of authority for leadership may be legal, as a high school principalship which is designated as a position in schools by state statutes and school board regulations. Such a definition of a leadership position gives to the principal what is called a "status" position. In it he may function only as an executive without assuming much responsibility for educational leadership; if so, the leadership function will be delegated to or assumed by others. Actually, the status position of the school principal is poorly defined in most state statutes; some states give the position no legal status, even though it may be mentioned in school legislation. On the other hand, the post is usually rigidly defined in the regulations of school boards, in the job descriptions formulated by superintendents of schools, and in the expectations of teachers and other employees of the school, as well as of pupils and parents.

A second source of authority for leadership is the group for whom leadership is exercised. Such leaders are usually elected to positions or assignments. The individual so designated for leadership responsibility may or may not hold a status position. For example, when teachers share in the selection of their principal, the legal status accorded by the appointment by the school board is bolstered by the endorsement by the group itself.

Authority of fact is another source of power for a leader. The status leader enjoys the force of legal enactments to enforce his efforts and the individual assigned to leadership by a group can rely upon the confidence and loyalty of the electorate in most situations, but any individual member of a high school faculty may exercise leadership based upon established facts or truth. It is from this source that the researcher, usually one who would hardly be thought of as an administrator, achieves power to change the direction of a group or to influence its decisions. A happy situation exists when the status or group-designated leader bases his leadership on fact rather than legal authority or group consent.

Function of Leadership

The image of a leader is further enhanced by the functions he performs. These may range from the selection of goals, the organization of human and material resources, gathering and interpreting information, establishing policy, implementing policies established by others, making decisions, and getting decisions made by groups, to evaluating outcomes. Or the leader's function may be one envisioned by Stryker: "He [the leader] has an innate propensity for change and innovation; . . . he manages to change men's beliefs, attitudes, and behaviors with benefits to many people."[1]

Some writers differentiate between the executive and leadership functions. They would classify men like Henry Ford and Cyrus Hall McCormick as leaders because of their creative impact on industry, whereas Andrew Carnegie and John D. Rockefeller would be considered as executives who were shrewd and gifted managers. According to this concept, some secondary school principals would qualify only as executives, capable of managing a school; others would qualify as leaders because of the creative impact their ideas and influence exert upon the educational programs.

Means of Accomplishment

Whatever a leader's source of power, and regardless of the function

[1] Perrin Stryker, "The Rarest Man in Business," *Fortune,* May 1959, p. 119.

he assumes, he utilizes certain means of accomplishing his mission. These processes of leadership are judged of particular importance in a democratic society that takes into account means as well as ends.

The traditional means of leadership is by mandate or command. Those who employ this means are sometimes strong, dominating persons to whom their subjects ascribe magnetic and perhaps magical or superhuman qualities. Such leaders often gain power by force—physical, political, economic, or social—and hold it by aggressive subjugation of those ruled.

Contrasted to the authoritarian leader who rules by mandate, a new type of leadership that depends primarily upon persuasion has emerged in the United States. It is based upon the precepts of democratic human behavior and relationships and is rooted deeply in the principle of self-government. The democratic leader is expected to encourage and to promote group decisions and subsequent actions, rather than to impose his plans upon the group. He is seen as an organizer, rather than a decision-maker; a member of his group, instead of a ruler. This type of leader persuades by helping members of a group to identify problems, assemble and interpret evidence, formulate possible courses of action, and select a plan to follow. The democratic leader aims at stimulating planning and action by members of a group and takes responsibility for coordinating their contributions.

Although the use of influence of others as a principal means of leadership is generally accepted educational practice, it has led to confusion and poor results in some schools where it has not been well understood. The difference between direction and outright but subtle command is often difficult to distinguish. Lack of clear-cut distinctions between these two means of leadership may weaken both leader and group contributions.

Impact of Leadership

What is accomplished is also an important element of leadership. In authoritarian situations, the end product is all-important. Democratic groups place more emphasis on means, but here, too, the outcome must be considered when judging the effectiveness of leadership.

The impact of leadership is usually first apparent in the response it evokes from those being led. For this reason, ability to get along with teachers, students, and parents is given high priority when high school principals are selected. The leader who is well liked is often assumed to be effective. Acceptance by members of the faculty is particularly vital to the principal. Being leaders themselves, teachers are often very sophisticated in their knowledge of the psychological mechanisms for influencing others and the philosophical theories of the sources of authority and means of accomplishing leadership. When leadership is accepted by teachers, their cooperation alone is usually sufficient to make the leader successful; when rejected, failure of the leader is usually inevitable.

Parents usually respond to school leaders through the eyes and attitudes of their children. If students carry home favorable impressions of the principal, parents typically accept them as their own. Yet every community has a minority of discerning citizens and parents who look beyond the popularity of a school official when appraising his impact on the educational program. These individuals are themselves leaders who function as opinion-makers among various subgroups in which they hold membership. Their judgment of the impact of leadership ranks, perhaps, next to that of teachers.

The final test of leadership, of course, is the results it produces: in the case of the secondary schools, the quality of the educational program provided and the efficiency of learning by students. An effective principal will develop a good school. The teachers who work under his leadership will improve from year to year. Students will be well prepared for post-high school opportunities. Community leaders will recognize that the quality of the educational program measures up to expectations.

It is not always possible to appraise the effectiveness of leadership on a school by assessing the reactions of teachers and students alone. A good leader may confront criticism, may even be dismissed, particularly if his objectives do not coincide with those of the group. On the other hand, it is possible for the weak leader to promote, for a substantial period of time, harmonious relationships among faculty members and within the student body. By endorsing the *status quo,* keeping pressures to a minimum on teachers and students, and providing opportunities for all to share in the governing of the school, a relatively high morale can be maintained even though the school does not achieve good educational results. Some leaders in recent years have established acceptance by focusing the attention of teachers and students almost exclusively on group processes—the means of working together democratically. Exclusive concern with group processes may obscure the results that group decisions and actions are intended to achieve. A leader who follows this course compromises principle and purpose in order to maintain harmony. Ultimately, of course, a day of reckoning occurs that upsets the temporary group rapport; yet much damage to students may occur before people become sufficiently aroused to evaluate the results being achieved.

Leadership Image

The various facets of leadership—source of authority, function, means of execution, and impact—combine in the minds of most people, with differing weights accorded to each by individual preferences and prejudices, to form what might be called a leadership image. Table 14-1 illustrates the manner in which such images and the terms used to describe them grow out of these various elements. These impressions of leaders represent practical definitions of leadership.

Table 14-1. *Elements Contributing to Leadership Image*

SOURCES OF AUTHORITY	FUNCTIONS
Legal enactments	Issuing mandates
Personal power	Making decisions
Group decisions	Organizing group
Truth	Getting decisions made by group
	Fact finding
	Evaluation

LEADER IMAGE

Boss	*Judge*	*Guide*
Forceful personality		Observer
Authoritarian		Team member
Politician		Educator
Laissez faire		Stimulator
		Group organizer
Servant		*Creator*
	Clerk	

MEANS	OUTCOMES
Creative ideas	Goal achievement
Coordination of group activities	Absorption with group processes
Stimulation	Acquiescence to authority
Persuasion	Frustration
Compulsion	Acceptance of leadership
Personal action	

DIFFERING CONCEPTIONS OF LEADERSHIP

Studies of the effect of leadership have documented the importance of agreement between the expectations held of a leader and the role he assumes. One investigation carried on in sixteen elementary schools in Illinois, Indiana, and Wisconsin led to the conclusion that:

> All aspects of staff relations, effectiveness, satisfaction and confidence bear a marked relationship to the extent to which the perceptions of expectations and behaviors held by principals and teachers coincide. If the principal views the behavior of teachers in a markedly different manner from that in which the teachers themselves view their behavior, or if the teachers report that markedly different expectations are held by the principal from those which they themselves report holding, there is an excellent chance that there will be a breakdown in staff relations, with a concomitant drop in levels of effectiveness, satisfaction, and confidence.[2]

The leadership success of the principal is even more specifically affected by the expectancies of teachers. The same study found that:

> The degree of confidence in the principal's leadership exhibited by a given teacher depends upon the degree of congruence between the teacher's perception of the principal's expectations and the teacher's expectations from an ideal principal. In this sense, confidence in the principal may be thought of as the obverse degree of satisfaction.[3]

The complicated circumstances of leadership in secondary schools make it difficult to arrive at leadership roles and relationships that are understood and consistently held by the many different individuals concerned. Concepts of leadership are shaped by clerical images of the principalship passed on by previous generations, by the growing tasks of professional leadership, by group-oriented conceptions penetrating the schools from the social sciences, and by the shared leadership becoming common in many areas of human activity as a response both to theory and to the growing complexity of organized effort.

Evolutionary Role—Chief Clerk

Principals, teachers, superintendents, school boards, students, and communities still think of the principal as a clerk responsible for many routine duties that make for the smooth day-to-day operations of the

[2] Egon G. Guba and Charles E. Bidwell, *Administrative Relationships,* Chicago (Midwest Administration Center, Univ. of Chicago), 1957, p. 50.
[3] *Ibid.,* p. 50.

school. This image has grown out of the outmoded functions of an earlier day, when the "principal teacher" consolidated the reports of attendance, marks, and promotion of pupils as prepared by the few other teachers of the school and summarized their simple requests for supplies. Such duties were usually assigned to a full-time teacher. To these simple clerical tasks was often added the matter of coping with problems of student behavior beyond the capacity or physical strength of less experienced or female teachers.

When one remembers that it is still possible to talk with men and women who not only attended but taught in schools organized in this way, it is not surprising that many people still expect the principal to concentrate largely on clerical and disciplinary matters. In larger, modern schools this conception of the principalship includes office management and marshaling the resources of other agencies to deal with problem youth.

Even recent definitions of the responsibilities of the secondary school principal stress heavily the role of handling routine duties. A statement by the Philadelphia Suburban School Study Council illustrates this point.[4] It lists the following eleven items under the heading "Administration of Routine Duties":

THE PRINCIPAL

1. is solely responsible for routine duties, even though he may supervise or approve plans of staff members or noncertificated personnel
2. organizes the total school program so that rules and regulations are cooperatively set up and fully understood by pupils, staff, and parents
3. is responsible for all pupil accounting, including registration, daily attendance, drop-outs, transfers, and promotions
4. supervises the preparation of reports to parents and superintendent, in areas such as pupil progress, conferences, educational and physical needs, fire and air raid drills, building inspection and maintenance, substitutes, and collections and receipts of money.
5. provides bus information to parents and sets policy regarding pupil behavior and keeps accurate records of those involved in bus transportation
6. sets up the cafeteria policy regarding behavior, time schedule, collection of money, and cooperates with the director of cafeterias in evaluating the total school lunch program

[4] Philadelphia Suburban School Study Council, *The Leadership Role of the Principal,* Philadelphia (School of Education, Univ. of Pennsylvania), 1957, pp. 4-5.

7. keeps records and approved requisitions for audio-visual aids, supplies, equipment, textbooks, and library books
8. sponsors the making and administration of the master schedule involving rostering of classes, use of rooms, health and dental examinations, and conferences
9. establishes the over-all school calendar concerning the use of school facilities to insure priority over nonschool activities
10. is responsible for the supervision of office facilities and personnel
11. arranges pertinent interviews and handles correspondence

This list states routine duties in professional or semiprofessional terms and seems to presume clerical help; nevertheless, it is so inclusive as to raise doubts as to whether such routine duties would ever leave time for creative leadership in improvement of instruction and personnel relations.

As a result of the "clerical chief" conception of the principalship, many secondary schools grew haphazardly, with little effective educational leadership from within, often expanding their facilities and curriculums at random in response to community pressures. New courses, extracurricular activities, and intrascholastic athletics were accepted as functions of the high school and were often given time and budgetary support equal to or greater than that given the traditional fundamental subjects. Educational theory, itself formulated largely by secondary school leaders, readily endorsed the chaotic development as basic to the democratization of schools and fundamental to the needs of students and communities.

Lengthening Shadow Concept

Out of the traditional image of the strong leader, as well as from the pattern of educational leadership that had developed in academies and colleges, came the "lengthening shadow" concept of educational leadership for the secondary school. This type of principal was more often found in private than in public high schools; nevertheless, such leaders existed in both and were instrumental in helping to establish strong and well-known secondary schools that served as models to others. The point of view that supported this conception of educational leadership held that the good school was largely a product of a great educational leader. Schools fortunate enough to have such leaders developed in accordance with the educational philosophy and wisdom of their principals.

The great secondary school principals not only shaped the character of the school—the quality of its staff, the substance of the curriculum, the academic standards it maintained—and influenced the lives of individual boys and girls who came under their direction, they affected the very shape of secondary education as an institution. A few examples of outstanding secondary schools that resulted from the leadership of strong principals are the Boston Latin School, under Ezekiel Chevers; the Evanston Township High School, under Francis Bacon; New Trier High School, led by Matt Gaffney; Scarsdale, New York, headed by Lester Nelson; the Science High School of New York City, under Morris Meister; the College Laboratory High School of Colorado State College in Greeley, Colorado, as directed by William S. Wrinkle; and the McKinley High School of Honolulu, Hawaii, as developed by Miles Cary.

Group Organizer

Emphasis on democratic leadership projected the image of the principal as a member of the teaching group who was assigned the responsibility of coordinating and organizing action resulting from decisions made by the faculty. Such a leader does not impose his will upon the group; rather he leads the teachers to arrive at agreements on educational policies and procedures and to delegate responsibility to members for necessary action.

Yet the principal, or department head, who strives to achieve the leader image of the group organizer often finds himself confronted with dual pressures: one from the group of which he is a member and to which he is obligated; the other from external forces and directives, often legal, to which he is expected to promote group compliance. In this sense, his position is similar to that of middle management in business as described by J. Erwin Miller, chairman of the board of a large manufacturing company.

> The special problem of the middle management man is this: On the one hand, he is required to discharge what in the past have been considered very great responsibilities. On the other hand, the need to conform to the broad programs of the whole organization, which are established without the possibility of his direct participation, deprives him of the power of determination and decision that his own people expect him to have and forces him at times to carry out policies and programs he may passionately believe to be wrong, at least in their local application. So the organization also becomes his special enemy, and appears always able to deprive him of genuine

accomplishment. This arouses his fears and induces in him a conformity which at times he despises and yet from which there is no escape, at least on terms he is willing to contemplate.[5]

Leaders are caught between roles and between groups. The principal attempts to arrive at decisions after democratic deliberation with the staff in his school, but additional considerations enter at a different point—where other schools are concerned, perhaps, or where community pressures must be taken into account. Parallel problems occur when the chairman of a mathematics department, for example, participates with his department in arriving at a decision which is to be considered later by people with different points of view, or where a representative of one segment of the faculty meets with a schoolwide group.

Schools attempt to overcome these difficulties by sharing decision-making with groups constituted to permit widespread participation. These representative bodies have to take into account overlapping authority and responsibilities; in this way an effort is made to reduce conflict and to arrive at decisions that are both better and, at the same time, more satisfying to those involved. Tead has observed:

> In every organization the tendency is both for the departmental heads and for the rank and file of members to see the organization's problems in terms primarily of their own functional effort. And as departments and functions become more elaborated and more cut up, this danger of a solely specialized interest increases correspondingly.[6]

Realizing some of these difficulties, school personnel have been as ready as people in business and government to have the kind of leadership that uses group resources. In its 1955 Yearbook, the American Association of School Administrators identified six considerations for improving the structure for administration:

1. Decentralization to place maximum responsibility at the operating level
2. Flattening of the hierarchal structure to shorten lines of vertical communication and make it possible for those at the operating level to influence general policy decisions
3. Involvement of as many staff members as possible in setting goals and formulating schoolwide and systemwide policies

[5] J. Erwin Miller, "The Dilemma of the Corporation Man," *Fortune,* August 1959, pp. 103-34.
[6] Ordway Tead, *The Art of Leadership,* New York (McGraw-Hill), 1935, pp. 8-9.

4. Creation of small work teams with definite responsibility for planning and effectuation of plans for defined areas of the program
5. Judicious use of committees in planning and coordination
6. Development of advisory and special services to assist the operating units[7]

Implicit in all of these considerations is the impact of leadership on groups. How a person with status or responsibility influences others is not presently as important a topic to scholars as the ways in which groups initiate courses of action, make decisions, and evaluate progress.

Leadership Team

Emphasis on group processes in the organization and administration of secondary schools, plus the growth of large institutions, has led to the development of the leadership team, where responsibility for school leadership is placed on both career leaders and classroom teachers. Those with leadership responsibilities coordinate their efforts, in teamlike fashion, to ensure smooth functioning of all aspects of the school program. The principal is usually responsible for organizing the leadership team, yet this duty may be assigned to another who is better qualified or who may have more time to coordinate the work of team members.

In secondary schools with the "schools within a school" pattern of organization, leadership may come from a number of teams, one for each school, with the activities of the various teams being coordinated by the principal or one of his assistants. Where several leadership subteams function in a multischool organization, various types of team relationships usually prevail. For example, heads of departments may work as a team for the entire system; they will also serve as members of the leadership team for their own school within the larger institution. In general, as groups become large and complex in structure, less general participation by teachers is possible and greater demands are made on leaders. Contact between group members and leaders in such situations may be maintained through representatives, rather than directly.

Education, taking a cue from politics, the armed forces, and industry, is developing a greater disposition to utilize team efforts, to analyze situations, to decide upon plans of action, to carry out the

[7] American Association of School Administrators, *Staff Relations in School Administration,* Washington, D.C. (National Education Association), 1955, p. 28.

plans, and to appraise the success of the endeavor. The same team may participate in all phases, different teams may accept responsibility for each phase, or there may be overlapping membership on the various teams. A team both organizes itself to provide leadership for others and seeks leadership for itself. Leadership within the team may be highly differentiated, with each member sometimes leading in the activity for which he is best suited. Such flexible provisions for leadership demand the maximum skill from the person with over-all leadership responsibility, the principal. The test of leadership is the ability to bring out "leadership"—initiative and dedication—in others. As Tead observed, "The proof of leading is in the qualitative growth of the led as individuals and as group members. Any other test is trivial and unworthy."[8]

NEW DEMANDS ON LEADERSHIP

The importance of leadership for secondary schools is accentuated by the new demands that are now being made on those in such positions. These demands require both higher levels of competence and greater versatility by those who prepare for or accept the responsibilities of leadership.

Larger Schools—Multiple Responsibilities

Although many small high schools still exist, the trend is toward large institutions with enrollments of from 500 to 5,000 students. With bigness come complex curricular problems, intricate class schedules, persistent personnel changes, extensive budgetary planning, plant expansions, and sensitive community relationships to challenge the most able leaders.

Large schools typically serve attendance areas of greater heterogeneity. They enroll pupils with sharp differences in home background, religion, academic abilities, motivation, interests, and vocational ambitions. At the same time that high schools are confronted with wider ranges in individual differences, they find themselves dealing with attendance areas—many in recently developed suburban districts—that are uncohesive, disorganized, and almost devoid of common goals and values. The small-town moral and spiritual values of a generation past do not exist today to stabilize behavior and to provide motivation for good scholarship to boys and girls. Furthermore, adult interests,

[8] Tead, *op. cit.*, p. 81.

activities, and goals may provide bad examples to young people. Against such a background, educational leadership is challenged to create schools that will elevate students to new heights in scholarship and intellectual development.

Complex Program Demands

The program of the contemporary high school makes demands on leadership unknown a generation ago when only a small percentage of youth of secondary school age attended school and the curriculum was oriented largely to academic preparation for further formal education. With about four-fifths of all youth now continuing in high schools, programs must be adapted to a wide range of abilities and goals.

In addition to the insistent program demands from various segments of the student population and the community, there are demands from industry, business, the armed forces, and colleges for emphases appropriate to their personnel requirements. Such crosscurrents of prescription for the secondary school force leaders to face highly controversial issues and decisions.

Personnel Selection and Development

Leadership of the secondary school must be concerned with the gigantic problem of maintaining a competent staff in the face of a critical teacher shortage produced by uncompetitive working conditions and what are considered inadequate salaries. This situation may be expected to deteriorate further as expanding college enrollments force the colleges to raid high school faculties for better instructors.

High school principals and supervisors face the choice of trying to create good teachers out of the best they can employ or of devising ways of stretching the talents of outstanding teachers to benefit greater numbers of students. Either course—and both courses will probably have to be utilized—places demands on secondary school leaders that challenge them to perform what appears to be almost the impossible.

Appraisal and Reward of Teacher Competence

Recent interest in recognizing and rewarding excellence in teaching illustrates another demand on secondary school leadership. Almost without exception, school boards and laymen endorse the idea that good teachers should be identified and rewarded. On the other hand, teachers themselves are fearful that such practices, which will produce unequal treatment, may be unfair to individual members of the profession. A major argument given by teachers against rewarding good teaching is their lack of confidence in those now in positions of educational leadership.

Between these two forces, the high school leader, particularly the principal, is trapped. All good administrators know who their outstanding teachers are, just as teachers themselves know. If principals agree that teachers should be rewarded for outstanding work, they may find themselves rejected by members of their staff. Deciding whether to stand on a principle that ultimately would benefit both students and teachers or to accept the mass verdict of the organized teaching profession against rewarding excellence in teaching is a dilemma that only individuals of strong character and sound educational convictions can resolve.

Pressures—Local and National

The secondary school is the focal point for pressures on education, regardless of their source or purpose.[9] Influential segments of the public would make of the high school a scapegoat for all the weaknesses of government, higher education, scientific research, technological development, national defense, international relationships, and religious devotion. To eliminate actual weaknesses in the school program, wherever they exist, and to preserve the recognized strengths in the face of persistent and often unreasonable pressures at both local and national levels, places a heavy burden upon educational leadership.

DILEMMAS OF LEADERSHIP

As is true with leadership in most fields, the secondary school presents to the administrator and supervisor a number of acute dilemmas. These are not new frustrations, but added to other factors they may become less bearable than they would be otherwise.

Authority and Responsibility

The principal is charged with legal authority for the execution of his duties. The school board and the community hold him accountable for the manner in which the school discharges its educational responsi-

9 David Riesman, *Constraint and Variety in American Education,* Garden City, N.Y. (Doubleday), 1958, pp. 120-42.

bilities. He is expected to establish high standards of scholarship and conduct, to set correct priorities in the curriculum, to make certain that all teachers give good instruction; in brief, to please everyone. If the principal takes action compatible with his authority, he may be censured by teachers and the public as a dictator; if he fails to act, he is charged with weakness. Teacher groups may share in the formulation of policies, in the making of plans for the school program, and in their execution; but if criticism results, the leader is held responsible for all.

Faced with the dilemma of trying to please everyone but being held solely responsible for all decisions, many principals elect to exercise their legal authority in making their own decisions. They may utilize the advice and judgments of teachers to help them decide on a course of action, but they make the actual decisions. Others throw themselves on the mercy of their faculties and attempt to hide behind the cloak of "committee actions." Either course leads to pitfalls and periods of stress.

The principal's maintenance of authority and responsibility is further complicated by the fact that teachers and communities expect educational leaders to give more vigorous direction than the group-organizer type of administrator does. They want the status leader to influence policy. Many recognize that often the most worthy causes and decisions are unpopular. They demand strong leaders, yet when the leadership is vigorous they may resist it.

Educator or Politician

In democratic institutions, many forces press the leader to resort to political devices to accomplish his objectives. Secondary schools are no exception. No matter how well prepared for his mission he is, the principal finds numerous temptations to abandon a scholarly and intellectual approach to educational leadership in favor of the more expedient procedures of marshaling popular support and aligning one group against another. Less able or poorly prepared administrators are even more susceptible to the temptations to introduce politics into educational leadership.

This dilemma of choosing whether to be "educator or politician" that confronts the high school administrator is further complicated by the fact that many communities still view educational institutions as they do governmental institutions to which representatives are elected. Some school officials still are elected by popular vote, or are appointed by political officials who themselves have attained their positions by appeals to the electorate. Under such circumstances, the task of making educational leadership a professional, rather than a political, assignment is difficult.

Sanctions or Helpfulness

In the relationships with students particularly, but sometimes also with teachers, the principal is torn between whether he should be the enforcer of sanctions or a helpful guide and counselor. Guidance counselors, and often teachers too, are eager to deal with students who have solvable problems and to leave the purely disciplinary cases to administrators.

The necessity for the principal to apply sanctions on occasion identifies him as an authoritarian figure and may well reduce his effectiveness as a guide and counselor, a role that is also expected of him. Yet he must be prepared to use both approaches if his leadership is to be successful.

NEW LEADERSHIP ASSIGNMENTS IN THE SECONDARY SCHOOL

An important aspect of the development of leadership for the secondary school is the expansion of defined status leadership positions. These other leadership positions offer assistance to the principal and career opportunities for teachers with leadership ambitions and potentialities.

In addition to the post of principal, the longest established position of leadership in the high school is that of departmental head. Although this post is sometimes opposed, about four-fifths of all secondary school principals have been found to favor its establishment.[10] Those schools that do not maintain permanent departmental heads usually provide for rotating chairmanships or subject field curriculum committees with either elected or appointed leadership.

Other types of leadership opportunities that are found in secondary schools, many of them new, are shown in Table 14-2. These include those that have official status and are assigned by the principal, superintendent of schools, or perhaps the school board; a variety of jobs that are assigned to teachers through election by members of the

10 Robert J. Keller, "Secondary Education—Organization and Administration," *Encyclopedia of Educational Research,* Chester W. Harris (ed.), rev. ed., New York (Macmillan), 1960, p. 1245.

Table 14-2. *Leadership Opportunities in Secondary Schools*

STATUS POSITIONS	Principal Assistant Principals Dean of Boys Dean of Girls Director of Curriculum and Instruction Supervisor of Pupil Activities Business Manager Director of Research Director of Public Relations Director of Guidance Director of Interscholastic Athletics Head of instructional teams Head of department Attendance Officer Director of Television and Audio-Visual Education
ELECTIVE ASSIGNMENTS	Subject field committees Curriculum revision projects Student Council advisers Class sponsorship Professional organizations Administrative councils Direction of student activities Professional organizations Parent-Teacher Association
INDIVIDUAL OPPORTUNITIES	Creative activities Research Instructional experimentation Professional writing and speaking

faculty or student body; and certain activities through which leadership may be exercised on an individual basis without either status or elective assignments.

The post of assistant principal is becoming a key position in the secondary school. Such personnel are given a wide range of leadership responsibilities in the fields of student personnel, administration, student activities, and program supervision. Many of the duties of this post are shared with the principal.[11]

The position of director of guidance is being added to secondary schools just about as rapidly as qualified personnel become available. Large schools aim at providing, also, a counselor for every 250-300

[11] Charles M. Long, "Duties of Secondary School Vice Principals," *Bulletin of the National Association of Secondary School Principals,* February 1957.

students. Smaller high schools often appoint a classroom teacher to serve as guidance director on a part-time basis. Such positions require specialized preparation and usually offer higher financial rewards than teaching.

The number and type of leadership assignments vary with the size of school, the character of its organization, and with the degree to which the community is able and willing to provide leadership services. Studies have shown that at least one full-time leader, or administrator, is provided or is needed for every 400 pupils.[12] Where more than one status leadership officer is available, either on a part-time or a full-time basis, the assignment of duties typically varies with the interests and abilities of those appointed to the positions.

Business managers, directors of public relations, and supervisors of curriculum and instruction are usually found only in the larger secondary schools. The position of head of an instructional team is a new one found only in high schools that are experimenting with the "team approach" to the organization of instruction. Similarly, a director of audio-visual or television education will be found only in those systems that are utilizing these mediums.

The number of leadership opportunities, in both status and elective positions, as well as the tasks that individuals can undertake, suggests the multitypes of leadership required in secondary schools today. It also suggests the complex task the principal must assume to coordinate the efforts of various people engaged in leadership. In addition, the list of these opportunities offers encouragement to the high school teacher with leadership aspirations to prepare for leadership positions inasmuch as they are increasing yearly.

THE PROFESSIONAL PRINCIPALSHIP

Over the years, the secondary school principalship has been moving toward professional status. Recent surveys and research studies have revealed progress in defining the qualifications, personal and professional, that principals possess, and the competencies required for successful high school administration. The rapid increase in the number of junior and senior high schools that will come in the next decade promises expanded career opportunities for able educators who prepare for this position.

[12] Robert E. Broyles, "What Is a Satisfactory Pupil-Administrator Load?" *Bulletin of the National Association of Secondary School Principals,* January 1942.

Status of the Principalship

In earlier times the emphasis in the principalship's work assignment was on instruction, rather than administration. He was first and foremost an educator; in fact, in certain parts of the country he was called "professor." The term "principal" is derived from the terminology "principal teacher." As we have seen, the original responsibilities of this position were to assist other teachers to perform this work.[13]

The secondary school principalship experienced periods of professional derogation during which educational leadership for the high school was supplied by the superintendent of schools or his assistants and the post was viewed largely as a managerial, or clerical, assignment. Eventually, agreement was achieved among educators that restored this position as the key educational leadership post of the secondary school.

Studies of the status and duties of secondary school principals have utilized such techniques as job analysis,[14] time apportioned to various activities,[15] and judgments of teachers and professional educators.[16] These various researches produce evidence that the principal's job now encompasses leadership responsibility for:

(a) The curriculum and program of instruction
(b) Staff selection, assignment, in-service education, and supervision
(c) Organization and administration of the school, including pupil activities, guidance, facilities, discipline, pupil accounting and records, and budgetary planning
(d) Interpretation of the educational program to the community

Such duties accord to the principal a position of maximum importance in secondary school leadership. In effect, more than any other individual the principal may determine the quality of program that a school will provide.

As secondary schools have grown in size, the authority, responsi-

[13] Egon G. Guba, "Research in Internal Administration—What We Know," *Administrative Theory as a Guide to Action,* Roald F. Campbell and James M. Lipham (eds.), Chicago (Univ. of Chicago), 1960, p. 115.

[14] Wilson F. Wetzler, "Use of Job Analysis Toward More Effective Educational Administration Practice," *Educational Administration and Supervision,* 1954.

[15] Stephen Romine, "The High School Prncipal Rates His Duties," *Bulletin of the National Association of Secondary School Principals,* May 1950.

[16] Bernice L. Cooper, *The Critical Requirements for the Principalship Based upon an Analysis of Critical Incidents Reported by Instructional Supervisors and Visiting Teachers,* unpublished doctoral dissertation, Athens (Univ. of Georgia), 1957.

bility, and influence of the principal have increased. Numerous highly competent and professionally prepared educators have been attracted to such positions. Inasmuch as some communities continue to maintain small high schools, the status and prestige of the principal, and the caliber of persons recruited to it, tend to vary with the size of school and the traditions in given communities. As a consequence, widely varying conceptions of the secondary school principal's job still exist across the nation.[17] Nevertheless, surveys of the status of the principal in recent years have revealed a continuing upward trend in the professionalization of the position as reflected by such factors as higher salaries, improved tenure, higher standards of professional qualifications, and increased interests of principals in the educational aspects of leadership.

Qualifications

Both personal and professional qualifications are judged to be essential to success in the secondary school principalship. Through surveys and a few research studies efforts have been made to identify the existence and relative importance of such characteristics. Programs of preparation have emphasized recruitment and selection to identify individuals with personal qualities and training suitable to truly professional principals. In a practical sense, these efforts are still in an embryonic stage since little differentiation has been made in such programs between principals, supervisors, and superintendents of schools. One study showed that 90 per cent of the emphasis in programs of preparation for educational administration should be identical for these three types of positions.[18] Failure to distinguish between the personal traits and professional qualifications unique to each of these three types of leadership positions is no doubt a strong factor in the tendency of administrators to move from one assignment to another—often with unfortunate results to the program of education.

Personal traits. Studies of personal traits appropriate to the secondary school principal have been concerned with such characteristics as intelligence, general knowledge and culture, creativity, originality, adaptability, initiative, persistence, ambition, judgment, responsibility, integrity, conviction, self-confidence, dominance, popularity, disposition, introversion-extroversion, social activity and mobility, economic

---

[17] Robert J. Keller, *op. cit.,* p. 1245.

[18] Prince B. Woodard, *A Study of Competencies Needed by School Administrators and Supervisors in Virginia with Implications for Preservice Education,* doctoral thesis, Charlottesville (Univ. of Virginia), 1954.

status, cooperativeness, verbal facility, and physical characteristics.[19]

Certain of these traits have been found to have a significant positive relationship to leadership: popularity, originality, adaptability, judgment, ambition, persistence, emotional stability, social and economic status, and communicative skills.[20] Lesser degrees of relationship seem to exist between leadership and insight, initiative, and cooperation. The traits and personal qualities that have been found to have positive relationship with administrative behavior tend to be those closely associated with personality of the leader as opposed to his position; they pertain more to interaction between people than to status. Possession of given traits does not assure successful leadership, yet, in general, good leaders possess at least several of such personal qualities.[21]

Professional qualifications. General agreement prevails, among educators at least, that the principalship requires professional preparation. This belief is reflected both in the certification standards for the position in most states as well as in the special programs of preparation that have been established in institutions of higher learning.

All states require some specialized preparation for certification for the principalship.[22] All but five[23] require more preparation than the bachelor's degree. Thirty-eight stipulate that the master's degree or its equivalent must have been completed, while five specify that work beyond the master's level must be submitted as evidence of professional preparation. Most states demand that applicants for this position complete courses in specified programs of preparation. About two-thirds of the states stipulate that a minimum of three years of successful experience as a teacher must be completed to qualify an individual for the principalship.

Interest in professionalizing the principalship has increased since World War II. Part of the momentum comes from steps being taken to upgrade the school superintendency.[24] Institutions of higher learning are experimenting with programs of preparation, some of which

[19] Truman M. Pierce and E. C. Merrill, Jr., "The Individual and Administrative Behavior," *Administrative Behavior in Education,* Roald F. Campbell and Russell T. Gregg (eds.), New York (Harper), 1957, pp. 318-31.

[20] *Ibid.,* p. 331.

[21] *Ibid.,* p. 332.

[22] W. Earl Armstrong and T. M. Stinnett, *Certification Requirements,* Washington, D.C. (National Education Association), 1959, p. 23.

[23] Colorado, Maine, Nevada, New Jersey, and North Dakota.

[24] Hollis A. Moore, Jr., *Professional Administrators for America's Schools,* Washington, D.C. (American Association of School Administrators, NEA), Thirty-eighth Yearbook, 1960.

require two years of graduate work, that draw upon their own inter-disciplinary resources as well as on the laboratory facilities for research and internships in public school systems.

Professional Competencies

Above and beyond concern for the personal and professional quali-ties that are apparently needed by the secondary school principal, con-siderable study has been made of the professional competencies that principals should achieve. School boards, for example, were found in one survey to look for such skills as ability to work well with both teachers and members of the community, initiative and ability to make prompt and careful decisions, ability to get things done efficiently, and the personal qualities of integrity, leadership, and personality.[25]

A synthesis of the competencies that are believed, or have been found, to be important to success in junior or senior high school prin-cipalships would include the abilities to:

(a) Analyze complex situations and identify key elements
(b) Combine separate forces into concerted action
(c) Reconcile conflicting elements, e.g., ideas, interests, or specializa-tions
(d) Balance varied purposes and goals
(e) Identify and make vivid purposes and aims
(f) Select individuals who can advance educational purposes
(g) Think of organization in terms of human activities
(h) Communicate and foster communication
(i) Inspire confidence, enthusiasm, and devotion
(j) Appraise accurately and objectively the success of a venture

Such abilities in the secondary school principal are the measure of the total impact of both personal qualities and professional prepara-tion; furthermore, they reflect the subtle human relationships involved when one individual exerts influence on group operations.

Opportunities Offered by the Principalship

Although the principalship, particularly in small high schools, will no doubt continue to be a steppingstone to the superintendency,[26]

[25] Gerald Bosch, *A Study of Some of the Factors That Influence the Selection of Public School Superintendents and High School Principals in Michigan,* doctoral dissertation, East Lansing (Michigan State Univ.), 1953.

[26] 83 per cent of the superintendents of schools reporting in a 1960 study indicated that they had come to their positions through the route of the building principalship; over half had been high school principals. Hollis A. Moore, Jr., *op. cit.,* pp. 36-37.

this job is coming rapidly to be recognized as a career position. As such it offers opportunities for important and satisfying educational leadership and rewards for successful attainment that are attractive to able individuals.

Top salaries for large secondary school principalships now range as high as $20,000 to $22,000 a year. Such positions usually go to persons with maximum training, e.g., the doctor's degree, and highly successful experience. They provide opportunities for professional contributions on state and national levels as well as within the school community itself.

The number of principalships and the number of positions in secondary schools of sizable enrollments are increasing rapidly. In addition, the creation of new junior high schools will provide administrative openings in city and surburban areas in most states. With the shortage of good teachers and capable prospective administrators, many good secondary school principalships promise to be open to able, ambitious educators who prepare for such work.

TEACHER'S ROLE IN LEADERSHIP

Opportunities for teachers to share in the leadership responsibilities of the secondary school, apart from those they assume in teaching, vary with the nature of the philosophy of administration. If the principal exercises authoritarian control over all functions, teachers may have little chance for leadership outside their own classrooms and the activities they sponsor. On the other hand, the emphasis on shared policy formulation which is characteristic of democratic groups provides all members of the teaching force chances to participate in the most important functions of leadership: the selection of goals, the agreement upon policies, and the appraisal of results.

Beyond the level of policy formulation, classroom teachers are called upon to assist with various phases of leadership. They play central roles in interpreting the program of the school to both pupils and the community. The implementation teachers give to school policies in curricular and instructional programs may determine the success or failure of group decisions. The insights teachers provide in appraising the effectiveness of the total school operation, as well as their evaluation of their own responsibilities, are usually the most valid of the observations offered by those who are connected with the school.

Through research and scholarship the teacher may identify knowledge and establish general principles that give direction to all secondary schools as well as the one in which he works. Here, perhaps, is the area in which the teacher assumes his most important role as an educational leader. To the extent that he engages in the continuous process of testing educational theory and established policies with systematic experimentation, he will be able to offer direction for the improvement of educational programs.

In many secondary schools classroom teachers actually assume major responsibility for leadership of such functions as curriculum reorganization, in-service professional improvement, improvement of personnel policies, student activities, intrascholastic functions, class sponsorship, yearbook and newspaper production, school assemblies, dramatic and musical performances, as well as numerous types of special projects. Few organizations, in fact, have as varied and competent resources for leadership as do junior and senior high schools; and few offer as many and important opportunities for leadership development and utilization.

SELECTED REFERENCES

American Association of School Administrators. *The High School in a Changing World*. Washington, D.C.: National Education Association, 1958.

BENT, RUDYARD K., AND LLOYD E. McCANN. *Administration of Secondary Schools*. New York: McGraw-Hill, 1960.

CAMPBELL, ROALD F., AND RUSSELL T. GREGG, eds. *Administrative Behavior in Education*. New York: Harper, 1957.

CAMPBELL, ROALD F., AND JAMES M. LIPHAM, eds. *Administrative Theory as a Guide to Action*. Chicago: Univ. of Chicago, 1960.

CULBERTSON, JACK A., PAUL B. JACOBSON, AND THEODORE L. RELLER. *Administrative Relationships*. Englewood Cliffs, N.J.: Prentice-Hall, 1960.

EYE, GLEN G., AND WILLARD R. LANE. *The New Teacher Comes to School*. New York: Harper, 1956.

HANSFORD, BYRON W. *Guidebook for School Principals*. New York: Ronald Press, 1961.

MILLER, VAN, AND WILLARD B. SPALDING. *The Public Administration of American Schools*. Tarrytown, N.Y.: World Book Company, 1958.

PIERCE, TRUMAN M., AND A. D. ALBRIGHT. *A Profession in Transition*. Nashville, Tenn.: The Southern States Cooperative Program in Educational Administration and its successor, The Associated Programs in Educational Administration, 1960.

TANNENBAUM, ROBERT, AND OTHERS. *Leadership and Organization: A Behavioral Science Approach*. New York: McGraw-Hill, 1961.

TEAD, ORDWAY. *The Art of Administration*. New York: Harper, 1951.

An intern teacher discusses his work with the master teacher who supervises his teaching.

One of the newest ways of improving teachers is a nation-wide television course to teach teachers the appropriate use of audio-visual resources.

CHAPTER 15

The Secondary School Teacher

THE TEACHER is the key to quality in secondary education. Public awareness of this fact is growing as economic conditions, population imbalances, and increased demands on schools make good teachers scarce. Nation-wide efforts are under way to recruit to the teaching profession able young people and to provide them with training programs and professional conditions that are challenging and rewarding.

The teaching profession must wrestle with the realistic fact that professional status requires a professional job. It is with mixed reactions that it views new experiments to adapt the variety of instructional tasks to the individual differences of teachers, with nonprofessional chores being assigned to noncertified personnel. As yet, teachers, unlike other professional people, have not strongly supported the principle that "only the best should teach." The incentives for capable people to choose secondary school teaching as a career are becoming greater, however, both in professional work and personal satisfactions.

TEACHER: KEY TO QUALITY EDUCATION

Severe shortages of qualified teachers during a period of rapid increases in school enrollments have alerted the nation to the danger of deterioration of its public education. A major effort is under way to find the means to attract to teaching the most desirable young people.

National Danger Recognized

Nonprofessional groups, as diverse as the American Federation of Labor, the Chamber of Commerce, the National Manpower Council, and the National Citizens Commission for the Public Schools, have reported to their members and to the public concerning the need to attract the talented to careers in teaching. Since World War II, economic advisers and highest level national leaders of every administration, Republican and Democratic, have recognized the close relationship of education to national progress. One statement representative of this thinking was made by Charles E. Wilson, former Secretary of Defense and President of General Motors Company: "The future growth of America, of our economy and of our security, is directly dependent upon our ability to continue to increase the level of education in the United States."[1]

Government economists regularly investigate the progress in the level of educational attainment of the adult population as an index of economic and social improvement.[2] They are able to relate family income, supply of potential skilled and technical manpower, and employment levels to the level of educational attainment found in the adult population of the country. In effect, the total social and economic advance of the nation is thought to be directly related to the ability of the educational system to enlarge the potential of its citizens. In 1960, slightly more than 42 per cent of the adult population had completed high school. At the present rate, the 50 per cent level will be reached in 1970. Whether this rate can be maintained while schools improve the quality of the education provided, remains a question.

Quantitative Dimensions of the Teacher Shortage

The national problem of the teacher shortage can be placed in perspective through the projection of certain known data and conditions. Often distorted or ignored in criticisms of public education are the

[1] Charles E. Wilson in a speech before the National Citizens Committee for Educational Television.

[2] U.S. Department of Commerce, *Projections of Educational Attainment in the United States: 1960 to 1980*, Washington, D.C. (Bureau of the Census), 1959, Series P-20, No. 91. Also, *1960 Census of the Population*, Vol. II, *Characteristics of the Population, U.S. Summary*.

extremely serious handicaps that have plagued schools since the economic depression of the '30's. Although only the staffing problem is presented here, serious deficits in buildings and equipment and in other facets of the educational enterprise have continued to accumulate. The current conditions relative to the supply and demand of teachers are described below.

Supply and demand: a double handicap. The fact of rising enrollments in the secondary schools is clear and predictable. Just as definite are the numbers of young people who form the pool from which new teachers are drawn. These data are available because the youth who will be in the secondary schools during the next decade and the teachers who will be available to teach them are already born. Babies born in 1946 entered the ninth grade in 1960; thus, the birth rates from 1946 to 1955 reveal, in general, the numbers of pupils the secondary schools may expect to enroll during the period 1960-1969. Likewise, the birth rates from 1936 to 1945 indicate the reservoir of manpower from which will be drawn the new teachers who will graduate from college from 1959 to 1968 and who will be available to teach during the same decade. These data, which are illustrated in Figure 15-1A & B, reveal a double handicap.

In the 1960's, the nation must draw its teachers from the lowest portion of the birth-rate curve; whereas the youth to be taught were born during a very high and increasingly higher portion of the curve. The birth rate of the 1920's was not reached again until after 1941. The period 1929 to 1941 produced an accumulated deficit of manpower which will plague public education through the 1970's.

Accumulated deficit—a complex condition. Several elements combine to complicate the process of determining the numbers of teachers needed yearly. Two of these elements are readily apparent. First, a certain number leave active teaching each year because of retirement, marriage, change of occupation, further training, or other reasons. Approximately 8 per cent of the secondary school teachers must be replaced each year to cover this turnover. In 1960, about 40,000 new teachers were needed for this purpose. Second, enrollment increases of about 500,000 pupils each year create a demand for an additional 20,000 teachers. This demand remained constant during the latter part of the 1950's and will remain so in the foreseeable future. Thus, in total, the secondary school demand for teachers amounts to approximately 60,000 each year to cover replacement and rising enrollments.

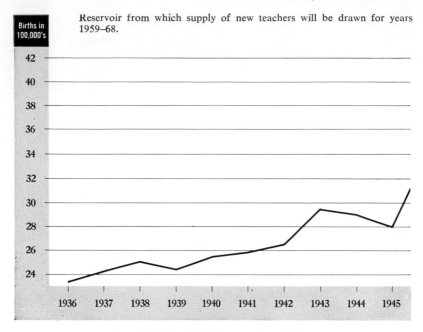

Reservoir from which supply of new teachers will be drawn for years 1959–68.

Fig. 15–1A. *Birth Dates, 1936–1945*

The number of bachelor-degree graduates from the nation's colleges who prepared for teaching during the period 1950-1960 averaged 65,000 yearly. However, less than 60 per cent of those who prepared to teach actually took positions in the public secondary schools. This left the nation with a yearly deficit, during this period, of from 15,000 to 20,000 qualified secondary school teachers. The deficit was made up by increasing class size and by the employment of those who could not normally qualify to take teaching positions. The threat to the quality of education through the erosion of the professional teaching corps becomes apparent.

Table 15-1 shows that the number of graduates per year rose steadily after hitting a low point in 1954 and that the 1960 graduates were almost sufficient to meet the demand. As the numbers increased, the percentage of those who actually accepted positions also increased. In 1960, 70 per cent of the graduates took positions in public secondary schools. If this trend continues, there is hope that the teacher shortage, as far as secondary schools are concerned, may be alleviated and the deficit somewhat recovered within a decade.

Section of the birth curve from which entering 9th graders will come, 1960–69.

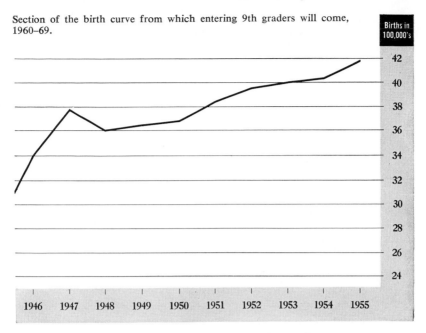

Fig. 15–1B. *Birth Dates, 1946–1955*

Further complications. Elements other than the two noted above contribute to teacher demand. Some schools would like to add services, decrease pupil-teacher ratios, replace unqualified teachers, and expand instructional programs in certain fields. Of these elements the most serious is that the supply of new teachers in such critical areas as English, foreign languages, mathematics, and science is gravely out of balance with the demand for them. Table 15-2 indicates the percentage of teachers in service in these fields compared with the percentage of graduates who prepared to teach in these fields in 1960. Merely to maintain the present numbers in each area the percentages should

Table 15-1. *Number of College Graduates Prepared to Teach in Secondary Schools*

Year	1950	1952	1954	1956	1958	1960
Total	86,890	61,510	48,916	56,785	69,093	80,465

S O U R C E : *Teacher Supply and Demand in Public Schools, 1960,* Washington, D.C. (National Education Association), Research Report 1960-R7, April 1960, p. 11.

Table 15-2. *Percentages of Prospective Teachers Compared with the Percentages Presently in Service in Secondary Schools*

FIELD	PROSPECTIVE NEW TEACHERS, 1960	TEACHERS IN SERVICE
English	11.7	15.5
Foreign Languages	2.7	5.2
Mathematics	7.0	12.9
Science	9.7	12.6

S O U R C E : Same as Table 15-1, p. 10.

be equal, or nearly so; to increase them the proportion of teachers entering each field should be considerably greater than that already in the field. Even though the total number of teachers needed should become available, the threat to quality education will remain until the proportions within critical areas come into balance with demand. Further increases in supply are required to replace unqualified teachers, to staff needed new programs, and to permit a greater degree of selectivity of the most able within the ranks of those preparing to teach.

Qualitative Dimensions of the Shortage

Numbers alone do not give an adequate, over-all picture of the importance of the teacher in secondary education. More important than numbers, yet closely related to them, is the continuous improvement in the quality of secondary school instruction. In the matter of quality, secondary education faces its severest test during the impending decade. In the concern for quality, however, it will be found that quantity—the high quantity of pupils, the low quantity of teachers and funds—is a prime consideration.

Teachers determine quality of education. Lack of full opportunity and challenge for the able students, curriculum gaps due to the shortage of teachers, and evidence of numbers of unqualified teachers—all these threaten quality in secondary education, with the teacher as the key element of the problem. All too often in secondary schools the development of a program or a needed change is delayed, modified, or canceled because of the lack of qualified staff to put it into effect. Teachers function as determinants of instruction in two ways: first, in their work as individual teachers within the classroom; second, collectively as a professional staff working to develop and carry out an integrated total program of instruction.

Instruction takes place through the relationship between the teacher and his students. The nature of this relationship is crucial to learning, and it is at this point that the teacher is revealed as the vital element in developing quality education. Whenever the teacher lacks knowledge or fails to understand learning problems or does not have the skills and techniques to solve them, the quality of education will suffer.

At the collective level, the effectiveness of the individual teacher can be thwarted if his work does not fit into a total plan for the students being served. Overlap, gaps in coverage, and lack of integration within the instructional program result when each teacher goes his own way. Even more serious is the threat to the effectiveness of each teacher if there is no opportunity to study cooperatively, conduct experimental projects, and participate in broader planning with colleagues. The teachers who conduct instruction are the logical ones to participate in its over-all planning and, in turn, to profit through personal development by such participation.

Effects of shortage. As we have seen, sufficient evidence is available to give warning that the teacher shortage is the major threat to quality education. Indexes of the erosion of quality may be listed as follows:

- (a) The shortage of qualified teachers is increasing and more emergency teachers are being hired
- (b) Expansion and improvement of foreign languages, science, and mathematics instruction are being hampered by an insufficient number of teachers
- (c) More schools are going on part-time or double-session schedules
- (d) Pupil-teacher ratios are increasing
- (e) Student achievement in certain subjects and in certain areas of the nation remains poor[3]

Quality—a restrictive factor. Despite shortages of teachers and increasing enrollments, the quality of the teaching corps has constantly improved. One index of this improvement is the requirements for teacher certification. Forty-seven states now require a minimum of a bachelor's degree for certification to teach in the secondary schools. In 1957, the Research Division of the National Education Association reported that the percentage of teachers holding master's degrees had

[3] During the Korean conflict, 34 to 58 per cent of the registrants in nine states failed to qualify for service on the Armed Forces Qualification Test. There is little evidence to indicate that this condition has improved.

increased steadily from slightly more than 10 per cent in 1930 to more than 40 per cent in 1956.[4]

Constant improvement in the quality of the teaching corps has served as a restrictive, but necessary, factor in teacher recruitment. Unfortunately, the better-qualified teachers have also become the most difficult to retain. However, the need for improved quality demands that only the ablest should be recruited and kept in teaching. As educators look ahead at the population curve and the national need for quality education, they seek imaginative solutions that will provide intellectual adventure and academic opportunity to able young persons now entering public education.

ATTRACTING THE MOST ABLE

Since the teacher is a key element in the problem of quality in education, larger numbers of able teachers who are well-prepared and who are given the opportunity to work under conditions of maximum effectiveness are essential to its solution. Arrangements for recruitment and selection, preparation, and development of the professional status of the teacher figure heavily in any effort toward long-range improvement in the quality of secondary education.

Recruitment to Teaching

Active recruitment to teaching is necessary if the profession is to get its fair share of the best talent. Attention to the problem of recruitment begins in the secondary schools, or earlier, and carries into the graduate programs of the universities. Unfortunately, very little effort has been made by the profession to recruit desirable young people into its ranks. At present it is not possible to imagine how large a share of the nation's abler young people could be attracted to teaching or what effect this might have on the quality of public education. No one knows because a concerted effort at recruitment has never been tried.

Teacher recruitment in secondary schools. Vocational guidance and educational planning in the high schools have begun to include the task of alerting capable students to the opportunities and satisfactions of teaching. Schools, through their guidance programs, are reaching

[4] Research Division of the National Education Association, *The Status of the American Public School Teacher,* Research Bulletin, No. 1, Washington, D.C. (NEA), 1957, p. 14.

more of the students who are not even considering college training.[5] More young people are encouraged to consider teaching as a career and to learn of the changes taking place in the field of public education. Some secondary schools, through activity programs (including formal organizations such as the Future Teachers of America clubs), provide firsthand information and experiences for their members. Positions as laboratory, library, and classroom aids, as well as tutoring experiences, are made available in these programs.

Universities: improved programs, wider interest. Teacher education institutions, including liberal arts colleges, have taken belated action to strengthen their programs in education and make them more challenging. These institutions have awakened to the crisis in public education and, through scholarship opportunities, improved curriculums, and programs articulated with secondary schools, they are beginning to take more seriously their responsibilities to the teaching profession. A significant new program in the universities is the "fifth year" of professional training for those who have completed a bachelor's degree but have taken no professional training. This program and others like it are tapping a large source of well-educated people who otherwise would have been kept from teaching.[6]

Prestige and Status: Major Considerations

The recognition accorded to a profession is generally a stronger incentive for entry into the profession than is financial remuneration. In this regard, education benefits greatly from the public trust that has been traditionally accorded to teaching (but not necessarily to *teachers,* as we shall see) in this country. Not less important are the increased emphasis now being placed upon learning, and the high value, no matter how vaguely conceived, that is attributed to an education. However, efforts from within the profession have recently been significant in increasing the prestige and improving the status of teachers. If these efforts are continued and redirected to meet the changed conditions of a new era, public school teaching will improve its ability to attract the able into its ranks and meet the challenge to provide a quality as well as quantity of public education unparalleled in history.

Quest for professional status. In the early history of the nation,

---

[5] Various estimates indicate that at least one-half of the top one-quarter of high school graduates do not at present enroll for college training.

[6] U.S. Department of Labor, "An Idea in Action: New Teachers for the Nation's Children," Washington, D.C. (Government Printing Office), 1956.

school teachers were itinerant workers, almost always men, who were incapable physically or mentally for other work. Washington Irving's Ichabod Crane is not too unfair a characterization of the early teacher. Later, women replaced men in practically all positions because teaching came to be looked upon as women's work and because women would work for less money than men. Fortunately, social forces operated to impress the public with the need for well-trained, independent teachers. By the beginning of the twentieth century, teachers were organizing into professional associations to better their working conditions. Certification laws were passed; minimum salaries were adopted; and tenure laws were enacted.

As late as the 1930's, teachers were still frequently fired for bobbing their hair, for smoking even in private, or for refusing to teach a Sunday school class as part of their teaching contract. Gains in professional status were won by tough, dedicated teachers and administrators with a vision of what the professional nature of teaching should be. Improved preparation for teaching and the demonstration of the results of better education consolidated these hard-won gains and increased prestige.

Status not automatically accorded. Unlike ministers and physicians, professional status is not accorded teachers just because they practice their profession. This is understandable, for the body of public school teachers includes some who are neither prepared nor interested in teaching, some who are using teaching as a stopgap or steppingstone to other employment, and a few who are almost ashamed to be called teachers. Because of these conditions, recognition is accorded on an individual basis, and it must be earned. To the extent that a teacher is prepared for, and dedicated to, the task of teaching and conducts himself according to the ethical standards of the profession, status is usually accorded.

Despite isolated cases of incompetence, few schools exist that cannot boast of teachers who have earned the respect and admiration of community, students, and colleagues. Years of improvement in the caliber of teachers have returned rich dividends. The competent individual, thoroughly prepared and personally self-sufficient, has become the recognized image of the high school teacher in most communities.

Changing Conceptions of the Teaching Task

As the level of preparation of teachers improved and as tenure, minimum salaries, and professional ethics brought a measure of security and stability, the traditional conception of the teaching task began to change. Schools traditionally sought teachers who conformed to a standard pattern. Like parts of a machine, they had to be interchangeable; one teacher could be taken out of the organization and another substituted without affecting the work of other teachers. The curriculum, even daily lesson plans, were prescribed in detail. Teachers were judged upon their ability to maintain order in the classroom and "cover the subject."

As a few schools began to view education in broader perspective and to develop programs which incorporated the purposes described in Part II of this volume, they found that a different kind of teacher was required. In fact, *many* different kinds were needed. Schools began to make use of the individuality of each teacher and sought those who could bring to the school talents and points of view not already found in its staff.[7] Such educational objectives as creating an informed citizenry, developing a sense of values, training in critical thinking and problem solving, and discovering and developing talent cut across subject and departmental lines and cannot be achieved without well-educated, highly sophisticated teachers who possess varying backgrounds and experiences and who can work together in a coordinated effort.[8]

THE BEST SHOULD TEACH

Who should teach? This is a question which must have existed ever since teachers first engaged in their work. Those who consider teaching as a career and others who train, employ, and supervise them must continuously ask and answer this question. A concise and ready answer is not available, if it is even possible, but certain guides for making judgments about teachers can be stated.

Teaching Undergirds All Endeavor

What is valued, what problems are viewed as important, in effect, what a society hopes to become, are reflected in its educational system.

[7] As early as 1950, Stiles and Dorsey presented evidence to support the point of view that this conception of teaching was needed and was evolving in the secondary schools. See Lindley J. Stiles and Mattie F. Dorsey, *Democratic Teaching in Secondary Schools,* New York (Lippincott), 1950, pp. 35-63.

[8] Studies conducted by the Thirteenth Yearbook Commission of the John Dewey Society reveal a wide variety of roles that teachers are now expected to perform. See Lindley J. Stiles (ed.), *The Teacher's Role in American Society,* New York (Harper), 1957.

The teacher is judged in the light of these social concerns. David Ryans points out this fact in an attempt to provide a framework for judging effective teaching:

> Teacher behavior is good or bad, right or wrong, effective or ineffective, only to the extent that the behavior conforms or fails to conform to the particular value system, or set of objectives, defining (1) the activities expected of a teacher in a given community or culture, and (2) particularly the kinds of learnings (attainments) and methods of teaching to bring about these learnings, approved by the particular culture.[9]

That the teacher has not been properly valued by the citizens of the United States cannot be argued. The value attached to an education has not been related, in the public mind, to either the material or the spiritual support of those who conduct it. The general low level of remuneration and of status, often summed up in the common phrase "anyone can teach," has long had an adverse influence upon the effectiveness of public education.

Federal interest—a proper perspective. The awakening of the nation to the intellectual needs of its scientific-technical society has brought about a sharp increase in interest in improving teacher status through efforts at the national level. Many believe that the national safety and future well-being may be sacrificed unless steps are immediately taken to strengthen federal assistance to education. There is little question that the federal government has an interest and a responsibility to public education. The slowness of the federal government to provide assistance has been due largely to the legal structure of the control of education and public resistance to centralization of any state functions.

So far, measures taken to strengthen public education through the improvement of teacher status have been, in the main, indirect or inadequate. Recent legislation, from the Smith Hughes Act of 1917 to the National Defense Education Act of 1958, has given attention to this problem. Direct aid from the federal government, through these measures, has provided funds to improve teacher salaries in vocational and home economics fields, for scholarships and loans to students and teachers, and to support training programs in science and mathematics, foreign languages, and guidance. Proposals have been made in Congress to allocate federal funds specifically to improve teacher salaries.

[9] David G. Ryans, "Theory Development and the Study of Teacher Behavior," *Journal of Educational Psychology,* October 1956.

Legislation embodying this kind of financial aid has been delayed due to resistance to a "general aid" program, but such aid could contribute to the elevation of teaching and serve to attract more able people to the profession.

Qualities Demanded in Teachers

An almost continuous search has been carried on to define the traits and abilities that distinguish effective from ineffective teachers. The literature of professional education contains considerable material describing the spiritual side of teaching. Horace Mann is purported, upon many occasions, to have expounded upon the need to find teachers who could "strike a victory for humanity," while others have asked for teachers who "gladly give of themselves." Dependable and significant measures of traits and abilities, however, must be obtained from careful scientific study.

Categories of traits and abilities. Traits and abilities judged essential for successful teaching have been classified into two categories. One includes skills and knowledge pertaining to psychological principles of teaching, competence in the liberal arts generally and in the subject matter to be taught, as well as general mental abilities. The other category includes the teacher's effectiveness in promoting good working conditions with pupils, his patterns of interests and commitments, and his personal adjustment. Although the categories are not mutually exclusive, for traits and abilities in one category influence those in the other, they do provide a framework for assessing the qualities likely to be important to teaching effectiveness.

High intelligence—the only trait education cannot supply. Those who hold that teachers are born, rather than developed, are correct as far as intelligence is concerned. Without a reasonably high degree of intelligence, the education of a teacher, in any field, is impossible. Given the necessary amount of intelligence, however, it is possible to develop in most young people the other traits essential to teaching. In fact, unless our present beliefs about the biological development of man are wrong, most of the other traits must be developed through the process of education.

Distinguishing abilities and traits. Through scientific procedures, researchers have been able to isolate the abilities and traits which distinguish between effective and ineffective teachers. Schultz and Ohlsen applied procedures used in the study of experienced teachers to a group of student teachers. They found that:

The outstanding student teacher . . . was a creative person who had an abundance of initiative and enthusiasm. He had a genuine interest in his pupils and a positive attitude toward teaching. He was able to adapt to new or unforeseen situations. In his classroom, his work was well organized. This ability to organize and plan was combined with a good understanding of the teaching-learning process, a knowledge of his subject matter and a knowledge of teaching methods. He understood his students and was able to involve them in classroom activities in such a way as to promote and hold their interest.[10]

This general description of the effective teacher is supported by the findings of other studies. Schultz and Ohlsen, in addition, give measures of those who have completed professional training, but who have not as yet become teachers. In this sense their study provides a means of locating the effective teacher before he assumes a regular teaching position.

A second and later study, also conducted with student teachers, reveals abilities and traits which distinguish the effective student teachers from the ineffective. The findings, given in Table 15-3, agree closely with those of the Schultz-Ohlsen study. Further, they suggest the importance of professional training in such items as organization and planning, identification and diagnosis of learning problems, understanding of students, and the like.

From Table 15-3 we can infer other skills and abilities, as well as personality factors, that are subsumed under the various traits. Imagination and resourcefulness, for example, imply not only a grasp of a wide range of techniques but also the ability to select these techniques appropriately and tailor them to specific learning conditions of the classroom. Revealed in the list is the interplay of the "personality" and "technical" categories of traits described above.

CHOICE OF SECONDARY SCHOOL TEACHING

Any person contemplating a vocational choice will properly attempt to assess his own potential for success, as well as his interests and preferences, in light of the information he can gather concerning possible career fields. This process is almost a continuous one for those who are fortunate enough to have the means and the ability to undertake a college education in the United States.

---

[10] Raymond E. Schultz and Merle M. Ohlsen, "How to Define a Good Teacher," *School Executive*, July 1954.

Table 15-3. *Discriminatory Traits of Best Student Teachers*

1. Imagination and resourcefulness
2. Organization and planning
3. Explanation of ideas
4. Leadership
5. Maturity
6. Identification, diagnosis of learning problems
7. Understanding of students
8. Quickness in assessment, reaction
9. Motivation ability
10. Initiative
11. Exercise of good judgment

SOURCE: Francis James Rybak, *The Identification of Discriminatory Traits in Behaviors Associated with Best and Poorest Secondary-School Student Teachers,* unpublished doctoral thesis, Ohio State University, 1958.

Steps taken in recent years to improve teaching as a profession have made secondary education a more attractive career for young people today. The opportunities and challenges in teaching and the kind of life it makes possible are qualities that those intellectually inclined will prize.

SOME ASPECTS OF TEACHING AS A CAREER

High school teaching compares favorably with any other field in the opportunities it offers to those with ability and initiative. Secondary education is booming—to say less would be an understatement.

The redefinition of the teacher-task, the phenomenal growth of high schools, and the increased public attention to education point to rapid changes and enlarged opportunities in teaching. Any person who gets more satisfaction from creative activity and new ventures than from repetitive work under unchanging conditions will find these kinds of challenges in the secondary school teaching. There is less competition for positions of responsibility and creativity than in almost any other field. Secondary education is developing opportunities which run beyond the imagination even of those who have been active in beginning the changes now under way.

Secondary schools employed 511,607 teachers in 1960, of whom the numbers of men and women were almost equal. No longer are high school teaching positions dominated by either sex. Improved salaries and working conditions, and opportunities for advancement contribute to holding able men in teaching. The stereotype of the old maid high school teacher is rapidly fading; most women in secondary school positions today are married, have families, and are pursuing teaching as a career parallel to homemaking.

An array of statistics has been gathered concerning the teacher's satisfaction with his job, restrictions upon his personal life, occupational mobility, and similar matters. In every case the stereotyped beliefs about the unhappiness of teachers and the unpleasantness of teaching were exposed as grossly exaggerated. In the main teachers are happy with their positions; they intend to remain in teaching and in the communities where they now work. They are not overwhelmed with petty details and activities, nor are they restricted in their personal lives. (One survey found that 65 per cent of the teachers felt positively no restrictions; only 2 per cent, serious restrictions.) They are active in politics; 84.8 per cent voted in the 1956 elections. They belong to a number of community organizations and participate in church work far more frequently than the average citizen of the nation. Over 90 per cent of the public school teachers are reported to have church membership compared to a national average of about 60 per cent.[11]

Practically all teachers, as is shown in Table 15-4, felt accepted in the social life of their communities. Those in small- to medium-sized population districts had the most uncertainty about acceptance. In addition, teachers reflect an enjoyment of their associations, and, above all else, a great love of teaching. In 1957, the National Education Association published the results of an extensive survey of public school teachers. In the questionnaire used to collect the data, a space was provided where respondents could freely express their feelings toward teaching. According to the analysts of the study, over one-third of the replies "dealt with one general theme—the love of teaching and the rewarding sense of achievement that comes from work with children and young people and contributing through their lives to a better world."[12]

[11] See especially, *The Status of the American Public School Teacher.*
[12] *Ibid.*, p. 40.

Table 15-4. Acceptance of Teachers into Social Life of the Community
(percentages)

GROUPS OF TEACHERS	ACCEPTED	PARTLY ACCEPTED	IGNORED OR REJECTED
Type and size of school district			
Rural	90.9	8.6	.5
Urban by population			
500,000 or more	92.6	6.6	.8
100,000–499,999	90.3	9.0	.7
30,000–99,999	85.2	14.0	.8
10,000–29,999	84.4	14.5	1.1
5,000–9,999	80.5	18.1	1.4
2,500–4,999	80.9	18.5	.6
All urban	86.4	12.7	.9

SOURCE: Research Division of the National Education Association, *The Status of the American Public School Teacher*, p. 32.

Remuneration in teaching. Education is a field that should not be entered by those whose primary interest is making money. Salaries in education do not compare well with earnings in other professional fields. However, the salary conditions in public schoolteaching require careful analysis if a realistic picture is to be obtained. National averages and minimum salary figures do not indicate the wide variations which exist between school districts or the range from minimum to maximum levels within districts. Teacher salaries from $6,000 to $10,000 are common in most suburban areas around large cities in the North and the Far West.

1. *Starting salaries and minimum levels.* Preliminary data indicate that the average starting salary for teachers in 1960 was more than $3,600 (with a range from $2,600 in the South to $3,800 in the Great Lakes region to over $4,200 in the Far West). The variation within a region can be indicated by a simple illustration: the authors averaged the beginning salaries of twenty-three school districts around Chicago and found the average starting salary to be in excess of $4,600 as compared with the regional average of $3,800. In general, suburban areas around large cities pay the highest beginning salaries; next in order are the large cities; then, smaller cities, towns, and rural areas (with differences depending upon the region of the country).

2. *Averages and comparisons with other groups.* During the decade

of the 1950's, average teacher salaries showed strong and continuous improvement. The gain was both well above the rise in cost of living and favorable in comparison with other salaried employees. Teacher salaries gained a level 10 per cent above that of all salaried persons during this period. These data are presented in Table 15-5 which

Table 15-5. *Teacher Salaries Compared to Other Groups (averages)*

YEAR	TEACHERS [a]	ALL PERSONS ON WAGES OR SALARIES [a]	EMPLOYEES IN MANUFACTURING [a]
1950	3,663	3,613	3,963
1953	3,904	3,867	4,373
1955	4,337	4,151	4,695
1956	4,487	4,297	4,873
1957	4,594	4,325	4,910
1958	4,792	4,324	4,911
1959[b]	4,935	4,421	5,033
Percentage increase of 1959 over 1950	34.7	22.3	26.8

[a] Earnings are shown in constant dollars based upon 1958 prices.
[b] 1959 earnings are estimates.

S O U R C E : Research Division of the National Education Association, *Economic Status of Teachers in 1958-59*, Report 1959 R-3, Washington, D.C., 1959, p. 21.

also indicates the relatively low level of salaries of teachers in 1950. There is reason, however, to speculate that the average teacher salary figure is low because of the very large number of beginning teachers whose starting salaries tend to weight the average toward the low side in the computation.

3. *Maximum salaries.* Able teachers who complete advanced training will find ample opportunity to obtain positions which improve their salary potential. In addition to increases in salary due to length of service, there are increases given for advanced professional training and for positions which combine teaching with related professional duties. One in six school systems also rewards excellence in teaching with merit increments. A survey of salary schedules (see Table 15-6) shows the median of scheduled maximum salaries for cities of various sizes. In the year 1959-60, this range was from $6,815 to $6,900 for full-time teaching. For other positions, occasionally combined with part-time teaching, maximum salaries range from that of Dean at $7,400 (median) to that of Director at $11,996 (median).

Table 15-6. *Maximum Salaries of Teaching and Related Professional Personnel, 1959-60*

POSITION	MEDIANS OF SCHEDULED MAXIMUM SALARIES FOR THOSE WITH MA DEGREES		
	Group 1[a]	Group 2[a]	Group 3[a]
Teacher	6,900	6,815	6,850
Counselor	7,700	7,957	7,675
Dean	7,400	8,400	7,885
Head of Department	8,230	7,900	7,495
Supervisor	9,518	9,060	8,200
Director	11,996	10,809	9,350

[a] Population of urban school districts: Group 1: 500,000 plus; Group 2: 100,000 to 499,999; Group 3: 30,000 to 99,999.

SOURCE: Division of Research of the National Education Association, *Research Bulletin*, Washington, D.C., May 1960.

4. *Final considerations.* Salary no doubt is a major factor in determining a career choice. It is appropriate that it be considered along with personal and social factors. Unless the means are found to bring teacher salaries within the range of occupations with which public education must compete, interested and able people will be lost to these other fields. At the same time certain conditions mitigate the salary differentials that do exist: one should not overlook the advantages of sound retirement programs, insurance plans, tenure, and substantial vacation periods. Finally, starting salaries and averages do not show the levels to which individual teachers can go in a given school system. Maximum salaries must be considered, and, for able high school teachers, the salaries which are paid for the positions shown in Table 15-6 are definitely possible.

The Teaching Profession

When the teacher accepts a position, he joins a large group of colleagues in a professional enterprise. Morally he is bound by the tenets of the profession which describe ethical standards and establish the limits of conduct and the obligations of service. Within the profession, associations are formed to educate the membership, improve their effectiveness, and look after their welfare.

United, strong, influential. In numbers, teachers in the United States comprise the largest profession. The profession exists to render a high and specialized form of social service. Together with law, medicine, and theology, it is regarded as one of the four great professions. One could argue that teaching is more worthy of this classification than are the other three professions. Teaching is an art and a science; like medicine, it has an empirical tradition, and it definitely has a stronger scientific basis than law or theology.

The profession has, in recent years, greatly improved working conditions and increased the knowledge and skills of its practice. In the process of making an intelligent decision about teaching as a career, the student must take into account this growth in professional strength and influence. By taking responsible action and by identifying closely with professional aims, teachers are increasing the influence of the profession on the educational mission it is privileged to serve.

Professional associations. Numerous organizations have been formed to unite and improve the profession. Nearly 600 state, regional, and national associations are in existence, and a large number (well into the thousands) of clubs and unions concern themselves with the welfare and interests of local groups. These groups, local, state, and national, perform significant services. They influence legislation, work to improve the conditions of teachers, and, most important, improve education through study and discussion. Almost every important program or proposal is discussed in numerous professional meetings.

The major national professional organization open to all teachers is the National Education Association. In 1957 this organization published the report of a survey of a large number of teachers which revealed the extent of the membership of teachers in professional educational organizations. These data are shown in Table 15-7. They indicate the large percentage of teachers (87.6 per cent) who hold multiple memberships in organizations, and the low percentage (4.8 per cent) who do not belong to formal associations.

The types and purpose of associations vary greatly. The National Education Association is open to all persons—whether teachers or not—who are in the profession. Another type is specialized in its interest in a particular field of instruction; the National Council of Teachers of English is an example. Other kinds include those concerned almost exclusively with teacher welfare (such as the American Federation of Teachers) and those which are concerned with certain segments of the profession, i.e., only teachers, only supervisors. Each type of organization contributes in its own sphere to the professional stature of the teacher.

Table 15-7. Membership of Teachers in Professional Education Organizations (percentages)

	MEN	WOMEN	ELEMENTARY	SECONDARY	TOTAL
Local, state, and NEA	53.9	60.3	59.5	57.0	58.5
Local and State	27.8	25.3	25.5	26.9	26.0
Local and NEA	.9	1.3	1.3	1.1	1.2
Local only	5.5	4.6	4.3	5.7	4.8
State and NEA	1.7	1.9	2.0	1.7	1.9
State only	2.3	2.2	2.4	1.9	2.2
NEA only	.3	.3	.4	.2	.3
Local teachers union	.5	.2	none	.6	.3
None	7.1	3.9	4.6	4.9	4.8
TOTAL	100.0	100.0	100.0	100.0	100.0

SOURCE: Research Division of the National Education Association, *The Status of the American Public School Teacher*, p. 62.

SELECTED REFERENCES

CHAMBERLAIN, LEO M., AND LESLIE W. KINDRED. *The Teacher and School Organization*. Englewood Cliffs, N.J.: Prentice-Hall, 1958.

CHANDLER, B. J. *Education and the Teacher*. New York: Dodd, Mead, 1961.

DOUGLAS, PAUL. *Teaching for Self-Education*. New York: Harper, 1960.

KLAUSMEIER, HERBERT J. *Teaching in the Secondary Schools*. New York: Harper, 1958.

MARSON, PHILIP. *Teacher Speaks*. New York: McKay, 1960.

REDEFER, F. L., AND DOROTHY REEVES. *Careers in Education*. New York: Harper, 1960.

ROGERS, JACK. *Automation: Technology's New Face*. Berkeley: Institute of Industrial Relations, Univ. of California, 1958.

ROGERS, VIRGIL M. *Do We Want Merit Salary Schedules?* Syracuse: Syracuse Univ. Press, 1960.

RYANS, DAVID G. *Characteristics of Teachers*. Washington, D.C.: American Council on Education, 1960.

STILES, LINDLEY J. *Teacher Education in the United States*. New York: Ronald Press, 1960.

STRANG, RUTH. "Every Teacher's Record." New York: Bureau of Publications, Teachers College, Columbia Univ. 1960.

New secondary schools provide excellent examples of aesthetic and functional, yet economical, architectural design.

CHAPTER 16

Secondary School Buildings

PROVIDING adequate and appropriate buildings to house secondary school programs and enrollments has been a persistent challenge to the United States since the turn of the century. The first high school buildings usually were simply old elementary school structures, adapted by the exchange of small desks for larger ones. Inasmuch as enrollments were small, these high schools were often housed in the same buildings with elementary school classes, usually in upstairs rooms. No provisions were made for libraries, laboratories, auditoriums, gymnasiums, or other specialized facilities.

As the public high school became popular, communities were forced to provide separate buildings intended only for high school use. These, although they were supposed to incorporate facilities appropriate to the functions being advocated for the secondary school, were usually composites of architectural designs borrowed both from the elementary school and the colleges. Their predominant feature was the room provided for certain extracurricular and competitive activities—auditoriums, concert studios, gymnasiums—that communities demanded. These areas, too, were patterned after designs made popular in institutions of higher learning. Central libraries, often too small, were added, justified frequently on the ground that the reading space could be used for study-hall purposes. Cafeterias became popular with the advent of government-subsidized hot-lunch programs during the depression years of the 1930's. Laboratories, shops, and occasionally guidance counseling rooms were other new features, frequently ill-designed for the purposes they were to serve.

Although most communities built new and larger high schools every ten or fifteen years, before 1940 the structures were almost always poorly adapted to the unique educational mission of the secondary school. The situation at the junior high school level was even worse; these institutions were shunted into the old senior high school buildings which were inadequate for their original purposes and even less well-suited to the intermediate level. Such practices have caused many junior and senior high school teachers and administrators to plead for secondary school buildings uniquely designed for secondary school pupils and programs.

After World War II, the accumulated shortages of school buildings that resulted from the lag in construction during the 1940's, followed by the rapidly expanding school populations, alerted public attention to the critical problem of providing adequate school buildings. As a consequence, an almost unprecedented interest prevails today in the building of schools. Congress is continually being called upon to appropriate funds to supplement the resources of state and local governments. Major architectural firms have assigned their most able personnel to the task of designing buildings appropriate to the rapid changes that are taking place. One leading philanthropical foundation has established a center for research on school buildings. Furthermore, people seem to have recognized that the provision of the high school plant is not a "one-shot" operation to be accomplished and then forgotten; building a secondary school is seen as a continuing task, subject to the changes that occur in enrollments, size of districts, school functions, and organization as well as in curricular emphases and instructional procedures.

Public interest in and attention to secondary school buildings, of course, is part of a general interest that extends also to the needs of the elementary schools and colleges. The expansion of housing for the lower schools forecasts the demands for high school facilities. Similarly, growth in secondary schools hints at the future college requirements. But unlike the elementary schools, which are relatively simple in design and facilities, or college structures, which are far removed from the close scrutiny and immediate use of most citizens, secondary schools tend to reflect the total educational aspirations of the community. Not only must they provide the space and facilities required for various aspects of the secondary school program, they serve also as community centers for adult education, cultural activities, recreation, civic meetings, and public entertainment. Any special interest of a town or city may well be reflected in the plans for a new high school. Changes in economic resources, growing urbanization, or industrialization may, similarly, dictate building specifications. Community pride may support aspects of plant design and facilities that contribute little to the utility of buildings. Furthermore, established conceptions of the high school's function may shape new buildings to fit out-of-date programs. In addition, pressure for local tax dollars more often than not reduces the space provided in new structures to below the actual need.

The forces that operate on secondary school buildings today, however, go beyond the usual concern for space, façades, and facilities for extracurricular and community functions. Nation-wide responses are developing that reflect the future shape and direction of secondary education rather than the past. Above all, these forces call for fresh, creative approaches to the design and construction of flexible and economic buildings to meet the demands of a secondary school program that is undergoing rapid changes.

ACCUMULATED SHORTAGES OF FACILITIES

The financial and instructional problems of secondary education have been greatly influenced by certain factors that have contributed to acute shortages of plant and instructional facilities in many communities. These include the changes taking place in enrollment patterns, economic forces, accelerating educational developments, and obsolescence in buildings. Efforts to overcome shortages continue to be unprecedented in scope and creativity, although they are often characterized by a kind of inverse inventiveness—ingenuity in freezing, modifying, or trimming educational programs to available facilities.

Causes of Shortages

Need for secondary school facilities has been peculiarly affected by widely divergent forces which converged only a few years ago. Increases in enrollment have both accompanied and followed economic depression and wartime upheaval. Deliberate efforts to reduce the lag between existing educational programs and methods and technological and social challenges have sharply stimulated both innovation and awareness of outmoded facilities.

Enrollment patterns and facilities. The twelve- to fourteen-year interval between each school generation's birth and its entry into the secondary school provides high school authorities time to prepare for enrollment increases—an advantage that elementary school officials do not have. The period from birth to preschool inventory and registration is so short that time is insufficient for the many steps that must be taken to provide school buildings—population surveys, site selection, bond issue referendums, drawing of architectural plans, letting of contracts, and construction.

Many secondary schools, however, have failed to take advantage of this extra time. Some communities have devoted these years, when buildings should have been planned and built, to debate rather than to constructive action. One reason for such time-wasting controversy in new residential areas around cities (where population increase is most rapid) has been the belief that families moving in with small children would not remain until their boys and girls achieved high school age. Some communities assumed that residents with children of elementary school age would undoubtedly move to larger homes or into the cities as their children reached the secondary school. As a result, high schools went unbuilt in the face of greatly expanded prospective enrollments. In a few instances, of course, mobility of families did reduce the size of anticipated secondary school enrollments; in most, however, families remained in their new suburban communities and others joined to swell the load on high school facilities.

Other communities, which took birth rates at face value for elementary school planning, discounted them at the high school level because of past experience with dropouts. The failure of schools to gain in holding power during the war years contributed to an underestimate of numbers who would continue in school when war conditions terminated. In 1947, 76.8 per cent of the boys and 79.1 per cent of the girls 14-17 years of age were in school. Ten years later 86.8 per cent of the boys and 86.7 per cent of the girls of these ages were in school. Projecting these trends, but allowing for substantial deceleration as a saturation point imposed by social and physiological limits is approached, the Bureau of Labor Statistics estimates 92 per cent of the boys and 90 per cent of the girls aged 14-17 will be in school by 1975.[1] This upward shift in percentages of attendance added to the very large increases in numbers of the 14-17 age group resulted in an increase of about 60 per cent between 1950 and 1960. This pattern of growth in enrollments was matched by an increase of about 58 per cent in secondary school teachers.[2] Thus, the schools' increased holding power joined with population growth to add large numbers of youth who had to be provided with learning space and equipment.

Another important cause of building shortage has been the continuing movement of families both within and among school districts. The major migrations have been from rural to urban and from city to suburban, with many variations within these patterns and minor departures from them. Both big city and rural high school districts have experienced a period of under-use of secondary school plants, extending in some cases into or through the 1950's. The explanation of this under-use was confirmed by the 1960 census which showed that net losses of population in the largest cities and in the rural areas exceeded estimates. In such communities the rise in the percentage of population of secondary school age did not offset the total population loss, partly because this age group figured heavily in the migrations.

Shifting enrollments are another common problem of the cities. As older neighborhoods deteriorate and are occupied by underprivileged groups, concentration of population in those neighborhoods goes up. The schools serving such areas frequently become overcrowded. Often they lack the facilities needed to serve the changed pupil population. Some cities that are unable to cope with the problem of integrating racial or social groups in their schools maintain rigid attendance boundaries, sometimes having crowded and under-used secondary buildings within blocks of one another. Many families, partly motivated by these unsatisfactory conditions, have moved to suburban school districts thus intensifying the shortage of facilities there.

Consolidation of schools has also contributed to the need for new secondary school plants. Between 1931 and 1959 the number of school districts declined from more than 127,000 to a little more than 40,000.[3] The change in Illinois, whose school districts shrank from

[1] Bureau of Labor Statistics, U.S. Department of Labor, *Population and Labor Force Projections for the United States, 1960 to 1975,* Washington, D.C. (Government Printing Office), 1960, p. 28.
[2] Research Division, *Estimates of School Statistics, 1959-60,* Washington, D.C. (National Education Association), 1959, pp. 7, 11.
[3] *Ibid,* p. 6.

12,000 in 1947 to 1,700 in 1959, was one of the greatest. While much of this type of change represented the elimination of very small elementary schools, the effort to achieve more efficient secondary school units was a major factor. Sparsely settled areas have difficulty achieving a high school with a graduating class of 100, the minimum size recommended by Conant.[4] The desirability of larger attendance units has brought about high school consolidation in many places, even where the population has been growing rapidly.

A good example of school district reorganization is provided by New Jersey, where in 1931 the legislature authorized regionalizing various types of educational services. Secondary schools have been the only educational agencies to take advantage of these provisions. The first regional high school was formed in 1935. By 1957, 115 separate school districts had merged into 25 regional high schools scattered widely throughout the state.[5] The median size of these schools was 850; they included both 7-12 and 9-12 grade patterns. In each case they have developed more comprehensive offerings—and require more varied facilities than the schools they replaced.

Economic forces. For a period of twenty-five years abnormal economic conditions have wrought havoc with needed school building programs. Figure 16-1 shows how public school building responded to the 1929 depression. In 1933-34 the expenditure for buildings and equipment dropped to about one-sixth of the 1927-28 level. While there was some resumption of building by 1939, it was curtailed to almost nothing during the war and did not return to the 1927 level until about 1950. Even though today expenditures are well beyond the 1927-28 level, the gap remains enormous. Most authorities consider that the building rate of the 1920's was inadequate. Thus there was an accumulated shortage even before twenty-five years of reduced construction.

People were generally apathetic about the lack of school building during the depression years. Demographers assumed a low birth rate would be permanent in the United States; therefore, the problem of providing new school facilities was conceived to be one of obsolescence only. Even during World War II realization of the extent and impact of the changed birth rate was lacking. Communities were encouraged

---

[4] James B. Conant, *The American High School Today,* New York (McGraw-Hill), 1959, p. 77.

[5] "Regional High School Development in New Jersey," *New Jersey State Department of Education Secondary School Bulletin,* March 1957, p. 1.

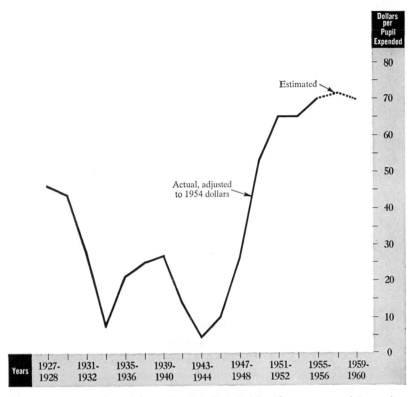

Fig. 16–1. *Capital Outlay Per Pupil in U.S. Public Elementary and Secondary Schools*

to delay building until "postwar inflation" was over. Respectable economists were among those who assumed that school districts could look forward to lowered building costs within a short time. But by 1958-59 costs of school facilities had risen until about $148 was required to buy what $100 had bought in 1948-49.[6]

School districts thus found themselves with shortages of school facilities, accumulated over many years, which could be corrected only at record costs. In many cases they also found themselves confronted by statutory limits on bonded indebtedness not geared to growing enrollments, to accumulated shortages, or to spiraling costs.

Educational changes. Some communities found their approach to

[6] Committee on School Finance, *What Everyone Should Know about Financing Our Schools,* Washington, D.C. (National Education Association), 1960, p. 11.

their critical need for secondary school buildings further impeded by an atmosphere of uncertainty and by unassimilated educational changes. One of the changes with considerable influence was the junior high school. Some students of the junior high school movement have concluded that it was from the beginning primarily a housing expedient that had been rationalized on other grounds. A new junior high school could take the overflow from both elementary and high school buildings, or perhaps occupy the old high school when new facilities were built for the upper secondary grades. At least one state legislature directed a study of departmentalization in grades 7 and 8 to determine whether it is superior at that level to self-contained classrooms.[7] Innovations in divisions of grade levels have tended to accompany periods of rapid growth in enrollments and consequent school housing problems. There can be little doubt that crowding has played a part in the promoting of various six-three-three, six-four-four, six-six, six-two-two, and other organizational schemes, or that available buildings have shaped the programs of reorganized schools. On the other hand, many communities have earnestly sought the plan of organization best suited to the development of youth of their areas.

A growing awareness of the value of the kind of "learning by experimenting" represented by laboratory learning procedures has added to the need for facilities. The learning laboratory has a long history in secondary education. Franklin and Jefferson wrote of scientific apparatus as essential to the kind of education they visualized. Franklin proposed that students be taught grafting as a part of "natural history." In such areas as science, agriculture, industrial arts, and home economics, schools quickly found the advantage of discovery, practice, and interpretation of what is observed by the learner himself. Teachers of other areas were not slow to see the advantage of instruction in which a student consolidates his knowledge by trying the techniques or applying the concepts, recording his success, and analyzing the data he has compiled. Slowest to find ways to use laboratory procedures were teachers of social science, English, mathematics, and foreign language. Within the past few years, however, the possibilities of richer learning experiences in laboratory settings have been extended even to these subject fields.

The learning laboratory has come to signify a heightened emphasis upon the student's self-direction in a school environment rich in

[7] J. H. Hull, "The Junior High School Is a Poor Investment," *Nation's Schools,* April 1960, p. 78.

learning materials: books, maps, globes, graphs, recordings, films, learning machines, and laboratory apparatus. This approach calls for more space, more varied learning areas, and a great deal more equipment. Some of these adaptations are quite inexpensive; others are quite costly. A well-equipped language laboratory may cost 25 per cent more than a language classroom of the older type; a physics laboratory with adequate laboratory stations for each student will cost one-third or one-half more than a room equipped only for lecture and demonstration. Either is less expensive than an industrial arts shop or a home economics laboratory of the kind that has been a part of secondary schools for years.

The full possibilities of the laboratory approach, combined with open-circuit and closed-circuit television, 16-millimeter films, and other audio-visual devices which free the teacher to guide the learning process, can only be guessed at as exploration and research go forward. What is certain is that all these developments call for modifications and additions to secondary school plants.

The influence of vocational education on high school facilities has been substantial. Even after a decade of lively school building activity, some communities show as the newest addition to the secondary school a building or a wing devoted to vocational education. The "manual training" high schools, built in certain urban centers in the early 1900's, in many cases have been converted to comprehensive high schools in which vocationally oriented students are only one segment of the student body; but some communities, particularly the largest cities, have continued to build vocational and technical high schools. Cities as widely scattered as Baltimore, Chicago, Cincinnati, and Salt Lake City have in the past few years built schools to concentrate on vocational training.

Facilities for vocational education usually require more space per pupil than other secondary school facilities, need extensive and elaborate equipment, and must be constantly re-equipped to prevent rapid obsolescence. Instruction in the use of office machines, for example, requires electrically driven typewriters, calculating machines, duplicators, and data processing equipment. Business establishments are quick to change to improved models, and the school must follow suit if students are to be vocationally prepared. Many buildings, even of recent construction, do not have adequate space in the vocational training rooms; nor do they provide an adequate supply of electricity for the power-driven equipment that must be added.

Although some educators would prefer to see vocational education postponed until after high school, the U.S. Department of Labor anticipates that a shortage of skilled workers will be one of the acute problems in the decade 1965-75.[8] Therefore, in the immediate future, as in the recent past, facilities for vocational training will likely be one of the requirements of secondary schools.

Obsolescence. In view of the long-term failure to build the needed physical plant, it is not surprising that outmoded facilities, even some that are unsafe, remain in use. During recent years only 16,000 or 17,000 rooms per year have been abandoned.[9] This is a much slower rate than would be expected even if school functions had remained static. A School Facilities Survey authorized by Congress included an inventory which disclosed that in March 1951, 62 per cent of the pupils in the United States attended school in buildings built before 1930; 68 per cent of the classrooms had below the minimum recommended space for each pupil; and 60 per cent of the pupils were housed in buildings rated by state departments of education as only fair or unsatisfactory.[10]

Many of the older buildings were constructed in a monumental manner which makes their remodeling or conversion impossible or uneconomical. Usually they are located on sites entirely too small and unsuited to modern programs of secondary education. A high proportion of the instructional space in American secondary schools is obsolete and imposes severe handicaps on efforts to attain universal, excellent, and efficient secondary education.

Efforts to Provide Facilities

Pressures of rising enrollments, depression and war-accumulated shortages, as well as rapid educational change, have presented the nation with herculean building tasks. During the 1950's serious attempts were made to reduce the discrepancy between what was needed and what was available. These efforts were ambitious in scope and influential in impact.

Scope. The annual expenditure on elementary and secondary schools increased in the ten-year period between 1949-50 and 1959-60 from

[8] Bureau of Labor Statistics, *op. cit.,* p. 49.

[9] "Enrollment, Teachers and Schoolhousing," *School Life,* January-February 1959, p. 23.

[10] Clayton D. Hutchins and Elmer C. Deering, *Financing Public School Facilities,* Washington, D.C. (Government Printing Office), 1959, p. 5.

$4,687,270,000 to $11,910,269,000, or 154 per cent. Capital outlay expenditures increased during this period from $1,014,176,000 to $3,255,171,000, or 220 per cent. Expenditures for interest increased proportionately.[11]

It has become customary to compare capital outlay expenditures in one year with averages built up over the years. This procedure can be very misleading at the local level, where major expenditures are relatively infrequent, and at the national level as well, where they have varied widely from year to year. The average expenditure for capital outlay, for example, over the 34 years from 1923-24 to 1956-57 was 19.9 per cent of the total expenditures for schools. But the percentage varied from a low of 6.1 in 1944-45 to a high of 26.6 in 1956-57. If interest charges are eliminated, the range is even greater, from 2.2 per cent in 1943-44 to 23.9 per cent in 1956-57.[12]

These figures indicate that since about 1949 school districts have been concentrating heavy shares of their economic resources on the effort to provide adequate facilities. During this period state and federal governments have also stepped up their support.

A more graphic illustration of the scope of secondary school building, and of the job remaining, is presented by a summary of the new schools that were opened in 1959 in the metropolitan area of Chicago. Twenty-seven new public high schools and some additions to existing schools provided 855 classrooms for 23,116 pupils at a cost of $47,924,661. Seven new parochial high schools were opened in the same area at the same time. Of the thirty-four new high schools only three were in the city of Chicago, where there was an actual decline of 662 in high school enrollment. Suburban Cook County, with less than a third the population of Chicago, spent 70 per cent more for schools and provided facilities for 8,075 against an enrollment increase of 4,772.[13] The suburban high schools were obviously built with an awareness of the 16,363 increase in elementary school enrollment for that year.

Impact. The extent of the school housing problem has forced many developments in school administration and community planning. Realization has grown that problems of school housing are continuous and call for long-range planning.

[11] Research Division, National Education Association, *op. cit.,* pp. 16-17.
[12] Hutchins and Deering, *op. cit.,* p. 8.
[13] "Chicago Area Gains 228 Schools in Year," Chicago Tribune, October 4, 1959, p. 26.

School personnel have learned that plant needs can be understood only in relation to the development of the whole community and that the widest participation by community representatives leads to the wisest decisions and the quickest acceptance of responsibility. Some communities have learned to conduct building programs that provide space as needed and to reduce the waste of unused space or space built before requirements can be fully anticipated.

A successful example is provided by Barrington Consolidated High School in suburban Cook and Lake Counties in Illinois. Barrington was the first high school in that state to undertake a complete new building after the World War II construction restrictions were removed. When the war ended, Barrington High School was cramped in an old building in a crowded residential area. The board of education and professional staff studied the community and its school needs intensively, employed experts from the University of Chicago to make an independent survey, gave wide distribution to the information gathered, carried on public discussion, and reached decisions. A series of eleven referendums were required to reorganize the district, to provide a realistic financial and attendance base, and to authorize the selection of a site and construction of a building. By 1949, 360 students were occupying a new building with a capacity of 450 on a 71-acre site. The architects had planned to accommodate expansion that could be clearly forecast but not programmed in detail. In 1955 a second stage brought the pupil capacity up to 900, and tentative planning was under way for the third stage. This was ready for occupancy in 1960 with a capacity of 1,500. Continuous planning plus careful communication with the people of the community made it possible to provide excellent facilities for a fourfold multiplication of enrollment within a period of twelve years. Figure 16-2 shows how the architects programmed this three-stage building project.

In the same period, less fortunate young people in other communities limited by the available space were forced to attend only half-day sessions. More commonly, students studied the kinds of subjects for which rooms were available, by the methods for which facilities had been designed, perhaps as long as fifty years previously. For example, the study of woodworking might have been limited to the use of hand tools for operations that are now usually performed by simple home-workshop type machines. Or the study of physics, chemistry, and biology was restricted to the lecture-discussion method forty years after individual laboratory experimentation was accepted as

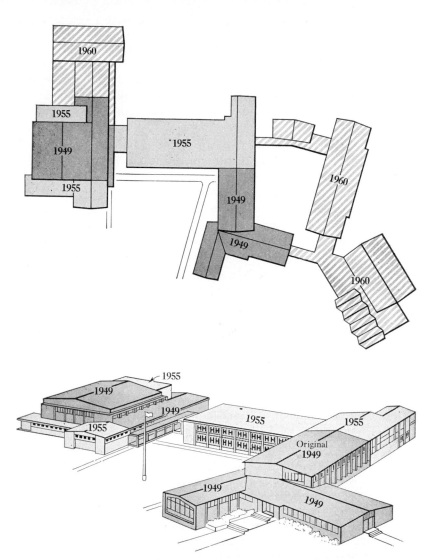

Fig. 16–2. *Layout of Barrington High School showing original 1949 buildings with additions made in 1955 (below) and in 1960 (above). The 1960 academic addition contains classroom, laboratory, and study facilities, and rooms for music, dramatics, and speech instruction. This frees classroom space in the old buildings. The auditorium seats 750 and is used for the school's general assembly program and for combined class instruction, concerts, operettas, and other programs presented by the high school. It is also available for civic, social, and cultural activities of the community.*

standard procedure for these subjects. Audio-visual resources were not used because of a lack of suitable viewing rooms and equipment. Students and teachers were compelled to "make-do" with obsolete books or inadequate supplies of books and instructional materials because proper facilities for centralizing and distributing supplies were lacking.

In a depressing number of cases insufficient and obsolete physical facilities not only negated the development of better learning methods, but even discouraged the use of standard procedures with which teachers were well acquainted, and were more than ready to use.

As educators reviewed the progress of the 1950's, they could not ignore the tremendous future population growth. The standard informational service for the construction industry reminded the nation: "How much must we build? That's easy—we have to build a second United States, and then some. We will have to double all the structures, all the facilities, that now exist. And we will have to do it before the babies born in 1959 reach middle age."[14]

DEVELOMPENT OF A PHILOSOPHY FOR THE SECONDARY SCHOOL PLANT

Any school building is built to advance certain educational purposes and to serve specific programs of instruction. One of the most important and most difficult of the planning tasks is to make these purposes and programs—and the values they serve—clear and explicit.

> Countless factors operate to produce widely varying programs, buildings, and costs. At the outset, the very value placed on education differs widely. Where books are revered, libraries will be bigger; and where basketball, gymnasiums. Different values produce different educational programs and different buildings; and so do different climates, frost depths, topographies, subsoil conditions, vegetation, distances, land costs, labor costs, community incomes, and pupil population—present and projected.[15]

Part of the delicate task of weighing these many factors belongs to the public, part to the educational staff, and part to architects. Coordinating the efforts of all those involved is a vital element of successful planning.

[14] George Cline Smith and others, *Sighting the Sixties: Launching a Second U.S.A.*, New York (F. W. Dodge Corporation), November 1959, p. 8-D.

[15] "Schools and Architects, Costs and Values," *Architectural Record*, October 1957, p. 173.

Sound programs of education provide a firm base for determining the facilities to be planned and constructed. New patterns for facilities have been slower to emerge at the secondary level than at the elementary level. Elementary education, in contrast, has a criterion in Crow Island school of Winnetka, Illinois, which dates from 1940. A journal for architects, re-examining this school in 1955, observed:

> We have never had a Crow Island in the high school field. But, a new kind of high school is in the making with the giant surge of adolescent population hot on its heels. This juxtaposition of concept and need has its providential side, but its unfortunate side, too. Who will have time to give to a high school prototype the patient, loving study that went into Crow Island?[16]

Examination of high school and junior high school buildings built in the past few years shows some freshness of design but, in the main, innovations are made without new underlying educational concepts. The major architectural trends have been refinements of the traditional massive secondary school building, experimentation with various ways of dividing the mass into smaller units, and various innovations in structural components and materials. It is in some respects surprising to see the major role architects have taken in proposing and interpreting the educational ideas which must undergird new schools.[17]

Two new agencies have recently exercised considerable influence on plans for future secondary school buildings: The Commission on Experimental Study of the Utilization of the Staff of the Secondary School and the Educational Facilities Laboratories, Inc. Both received support from the Ford Foundation. The Experimental Study of the Utilization of the Staff, under the leadership of J. Lloyd Trump, projected new conceptions of teaching that require adaptations of space to both small and large groups, with provisions for the use of television instruction as well as teaching machines and laboratory equipment.

The Educational Facilities Laboratory, Inc., directed by Harold

[16] "Schools: A Look Backward and Forward," *Architectural Forum*, October 1955, p. 129.

[17] A few examples are: John Lyon Reid and Archibald B. Shaw, "The Random Falls Idea," *School Executive*, March 1956, pp. 47-86; Charles Bursch and John Lyon Reid, *High Schools Today and Tomorrow*, New York (Reinhold), 1957; Lawrence B. Perkins, *Work Place for Learning*, New York (Reinhold), 1957; and Charles William Brubaker and Lawrence B. Perkins, "Sketch Book: Space for Individual Learning," *School Executive and Educational Business*, February 1959.

Gores, is conducting experimentation on school buildings and facilities to ascertain the validity of both designs and materials in terms of educational utility. This agency has already projected specifications to guide communities in the planning of new secondary schools. Late in 1959 two proposals were presented jointly by these bodies at a meeting of educators and architects at the University of Michigan. The interest of educators and architects in the proposals reflects their readiness to accept new concepts in secondary school buildings.[18]

Some aspects of the new proposals for secondary school buildings are radically different, but they generally depend upon several time-tested assumptions. The most important of these are that facilities should be adapted to the educational program; design should be appropriate to location, community, and site; facilities should be sufficiently flexible to allow for changes in educational usage; educational utility should hold priority over other factors; and economy is essential.

Buildings and Facilities Appropriate to Educational Use

Suiting the facilities to the educational program is one of the most difficult requirements for school buildings. There is a natural tendency for school staffs to want to incorporate into new buildings all that was lacking in old structures. Educational consultants and architects, on the other hand, are likely to favor advanced ideas that may be unsuited to the use by particular teachers in given communities. Both tendencies are unfortunate. Sometimes communities in their eagerness to adopt the latest developments accept ideas for buildings that are untested or transient in terms of educational theory.

Buildings and facilities should be designed to suit the needs of students and to provide for the educational purposes, student services, faculty facilities, related pupil activities, and auxiliary services of a particular level of the school system.

Needs of high school students. Secondary school students need suitable places for individual and group study. Each student requires a school "home" where personal belongings may be kept, relationships with the school maintained, individual study carried on, and healthy associations with an established class or group enjoyed. In contrast to the traditional high school building in which the student's school home

---

[18] Brubaker and Perkins, *op. cit.;* and John Lyon Reid, "Two Loft Schools: New Instruments of Education," *Architectural Record,* February 1960, pp. 196-203.

was nothing more than a hall locker, a new building should provide each student with a desk and locker space in a home room that has accompanying facilities to encourage wholesome scholarship.

Educational purposes: curriculum and instruction. A school building reflects the purposes envisioned for the educational program. Inasmuch as the central mission of the secondary school is intellectual development, libraries, laboratories, group and individual study rooms, instructional materials, evaluation instruments, and workrooms should have priority in space and facilities. Traditional school buildings, with their inadequate libraries, overcrowded laboratories, small classrooms, lack of storage and individual study space, and poor provisions for audio-visual resources, have encouraged a type of rote learning that depends upon memorization, recall, and recitation. In contrast, secondary schools of the future are envisioned as requiring a variety of learning laboratories, among them:[19]

(a) Library, including audio-visual resources

(b) Individual study, studio, and practice rooms for reading and research; practice in music, art, speech; picture viewing; record listening; tape recording

(c) Group study and meeting rooms provided with a variety of appropriate books and other printed material; audio-visual resources, including television receivers, tape recorders, talking books; other kinds of equipment, e.g., manual, scientific; mock-ups, visualizations of concepts, displays; instructional supplies—in short, everything needed to make possible multisensory approaches to learning

(d) Laboratories for group creative, experimental, and skill activities— for art, science, home economics, industrial arts, agriculture, vocational education, mathematics, business education, creative writing, music—any subject that requires this type of learning

(e) Special practice and large-group activity rooms—for band, orchestra, choir, dramatics, physical education, dance, political science

(f) Audio-visual response, self-teaching laboratories equipped with individual private stations that permit simultaneous practice with, and responses to, tape-recorded material or other types of self-teaching machines by all members of a group, each according to his own rate and level of mastery

(g) Telemation auditoriums that permit large groups to receive simultaneous multisized, multidimensional, colored, still, and motion

[19] Lindley J. Stiles, "Relationship of Instructional Teams and Learning Laboratories to New Directions in Education," *Report of Seminar on the National Defense Act, Title VII,* Boulder (Univ. of Colorado), April 1960.

pictures, with synchronized verbal presentations, either via television or personal lecture

(h) Outdoor laboratories, e.g., forest, farms, building projects, practice
fields, various community resources

The value of this approach to high school instruction has been established; it remains for buildings to incorporate facilities that permit it.
Educational planning now under way calls for a shift from classrooms
to laboratories for all high school subjects, from uniform to multisized
space arrangements, from sparsity to variety of learning materials and
instruments, and for the use of telemation and television to strengthen
and broaden the impact of good teaching.

Student services. Provision of space, equipment, and supplies for
student services such as guidance, records and accounting, health
checks, placement, and follow-up is required for the comprehensive
secondary schools both as they are envisioned and as they exist in some
communities today.

Faculty facilities. If secondary schools expect to have scholars as
teachers, provisions must be made for space and facilities that encourage staff members to continue their scholarship. Without offices, laboratories, and places for individual study and research, secondary school
teachers have little opportunity to be the kind of creative, intellectual
leaders that quality high schools require.

Suitable space and arrangements are needed also for the administrative staff. Contrary to past practice, provision needs to be made
for secretaries to serve teachers, as well as administrators. Emphasis
on instructional teams requires room for groups of professional people
to plan together. Workrooms are needed where technical assistants can
help design equipment and instructional aids to serve the professional
staff. Perhaps the best model for buildings and equipment for the
future secondary schools of the United States exists today in some of
the outstanding educational programs that have been developed by
the various branches of the armed services. In such programs the goal
is maximum learning at a maximum rate, and a high priority is
accorded to space and equipment in which instructional programs may
be designed.

Related activities. Certain student activities have come to exercise
an increasing influence on school building designs. The tendency of
subject-related activities to flow out of and back into the formal program of the curriculum requires a high degree of versatility in the use

of space. Laboratories must provide for student groups to carry on sustained experiments that grow out of classwork. Auditoriums, gymnasiums, libraries, and even cafeterias are being used in ways related to the academic program of the high school. Swimming pools, for example, may need special lighting arrangements to permit the artistic presentations of water ballet. Nearly every subject area requires flexible and expandable areas where either small or large groups of students may engage in educationally beneficial activities.

Auxiliary services. In some districts, most or nearly all the students ride school buses. Access to and safety of buses thus become important factors in building design. Multiple use of vehicles or uncertain weather conditions frequently lead to early arrivals or late departures which cause students to wait. Thus, there must be provision for profitable use of student time in study, wholesome recreation, or other worthwhile activity.

Health services and student feeding operations pose similar problems. Larger school districts and local, state, and federal interest in good nutrition, as well as increased employment of mothers, have contributed to the expansion of school lunch programs. School enrollments rose 44 per cent between 1947 and 1957, but numbers of children being fed at school rose 133 per cent.[20] It is not uncommon even for urban high schools to operate "closed" lunch hours with all students required to eat at school. In areas where students travel long distances and in underprivileged city neighborhoods the "school breakfast" is becoming popular. Space for preparing and serving food, dining space, and the many sanitary requirements of wholesome food service require expensive adjuncts to the school plant. Efforts to capitalize on the learning aspects of the school lunch and to make cafeterias suitable for other uses stimulate the ingenuity of school planners. A growing solution to feeding students at school has been the central kitchen with decentralized dining. Campus high schools have begun to experiment with this approach to breaking up mass feeding while preserving the advantages of quantity food preparation.

Appropriate Architectural Design

The climate of the United States ranges from tropical to arctic. Its topography ranges from rugged mountains to plains and swamps. Some of its regional architecture reflects imported influences of various

[20] "More Mouths to Feed," *School Planning,* January-February 1958, p. 14.

kinds, such as the Spanish style seen in the Southwest. Different schools of architecture have influenced the homes and public and commercial buildings in different areas and communities. All these natural and cultural variations are properly represented in school architecture.

Differences in climate, site, and local conditions lead to the kinds of differences shown in Figures 16-3 and 16-4. In designing the Mirabeau B. Lamar Junior High School in Laredo, Texas, for instance, the architects kept the climate in mind and sought to control the strong sunlight without sacrificing a close relationship with the outdoors. Warren H. Ashley, designing a high school for Groton, Connecticut, had less sunshine and colder weather to take into account. In his plan, he took advantage of the site's unusual natural beauty.

Figure 16-5 shows the Sarasota, Florida, High School which attempts to utilize the good features of the climate while minimizing the undesirable. The building is oriented north-south to catch prevailing breezes and help reduce direct sunlight. Unusual design of openings and clerestories provides for ventilation. Provision is made for drawing air into the rooms in the absence of breezes.

Flexibility for Changes in Educational Usage

Flexibility is the first criterion of present-day secondary school planners. Flexibility is a word of many meanings, particularly when it is applied to high school buildings. It denotes the suitability of a facility for varied methods of accomplishing the same purpose; it suggests the suitability of a facility for multi-uses; and it connotes ease and economy in converting a facility to new and perhaps unanticipated purposes. There is no phase of school building which these ideas have not influenced.

The simplest use of the word flexibility is in the sense of providing for varied activities in a particular space. Flexibility, so used, supports improved quality of educational experience; a flexible building is a more spacious, better equipped, and more costly one. The learning laboratory is an example, just as were earlier the larger and differently arranged science and home economics laboratories, industrial arts shops, and business education rooms.

The use of the term flexibility to designate multi-use areas has a long, and somewhat confusing, history. A great many schools that were built in the 1920's or later tried to combine expensive large units, such as the gymnasium and auditorium. A great deal of ingenuity was expended to justify space allocations for what, in retrospect, apparently

Fig. 16–3. Large-Area Structures Retain Indoor-Outdoor Relationship Without Sacrificing Sun Control

Fig. 16–4. Perspective, Senior High School, Groton, Connecticut. Architect Warren H. Ashley, 740 North Main Street, West Hartford, Connecticut

Fig. 16–5. *Sarasota High School, Sarasota, Florida*

were efforts to combine incompatible elements. The usual result was a gym with some utility as a place for large gatherings. Other common examples are a combined cafeteria and auditorium, or cafeteria and gymnasium. Where these combinations have added some utility that otherwise might have been omitted because of expense, they have been worthwhile; but they must be considered compromises rather than solutions.

A newer influence has been an attempt to combine units with more closely related activities and purposes. A good example is a trend toward multi-use auditoriums. *Architectural Record* reviewed the various efforts of five high schools in Nevada, Michigan, New York, and Oregon to build such an auditorium.[21] Figure 16-6 shows the plan for the auditorium of Boulder City, Nevada. This plan does not provide for widely different activities, but by careful arrangement and use of folding doors it does permit meetings of groups of different sizes.

The third approach to flexibility cuts deeper into theory and design. It assumes that space will be used not only for varied activities and purposes but also that these activities and purposes will be so changed during the life of the building that facilities must be completely malleable. Of this approach, Reid, an architect, observes:

> Our years of working with educators have resulted in a belief that a school building must not stand in the way of program changes and educational progress, that the building must be ready to adapt itself not only to minor but to major program changes. We believe that

21 *Architectural Record,* November 1959, pp. 206-28.

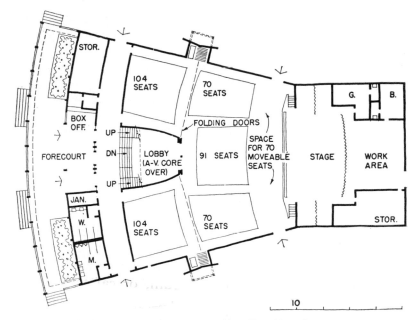

Fig. 16–6. *Multiple-Use Auditorium, Boulder City, Nevada*

total flexibility—or as close to that as possible—is a necessary attribute of the secondary school building of today, facing, as it does, the problem of a growing, changing, improving educational philosophy.[22]

There can be little doubt that flexibility is to be an increasingly important factor in secondary school design. Concern with it has brought one undesirable influence: a loss of care and specificity in defining the functions each facility is to perform immediately. Good buildings cannot be constructed without a clear understanding of function. Utility still must be more important than adaptability.

The Priority of Educational Utility

In a period of enrollment expansion, rapid educational change, and unprecedented building activity, it is difficult to keep a firm focus on function. Nevertheless, educational usefulness must have first place in all planning. A greenhouse may be essential to experimental work with plants or an electrical shop indispensable to study of electrical mechanics, yet neither may be flexible, economical, or add to the

---

[22] John Lyon Reid, "Two Loft Schools," p. 196.

beauty of the building. If these facilities provide a vital part of a student's learning, they need be justified on no other terms except their educational utility.

Since no school can teach everything and local conditions and individual students vary so widely, a large part of school planning must be done at the local level and should be sharply focused on utility for particular students in specific situations. A danger in the pressures created by change and financial stress is that they may produce less emphasis upon harmony between facility and function.

Economy Is Essential

It is not necessary to restate the unfortunate coincidence of sky-rocketing school enrollment and spiraling inflation that has made the search for economy in school building so assiduous and so imperative. In a situation where necessity has been the mother of invention, school systems have made fine progress in finding economical ways to build. The index of school building costs, using 1939 as 100, rose by 1947 to 170 and by 1957 to 226. However, while the cost of school buildings increased two and a half times, the cost of all other buildings increased three times.[23]

Some of the economies accomplished in school buildings have meant sacrifice. For example, it is reported that high schools constructed prior to 1957 provided an average of 150 to 160 square feet per pupil, but that buildings are now being designed with as little as 130 square feet per pupil.[24] While much of this decrease in space per pupil has been accomplished by reducing nonteaching areas, the effect has been to cramp space for student services, staff work, and informal student study and activities.

Other economies have been accomplished by lowering ceiling heights, made possible by improvements in lighting and ventilating; simplifying building outlines and eliminating ornamentation; multi-use of space; using materials standardized in size and shape; and simplifying or eliminating finishing materials and operations.

There are indications that improvements in materials and building design will continue to contribute to school building economy. Conditions in the immediate future promise a continuing thorough search

[23] Walter D. Cocking, "The School Building Situation," *School Executive,* November 1957, pp. 21-24.

[24] School-Building Commission, *Planning America's School Buildings,* Washington, D.C. (American Association of School Administrators), 1960, p. 188.

for such improvements. Increasing enrollments, demands for improved educational performance, and concern for efficient use of resources require that costs be kept as low as is practicable.

PLANNING THE HIGH SCHOOL

The legally constituted governing body of the school district, the board of education, is responsible for the planning of the school plant as for all other phases of education. Since all authority in a democracy derives from the people, the board is charged with establishing policies under which the public can be kept informed and can participate effectively as plans are developed and approved. Defining conditions under which these obligations may be accomplished becomes the first step in the school building planning process. The second step is organizing the professional staff for its leadership responsibility which will require thorough, laborious, and lengthy effort; this step may include the selection and employment of consultants. The third step is selection of an architect. Even if the district has retained the continuing services of an architect, additional professional help may be needed for particular projects. With these preliminary steps accomplished, the district is ready for a major planning venture, the results of which may well outlive all those who participate.

A Cooperative Venture

Planning a new school building, a sizable remodeling project, or a major addition to an existing building has far-reaching consequences and many complexities necessitating the cooperation, at appropriate times and levels, of many people. Figure 16-7 suggests schematically one way of organizing for this task and indicates the chief considerations that influence plans. The ideal coordinator is the person who will serve as principal of the new unit. When the new building requires a new staff, a growing number of school districts have succeeded in designating the new principal, and often other key staff members, early enough so that they may participate in the planning process. This type of prestaffing ensures interested, vigorous leadership that cannot be provided by the existing staffs who have other heavy responsibilities.

The principal who serves as the planning coordinator will give first attention to setting up ways in which all available resources can be used in planning the educational program which will determine the design of the building. This planning process may require two years

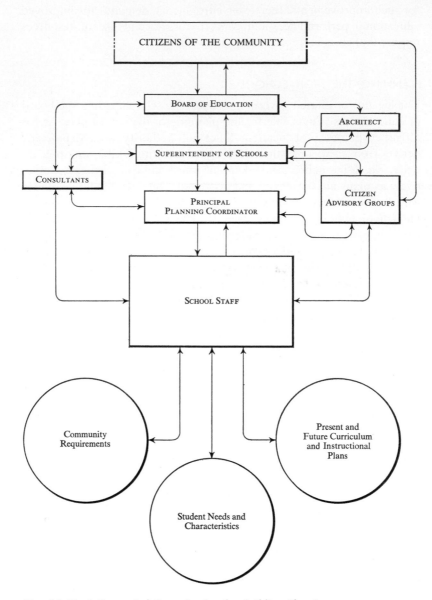

Fig. 16–7. A Suggested Organization for Building Planning

or more. The role of teachers is central in educational planning and all procedures must take this principle into account. Teachers will suggest many of the factors that need to be considered during planning. Others who help with the planning of secondary school buildings may include, in addition to the architects, representatives of the central administration, the city planning department, and the state department of public instruction. Close contact will be maintained with local health, social, and recreational agencies. Representative citizens and students will help determine the total facilities to be included. Consultants from colleges and universities may assist. Key service and office personnel will help plan space and equipment for their work assignments. In complex building projects, national educational agencies may be employed to research some of the problems related to the building plans.

Communities differ widely in human resources available for planning, as do school staffs. Large schools have available specialists of various kinds in their supervisors, department heads, and coordinators. The important thing is to use all of these resources without shutting off or stifling the ideas of others, particularly classroom teachers who are vitally interested and frequently have the most know-how about the ways young people learn.

Some communities, for example Brownwood, Texas, have found citizens' advisory committees valuable in planning school building for at least three reasons. The community is often not fully aware of the need for new facilities, the board and professional staff often do not fully understand public attitudes, and much sound and needed advice can be supplied by the public for all phases of the building program.[25]

The amount of independence allowed school staffs varies according to local organizational structure. Building planning is not one of the areas likely to be completely delegated either by the board of education or the central office staff. Coordination with the central office leadership is one of the essentials of successful planning. The large sums involved, the intense community interest, the inevitability that requests for space and equipment will be trimmed even under the most ample budget—all put a premium on effective communication, mutual confidence, and cooperative teamwork. However useful the principal can be in coordinating detailed planning, he will be wise to depend heavily on the superintendent and his immediate staff for the major

[25] Joe B. Rushing, "Involving the Community in School Planning," *American School Board Journal,* July 1960, p. 18.

share of financial decisions: contracts, negotiations, and interpretation of the building program to the board of education and the public.

It is helpful to have the architects share in all stages of planning and to keep the school staff actively involved in all decisions until the building is ready for occupancy. While the educational planning is going on, the architect's function is principally to listen, read, and absorb the ideas developed. It is essential that the educational planners remain active in checking, criticizing, and modifying the architect's plans for housing the program. Only in this way can the people who are to conduct the educational program be sure their efforts to communicate have been successful.

The Importance of Explicit Plans for the Educational Program

With such complex and diverse problems involved in communication, it is essential that the educational program be expressed in clear, complete, exact, and definite educational specifications. Written descriptions of the educational program guide the architect in developing his sketches, preliminary plans, layouts, working drawings, and architectural specifications to be incorporated in contracts. They also permit evaluation at each stage of the work. For this reason each person who participates should have copies of the portions of the educational specifications to which he contributes and should have an opportunity to examine each step of progress from educational specifications to architectural specifications, with the help of experts to interpret technical data.

Educational specifications should be written in understandable non-technical language with the conventional aids, such as a table of contents and index, for easy reference; all pertinent background and factual information should be included. Specifications should include aims, objectives, and underlying points of view. They should indicate anticipated methods of teaching and materials and equipment to be used. They should supply number and types of rooms and spaces and all other pertinent quantitative data. Anticipated future expansion should be included in as much detail as possible. All special types of equipment and services should be enumerated.

It is within the scope of educational specifications to state preferences and requirements for materials or relationships of areas; but it is beyond the scope of educational specifications to include material specifications, room layouts, and engineering details. These are the special tasks of the architect.

Allocation of Space

Traditional methods of allocating space for instruction in the secondary school are today inadequate. Until very recently, the commonly accepted method was to forecast enrollment, to analyze the previous pattern of enrollment both in required and elective courses, to estimate corrections based on anticipated changes in this pattern, and to project these data into a number of rooms for each subject field, dining spaces, or student lockers. This method was used both for "pupil-period enrollment" and an "estimate of teaching spaces."[26] The entire procedure has recently been questioned.

A new approach, creative in concept but as yet very thinly founded on successful practice, has recently been widely accepted. Apparently derived from the work of the "Trump Commission" and a few very articulate and experimentally minded architects,[27] this approach, which might be called a trend toward "cluster-space" assignments, is being advanced aggressively by the Educational Facilities Laboratories,[28] and has been endorsed implicitly by the Building Commission of the American Association of School Administrators.[29] The following statements illustrate the thinking of its advocates:

> At the moment a number of schools are being designed and erected to accommodate clusters graduating in size from individual work spaces—to the seminar-space for 10 pupils and a teacher around a table—to the standard classroom—to the 100-pupil lecture-discussion space—to the divisible auditorium where two or more large groups may be instructed simultaneously and without acoustical interference.
>
> A new high school in Wayland, Massachusetts, is another example of how the changing deployment of staff and student body is bringing about the re-arrangement of space. When the building is first occupied (1960), the academic program of the typical student will consist of 10 per cent of his time in small group seminars, 80 per cent in the traditional classroom, and 10 per cent in large-group lecture discussions. Within five years, when an addition to the building will be required, the proportion of academic time will have evolved to

[26] American Association of School Administrators, *The High School in a Changing World*, Washington, D.C., 1958, pp. 256-64.

[27] J. Lloyd Trump, *New Horizons for Secondary School Teachers*, 1958; *Images of the Future*, 1959; *New Directions to Quality Education*, 1960. All published in Washington, D.C. by the National Association of Secondary School Principals.

[28] Educational Facilities Laboratories, *Here They Learn*, New York, 1959.

[29] American Association of School Administrators, *op. cit.*, pp. 35-36.

20:60:20, and ultimately the division may become 30 per cent seminar, 40 per cent classroom, and 30 per cent large-group instruction. Physical education will be housed in a geodesic dome.[30]

This trend is highly experimental; under its influence new procedures can be expected to evolve as experience accumulates. And other approaches are certain to be developed, for the entire question of the best way to house the high school of the present and future has clearly been opened and is being studied in new terms.

CURRENT TRENDS IN ARCHITECTURAL TREATMENT OF EDUCATIONAL DEVELOPMENTS

This brief survey of the problem of housing the secondary school would be incomplete without some attempt to summarize some of the important recent developments, even at a time when it is apparent that new forces may well make the major changes of recent years appear minor by contrast. The chief trends now in evidence and most likely to be lasting are efforts to humanize and personalize education by breaking down and abolishing the institutional atmosphere; efforts to improve flexibility and economy through modular units and malleable interiors; efforts to improve teamwork, adapt to varied teacher talents, and to serve individual student needs through varied relationships of learning spaces; and efforts to capitalize on technological advances by incorporating all kinds of mechanical and electronic aids to learning.

Campus Plans and Schools Within Schools

One of the best established trends in high school buildings is the use of the campus plan—that is, a series of small, decentralized units in place of the traditional massive single building. This plan is based on conviction that a good atmosphere for learning is dependent to a large extent on physical environment. It has been made possible by technological advances which permit building the various units as economically as more massive buildings were constructed earlier. Under this plan decentralization gives the individual student a relatively more important place in relation to the mass. It allows for more independent attention to each of the parts and subdivisions of the building, thereby accomplishing a greater harmony between form and function.

[30] Educational Facilities Laboratories, *op. cit.,* pp. 8-11.

Many other recent trends can be traced to the campus plan and its various modifications which have made it possible to isolate noisy units or to group related elements in convenient juxtaposition. A good example is provided by J. Sterling Morton High School West in Berwyn, Illinois, built in 1958 in a finger-wing arrangement inspired by the campus plan. Figure 16-8A & B show how art, music, drama, and the speech arts were clustered together to facilitate coordination among them. At the same time, the design makes access convenient for students after normal school hours as well as for the public, and it isolates

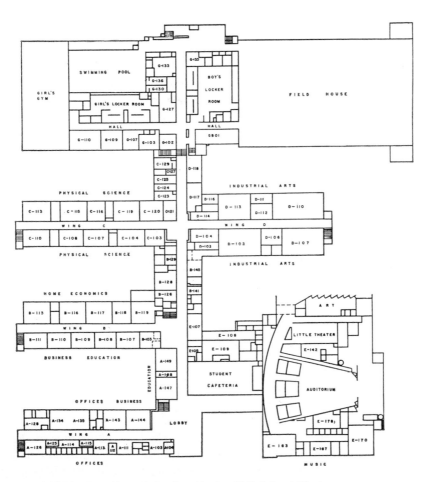

Fig. 16—8A. *First Floor, J. Sterling Morton High School West*

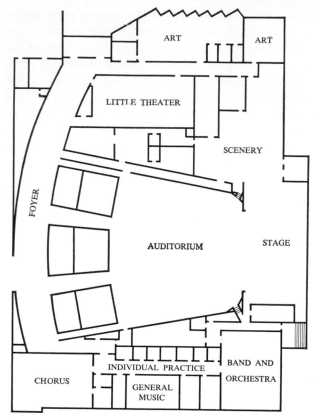

Fig. 16–8B. *Auditorium, J. Sterling Morton High School West*

the noise of band rehearsals and other activities from the rest of the school plant.

The campus plan and its modifications also lend themselves to new organizational concepts, particularly "schools within schools." This popular adaptation is based on the concept of "small within big"— maintaining the advantages of economy and comprehensive facilities available in large schools, while providing for students the warmth and closeness of smaller organizational units. The school within the school provides for closely knit operating teams. The student spends most of his time for four years or longer in one physical subdivision of the school, associates with a portion of the faculty who get to know him and he them, but enjoys the use of special facilities and services available only in a larger school. Figure 16-9 shows an architectural adaptation of the schools-within-schools idea in Maine Township High School West in Des Plaines, Illinois. This large plant provides for 3,000 students, each of whom spends most of the day in one wing which has its own classrooms, laboratories, faculty, and subordinate administration. A central core contains the cafeteria, central administration and coordination, library, and the like. Units that need not be duplicated—swimming pools and shops—are housed in separate wings. A desirable feature for a school in this area, which is close to the

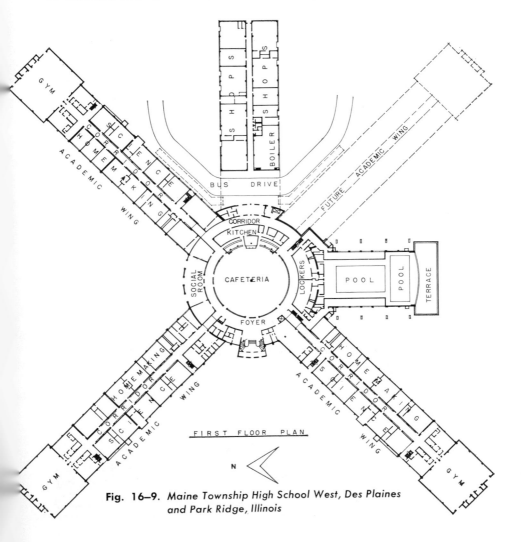

Fig. 16–9. *Maine Township High School West, Des Plaines and Park Ridge, Illinois*

Great Lakes with their extremes of temperature and many rainy days, is the convenience and ease of movement from one part of the sprawling plant to another along interior routes.

Neither campus plans nor schools within schools are limited to the extremely large high school. Boonsboro High School in Washington County, Maryland, was planned to accommodate an enrollment of 600-700 in a campus-type plant composed of two little schools of about 350 each. It is expected to expand to 1,200-1,400 in 5 or 6 years. The campus plan is well suited to expansion.[31]

Modular Units and Malleable Interiors

Other well-established trends are the use of modular units and interiors with easy rearrangement. The use of modular units resulted from the search in architecture and construction for economy of material and labor. Basically, it is an effort to apply the American industrial techniques of interchangeable parts to the building industry. When architects learned how to build a large expanse without the necessity of having interior partitions to carry the weight of the roof, it became possible to use many movable and interchangeable units. This trend is well established but far from its full development in this country, in contrast to England where standardization of school parts is far advanced.[32]

Architectural progress has stimulated and facilitated educational thinking about learning modules. Folding partitions and movable partitions make it possible to use the same space for groups of different sizes. The possibilities inherent in this concept are being endlessly extended.

Malleability of interiors and growing mastery over lighting, ventilation, and temperature control have led to controversy between those who wish to control and utilize the natural environment and those who wish to eliminate it in favor of completely artificial environment. Some architects are still striving for a beautiful view from a library or a sunny atmosphere free from glare while others are building windowless schools.[33] An architect reports that after several years of using rooms

[31] John W. McLeod, "A Campus Plan for a Small School—With Space to Grow," *Nation's Schools,* August 1960, pp. 57-63.

[32] Ezra D. Ehrenkrantz and John K. Kay, "Flexibility Through Standardization—Part I: The Hertfordshire Prefab Schools," *Progressive Architecture,* July 1957, pp. 105-11.

[33] Charles L. Mills, "The Windowless School," *School Planning,* September 1958, pp. 14-15.

of both types at Hillsdale, California, teachers preferred "inside" rooms to "view" rooms.[34]

West Leyden High School in Northlake, Illinois, made extensive use of modular concepts. Removable prefabricated partitions not only provide for ease of altering spaces as educational needs change, but they permitted planners to look at spaces as shells in which it was possible to create the learning conditions desired. Some results were outstanding. An example is the comprehensive library facility shown in Figure 16-10, which incorporates traditional library services, audio-visual services, textbooks, and a teachers' work area in a flexible environment which the future may reshape.

Teaching Teams and Teaching Spaces

The rapid extension of team teaching is revolutionizing relationships among teaching spaces. The old egg-crate design of rows of rooms of equal size is breaking down. A trend which started timidly with inter-connecting doors and occasional folding walls is now flourishing in a multitude of bolder designs. Figure 16-11 is one illustration of efforts to provide for teaching teams at the Olympia Fields Campus of Rich Township High School in Park Forest, Illinois. This school also was planned with heat pump temperature control permitting both heating and cooling of classrooms—simultaneously when necessary.

Mechanical and Electronic Aids to Learning

Experimental work with closed-circuit and open-circuit television has as yet failed to delineate a place for television in secondary education. Closed-circuit television has been improved and simplified, thereby reducing cost, but it remains relatively costly as an aid to conventional teaching. In the future, it and educational television in general will probably be used in combination with team-teaching techniques as one way to vary teaching and utilize teaching talents more effectively. For several years new schools have hedged against the future by installing conduits for closed-circuit lines while educators watch the pioneering experiments and study results.

Other developments, like the Airborne Classroom experiment, which has blanketed major parts of several states with several hours of educational broadcasts tailored to the requests of schools, have added to the attention given to television. They have also strengthened the belief,

[34] John Lyon Reid, "Two Loft Schools," p. 197.

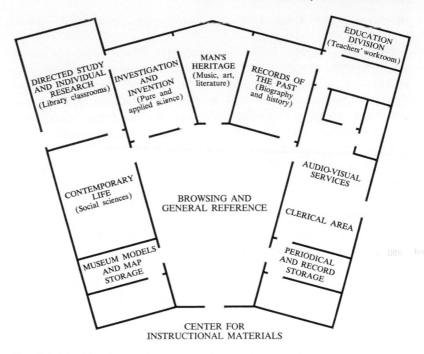

Fig. 16–10. *The Center As an Integral Part of Every School Department*

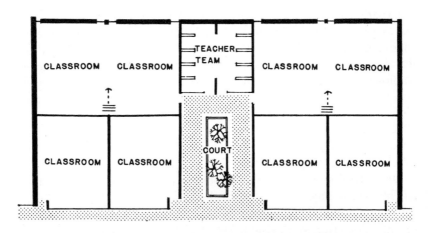

Fig. 16–11. *A Classroom Cluster Shares an Interior Court. All Teaching Spaces Are Readily Available to the Team*

which has existed for a decade, that television is on the threshold of an educational break-through.

Unlike television, laboratories for learning have been widely accepted by educators and have become increasingly important in new buildings. The language laboratory of J. Sterling Morton High School West, shown in Figure 16-12, was one of the first complete laboratories to go into a high school when it was installed in 1958. It brought eleven different sound sources—tapes, radio, television, phonograph—to each of thirty-five student booths with two-way communication. This laboratory has been used with five modern languages, Latin, and shorthand. Laboratories of this kind and laboratory facilities for almost every conceivable subject are going into new buildings at a record rate. Older buildings, including some of recent date, are being remodeled and given additions to bring to students the accelerated, broadened, and deepened learning made possible by laboratory settings.

Risks

As early as 1955, at least, careful observers predicted that the flood of building and financial pressures and the perplexity about high school programs would lead to hasty construction and pat solutions. These fears are being realized. The dangers are the same old dangers that

Fig. 16–12. *Language Laboratory, J. Sterling Morton High School West*

have confronted high school planners throughout the years, intensified in speed and magnitude. The risks call for the old remedies to be applied in new ways. The principal remedies are to spell out carefully the educational functions facilities are to perform, to guard against rigidity of design, and to utilize the best architectural services. As each year passes, the methods and materials available and the creative solutions to educational problems become more numerous and more nearly adequate to the tasks. For this very reason they are more difficult to select from and to incorporate successfully into an integrated school plant—a total environment for learning in harmony with the best of the other educative forces of the community.

SELECTED REFERENCES

BURSCH, CHARLES W., AND JOHN LYON REID. *High Schools Today and Tomorrow*. New York: Reinhold, 1957.

Estimates of School Statistics, 1959-60. Research Report 1959-R23. Washington, D.C.: National Education Association, December 1959.

HUTCHINS, CLAYTON D., AND ELMER C. DEERING. *Financing Public School Buildings*. Washington, D.C.: Government Printing Office, 1959.

SCHOOL-BUILDING COMMISSION. *Planning America's School Buildings*. Washington, D.C.: American Association of School Administrators, 1960.

Secondary School Plant Planning. Nashville, Tennessee: National Council on Schoolhouse Construction, 1957.

TRUMP, J. LLOYD. *New Directions to Quality Education*. Washington, D.C.: National Association of Secondary School Principals, 1960.

U.S. Department of Labor, Bureau of Labor Statistics. *Population and Labor Force Projections for the United States, 1960 to 1975*. Washington, D.C.: Government Printing Office, 1959.

PART V

Current Concerns in Secondary Education

Bright high school students in Wisconsin High School study Russian history under Beth Arveson, an authority on the subject.

The Bronx High School of Science in New York City is noted for its strong academic programs for academically talented students.

CHAPTER 17

Challenging the Gifted Student

MOST of the future creative talent and leadership of the nation will come from those now in school who can be identified as possessing outstanding potential. Research evidence[1] supports educators who take the position that intellectual talent can and must be identified in the young. If individuals with extraordinary potentials, who will later become the most productive for society, can be identified, shouldn't the system of public education pay particular attention to the kind of instruction needed to develop their talents fully? Indeed, the secondary schools are being pressed, as in no other period, to provide programs appropriate to the education of this group.

Creative innovations[2] now undergoing trial, and research and professional experience, offer some useful principles and guides for the fuller development of the abilities of the gifted. At the same time there exist both practical problems and philosophical issues as yet unresolved. Those who seek to design instructional programs and those who attempt to challenge the gifted through their teach-

[1] Harold D. Carter, "Gifted Children," *Encyclopedia of Educational Research,* 3rd edition, New York (Macmillan), 1960, pp. 583-93.

[2] "Progressing Toward Better Schools," *Bulletin of the National Association of Secondary School Principals,* Third Report on Staff Utilization Studies, January 1960.

ing require current knowledge of developments in this important area. Perplexing problems exist, but the rewards to society are great; the task is urgent.

URGENT EDUCATIONAL GOAL

Social forces have suddenly brought to prominence the serious and irreparable damage to the nation caused by loss of human talents. The conviction that special educational provisions are necessary for the development of highly gifted children and youth seems now to be widely held by public and educators alike. In the past, the case for special attention to the gifted was based upon the democratic ideal that each individual should be educated to make the fullest use of his potential. This argument, even when backed with sound research evidence,[3] did not stir widespread effort. Although the position of the few educators and social scientists who advocated special treatment remains valid, the urgency felt today is a result more of society's need for talent than of its concern for individual opportunity.

Neglect of Talent: Threat to Modern Civilization

The conditions which have served to arouse educators to the needs of the gifted are largely of post-World War II origin. Rapid technological changes, tense international relationships, and a phenomenal growth of knowledge have caused a severe and continuing shortage of top leadership in education, science, administration, technological research, and other vital areas. So serious has the lack of the very top talent become that many scholars concerned with the problem view it as an immediate threat to our way of life. Representative of this point of view is a statement by Ralph W. Tyler, Director of the Center for Advanced Study in the Behavioral Sciences, Stanford, California:

> It becomes quite clear that the greatest threat to the continuation of modern civilization is the neglect of human potential. Failure to identify individuals with talent, to motivate them to develop their abilities, and to provide the education that they require would result in the most serious damage society could suffer.[4]

[3] See Lewis M. Terman and others, *The Promise of Youth*, Vol. III, Genetic Studies of Genius, Stanford (Stanford Univ. Press), 1930; and Leta S. Hollingworth, *Gifted Children: Their Nature and Nurture*, New York (Macmillan), 1926.

[4] Ralph W. Tyler, "Meeting the Challenge of the Gifted," *Elementary School Journal*, November 1957.

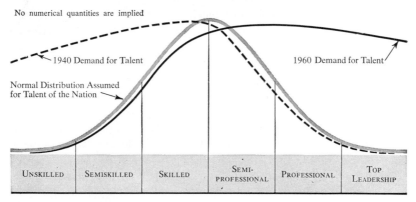

Fig. 17–1. *Demand for Talent, 1940 and 1960*

Demand for intellectual talent. Within the past two decades the proportions of the demand for talent, from the unskilled categories to the top leadership categories, have almost exactly reversed themselves. If one views job classifications as arranged on a continuum from unskilled to top leadership (see Figure 17-1), the demand for unskilled labor has fallen and the demand for top leadership or intellectual talent has increased in an inverse proportion. Prior to 1940, many individuals had to accept jobs requiring talents below their levels of ability. Some, even with training appropriate to a higher job classification, could only obtain employment as unskilled or semiskilled workers. Today this condition does not exist. The demand in the higher job classifications has far outstripped the supply. There are no indications that future conditions will alter this demand. The nation's economic, social, and educational growth has now reached a point at which everyone must be trained for the highest position which his ability and motivation will permit him to attain.

Expansion of knowledge. Perhaps the most pervasive changes which place a premium upon the development of giftedness are those that arise from the discovery of new knowledge. In 1952, after several years of study, John McPartland estimated that within each present two-year span of time more new knowledge is gained than in all of previous history.[5] The massive cumulative nature of the discovery of knowledge and its accelerating effect defies comprehension. Entire fields of study have come into existence and have been subdivided into further, almost discrete fields within the past decade.

[5] John McPartland, "No Go, Space Cadet," *Harper's,* May 1952.

The rapid advance of knowledge has multiplied in geometric proportion the numbers of highly gifted and well-educated individuals needed to maintain it. The phenomenon of specialization which accompanies growth of this kind has brought about the need for team and subgroup attack upon problems. In medicine, science, and industry no one can master all the knowledge and techniques of the complex problems and processes of a given field. Therefore, groups of experts are formed to plan and conduct most undertakings. The clinic, the research team, and the technical staff are recent developments in medicine for integrating the work of specialists, the work of each group being formerly the domain of one individual. In industrial management and administration, both public and private, a similar phenomenon has brought about reliance upon group decision- and policy-making.

The concomitant of specialization is interdependence. In order for each specialist to work efficiently and effectively, all the specialists required for a particular enterprise must be available and properly coordinated. A shortage of one kind of talent can seriously hamper, even halt, work in a given area of knowledge. Interdependence, like specialization, seems to be at once a result and a contributing factor to the phenomenal growth and continued acceleration of the development of knowledge.

Problem for secondary education. The conditions described above are beginning to make an impact upon the secondary schools. International tensions have, of course, provided the element of dramatic urgency to the problem. However, even if international tensions should subside, a matter which seems to be beyond the realm of hope, demand for intellectually able youth would not diminish. This is the situation faced by the secondary schools as they seek to determine the best educational plan for the gifted.

False Assumption: Gifted Require Little Instructional Help

Even at a time when public schools were highly selective, a few schools made special provisions for the gifted.[6] Little scientific justification for special attention was available, however, until the advent of the Stanford-Binet intelligence test in 1916 and its use by Terman

[6] The first major effort is generally acknowledged to have been made by the St. Louis Public Schools in 1868 when a plan of acceleration was adopted on a large scale.

in the 1920's.[7] Meanwhile, increasing enrollments had brought about some demand for special classes for the academically able. This demand met with considerable resistance from both parents and educators. Although the arguments took several forms, they were based on a general assumption that the gifted required little in the way of special instructional help and should be left alone.

Arguments opposing special considerations. The arguments against programs for the gifted generally took three forms. First, it was maintained, such provisions are undemocratic and not in the interests of either the gifted student or the remainder of the school population. Gifted students should not be set apart since they need to understand and communicate with less able students and, in the process, learn to lead others. In addition, the danger of creating an elite is introduced. Second, ability will inevitably show itself. Extra effort is only a waste; what is needed is a basic education for all, and the needs of the gifted will be taken care of automatically. Finally, too little is known about the gifted to warrant special treatment, and departures from traditional practices may be harmful. Until definitive research is conducted and reported, it is educationally unsound and dangerous to attempt experimentation with the gifted. These arguments are still strongly raised and need to be taken into account.

Individualization of instruction: an unattainable ideal. The tailoring of instruction to the individual differences found within each class group is valid as an ideal but difficult to carry out in practice. It has, nevertheless, been a major rationalization for lack of special attention to able students, and low-ability students as well. Experienced, well-trained elementary teachers, backed up by special teachers in certain fields, have generally been successful in individualizing instruction, but even at the elementary level the need for special provisions is being carefully studied.[8] The general failure to individualize instruction in high schools is usually attributed to the widening range of differences among students as they proceed through school, to the concentration upon subject matter more than upon individuals, and to

---

[7] Lewis M. Terman and others, *The Mental and Physical Traits of a Thousand Gifted Children*, Vol. I, Genetic Studies of Genius, Stanford (Stanford Univ. Press), 1925; and Catherine Cox, *The Early Mental Traits of Three Hundred Geniuses*, Vol. II, Genetic Studies of Genius, Stanford (Stanford Univ. Press), 1926.

[8] Ruth Strang reviews the issue of ability grouping in the elementary grades in "How About Separate Classes for Gifted Children?" *Grade Teacher,* November 1957.

the larger number of students with whom each secondary teacher must become familiar under present scheduling practices. Most authorities now agree that special provision for the gifted is an essential element of an adequate secondary school program.[9]

New Theory: The Greater the Ability, the Sounder the Investment of Instructional Services

Rejection of the arguments noted above and realization that it is impossible to rely completely upon the ability of each teacher to individualize instruction have led to an examination of appropriate courses of action to ensure adequate instruction for the gifted in the secondary schools. As a result of such examination, a multitude of new projects has blossomed across the nation. This experimentation is providing an array of answers to the question of what secondary schools can and should do for the gifted. Many of these projects have been designed to permit sound evaluation of results, and the findings may thus be generalized for use by other schools. The moving force behind this development is, in effect, a new theory that the greater the ability a student possesses, the sounder is the investment of educational resources. From this new point of view schools are developing innovations of value to all students.

Secondary school response. The Research Division of the NEA, in 1960, reported the results of a survey of new practices in the secondary schools. The provision of special programs for the gifted led the list with almost eight out of every ten systems reporting such practices for both junior and senior high schools. Results of the survey are given in Table 17-1[10] They reveal that the larger the school district, the more likely that special provisions will be found, but in districts of all sizes throughout the country extensive movements are under way to improve the educational opportunities of the gifted.

Special provisions: danger or opportunity? In education there is the tendency to focus so much attention upon one facet of a task that the need to maintain a balanced program for all students is forgotten. This constant swing of emphasis is a recognized phenomenon. In the public

[9] See Robert Havighurst and Robert DeHaan, *Educating Gifted Children,* Chicago (Univ. of Chicago Press), 1957; Harry Passow and others, *Planning for Talented Youth,* New York (Teachers College, Columbia Univ.), 1955; and National Society for the Study of Education, *Fifty-seventh Yearbook: Education of the Gifted,* Chicago (Univ. of Chicago Press), 1958.

[10] *Research Bulletin,* Washington, D.C. (National Education Association), May 1960, p. 47.

Table 17-1. *Special Programs for the Gifted*

SIZE OF SCHOOL DISTRICT	JUNIOR HIGH SCHOOL	SENIOR HIGH SCHOOL
500,000 and over	100.0%	100.0%
100,000–499,999	93.7	96.5
30,000–99,999	91.3	93.7
10,000–29,999	84.2	82.6
5,000–9,999	65.9	66.4
2,500–4,999	55.9	57.9
ALL DISTRICTS	76.8	76.7

schools there is always more to be done than can be done in any chosen direction, and a proper sense of proportion is difficult to maintain. The problem of priorities is ever-present, for schools have limits to their resources. Special provisions, whether for gifted, handicapped, retarded, or other groups, carry the danger of overemphasis and eventual restriction of the scope of the total program. At the same time, special provisions are a necessary part of any program that holds the individual paramount in its consideration. This is the great ideal of public education and its source of opportunity. As the secondary schools study their students and prepare programs that emphasize the challenge and enjoyment of working to capacity and the fun of using developed skills, whether aesthetic, practical, or intellectual, the opportunities inherent in special provisions become clearer, and the dangers become minimized.

CHARACTERISTICS OF THE GIFTED

Little can be done to prepare adequate plans for instruction until the nature of the student population in question is known. Research gives a reasonably clear indication of the attributes of gifted students. With this knowledge, means of identification, planning of instruction, and services for the gifted, as well as evaluation procedures, can be considered for specific schools.

General Intelligence: First Mark of Giftedness

Intelligence, however defined, is accepted universally as the first criterion of giftedness. Assuming that general intelligence is normally distributed throughout the total school population, as it seems to be, the top 1 or 2 per cent are considered intellectually gifted; the top 10 to 15 per cent are solidly superior. Since the distribution of a trait is continuous, marking off a particular segment of the distribution is an arbitrary matter.[11] In selecting students for special instruction in secondary schools, specific "cutoff" points, as long as they are kept reasonably close to those indicated above, can be adjusted to meet other considerations, such as having adequate numbers to form groups.

A very strong relationship occurs between measures of general intelligence (I.Q.) and high school and college marks, college degrees, occupational level reached, and productivity in adult life. The factor of general intelligence seems to be a major component of many special abilities and to be essential to the highest achievement in all fields of endeavor that have been subjected to research investigation.[12] This and other evidence permits the use of general intelligence as a means of identifying the total reservoir of talent for all areas.

Assessment of general intelligence. Various methods have been used to locate the students who might be intellectually gifted. Teacher nominations, grades, group and individual intelligence tests, peer selections, and expert judgments of student projects have all been tried. Pegnato and Birch have done research upon what they term the "effectiveness" and "efficiency" of a number of these procedures.[13] They conducted their study by applying several methods to a population of 1,400 junior high school students and checking the results against individual Stanford-Binet intelligence test scores. Teacher nominations were surprisingly poor, both because many gifted students were overlooked and because many were nominated who were not gifted. By combining group intelligence and group achievement test results, 97 per cent of

[11] For research purposes Stanford-Binet I.Q. scores over 132 are frequently used to denote the intellectually gifted because statistically this point in the scale is two standard deviations above the mean of the total population and is expected to mark off the top 2 to 4 per cent. A Binet I.Q. score above 116 is one standard deviation above the mean and is expected to mark off the top 15 to 20 per cent.

[12] Lewis M. Terman, *The Discovery and Encouragement of Exceptional Talent,* Test Service Notebook: an abridgment of Terman's Walter Bingham lecture delivered at the University of California (Lecture copyright held by *The American Psychologist*), Tarrytown, N.Y. (World), 1954, p. 2; also P. F. Brandwein analyzes research evidence bearing on this point and reviews the importance of general intelligence in his book *The Gifted Student as Future Scientist,* New York (Harcourt, Brace & World, Inc.), 1955.

[13] C. W. Pegnato and J. W. Birch, "Locating Gifted Children in Junior High Schools: A Comparison of Methods," *Exceptional Children,* March 1959.

the gifted students were identified. The researchers concluded that the combination of these two screening devices would produce the best method available to most school systems. Their findings are strongly supported by other research.

Research results should not lead to the conclusion that teacher judgments, school performance, or other measures are of no value. On the contrary, these kinds of additional information are useful in discovering specific abilities, in affording data for recommendations in program planning, and in supplying clues to the development of individual students. Identification and refinement of information relating to individual student progress should be a continuous and regular process in the development of the abilities of all students.

Use of standard tests. There are many kinds of standardized group tests which are inexpensive yet yield fairly accurate measures of general intelligence (I.Q.). These tests are safe to use whenever it can be assumed that the students have had a cultural background comparable to that of the subjects on whom the tests were standardized, or when the school district can develop its own local norms for a particular test.

Group intelligence tests are often designed to yield a single total measure or index, often expressed as an "intelligence quotient." This measure is the best single predictor of future *academic* achievement. When it is used together with some measure of achievement, either school marks or standardized achievement test scores, accuracy of prediction is further improved. In general, high measures in both intelligence and achievement give the greatest expectancy of academic success; high measures in one but not the other reduce the expectancy of success; low measures on both offer least hope of future academic achievement. Henry Chauncey, president of Educational Testing Service, commented on the effectiveness of the use of intelligence tests as predictors in discussing the effectiveness of test results of fourteen-year-olds in predicting college success:

> While the results of specific studies vary, we can say with confidence what is *usually* found. Typically, of the students in the top 20 per cent on the test (at age 14), about 45 per cent will do honor work (in college), 52 per cent will do satisfactory work, and only about 3 per cent will fail. Of the students in the bottom 20 per cent on the test, only about 3 per cent will do honor work, 52 per cent will pass and 45 per cent will fail. . . .
> Not a perfect record, obviously, but as actuarial forecasts go,

reasonably good; especially when we consider that predictions are based only on aptitude-test (intelligence) scores and do not take into account such factors as interest and motivation.[14]

Cautions in the use of group intelligence tests. Certain shortcomings of group intelligence tests as devices for identifying the gifted should be noted. The meaning of any I.Q. score cannot be fully understood unless the user is familiar with the content of the test and its limitations. At the extreme ranges, the crucial area for identifying the gifted, group scores are generally much lower than scores obtained in individual tests. In fact, some group intelligence tests do not permit an I.Q. score above 130 no matter how many items are answered correctly.

Interpretation of a group test score of an individual is extremely risky unless considerable supplementary data are available. Special abilities, verbal fluency, and creativity, particularly, are not measured by present group tests. The extent of specific abilities, even within the configuration necessary for academic success, is often not amenable to measurement by group intelligence tests. Some excellent tests are available which yield subscores indicating measures of these abilities, but even these tests do not purport to measure separate abilities with high reliability or completeness.

Special abilities. Our educational system requires that students make curriculum choices in the junior and senior high schools. Their decisions are vital to future educational and career choices. The differentiation of secondary school programs, particularly those that include special programs for the gifted, makes it necessary that any special abilities be recognized. Gifted students usually possess, in addition to high general intelligence, some special abilities to a greater degree than others. First, special intellectual abilities become highly developed; and, second, abilities that contribute to outstanding achievement in nonacademic pursuits appear. Each of these kinds of special ability is important to educational program planning and to guidance of the gifted student.

Specialization of intellectual abilities. Grasp of spatial and numerical relationships, reasoning, vocabulary, conceptualization, generalization, and word analogy are a few of the mental abilities measured by intelligence tests. Since the ability to function well in dealing with problems in each of these areas, taken together, correlates highly with academic

[14] Henry Chauncey, "How Tests Help Us Identify the Academically Talented," *Research Bulletin of the National Education Association,* April 1958.

achievement, it is assumed that they are the components of intellectual giftedness. By the early secondary school years individual interests, motivation, and personality factors, coupled with instruction, have usually caused the development of some intellectual abilities to a far greater extent than others.[15] Unusual achievement in languages, science, social studies, literature, and mathematics can serve as an indication to teachers that intellectual abilities are becoming specialized and that educational opportunities which take this condition into account might be particularly fruitful.

Nonacademic abilities. Aptitudes in all areas of the arts, in mechanics, and in leadership are not amenable to identification by standard intelligence tests. Although authorities agree that general intelligence is probably a factor in all areas of giftedness, special abilities undoubtedly exist in those students who show giftedness in nonacademic pursuits. Creativity, originality, verbal fluency, and certain kinds of critical judgment, all of which contribute greatly to nonacademic achievement, must largely be identified in students by study and observation in the school setting.

Personal Adjustment, Interests, and Motivations Characteristic of the Gifted

The possession of outstanding abilities does not guarantee achievement. Personal and social factors, including events which can only be labeled accidents of fate, affect the productivity of individuals. However, the extent to which personality, interests, and motivations contribute to achievement is not known. It is, nevertheless, just as important to study these factors as it is to identify the abilities of the gifted, inasmuch as those traits generally found in gifted students can serve as a guide both in general planning and better understanding of individual cases.

Personal adjustment. As a group, gifted youth present a picture of sound emotional and social development. Contrary to popular belief, the gifted rate well above the normal population in every respect. Lewis Terman cogently summarizes the evidence as follows:

> [Gifted children] are, in general, appreciably superior to unselected children in physique, health, and social adjustment; markedly superior in moral attitudes as measured either by character tests or by trait

[15] J. E. Doppelt has investigated this phenomenon and reports his findings in *The Organization of Mental Abilities in the Age Range 13 to 17,* New York (Teachers College, Columbia Univ.), 1950.

ratings; . . . Moreover, the gifted child's ability as evidenced by achievement in the different school subjects was so general as to refute completely the traditional belief that gifted children are usually one-sided. . . .

Results of thirty years' follow-up . . . show that the incidence of mortality, ill health, insanity and alcoholism is in each case below that for the generality of corresponding age, that the great majority are still well adjusted socially, and that the delinquency rate is but a fraction of what it is in the general population.[16]

There is a considerable body of research on the question of the social and emotional development of the gifted. Certain of these studies are cited below; however, there is no research evidence that refutes any aspect of Terman's statement.

Studies of social adjustment measured in terms of peer acceptance, although inconclusive, lead to the belief that the secondary school years may be the period of the lowest popularity in *intellectually* gifted youth. Martyn, in a study, found that gifted junior and senior high school students were given social acceptance ratings no higher than the averages received by all of their classmates.[17] Leta Hollingworth, through case studies of highly gifted children (I.Q.'s above 180), reached the conclusion that these children faced special problems because they were not understood by those with whom they associated.[18] She examined the problems of the imbalance of development of a child with an intellectual age of fourteen or fifteen years but with the physical development and social skills of an eight- or nine-year-old. Some authorities believe that the creatively gifted have some adjustment problems because they are often viewed by the less gifted as having silly ideas. In various studies, teachers have shown preferences for the less creative even though they say they like creative students. The gifted student is not likely to be a conforming one, and frequently teachers and other adults are unable to distinguish nonconformity from poor adjustment. In conclusion, it can be said that although the gifted, as a group, show no unusual personality difficulties, they are in danger of being misunderstood and frustrated by the conditions of the normal classroom.

[16] Lewis Terman, *The Discovery and Encouragement of Exceptional Talent,* p. 2.

[17] K. A. Martyn, *The Social Acceptance of Gifted Students,* Stanford, California, unpublished doctoral dissertation, Stanford University, 1957.

[18] Leta Hollingworth, *Children Above 180 IQ,* Tarrytown, N.Y. (World), 1942.

Interests. The interest patterns of the gifted have not been conclusively studied. Instruments are available for measuring interests in the secondary school age range, and there is evidence that interests shown after age fifteen remain reasonably constant throughout life.[19] This fact alone has import for guidance and program planning. It appears reasonable to assume that an interest develops through satisfying experience and that the interest, in turn, motivates the student to concentrate upon the development of particular abilities.

One of the authors grew up in a very small town which valued basketball highly. Basketball hoops were about the only equipment on the school grounds. The gymnasium was open before and after school, and boys were strongly encouraged to practice basketball at every opportunity. A program for teaching basketball skills and providing team play ran throughout the elementary grades. Needless to say, boys developed a strong interest in basketball and expended considerable effort to do well in the sport. As a result the school regularly excelled in interscholastic competition, and a large number of boys received athletic scholarships to colleges. If this same effort had been undertaken for science, music, art, and other areas, it is likely that the results would have been similar.

Gifted students develop intense interests which can sustain unusual and extended effort. The school which is sympathetic to individual activity and provides freedom of schedule and facilities can often obtain startling results. Since interests channel effort, which in turn leads to concentrated development of certain patterns of abilities, school programs should provide opportunities for the development of a variety of interests.

Motivation. Whether or not great capacity leads to great achievement may depend upon family or social pressures as well as upon internal drives. Socioeconomic status, membership in a particular ethnic group, and family relationships are among the important areas that influence motivation.

The unmotivated student is to many counselors and teachers the most annoying and puzzling of their professional problems. This group of students seems to be divisible into two broad categories easily recognizable by the perceptive teacher. One category includes those whose attitudes and emotional make-up, largely determined outside of school, cause achievement well below ability, resistance to any expectations

[19] Lewis Terman and others, *The Gifted Child Grows Up*, Vol. IV, Genetic Studies of Genius, Stanford (Stanford Univ.), 1947.

of better performance, and rejection of imposed standards. The other category includes those who are not challenged by the work they are given in school; they either rebel and create problems or accept what is for them uninteresting and routine until their enthusiasm and work habits become dulled.[20]

The effects of social emphases and socioeconomic status upon motivation have been presented in Chapter 7. In addition, it should be noted that different groups motivate their young people differently. Environmental influences, particularly those of family relationships, seem to have an important bearing upon motivation. Highly motivated, gifted individuals are known to possess the characteristics of independence, drive, perseverance, and foresight, and to be relatively free of inferiority feelings.[21]

Through insights into the various factors which contribute to the motivation of students, schools can influence the direction and the extent to which individual students pursue their studies. In the matter of motivation the school is not neutral. The ways in which achievement is rewarded, establishment of high expectations, concern for the relationships of gifted students with their peers and teachers, and the stimulus of challenging programs can serve to modify and to build upon deep-seated attitudes and predispositions. Intelligent understanding and flexible, imaginative action are necessary to challenge gifted students.

SECONDARY SCHOOL PROGRAMS: ADAPTATIONS FOR THE GIFTED

With methods available to identify the gifted and specify their abilities and with knowledge of the characteristics which set the gifted apart from their fellow students, secondary schools face the problem of establishing appropriate services and programs of instruction. Because

[20] The results of research into the problem of chronic underachievement up to this time have been discouraging in terms of improved performance in school. However, Professors Merle Ohlsen and Fred Proff at the University of Illinois and Miriam Goldberg of the Horace Mann Lincoln Institute of Teachers College, Columbia University, are currently making separate investigations of this problem.

[21] See E. P. Torrance, "Personality Development of the Highly Creative Child," *The Minnesota Studies of Creative Thinking in the Early School Years*, Minneapolis (Bureau of Educational Research, Univ. of Minnesota), 1960, pp. 27-29; and F. L. Strodtbeck, "Family Interaction, Values and Achievement," *Talent and Society* (McClelland et al., eds.), New York (Van Nostrand), 1958, pp. 135-94.

of the current intense interest in programs for the gifted, many tested materials and procedures have become available. What steps a given school will take, if any are taken at all, will depend upon local conditions. Approaches described in this section are widely used and readily adjusted to most local situations.

Considerations in Planning for the Gifted

Organizational conditions in the junior and senior high schools make possible certain program adaptations for gifted students not readily attained in the elementary schools. The departmentalized structure of secondary schools replaces the self-contained elementary classroom. Secondary school teachers are subject specialists and usually instruct in only one or two subjects. This kind of structure permits the development of a different program of study for each student merely by the selection of different course patterns. Further, wherever multiple sections of the same course are necessary, ability grouping can be easily provided by having certain class sections of the same course designated for low ability or for honors study.

The educational patterns of the secondary school, as well as the organizational conditions, permit adaptations to the gifted student. Attention to general educational goals tapers off during the early secondary school years, and specialization comes increasingly to the fore. Sequences of learning allow, indeed require, students to choose programs that fit their particular needs. By and large, the gifted student uses his secondary school years as preparation for advanced training.

The choices students make or their placement by school authorities in certain sequences of learning are heavily influenced by a well-organized phenomenon of maturation. That is, as students mature, the range of difference between the most able and the least able increases sharply both in ability and in achievement. Within the ninth grade in a normal public school a few students may be reading at fourth-grade level; another few, at college level. Likewise, in a particular individual, differences widen in the level of achievement from one area to another; a student skilled and interested in creative writing may require remedial instruction in mathematics. Wide ranges of ability and achievement impose the need for qualitative differences in instruction and flexibility in their application to students.

Factors peculiar to local schools set limits upon the extent and type of adaptations which can be carried out successfully. Size of enrollments, for example, may rule out the possibility of ability grouping in all but a few courses. Most important perhaps is the willingness of the community to provide the financial resources for special programs. After making an extensive study of the educational needs of gifted youth for the State of Illinois, Department of Public Instruction, James J. Gallagher reported:

> It is certainly wishful thinking to suppose that well meaning and hard working teachers without sufficient content knowledge, without special knowledge of gifted children, without time for planning programs, and with limited assistance from supervisory personnel could alter in any meaningful degree the educational situation for gifted children. . . . There is no reason to suppose that the educational system is exempt from the precept "you can't get something for nothing." To improve the system, money must be spent. It must be spent judiciously and with an eye toward value received, but it must be spent.[22]

Experience indicates that schools are more likely to make successful improvements if they select carefully procedures appropriate to local conditions, provide a trial period for adaptation and refinement of procedures selected, and evaluate objectively in the local setting before incorporating proposals into the total program.

Administrative Provisions

Several types of special provisions for the gifted do not require major alteration of the normal instructional program. Their effectiveness depends primarily upon the organization of classes, and for this reason they are considered to be administrative plans. Three types, either in "pure" form or in various combinations, are in popular use. These are acceleration through the normal program, ability grouping, and enriched experiences within heterogeneous classes. The percentage of senior high schools employing each type or combination can be found in Table 17-2.[23] Acceleration, even when combined with other forms, is the least popular practice. Enrichment seems to be the most favored single provision, although most schools employ some combination of the three types.

Enrichment within heterogeneous classes. Enrichment consists of providing the gifted student with opportunities to pursue interests at

---

[22] From an advance release of James J. Gallagher's unpublished report, pp. 167-68. Permission to quote from the typed copy was given by David M. Jackson, Director, State of Illinois Project for the Gifted, Urbana, August 1960.

[23] *Research Bulletin,* National Education Association, May 1960, p. 48.

Table 17-2. *Special Provisions for the Gifted*[a]

Enrichment in heterogeneous classes only	24.7%
Separate classes only[b]	9.8
Acceleration	1.3
All of the provisions above	10.5
Separate classes and enrichment	21.4
Separate classes and acceleration	2.5
Enrichment and acceleration	6.5
TOTAL SCHOOL DISTRICTS WITH SPECIAL PROVISIONS	76.7

[a] Only senior high schools were included in this survey.
[b] Separate classes refers to ability grouping.

greater depth or to develop abilities through wider experiences than are given the average student. When enrichment is undertaken as an administrative device, the teacher normally is not required to alter significantly the scope or sequence of regular classroom instruction. Enrichment in depth is provided by augmenting class instruction with club work, projects, reading programs, and other related study carried on by community agencies, special teachers, or regular teachers in their activities work. Lateral enrichment includes allowing the student to carry extra course work beyond the normal schedule of classes, providing instruction in areas such as art or music, and setting up projects or activities apart from the regular classroom.

Administrative provisions for enrichment are perhaps the cheapest and easiest for the school to develop. They are often used in communities in which there is resistance to programs which single out the gifted. Administrative enrichment plans are criticized primarily because they do not in themselves bring about qualitative changes in classroom instruction; they are, in the main, quantitative additions. A practical disadvantage is that the added work generally becomes the burden of already overloaded teachers.

Ability grouping. Grouping procedures vary greatly. There is disagreement about the merits of grouping in the secondary schools, and unfortunately, most criticism is leveled at ability grouping *per se* rather than at the kinds of grouping attempted under particular circumstances. Recent research and the opinion of recognized authorities seem to be on the side of grouping gifted students, at least for part of the instructional program.

The least extreme form of grouping comes about through the interests and choices of students. Advanced courses of sequential studies are organized upon the basis of "natural" selection. Students tend to drop out of those areas of study in which they have little interest and ability so that the advanced classes contain the more able students. Few students who have had difficulty with geometry will elect trigonometry.

Other types of grouping, however, depend upon administrative arrangements. The most extreme form of grouping is the special school in which gifted students are segregated in completely separate plants and organizations. New York City has separate high schools for the talented in science, mathematics, art, music, technical training, and the performing arts.

1. *Separation within the comprehensive school.* "Multiple-track" plans, subschools, and separate curriculums are all devices presently in use for grouping students. The multiple-track plans depend upon classifying students as "honors," "regular," and "opportunity," or some other appropriate designations. Students then remain in their particular track for all of their subject instruction, although homerooms, physical education classes, and student activities are often organized heterogeneously. The separate curriculum plan involves the selection of students for college-preparatory, general, vocational, business, and other curriculums. Each curriculum provides the basis of a subschool with an independent program of study and assigned professional staff; students seldom change from one curriculum to another. A very small number of schools operate a completely separated subschool organization in which even guidance, administrative, and supervisory functions are retained in the subschool so that a school-within-a-school exists for each group of students.

The separation of gifted students either into separate schools or into one of the plans described above is generally favored by the extreme critics of American secondary education. They view the curriculum of the comprehensive high school as watered down and fragmented; they discount the social dangers of segregation and argue for a "democracy of real talent"; finally, they believe that standards have been lowered and rigorous examinations eliminated which, they say, has resulted in a loss of challenge.[24] Opposed to this point of view are those who wish to retain the comprehensive nature of American sec-

[24] See Paul Woodring, *A Fourth of a Nation,* New York (McGraw-Hill), 1957; and Arthur Bestor, *The Restoration of Learning,* New York (Knopf), 1955.

ondary schools. They recognize the need to challenge students more fully, particularly the gifted; and they wish to increase the intellectual and scholarly emphasis of secondary education and improve the quality of instructional procedures. However, they believe that necessary improvements should be made within the structure of the comprehensive high school to retain flexibility and a broad educational offering while, at the same time, ensuring quality of opportunity.[25]

2. *Flexible grouping.* One modification of the grouping plan is a flexible track plan in which no sharply defined curriculums comprise the total program. Instead "honors," "regular," and "opportunity" class sections are provided, where appropriate, in each course with enrollments large enough to require multiple class sections. Students are placed in a particular class group according to criteria established for each course. Thus, a student might be assigned to an honors class in mathematics but to a regular class in English. A student might find himself in one or many honors classes depending upon his abilities. Each student would have some heterogeneously grouped classes and opportunity to mix with all students in homeroom and activities.

Acceleration. Under "lock-step" educational conditions acceleration is synonymous with skipping whole grades or courses. This has excited much opposition and has been replaced generally by other forms. Acceleration has come to mean rapid progress through programs of instruction *in order to devote time to other purposes.* The principal argument raised against grade skipping has been that the gifted student, who could profit most from school, is passed through the quickest. The logic of this argument fails when applied to the newer forms of acceleration. In junior high school, grouping gifted students into rapidly moving classes to complete two years of a given subject in one, giving extra courses, and providing early admission to high school are current practices. In the senior high school, present practices allow gifted students to take extra courses (to accumulate more credits), to make rapid progress through a given subject sequence (mathematics, foreign language, science), and to complete their normal high school work early in order to take college courses in high school,[26] or to enter college early.

[25] See James B. Conant, *The American High School Today,* New York (McGraw-Hill), 1959, pp. 40-76.

[26] The Advanced Placement Program of the College Entrance Examination Board, Princeton, N. J., administers a program that grants college credit for work completed in high school. See W. H. Cornog, "Initiating an Educational Program for Able Students in the Secondary Schools," *School Review,* Spring 1957.

The pressing need to have gifted students pursue studies to greater depth and the desire to introduce them to more fields of knowledge are important points in favor of acceleration. Another consideration is the extended period of academic training facing most gifted youth. Irving Lorge has addressed himself to the problem of the social loss of productivity due to extended education. He estimates that "saving a year for one per cent of 25,000,000 children in elementary and secondary school would mean an additional 25,000 man years of productivity, or an additional 6,500 men for 40 professional years."[27] The educational and social advantages of acceleration seem great. But there is another facet of the problem: the effect of acceleration on the individual. Is the individual likely to be damaged in his personal, social, or intellectual development? The weight of research evidence is again strongly in favor of acceleration. Gallagher and Shannon each have recently made studies of the research bearing upon this point.[28] Gallagher sums up the case for acceleration: "It is very difficult to find any study which has reported any negative effects of acceleration when the acceleration is done as part of a planned program and is limited to reducing the student's total educational program one or two years."[29]

The practice of acceleration seems to merit more consideration than it has received in professional circles up to this time. Perhaps students in the future will ponder the reason for the long period of inactivity regarding it, and will question the wisdom of ignoring such a simple yet effective method of strengthening the nation's resources of talent.

Provisions in the small school: critical problem. No attempts have been made to study the educational effects of the very small secondary school. Cursory examination of the offerings of small schools, particularly rural schools, gives the impression of minimum opportunities. It is known that schools with less than 100 in their graduating classes send a much smaller percentage of their students on to college than larger schools, and of those who do enter, large percentages meet academic failure. James Conant in his widely acclaimed study of the comprehensive high school, voiced unequivocal opposition to the small high school and recommended its prompt elimination from the educational scene.[30] It is doubtful that any of the special provisions for the

[27] Irving Lorge, "Social Gains in the Special Education of the Gifted," *School and Society,* January 1954, p. 5.

[28] James Gallagher, see footnote 22 for reference; and Dan C. Shannon, "What Research Says about Acceleration," *Phi Delta Kappan,* November 1957.

[29] Gallagher, p. 146.

[30] James Conant, *op cit.,* pp. 77-85.

gifted presented thus far could be employed effectively in the small secondary school.

Small high schools can make use of such resources as correspondence courses or combination television-correspondence courses to further the development of gifted and highly motivated students. Research conducted in Wisconsin by Wittich and others[31] documented the fact that an able student can master high school physics with the aid of a television-correspondence course to a level equal to the achievement of students of comparable ability who have the benefit of conventional instruction.

The task of reorganizing schools will not be completed overnight. In the meantime, those responsible for the administration of the small schools are under obligation to make certain that academic talents of students do not go undiscovered and undeveloped.

Instructional Considerations in Special Programs for the Gifted

Administrative provisions can only provide the structure through which teaching is organized. At the instructional level, the effectiveness of the individual teacher is of primary importance. A scholarly command of the subject, important as it is, is useless unless the teacher holds high standards, has the personal qualities to teach without dominating or enforcing conformity, clearly understands and believes in his students, and can motivate them to make unusual effort.

Qualitative differences in the instruction of the gifted. Differences in the quality of instruction between what is appropriate for the average and for the gifted are not sharply defined. A difference in quality suggests more rapid mastery of content, more attention to detail, and higher standards of work. Although these aspects are important, they are not the principal outcomes of special instruction, since they would be expected as well in the instruction of gifted children in the regular classroom.

Consideration of the characteristics of the gifted leads to such instructional practices as reducing the number of concrete experiences and applications necessary to attain understanding; centering upon conceptual and problematical elements instead of factual ones; eliminating rigid standards such as writing out all steps to the solution of a problem; employing drill and memorization sparingly and only when

[31] Walter A. Wittich, *The Wisconsin Physics Film Evaluation Project,* Madison (School of Education, Univ. of Wisconsin), April 1959.

necessary to retention for later use; and assigning independent study where possible to allow the exercise of student judgment as to what constitutes satisfactory solutions. Quality of teaching, not quantity of material covered, is the goal.

Instructional opportunities provided by special provisions. The crucial test of the merit of special provisions is whether teachers use them to make real adjustments in the learning conditions of gifted students. The question arises as to how different instruction should be. Are the instructional needs of gifted students so qualitatively and quantitatively different that they are actually different in kind? Gallagher and Lucito have found sizable differences in the patterns of intellectual traits among the gifted, average, and mentally handicapped. Gallagher lists the outstanding strengths of the gifted in comparison to other groups:

(a) Association and interrelationship of concepts
(b) Critical evaluation of facts and arguments
(c) Creation of new ideas and origination of new lines of thought
(d) Ability to reason through complex problems
(e) Ability to understand other situations, other times, and other people; to be less bound by one's own peculiar environmental setting[32]

Creativity, originality, sensitivity to problems, flexibility of thought, critical thinking, and abstract thinking seem to be areas of important differences between the gifted and other groups. These seem to be the abilities through which the gifted will likely make their greatest contribution. The problem for the teacher might then be stated another way. What teaching procedures will raise these abilities to their highest level of use? Some promising, experimentally produced instructional materials are available for adaptation by teachers to help them meet this problem.

Scholars, professors of education, and secondary school teachers have combined their knowledge, talents, and special skills to study the content, learning problems, and materials necessary to high-level scholarship in the physical sciences, mathematics, and foreign languages. They have produced films, texts, experimental kits, manuals, tapes, and other instructional materials of excellent quality, coordi-

[32] James Gallagher, *op cit.,* p. 25.

nated for direct instructional use.[33] Materials available for classroom use, particularly in mathematics and science, are geared to critical analysis, discovery, and conceptual learning. They serve especially well the aims of education for the gifted described above.

Those who have formulated the pedagogical theories and the materials that emphasize "discovery" learning believe that teachers need special training for such work. This type of instruction omits verbal learning of rules and precise definitions and postpones the requirement that students state principles and concepts until they have discovered them and observed special cases and refinements. Beberman of the University of Illinois School Mathematics Program describes his experience in training teachers in his methods:

> Now, it is not an easy task to convince teachers that students can operate successfully (with mathematical constructs) in the absence of formalized rules. There is the tendency for teachers to "tie things up in verbalizations." Usually the first trial is enough to convince teachers that many of their favorite rules are unnecessary.

Of the students he observes:

> They [students] are astounded when their teacher tells them that it is their job to bring students to the point where they believe that they do not have to depend upon textbooks or teachers to operate successfully. But, it is possible, and rewarding.[34]

Theoretical formulations of method and tested teaching materials for a new and stimulating type of teaching are being rapidly developed. The general approach of the teacher will fit well with new practice if he can establish in his students a breadth of understanding of a particular field sufficient to provide the orientation for study in depth of significant aspects of that field; stimulate sensitivity to problems and the intellectual tools of problem solving; seek out class learning activities to extend classroom study and promote independent scholarship; and stress creativity, problem solving, and critical thinking as outcomes

---

[33] For information refer to: the Physical Science Study Committee, 164 Main Street, Watertown, 64, Massachusetts; the University of Illinois School Mathematics Program, College of Education, Urbana; and the Foreign Language Project (elementary and junior high school level only), Charles Johnson, Director, College of Education, University of Illinois.

[34] Max Beberman, et al., "The University of Illinois School Mathematics Program," *School Review,* Winter 1957, p. 463.

more essential than conformity to fixed rules and procedures. By these methods the gifted can be challenged to reach the highest potential, and in turn, meet the challenges which society will pose for them as adults.

EVALUATION OF PROVISIONS FOR THE GIFTED

The weakest point in special programs, whether for the gifted or other groups, is evaluation of their effects. Those responsible for planning a new program are, understandably, concerned about the immediate task of implementation. The weight of pressures to get started usually causes the matter of evaluation to be postponed. Too frequently it is an afterthought; often it is undertaken only when a program is called into question. A part of the planning of every new program should include preparation for an assessment of the results.

Importance of an Evaluation Design

The evaluation of a program involves two different kinds of questions. First are the "what" questions. What does the program aim to produce? In a program for the gifted the aim might be higher achievement, greater creativity, improved performance in problem solving, or new learning not provided before. What elements of the present program would it be most serious to lose or impair? Healthy student attitudes toward others, factual knowledge, or loss of interest in important out-of-class activities could be crucial elements. Second are the "how" questions. How can each of these elements be defined so that they can be measured? How can the needed evidence be gathered to ensure complete and acceptable evaluations?

Answers to the two kinds of questions provide the basis for a design. They will indicate to the evaluators the instruments to be used, the "base line" data to be collected, the "controls" to be selected, the timing of collection of data, and their analysis. From this brief discussion of the preparation necessary to sound evaluation, the importance of early planning becomes clearer. It is apparent that, in many cases, lack of prior preparation precludes validation of results.

Problems of Evaluation

The evaluation of certain educational programs—especially those providing for the gifted child—presents unusual problems, even when the programs are planned in advance. First, a suitable design is frequently difficult to evolve. Measuring the achievement of the gifted in comparison to that of average students is, of course, invalid, for the gifted might do as well in a regular program. To show simply that the gifted have made large gains is likewise invalid. Second, measurements of important variables may be ignored or found to be too difficult. The important abilities of creativity, problem solving, and critical thinking are not amenable to easy measurement. Often variables such as the stimulus which gifted students bring to regular classes or attitudes engendered by segregation of groups are not taken into account. Third, spurious data may be collected and accepted as valid. Opinions of teachers and students in special programs are sometimes reported in attempts to prove the merits of special provisions. Generally this kind of data must be rejected because of the biases of the subjects surveyed. Finally, statistical treatment and interpretation may lead to incorrect conclusions. Simple, descriptive statistical procedures generally do not permit decisive judgments leading to the acceptance or rejection of a given treatment.

Essential Elements of Evaluation

The previous statements relating to evaluation give clues to some points to be considered. Knowledge of research design, of the distinctive characteristics of the gifted, and of the particular program being undertaken and skill in the use of instruments and techniques are of primary importance. If this knowledge is not available within the school staff, wisdom dictates that those responsible seek the assistance of outside consultants.

Two general approaches can be recommended for evaluation designs for use in public schools. First, the use of control groups seems best to ensure valid findings. Use of controls requires that only a portion (usually one-half) of the students who actually qualify for the special program can participate in it during the period of evaluation. Further, the control group must match the experimental group on every important characteristic. In this type of evaluation pre- and post-testing is normally conducted, and the gains or losses on predetermined variables compared. The importance of obtaining measures of those aspects of the program which are planned deviations from the normal has been indicated. Second, some plans should be made to investigate the cases in which the experimental treatment worked unusually well or did not meet expectations. Often a case study approach is suitable for this work. Frequently the deviant cases provide important information for future planning and yield the most useful information.

Evaluation establishes a sound basis for program development. It is an integral part of the process of promoting significant educational change. It provides a needed element of stability and ensures a proper emphasis upon the planned aspects of new programs. Conducted in this spirit, evaluation can become the means of a continued, consistent search for improvement.

SELECTED REFERENCES

BROUDY, HARRY. "American Problems and Russian Solutions." *Improving Science Programs in Illinois Schools,* Urbana: Univ. of Illinois Press, 1958.

CONANT, JAMES B. "The Academically Talented Pupil." *Journal of the National Education Association,* April 1958.

COOK, WALTER W. "The Gifted and the Retarded in Historical Perspective." *Phi Delta Kappan,* March 1958.

CROWDER, THORA, AND JAMES J. GALLAGHER. "The Adjustment of Gifted Children in the Regular Classroom." *Exceptional Children,* May 1957.

DREWS, ELIZABETH, AND J. E. TEAHAN. "Parental Attitudes and Academic Achievement." *Journal of Clinical Psychology,* October 1957.

EVERETT, SAMUEL. *Programs for the Gifted.* New York: Harper, 1961.

GOLDBERG, MIRIAM. "Motivation of the Gifted." *Education of the Gifted: The 57th Yearbook of the National Society for the Study of Education,* Chicago: Univ. of Chicago Press, 1958.

GUILFORD, J. P. "The Structure of Intellect." *Psychological Bulletin,* July 1956.

HAVIGHURST, ROBERT, AND ROBERT DeHAAN. *Educating Gifted Children.* Chicago: Univ. of Chicago Press, 1957.

HERSEY, JOHN. *The Child Buyer.* New York: Knopf, 1960.

KORAL, ALEXANDER G. *Soviet Education for Science and Technology* New York: Wiley, 1957.

MARTINSON, RUTH, AND L. M. LESSINGER. "Problems in the Identification of Intellectually Gifted Pupils." *Exceptional Children,* January 1960.

PASSOW, HARRY, AND OTHERS. *Planning for Talented Youth.* New York: Bureau of Publications, Teachers College, Columbia Univ. 1955.

SUMPTION, MERLE R., AND EVELYN LUECKING. *Education of the Gifted.* New York: Ronald Press, 1960.

TERMAN, LEWIS M., AND MELITA ODEN. *The Gifted Group at Mid-Life.* Stanford, Calif.: Stanford Univ. Press, 1959.

Microphone, amplifier, and earphones make it possible for these deaf-oral students to keep up with their fellow students in regular high school classes.

Providing Educationally for the Handicapped

THE SECONDARY school's responsibility for the education of the handicapped has been recognized, but only sparsely implemented. Most states delegate to high schools the obligation of educating all youth up to the compulsory attendance age and beyond that age on a voluntary basis; a child cannot be excluded from school solely because of a handicap. Despite legal recognition of the handicapped adolescent's right to attend high school, educational practice in many communities falls short of providing suitable training programs for them.

Yet the growing concern of society for providing educationally for its disabled young people is forcing consideration of what can and should be done for such individuals in local schools. Already some training programs for handicapped youth are developing in junior and senior high schools, without benefit of sufficient research, or established policies, and often in the absence of suitable facilities and qualified teachers. These haphazard programs ultimately will force other secondary schools to face their responsibilities for handicapped students and to design programs for those among them who can benefit from the resources that high schools can offer.

SOCIETY'S CONCERN FOR THE HANDICAPPED

Natural human sympathy for the handicapped child, combined with the democratic belief that each individual, regardless of his lot, is entitled to educational benefits that will help him to develop his capacities—meager though they may be—generates strong public sentiment for secondary schools to do as much as they can for adolescent boys and girls with mental, emotional, physical, or social impairments. Evidence of society's concern for the handicapped is found in the unstinted support for education designed for such individuals, including legislative provisions for special state aids in all states, and in the fact that of the first federal funds appropriated for educational research a large share was earmarked for the study of mental deficiency in children and youth.

Definition of the Term "Handicapped"

As is often true, unfortunately, in the field of education, confusion in definitions and terminology has retarded the development of suitable educational efforts for the handicapped.

Two titles have been given to programs of education for the handicapped that compete with each other for popularity, but neither of them is precise in its meaning. These are "exceptional education" and "special education." The use of the first to designate categories of instruction designed for two distinct groups with completely different capacities for academic progress, different problems of learning, and different educational requirements—the gifted and the handicapped—has long been a source of confusion to educators. The gifted child has superior assets or abilities; all other categories of pupils included under the heading "exceptional" possess deficits or impairments in mental or physical capacities. Youth with deficiencies have much in common. Their handicapped conditions, also, are frequently multiple[1] in character and must be treated in a conceptually unified fashion. On the other hand, giftedness rarely exists in conjunction with a handicapped condition; consequently, in terms of educational treatment there is little in common between the gifted and the handicapped pupil.

The misuse of the term "exceptional education," is given support by the administrative structure of school systems, state departments of education, and even by the United States Office of Education. Similarly, institutions of teacher education have sought to prepare teachers and

---

[1] The term "multiple" as used here means that some conditions, such as emotional disturbance or social maladjustment, may only be the overt symptoms of other unidentified types of handicaps.

specialists to deal with these two extremes of the population as though their educational needs were closely related.

The second term, "special education," would perhaps be more appropriate were it not that it becomes confused with education provided in certain special fields, e.g., art, music, business education, agriculture, home economics, and physical education. It has the further limitation of suggesting to some people that all such services should be separate from the general program of the school. Such interpretations have sometimes led to the establishment of different schools for the handicapped, at heavy costs to taxpayers, without reference to whether the students could be accommodated within the facilities and resources of the comprehensive secondary school.

For purposes of reference here and without intending offense to or hoping for endorsement from those educators who champion either of the above terms, the designation "handicapped" will be used to identify all individuals whose mental or physical capacities, educational attainments, or personal and social adjustments deviate sufficiently from the normal range to require therapeutic educational treatment. This definition is intended to exclude children whose progress is below average to the point that they are called slow learners. It should be noted, however, that in some states the mentally retarded are legally defined as slow learners. For the purposes of this discussion slow learners are seen as being one level above handicapped youth.

The focus of attention in this chapter is on youth who have the potential for making independent social and vocational adjustments in the community upon termination of formal schooling. Which handicapped youth can be accommodated in a high school depends largely on the philosophy of the school and, in part, upon the services available. Some secondary schools are organized so rigidly that they cannot deal with even mild deviations from normality in students. The key question secondary schools must face is: who ought to be provided educational services? Once a school has accepted its obligation to all youth, which legally it is expected to fulfill, it can move toward developing a program with sufficient flexibility to serve the handicapped as well as the normal and the gifted.

Some youth, of course, possess deficiencies so great that they are incapable of becoming independent; they must be cared for in special institutions. Research in recent years,[2] however, has revealed that

[2] Richard L. Masland, Seymour B. Sarason, and Thomas Gladwin, *Mental Subnormality*, New York (Basic Books), 1958.

many children who formerly were diagnosed as noneducable with proper training are capable of sufficient development to assume responsibility for themselves.

Included in those classified as handicapped, by the definition above, are some youth whose major symptoms of deficiency will be poor academic achievement. In many such cases unidentified mental and physical deficiencies, or poor home environments, have produced lack of motivation for academic work; these boys and girls come to secondary schools hindicapped educationally, and often socially as well.

Traits That Require Educational Therapy

Traits that require educational therapy are related to three stages of the process of learning: the *input* phase, which is dependent upon sensory reception, e.g., seeing, hearing, feeling, and occasionally smelling; the *integrative process,* during which perceptions, impressions, and sensations are assimilated as knowledge, understandings, relationships, or principles; and the *output* stage, which is dependent upon vocal or motor responses.[3] For example, blindness or deafness seriously interferes with the input operation; brain damage or an insufficient level of mental functioning or social and emotional strains reduces the efficiency of the integrative process; crippling that restricts the use of the voice or motor skills hampers effective output. Inasmuch as such factors interfere with learning and necessitate special educational therapy, they are looked upon as handicaps. In this sense, such conditions as poor vision, speech imperfections, impaired motor skills, and perhaps chronic illness and low vitality may become handicapping traits that reduce effectiveness in learning.

With proper therapy, the difficulties caused by handicaps can often be removed or greatly reduced. Experience with day-school programs at the elementary school level has demonstrated that vision and hearing handicaps can be counteracted to the point that blind and deaf youth can succeed fairly well in integrated programs in the secondary school in which some work is taken in regular classes and therapeutic supplementary training is provided by resource-room teachers[4] or itinerant specialists.[5] Similarly pupils with speech and motor functioning deficits can be helped to succeed in normal programs of study by

[3] Interpretation supplied by Dr. Rick Heber, University of Wisconsin.
[4] Teachers who manage a specially equipped room in which the handicapped are given instruction.
[5] Teachers who serve several schools, traveling from one to another.

the treatment of their limiting handicaps. Emotional disturbance, often a temporary condition, may respond to therapy to the point where progress in high school is not seriously interrupted.

Mental retardedness limits the integrative aspects of learning so that pupils are unable to keep pace with the academic standards of most secondary schools. Pupils with such impairments, for various and perhaps multiple reasons, exhibit levels of functioning that make it necessary for their programs of training to be adapted to the level of individual responses. Some children with mental impairments are incapable of developing independent behavior. Those classified as educable, however, can learn, and some make surprising gains in intellectual functioning under proper instruction. Whether or not a particular pupil can be served by the secondary school will depend upon the level of mental functioning he demonstrates, the willingness of the school to establish training programs adapted to that level, and the availability of trained and sympathetic teachers.

The term "social maladjustment" is often used to identify a cluster of conditions that range from poor social adaptation to incorrigibility and delinquency. Such symptoms are common in high school populations. They require diagnosis and treatment just as do other types of handicaps to learning.

Another type of handicapped youth, whose problems may be related to or grow out of other traits, is the pupil whose scholarship skills and level of achievement fall below those required for successful high school work. Such individuals have been advanced through the elementary school because school officials have believed that it is better for them to keep pace with their age groups than to remain at their levels of achievement. They reach high school with little chance of success in regular programs but still below the legal school-leaving age. Such students require programs of training designed for their needs just as do others with more severe handicaps to learning.

Actually, the impairments to learning that are called handicaps are found to approximate a continuum from mild to severe; there is no sharp, definable dichotomy between "normal" and "abnormal." In fact, emphasis on these two classifications has led to the neglect of the borderline degrees of handicappedness. One serious result of ignoring pupils with only mild degrees of defects or impairments, mental or physical, is illustrated by the extent to which delinquent youth possess such limitations.

Number and Distribution of the Handicapped

Almost 12 per cent of the school-age population of the United States is educationally handicapped, either mentally or physically. A distribution of the estimated numbers and percentages of these pupils, according to the standard classifications of handicaps, is shown in Table 18-1. These estimates are conservative; studies of particular situations and reports of groups concerned with different types of handicaps have shown higher ratios. Also, these figures do not include pupils with academic handicaps that result from failure to keep pace with school

Table 18-1. *Estimated Proportion of Handicapped Youth of School Age in the United States*[a]

TYPE OF HANDICAP	ESTIMATED NUMBER	PERCENTAGE OF TOTAL SCHOOL-AGE POPULATION
Blind	12,000	0.03
Poor vision	80,000	0.20
Crippled or health deficiencies	800,000	2.00
Deaf and hard-of-hearing	800,000	2.00
Speech deficiencies	1,200,000	3.00
Emotionally disturbed and socially maladjusted	800,000	2.00
Mentally retarded (educable and trainable)	1,000,000	2.50
TOTALS	4,692,000	11.73

[a] Estimates based on percentages for each type of handicap that has been found dependable by various past surveys applied to an estimated school-age population of 40,000,000.

achievement standards. They are subject, too, statisticians believe, to difficulties in identification and classification, particularly for youth of high school age, many of whose handicaps do not become wholly apparent before they reach adolescence.

Enrollments of handicapped youth in secondary schools increased from 17,423 in 1937-38 to 88,825 in 1952-53.[6] By 1958, there were

6 Mabel C. Rice and Arthur S. Hill, *Statistics of Special Education for Exceptional Children, 1952-53,* Washington, D.C. (U.S. Department of Health, Education and Welfare), 1954, p. 13. Mentally gifted youth are excluded from these figures.

110,667 handicapped youth receiving instruction in secondary schools, as shown in Table 18-2. The distribution of types of defects included 48,910 pupils who were classed as mentally retarded at the upper range level, 37,422 with speech deficiencies, and 10,651, who were either crippled or had health deficiencies. These three classifications combined represent almost 88 per cent of all handicapped children being served in high schools.

Table 18-2. *Actual Enrollments of Handicapped Students in Elementary, Secondary, and Other Types of Educational Programs, 1958.*

TYPE OF HANDICAP	ELEMENTARY (INCL. NURSERY AND KINDERGARTEN)	SECONDARY	OTHER OR MIXED TYPES	TOTAL
Blind	2,252	425	65	2,742
Poor vision	6,222	1,821	223	8,266
Crippled or health deficiencies	38,176	10,651	1,242	50,069
Deaf and hard-of-hearing	15,013	3,267	919	19,199
Speech deficiencies	432,903	37,422	4,318	474,643
Emotionally disturbed and socially maladjusted	18,170	7,014	2,263	27,447
Mentally retarded: Upper range (approx. 50-75 I.Q.)	129,770	48,910[a]	18,105	196,785
Middle range (25-50 I.Q.)	10,555	324[a]	5,738	16,617
Not separately classified[b]	10,630	833[a]	1,578	13,041
TOTALS	663,691	110,667	34,451	808,809

[a] Housed in secondary school buildings.
[b] Includes pupils with multiple handicaps.

SOURCE: Preliminary figures for 1956-58, Biennial Survey of Education in the United States. Prepared by Romaine Mackie, Harold M. Williams, and Patricia Robins, Office of Education, U.S. Department of Health, Education and Welfare, September 7, 1960.

The number of handicapped youth actually enrolled in schools represents only about 11 per cent of the estimated number of school-aged handicapped in the United States, shown in Table 18-1. Furthermore, the number being provided for by high schools in 1958 was only slightly over 17 per cent of the enrollments of handicapped youth in elementary schools.

Education of the Handicapped

The care of the handicapped is a characteristic of a civilized society. In a democratic nation, where individual development and freedom to utilize one's abilities in the pursuit of personal dignity and happiness are cherished goals, education has a vital role in the habilitation of the unfortunate. Every individual is privileged to share in the benefits of free schools: to achieve literacy, cultivate his intellectual resources, become acquainted with the cultural heritage, to attain competence in his citizenship responsibilities, to refine his moral and spiritual values, and to develop useful and marketable skills. The right to learn is not predicated on intellectual, social, or physical normality. It belongs to the sick, the dull, the blind, the deaf, the crippled, and the disturbed, as well as to the genius with perfect health and physique—just because they are human beings, alive in a free society that is dedicated to humanity and justice.

The rationale for the education of the handicapped, however, goes beyond the right of the individual to share in the advantages of education. It takes into account the benefits that accrue to the total society when the talents of all people—even those with impairments—are refined to a maximum. A handicapped person who does not receive proper training may spend fifty years in an institution at public expense, at a cost of $3,000 per year. With the aid of education he can be converted into a self-supporting citizen who earns each year as much as he might otherwise cost the state—the difference is a $150,000 asset to society as compared to a $150,000 liability. Similarly, the uneducated and unemployable, almost as much as those who must be institutionalized, are social and economic burdens on the community. A basic goal of public education is to help all to learn to care for themselves, to perform useful work, and to share in civic duties.

RESPONSIBILITIES OF THE SECONDARY SCHOOLS FOR THE HANDICAPPED

Concern for the education of the handicapped is generating pressures on school faculties and administrators, as well as on school boards, for the expansion of efforts to provide programs integrated into the total offerings of high schools. The importance of incorporating such training into public high schools is supported by the evidence that an individual cannot be prepared for community adjustment in a residential school that separates him from family, school, and neighborhood life. Another reason for educating the handicapped in local schools is the advantages that accrue to all other high school students when they are permitted to adjust to, associate with, come to understand and accept, and in many instances, provide assistance to classmates with intellectual and physical impairments.

The philosophy prevailing in some other nations, such as Sweden, that the handicapped should be treated as normally as possible is making Americans realize that our practices are often, by comparison, almost medieval. Swedish policy is to treat the handicapped with complete acceptance. They continue in school, participate in family and community life. The adaptations necessary to help them to learn are made without indication that they are unusual or "special." As a result, handicapped children and youth do not become segregated from normal life; they retain the close associations of family and friends that are so essential to emotional stability. They gain confidence from facing the task of remedying or relieving their impairments with maximum assistance and encouragement. The Swedish approach and similar practices in other European countries call attention to deficiencies in philosophy and programs of education for the handicapped in secondary schools here.

An encouraging sign is the interest in this field being evidenced by secondary school principals. In 1955, for the first time, an entire issue of the *Bulletin of the National Association of Secondary School Principals* was devoted to the high school's responsibilities to handicapped youth.[7] In introducing the issue, Lloyd Dunn of George Peabody College for Teachers pointed out:

> In view of the common needs, problems, and similarities of all adolescents, in so far as possible the educational program and activities for exceptional pupils should be a part of, and not apart from, the high school program for the usual pupils. Some pupils may require special classes for academic instruction for part or all of the school day; others may be enrolled in regular classes.[8]

While only a few of the secondary schools have fully developed

[7] January 1955, Vol. 39, No. 207.
[8] Lloyd Dunn, "The Exceptional Pupil—A Challenge to Secondary Education," *The Bulletin of the National Association of Secondary School Principals,* January 1955, p. 10.

programs for handicapped youth,[9] testimony of high school principals indicates that most schools must provide for severely handicapped boys and girls. In spite of the newness of the developments at the secondary level, a number of responsibilities of junior and senior high schools in this field are coming to be recognized.

Research, Identification, Diagnosis, and Classification

Knowledge about handicapped youth and their educational habilitation is pretty much in a pioneer stage. Secondary schools enroll students at an age when much can be learned about the responses of those with various kinds of impairments to learning. The opportunities for research are practically unlimited.

In spite of the increases in handicapped youth attending high schools, according to conservative estimates, as many as 85 per cent of these young people still are not in school. Many are unknown to school authorities. The task of identifying these young people, who need to be in school even longer than normal students, places an added burden on high school authorities.

Classification of mental and physical defects usually is done by medical advisers, at least it is their function to describe the degrees of deviation from average. Social maladjustments often are even more complex than physical or mental deficiencies and require a broader range of professional resources to determine their nature. Educational classification is the responsibility of school authorities.

Diagnosis of the educational needs of handicapped adolescents is a task that requires the combined professional skills of specialists, school psychologists, guidance counselors, medical and social experts, as well as teachers and administrators. Often the process of diagnosis must

[9] One outstanding program has been developed at Lansing, Michigan, where each of four junior high school buildings contains a special three-room unit that serves as a resource center in which both girls and boys—ages 13-16—learn practical arts, academic studies and skills, and attitudes and behaviors necessary for adjustment to community life. The senior high school program is designed to continue the training for community adjustment through activities that reach beyond the traditional confines of the school. It also provides work training for youth aged 16-21.

Other programs that have received national recognition are found in Cincinnati, Ohio, Jacksonville, Florida, New York City, Santa Barbara, California, Sidney, Nebraska, Mason City, Iowa, Hartford, Connecticut, Des Moines, Iowa, Knoxville, Tennessee, and Minneapolis, Minnesota. See Romaine P. Mackie, Donald H. Dabelstein, and Rick F. Heber (eds), *Preparation of Mentally Retarded Youth for Gainful Employment*, Washington, D.C. (U.S. Department of Health, Education and Welfare), 1959, pp. 59-64.

continue over a period of time until responses can be thoroughly documented by observation in school situations.

Continuation of Elementary School Training Patterns

The responsibility of the public schools for providing elementary school education for handicapped children is fairly well established. Many school systems, even some in rural areas, have established "adapted" programs of instruction and guidance, either as a part of the general pattern of instruction or in what are called "ungraded rooms," in their elementary schools. These are open to all children who have been diagnosed as educable or trainable, including the mentally retarded, perhaps one of the most difficult types of handicaps to deal with educationally. Most states admit handicapped children to classes at age six and nearly all permit them to continue until they reach the age of seventeen. Twenty-three states permit mentally retarded children to remain in special programs until they reach the age of twenty-one. Recently the trend has been to extend the age limits even beyond twenty-one years, and one state, Louisiana, has set thirty-five as the maximum age to which local districts can be reimbursed for special education services. State aid to such programs has been provided in all states since 1955.

The first responsibility of the secondary school in educating the handicapped is to continue the training patterns established for such pupils at the elementary school level. A further task is to provide the vocational and civic preparation needed to permit these pupils a fair chance to be assimilated into the world of work and to adjust to a competitive society.

The comprehensive secondary school affords the flexibility that is needed to provide for the handicapped. It offers various programs designed for pupils of different abilities and educational interests. Its resources, both human and material, are extensive. Centers for handicapped youth in such institutions can be included within both the philosophy of the school, which is to provide differentiated types and levels of instruction within one school, and the facilities of its plant.

Differentiated Training for Pupils Incapable of Carrying Regular Courses

The blind, the deaf, the emotionally disturbed, the physically defective, and the intellectually retarded, if their handicaps are extreme, may be unable to carry any of the regular courses in the high school. For them all training must be planned in the resource center, with the help often of itinerant teachers. The program for such pupils is frequently elementary, and highly practical, in comparison to the rest of the high school curriculum.

It is important that the severely handicapped student recognize the value of his schoolwork to him, that the skills and the content of his courses be within the range of his level of response at a given time, that the rate of progress be adjusted to his individual needs, and that he gain a sense of achievement. Handicapped pupils require more time than other pupils; they need more highly specialized teachers, greater understanding, stronger psychological reinforcement, more individualized instruction, specially designed space and equipment, and team efforts by various personnel. Such programs are expensive in comparison to the average cost of other high school offerings, but economical in terms of their conservation of human beings and the ultimate savings to communities and states.

Counseling

Awareness of the need for specialized counseling services for handicapped youth is developing. One evidence of the expansion of interest is found in various studies by counseling specialists. Patterson's book[10] on the emotionally disturbed, for example, deals with an area in which psychiatrists have long had a proprietary interest.

Various agencies and individuals share in the counseling service. In fact, competition is currently developing between some professional groups over who should take responsibility for counseling: specialists in handicapped education, school personnel officers, rehabilitation counselors, placement and employment officials, school psychologists, classroom teachers, psychiatrists, or social case workers. Heber has stressed the point that counseling of the retarded requires the professional contributions of various personnel:

> Counseling is accepted as an integral part of the total program of education and vocational preparation of retarded adolescents. Effective counseling and guidance can occur through both formal and informal contacts with students and thus all persons engaged in education and habilitation of the mentally retarded have some degree of counseling responsibility.[11]

[10] C. H. Patterson, *Counseling the Emotionally Disturbed,* New York (Harper), 1958.
[11] Mackie, Dabelstein, and Heber (eds.), *op. cit.,* p. 23.

Most professional people interested in counseling the handicapped accept Heber's point of view. They realize that a range of services must be provided and that the knowledge required for these services is highly complex and extensive. The debates over prerogatives seem to revolve around who is to help with the process, and to what extent.

Ultimately, it can be assumed, reason will dictate a close collaboration among all who supply counseling services. Particularly must this be true for those who provide either educational or medical treatment. In addition, vocational counseling must be strongly emphasized. Inasmuch as the ultimate goal of the school is to help handicapped pupils learn a job that they can perform successfully, job placement, employer-student counseling, and postplacement follow-up all become important aspects of counseling services.

Vocational Training

High school programs for normal students usually provide some prevocational orientation and training; for the handicapped, the major emphasis is on preparing individuals for work and on other aspects of adjustment to the community. Those secondary schools that have inaugurated programs for the handicapped are experimenting with work-training arrangements that relate school study to on-the-job apprenticeships.[12]

A particular responsibility of the high school, in these times of rapid technological development, is to identify the types of jobs that handicapped youth can perform that are likely to have the greatest permanence. Even so, as observers of industrial development have pointed out, there is a danger that automation may force unemployed skilled and semiskilled workers into competition for the jobs for which the handicapped have been trained. A study of the employment problems of the mentally retarded, sponsored by the U.S. Department of Health, Education and Welfare, led to the conclusion that:

> Both the immediate and long-term implications of technological and social change must be considered in planning the program. Neither of the extremes of optimism or pessimism concerning the occupational market for the mentally retarded is warranted. A realistic view that will permit flexibility in planning is required so that a close relationship will exist between the preparation of a student and the nature and range of occupational opportunities available to him.[13]

[12] Mackie, Dabelstein, and Heber (eds.) *ibid.,* pp. 43-82.

[13] Herbert Goldstein and Rick F. Heber, "Summary of the Conference," in Mackie, Dabelstein, and Heber (eds.), *ibid.,* pp. 35-36.

INSTRUCTIONAL PROVISIONS FOR THE HANDICAPPED

Patterns for the provision of instruction for handicapped youth at the secondary school level are not as yet very clearly established. Those discussed here may exist in only a few schools, or individual programs may include aspects of one or more provisions.

Adaptations Within Regular Classes

The most common and rudimentary step in providing for the handicapped is to attempt to work out adaptations of instruction for them within the regular classes of the school. Such a procedure is followed by practically every secondary school that enrolls pupils with disabilities and that does not have an established program for them. Small high schools, particularly, are forced to follow this method.

For students with minor intellectual deficiencies, or those whose handicaps are physical or social, it is often possible to adapt the work of regular classes. The pupil with poor vision or faulty hearing, the physically deformed, the person with low energy or chronic illness, the individual with speech deficiencies—all can make fairly normal progress in the regular school program given sympathetic and understanding teachers who are willing to adapt instruction, to give extra time when needed, to promote with other students a climate of acceptance, and to help the individual utilize his unimpaired sensory and motor capacities to compensate for those that are weak or disabled. Equally essential is the work of itinerant specialists who can provide therapy and technical training for pupils as well as professional advice and assistance to the teacher.[14]

Even pupils with acute impairments can often make satisfactory adjustments to regular classes with the help of itinerant teachers who provide special instruction as needed. The deaf usually require special help in speech reading (lip or touch reading), auditory training, speech training; they may need to learn more by reading and to communicate more through writing than do other pupils. The blind can often adjust to regular classes in high school, particularly if they have had proper training in the elementary school program. When full-time resource teachers are not available, they need from the itinerant specialists continued training in advanced Braille, lessons planned for

---

[14] See Flora M. Daly and Leo F. Cain, *Mentally Retarded Students in California Secondary Schools, Sacramento* (California State Department of Education), 1953, pp. 80-81.

them in Braille, or the services of a reader when such lessons cannot be prepared, and supplementary help in subjects that require laboratory work. Similarly, youth who are crippled or have severe health problems, with supplementary assistance from a specialist in handicapped education, can often be successful in regular classes.

Use of regular classes has decided limitations only for pupils whose handicaps are so severe that adjustment to normal academic work is impossible. Such arrangements can do little for the mentally retarded boy or girl whose intelligence level is insufficient to permit the mastery of normal high school work.

Ability Grouping

The practice of grouping students on the basis of intelligence or academic achievement is seen by some schools as a partial means of adapting programs to the handicapped. Actually, such procedures may only camouflage the problems presented by handicapped youth. A common error in ability grouping is to attempt to teach the same content to all groups, with the low-ability classes taking more time to cover the material while the brighter pupils are given enrichment content related to the subject. For example, world history may be taught to all groups, even though it is well beyond the intellectual grasp of borderline mentally retarded pupils in the low-ability groupings.

Teachers of low-ability groups face the educationally impossible task of trying to instruct retarded children in content that is, for them, too difficult, too abstract, too verbal, and too far removed from their level of interest and immediate needs. Also, the range of abilities, even in grouped retarded classes, may actually be wider than it is in some heterogeneous groups. For example, I.Q. scores for some low-ability groups, which include the mentally retarded who are barely educable along with pupils at the lower end of the scale of normality, may be from 50 to 90—a spread of 40 points. The instructional problems created by such a range among handicapped children are substantially more complex than they would be for an ungrouped class with I.Q. scores ranging from 90 to 130. This is particularly true because the intellectual disabilities in a class of retarded pupils are heterogeneous, rather than unitary. Six children with identical I.Q.'s of 75 are likely to present quite different profiles of specific intellectual responses and disabilities with which the teacher must deal.

Integrated Programs Designed for the Handicapped Within a Comprehensive High School

Authorities on the education of the handicapped generally agree that the best arrangement for providing for such youth at the secondary school level is to develop programs of instruction uniquely designed for them.[15] Such programs are integrated into the general comprehensive high school with the emphasis on student needs for interpersonal experience with normal peers, preparation for independent living, and competitive employment.[16] Typically, these programs require a resource center, which consists of a number of laboratory rooms, to serve as the school home for handicapped youth. In this center, specialists work as a team to provide training in the basic core of the curriculum—communication skills, practical academic studies, and accessory vocational skills. Depending on the nature of their mental and physical deficiencies, students take other courses outside their basic curriculum. Those with normal mental responses may take academic work. All may be able to progress in regular classes in such fields as art, music, physical education, and possibly typewriting, shop, and home economics, thereby gaining opportunities to associate with nonhandicapped students.

In the later years of the high school, emphasis is on vocational training. This later period may last until the student is 21 years of age, or older, or until vocational placement, whichever comes first. The student normally spends from half- to full-time on a job under the supervision of school personnel so that activities in the school resource center and on-the-job training can be closely correlated.

Separate Schools for the Handicapped

Until recent years, handicapped adolescent youth were provided for, if they continued in school at all, in separate schools or "institutions." Public institutions of this kind are residence agencies to which acutely retarded pupils are sent or committed. A number of private schools for the handicapped are also available throughout the nation. The recent shift of the burden of education for the handicapped to the local

[15] Dorothy F. Pasch, "Trends in Establishing Secondary Programs for Mentally Retarded Adolescents," *Bulletin of the National Association of Secondary School Principals,* January 1955.

[16] Herbert Goldstein and Rick F. Heber, "Summary of Conference," in *Preparation of Mentally Retarded Youth for Gainful Employment,* ed. by Mackie, Dabelstein, and Heber, Washington, D.C. (U.S. Department of Health, Education and Welfare), 1959, pp. 20-39.

public schools has tended to change the responsibility of the separate institution to that of dealing largely with the uneducable and the child who possesses such serious defects that he cannot be assimilated into a day-school program. Such institutions are also giving service to the multihandicapped child and to rural children who do not have available special services or programs adapted to their needs in local schools.[17]

The practice of sending pupils with particular types of impairments, e.g., blindness or deafness, to special institutions for periods of training and treatment prior to placement in public school has been common in the past. Since World War II, however, a trend has developed toward establishing more special classes for the blind and the deaf in local schools. There are now as many blind pupils in public schools throughout the nation as there are in state residential institutions. Where facilities do not exist in public schools to care for such pupils, close cooperation with residential institutions is essential to assure that youth may transfer to the day schools whenever institutional training programs have helped them establish sufficient skills, or make sufficient adjustment, to return to community life.

Hospital and Home Instruction

Another type of instruction for the handicapped, which usually must be provided for only relatively short periods of the student's educational career, is that made available in hospitals, or in the home, for those unable to attend school. This type of service is particularly vital for the pupil with chronic illness, or one whose disability keeps him in bed. Teachers commute to homes or hospitals to provide instruction until such time as the pupils are able to attend school. On the average, three to five hours of instruction is provided each child per week; the patient is taught how to study independently with help as needed from the teacher.

FACTORS PERTINENT TO THE SECONDARY SCHOOL'S PROGRAM FOR THE HANDICAPPED

The task of providing suitable education for the handicapped at the secondary school level is related to a number of factors that may accelerate or retard the programs now being developed.

[17] Leo F. Cain, "Special Education," *Encyclopedia of Educational Research,* Chester W. Harris (ed.), New York (Macmillan), 1960, pp. 1324-28.

State and Federal Assistance

The deep interest of citizens in the welfare of handicapped children and youth has led to state aid for local programs of education as well as to support from the federal level for research and teacher education. The continuation and expansion of both state and federal assistance will be vital to the development of programs for the handicapped in high schools.

Special programs for the handicapped are expensive. They require support beyond the pattern for normal educational offerings. Because they care for pupils with difficulties that are not well understood, research and experimentation are required to develop educationally sound procedures.

Qualified Teacher Personnel

The general shortage of teachers is reflected more acutely in the ranks of those qualified to teach handicapped high school students. At present, public schools, residential institutions, private schools, and hospital programs compete for the services of good teachers in this field. Training programs in colleges and universities are insufficient in number; those that exist are unable to recruit enough candidates to meet the demand.

In 1959, Congress appropriated funds to establish graduate fellowships to train specialists in the field of mental retardation. Those entering such programs will be prepared for leadership positions and for teacher education so that they can in turn train classroom teachers. Time will be required, however, to recruit and prepare specialists-teachers for classroom instruction. One promising development in teacher recruitment is the effort to persuade successful teachers of normal students to prepare through graduate study for work with the handicapped. To the extent that positions in this field offer rewards commensurate with the preparation and specialization required and the responsibilities assumed, such attempts may prove fruitful. It must be remembered, however, that they compete with strong demands for educational personnel in practically every phase of the secondary school program.

Availability of Related Professional Resources

Sound programs of education for the handicapped require assistance from various types of professional personnel, including doctors, occupational therapists, rehabilitation counselors, psychologists, social workers, and employment officers. Cooperation from such professional practitioners is not always available. Even when professional services are at hand, costs may be prohibitive for school budgets.

Size of School

Much has been said and written in recent years about the disadvantages of the small school for academically talented students. For most of the same reasons, small high schools are equally at a disadvantage when programs of education for the handicapped students are contemplated. When enrollments are small, the number of pupils requiring specialized treatment may be too small to make a special program economically feasible.

City and county school systems can counteract the burden of small enrollments in particular situations by establishing programs in centralized high schools to which pupils may commute. Small high schools in rural areas are not so fortunate.

Academic Standards

One factor that no doubt deters some secondary schools from developing programs of instruction for the handicapped is the traditional concept of academic standards. Debates over what the high school diploma should represent in terms of amount and quality of education reveal how deeply rooted is the belief that to be admitted and graduated from high school students should achieve minimum levels of intellectual development and content mastery. Academic ability should be demonstrated in certain required courses that are basic to the curriculum and essential for liberal or general education. Such views exclude from the secondary school students who are mentally handicapped and many whose social, emotional, and physical deficiencies have caused scholastic retardation.

Competing with the concept of rigid academic standards is a point of view that has developed as secondary school populations have become more heterogeneous, and that is popular with some proponents of the comprehensive high school. It holds that secondary education should represent a period of educational service to adolescent youth, with each pupil being given the kind of instruction that is most appropriate in terms of his individual abilities, achievement, interests, and vocational prospects. It holds further that the high school diploma should signify the completion of a period of educational effort, or of a program adapted to the individual; the subjects studied and quality of achievement should be shown by the student's transcript of credits.

A compromise practice that has been adopted in a considerable number of secondary schools is that of awarding differentiated diplomas to indicate the type of program of studies completed.

Table 18-3 shows the practice according to size of school in awarding more than one diploma or certificate of attendance. It will be noted that about 80 per cent of all high schools issue single diplomas to all

Table 18-3. *Number and Types of Diplomas*

ENROLLMENTS IN HIGH SCHOOLS	PERCENTAGE OF SCHOOLS, BY TYPES OF DIPLOMAS AWARDED		
	SINGLE DIPLOMA	DIPLOMA OR ATTENDANCE CERTIFICATE	DIFFERENTIATED DIPLOMAS
Fewer than 300	81.7	14.4	3.9
300–999	78.5	8.8	12.7
1,000 or more	73.2	14.5	12.3
ALL SCHOOLS, WEIGHTED	80.3	13.0	6.7

S O U R C E : Research Division, National Education Association, December 1959.

who complete planned programs of study. Certificates of attendance are awarded to pupils who fail to achieve the graduation requirements. Differentiated diplomas, awarded in only 6.7 per cent of the schools, reflect the types of programs of studies completed by students. Even the concession of awarding a differentiated diploma to indicate the differences in ability that prevail within a high school student body may not offer sufficient latitude to permit the inclusion of programs for the mentally handicapped in secondary schools in many communities.

The standards for graduation for retarded students in Lansing, Michigan, senior high school are:[18]

(a) School attendance for a three-year period
(b) A minimum of eight credits for the first two years of the high school program
(c) Approximate full-time employment for the third year, or four hours of additional high school credit
(d) School attendance for two hours per week during full-time employment or its equivalent

[18] Marvin Beekman, "Lansing, Michigan," Mackie, Dabelstein, and Heber, eds., *op cit.,* p. 61.

(e) Satisfactory achievement in the subjects in which the student is enrolled

(f) Completion of a successful work-training program

(g) Recommendation of the principal

PROBABILITIES

Concern for the training of the handicapped within the facilities of local secondary schools promises to grow. It may be obscured, and perhaps even frustrated for a time by the current wave of interest in strengthening academic standards and the designing of special programs for gifted students. The trend, however, toward the integrated type of service to handicapped youth, within the comprehensive high school, is likely to continue.

State and national policies are being developed to serve as guides to programs for the handicapped in secondary schools. Research related to the educability of such young people is providing knowledge on which reliable practices may be established in schools. Vigorous efforts are being made to establish strong programs of teacher preparation and to recruit able personnel to prepare for work with the handicapped.

Already city school systems are responding in various ways to public demands, and in some cases to legislative provisions, for appropriate training for the handicapped, including the mentally retarded, in secondary schools. The formal inclusion of work of this type in high schools usually starts in the area of speech correction. A second step frequently concerns physically handicapped pupils. Providing services for the chronically ill and emotionally disturbed may be the next step. School systems that have entered into any of these phases are on their way toward ultimately designing a unified, integrated program of study and training for all handicapped pupils. As they move in this direction, they will find strong support from community agencies that must also serve such youth and from parents as well as other citizens who devotedly believe that the democratic concept of "education for all" should include those in most need of instruction—the handicapped.

SELECTED REFERENCES

CAIN, LEO F. "Special Education." *Encyclopedia of Educational Research,* Chester W. Harris, ed., New York: Macmillan, 1960.

Parents' Night offers wide range of opportunities to extend relationships between the school and the home.

A new development in school and community relationships is the use of television to improve communications. Here a school board meeting is telecast so that all members of the community may understand better the problems of the schools.

CHAPTER 19

School-Community
Relationships

PUBLIC schools are the property of the total society, operated in most states through a decentralized organization to keep them close to the people they serve. Their strength and the material support they receive depend squarely upon the degree of public understanding of their specific problems, needs, and possibilities.

Although it may be aided by many outside sources, the local professional staff remains largely responsible for the task of maintaining an interested and informed public. Unfortunately, in some schools teachers and administrators either do not accept the responsibility to develop public understanding of their work or else they look down upon it as a "selling" operation comparable to publicity campaigns of modern advertising. Even in schools where the importance of good school-community relationships is recognized, those in positions of responsibility frequently have not acquired the knowledge and skills necessary for successful communication with the public. Despite such conditions, the public is predisposed to view education in a favorable light, and within each community numerous opportunities exist for the development of relationships between the community and the school. These relationships can be broadened and used for the mutual exchange of information and points of view. It is out of such a climate that educational progress is made.

PUBLIC EDUCATION REQUIRES AN INFORMED PUBLIC

Because of the nature of the control and organization of public schools, considerable latitude is given the local community in all states except Hawaii to determine the educational program and the extent of its support. Although the public has a general commitment to schools based on state and national conditions, its attitudes toward and opinions about education are largely formed from a knowledge of local schools—their program, pupils, and personnel. Thus, the responsibility for an informed public rests primarily upon the community relationships that schools develop and maintain.

Right and Responsibility of Community Participation

Central to the political theory, out of which was formulated the legal structure for the control of public education, is the tenet of the enlightened, participating citizen. According to this philosophy, the freedom and well-being of the individual, and in turn the total society, are best assured when each citizen retains as much of the power and responsibility for decisions as possible. Laws guaranteeing rights and fixing responsibilities for the operation of public schools have not only been written to ensure a broad educational opportunity but have, at the same time, respected these principles. Responsibility for decisions and actions has been placed as close to their point of execution as effectiveness and efficiency permit. Thus, a wide range of decisions relative to education is left to the local community.

Local control. Local controls upon education operate in diverse ways. The legal controls exercised through boards of elected citizens, and described in Chapter 3, represent only one avenue of local supervision. Certain educational decisions are made directly by citizens voting in elections; some are placed in the hands of other elected local officials or the courts. In addition, there are numerous social controls derived from the community. Sometimes these latter influences are subtle expressions of public expectations about programs or activities which the school is to provide or not provide. Often they are the expressions of groups or individuals whose opinions and desires are presented before meetings and hearings at which decisions are made by constituted authorities.

The board of education is, of course, the focal point of policy making. Questions of level of financial support such as approval of tax rate increases or building bonds are universally subject to direct voter approval. Also, questions relating to the provision of certain programs, i.e., whether to provide a junior college, special classes, or kindergartens, frequently require approval at the ballot box. Such questions must usually be put on the ballot by school-board action; and in all cases, the proposition voted upon is either one permitting the board to take action or one directing it to do so. In any event, the board of education, as the body representing the public, is not likely to approve policies contrary to strong public opinion even in cases where it could legally do so.

Assuring responsible action. It is generally true that a school cannot advance much beyond the limits of understanding of the citizens of its community. When changes are made without concern about informing the public, the danger of suspicion and reaction is introduced. Under these conditions minor dissatisfactions are easily magnified and turned into important issues. Attacks upon schools are often spawned in this type of a poorly informed public.

Although schools cannot, with certainty, protect themselves from irresponsible attacks, they can make every effort to avoid the difficulties which are likely to result when the public is not kept informed. Citizens have a right to information about decisions that they must either make or support. For educators to neglect to provide it is not only dangerous but an evasion of professional responsibility. The profession is obligated to use all appropriate and honest measures to aid the public in understanding the educational task and supporting it adequately. Responsible action, supported by public understanding, offers the greatest hope for educational advance.

Home-school partnership. In addition to the political conditions which require communication with the public, schools carry a heavy responsibility for the development of wholesome home-school relationships. Much of the time of every young person is shared by home and school since both are concurrently attempting to shape his life. A partnership naturally exists between these two agencies. Whether a suitable climate for growth and learning will be maintained depends upon the manner in which the partnership is shared.

Parents naturally seek to guarantee opportunities that will enable their children to make the most of their lives; they recognize education as the surest avenue to this end. Parental interest provides a strong basis for good home-school relationships, but this interest does not mean that parents will permit unquestioned direction by the school, nor does it assure that they will give the school unqualified support. Regardless of how effective educational services may be, parents' confidence and support rest largely upon an understanding that the school's interest in their children is in harmony with their own. The relationship between home and school, to be of value, must provide for a mutual exchange of information and must include means for the development of understanding and the resolution of differences. Within these relationships with parents, teachers can make their most valuable contribution to public understanding.

Role of Professional Personnel in Policy Making

The statement, often used, that the public decides educational policy and professional personnel excute it is an oversimplification of fact. From policy making to the application of policy in minute decisions, professionals have important responsibilities which must be exercised if wise planning and sound programs are to result.

Educational policies too vital to be delegated to professionals. The power of education for good, or ill, has been amply demonstrated. In Nazi Germany prior to World War II and since that time in many other parts of the world, systems of education have been used primarily as instruments of national policy. In some countries instruction is intended to indoctrinate rather than to develop independent, reflective thinking; the right to an education is largely reserved to those in favor with the party in power; and programs of preparation are limited to the needs of the state. Fortunately, in the United States the concepts of the individual's right of self-determination and the state's duty to provide educational opportunity for the fullest development of each individual undergird the political devices by which policy decisions are made. The locally elected school board operating within limitations set by state constitutions, legislative enactments, state board regulations—all of which are bolstered by judicial decisions—has generally served its function well.

The central purpose of public education is development of the minds, with concomitant shaping of the personality and character, of the young. Policy making for such a task is too important to be delegated to any one group of citizens. Even though the professional educator is specially trained to conduct the educational enterprise, he does not make the final decision about the ends that education is to serve. On the contrary, it is the professional who should be most concerned that all matters of public interest receive the widest hearing. The choice of educational policy must reside with all the people.

Provision for professional participation in policy formation. The members of the professional staff are prepared through training and experience for educational leadership. The public and members of boards of education recognize this fact and usually give considerable weight to their judgments. The superintendent is employed as the professional adviser to the board. Through him the board has access to the knowledge and professional opinions of teachers and other administrative officers, and as executive officer, he is responsible for bringing problems to the board's attention. He and other members of the staff collect information, report research results, and translate decisions into plans of operation.

A common practice of boards of education is to reserve certain meetings, sometimes as many as one-half of the total, for consideration of problems of instruction. In these meetings members of the professional staff are invited to discuss their work and to present proposals. Whether or not such a practice is followed, the professional staff, through the superintendent of schools, has access to the board of education and to other officials and legal bodies that influence educational policies and decisions. Once a course of action has been determined, judgments of teachers are generally acknowledged, and specific plans and proposals are usually prepared by that portion of the staff directly concerned with a given problem.

Flow of information between school and community. Enlightened public action requires that pertinent facts, relevant information, and promising solutions be known. Without such knowledge, informed public opinion is impossible. On the other hand, laymen are neither interested in nor inclined to learn large amounts of technical detail relating to any given problem. Therefore, the professionals' task is to determine what information is likely to result in the understanding necessary to sound judgment. To a large extent what is communicated will depend upon current local problems and long-range objectives.

Although specific mediums and techniques are suggested in later sections of this chapter, certain general requirements relating to the flow of communications between school and community may be stated at this point. First, the moral support for public education already present in the community can be maintained and strengthened by reports of genuine accomplishments in the schools. The predisposition of the public to react favorably to educational needs is a positive factor that must be nurtured. Next, information relating to specific problems and issues must reach those who are concerned with deciding an issue at the right time and in a form which will be helpful to *them*. Finally, a continuous flow of pertinent information will maintain a favorable attitude and help avoid the necessity of using large amounts of time and energy in correcting misunderstanding. The goal of professional personnel in its relationship with the public is to prepare them to make sound judgments of policy and to create confidence in the staff's ability to execute action without undue restriction or detailed direction.

Translation of community decisions into sound educational practices. Every decision requires the means and the leadership to bring it to realization. Decision making by the community, important as it is, remains only an expression of approval of a particular course of action. Numerous steps successively involving more of the local professional staff follow the original approval. From the provision of funds, time, staff, and materials to the evaluation of results, constant professional attention is required. Often original plans omit important considerations; funds or other provisions are inadequate; better ways to accomplish the original purpose are found. These and many other problems frequently occur in complex undertakings, and the professional must handle them with good judgment if proper execution of decisions is to result in sound educational practice.

School-Community Communications: Complex Two-Way Process

Communication is the process by which ideas, attitudes, and opinions, and information are transmitted or exchanged. It is such a natural phenomenon that even teachers, whose work depends so completely upon it, seldom give thought to its crucial significance. Every relationship between school and community, whether through personal or mass mediums, is a channel of communication. The total effect of the school upon its community and the community upon the school depends upon the number, the nature, and the use of these communication channels.

Mass mediums and the public: new opportunities. With the introduction of new instruments of mass communication—radio in the last generation, television in this one—considerable speculation was raised about their effects. On the one hand, some people claimed that these instruments would put an end to democratic processes, that they would "rubber-stamp" ideas upon the minds of the public and that freedom of individual choice would be destroyed. Others felt that a new and better form of "town-meeting" type of civic activity would result, that these mass mediums would overcome the problems of numbers and provide the means to inform the citizen upon every public issue. It is now clear that each of these reactions is extreme. Powerful as they are, all mass mediums—radio, television, books, newspapers, etc.—are communication tools. They have opened new avenues and thus made new opportunities, but like most tools, each has its usefulness and its limitations. At one end, the ideas communicated must stem from *people* actively engaged in worthwhile effort; at the other end, the ideas are received by *people* who have needs and concerns and who do ultimately decide for themselves.

A conception of the community in communication terms. Interestingly, both "community" and "communication" derive from the Latin *communitas,* meaning that which is common or shared. It is helpful to keep the derivation of these two words in mind, for each community is an aggregate of individuals who are linked together by networks of communications.

1. *Importance of people—the primary group.* Every individual in every community is a member of a number of relatively small groups. Whether based upon family ties, vocation, school, church, neighborhood, social or other interests, these groups are held together by face-to-face (interpersonal) relationships; they are referred to by sociologists as "primary groups." These relationships, which serve each member in many ways, are in reality networks for interpersonal communications. Their primary interest, for communication, is that they are the principal source of the individual's attitudes, opinions, values, and beliefs; that is, individuals use others within their primary groups to obtain and try out ideas and to form their opinions.

2. *Mass mediums and interpersonal relationships.* The reason why the alarming speculations about the effects of the mass mediums did not become reality is that the mass mediums did not replace the primary group as the best or final source of ideas and opinions. Individuals continue to refer to their primary groups to *interpret* the information carried by mass mediums. Individuals, in effect, use mass mediums information, but they form their own opinions largely within the context of their personal relationships.

3. *Diverse subgroups—special concerns.* The conception of the community as a large number of "atomized" individuals, each deciding issues and forming opinions pretty much in isolation from each other, or the idea that individuals accept mass mediums or interpersonal com-

munications and immediately act according to directions given to them is false. Rather, the community is an aggregate of individuals whose interests and concerns bring them together into numerous and varied subgroups. The total pattern of interpersonal relationships forms networks of communication that are linked to, and serviced by, the mass mediums. These networks of relationships are the principal source of public opinion.

4. *The out-of-touch and uninformed.* Sometimes the communication links between subgroups break down; then, a number of "publics" exist, each of which develops its own "public opinion" relative to an issue. Generally, the cause of breakdown of communications within a community can be explained by the way in which subgroups form around special interests. If there are not enough individuals maintaining relationships in several groups, intercommunications between groups are reduced and "common" points of view cannot be developed. When this condition exists, some groups will be out of touch and largely uninformed regarding many issues. Each will tend to form opinions and reach conclusions about community problems (including schools) within its own narrow context. Isolation reduces the opportunity to test out opinions; the group's conception of reality is likely to be out of focus, and its conclusions about a given issue may be faulty or unacceptable to others.

School-individual contacts. The importance of continuous individual contacts between school and community becomes more apparent when viewed in the light of the conception of the community given above. Understanding and support from the community largely depend upon such contacts. The school must consciously develop its communications networks in the community not only because of its own interest in youth but also out of a professional responsibility to the citizens of the community.

Apart from the dynamics of opinion formation and decision making that are natural concomitants of interpersonal communications, continuous individual relationships provide the school with a two-way communications process, a service too little taken into account by school personnel. Unlike the mass mediums, which function in only one direction, interpersonal relationships allow an exchange and a sharing between school personnel and citizens. Through individual contacts, school personnel can obtain "feedback" and thus keep in touch with the community. Information needed by the school, which only "feedback" can supply, relates to such questions as: How well are messages from the school received? Are any misunderstandings developing? Which segments of the community are not being reached? What information do citizens seem to need most?

CONSCIOUS CULTIVATION OF HEALTHY COMMUNITY RELATIONSHIPS: A SCHOOL RESPONSIBILITY

The school cannot separate itself from the community. It is welded into it by naturally existing relationships. As a part of the community and because of its function, the school bears a heavy responsibility for maintaining the broadest, most useful relationships with citizens that it is possible to produce. The school is in a favorable position to do this, but it must go about the task deliberately.

Leadership from School Board and Administrative Officials

The board of education, the superintendent, and other administrative officials provide the leadership for school-community relations. These officials occupy key communications positions. Officially their duties require that they maintain certain relationships with the community. They are charged with the responsibility for keeping records and other information of public concern. Perhaps most important, the members of the board of education, with the superintendent, are the policy makers, and this function requires close contacts with the community if wise policies are to result. Thus, the school leaders influence the development and use of school-community relationships both by their own conduct of school affairs and by the leadership they provide to the professional staff.

Provision for interaction between school and community. The superintendent and the administrative staff become the focus of most community forces that impinge upon the school. Whether they can use these forces, favorable and unfavorable, for constructive action, will determine to a large extent how much the schools can improve. In some school districts the administrative staffs have led the boards of education to recognize the importance of using every opportunity to improve relationships with every level of the community. Too often, however, the leadership by both boards and professional staffs has unduly limited interaction through the simple lack of provision for it.

Programs of information and interpretation. Perhaps the chief provision which the leadership of a school district can make toward healthy school-community relations is the development of deliberate programs to inform the public about its schools. Democratic processes are based upon the principle that those in authority are responsible to the people for their actions. Experience indicates that confidence and support for schools cannot be maintained at a high level for long periods without public understanding. When rapid changes in educational programs are made, as they must be made under present conditions, public understanding can be easily lost.

1. *New frames of reference.* Judgments relating to all areas of human activity are made in terms of past experience, current information, and the context of prevalent attitudes and opinions. These elements comprise what might be termed a frame of reference for the formation of opinion. The leadership of the schools, through the use of regular communications, can build constructive frames of reference for the consideration of school needs.

In efficiently administered schools, needs can be anticipated and the public can be prepared for change. Time is available to inform citizens of practices which were not a part of their own school experience. Favorable attitudes can be created by clearly indicating how decisions will be made and what problems are to be faced. Under these conditions, positive frames of reference are created, and public reaction is more likely to be based upon sound educational values and choices than upon faulty perceptions of problems and conditions or vague notions about "frills" and "high taxes."

2. *Guides to specific activities.* So many possibilities exist for bringing information and interpretation of school programs to public attention that specific activities hardly require listing. Such activities include public hearings by the board; speeches, interviews, and other presentations by the superintendent and staff; lay committee studies and reports of specific school programs; and planned programs and visits which bring citizens into the school. In one community known to the authors, each school board member periodically brings small groups of citizens to visit one of the schools. The board members personally conduct their groups, explaining features of the school program and showing those things of which the school is proud as well as those requiring improvement.

At their best, programs of information and interpretation are tailored to the needs of the particular community, but principles upon which successful programs have been built can be helpful guides to planning and appraisal. These principles are:

(a) Communications flow regularly to the public so that messages come to be anticipated
(b) Professional staff and laymen participate in communications activity
(c) The professional staff is briefed upon the details of all important plans and information being released
(d) Balance is maintained between reports of accomplishment and needs for improvement
(e) All possible mediums are used
(f) Important messages are repeated in a variety of ways
(g) Short-term and long-range needs are covered
(h) Key communications are checked to determine effect, blocks, and misunderstandings
(i) Rumor and criticism are analyzed; then countered with facts and objective accounts
(j) Periodic appraisal is made to ensure that effort and coverage are adequate

Consideration of community attitudes and points of view. Effort is wasted and the risk of misunderstanding is increased unless attention is given to community attitudes and points of view. Consideration does not imply that community attitudes determine educational programs or that the leadership of the schools rush to satisfy public sentiment or relax concern for vital educational matters when confronted with public lethargy. Public attitudes and points of view need be neither accepted nor rejected. They must, however, be ascertained with as much reliability and accuracy as possible, for they become the points of departure for the development of further understanding. They are the base line for the planning of communications.

Too often the determination of community attitudes is left to chance or informal means. School leaders through their interpersonal contacts frequently believe that they have an accurate "feel" for public opinion. Status leaders are subject to the frailties of all human beings, and most people hear those things which they wish to hear and listen to those who shout the loudest. The range and strength of feelings and opinions are difficult to determine and can rarely be estimated accurately from informal contacts alone. Objective instruments including structured interviewing and questionnaires can be used to sample attitudes and opinions. Numerous devices, such as lay councils, special study committees, and board hearings, are often effective in eliciting points of view. Scientific procedures can aid school districts to conduct studies or to improve the use of local groups to determine community interests and opinions.[1]

Use of specialists in communications. Most large school districts employ one or more staff members who have special training or experience, usually in journalism, to direct the public relations program. Although useful, these individuals have not been involved in the broader aspects of school-community relations described in this chapter. They are almost universally employed to prepare mass mediums communications; radio programs, news releases, school publications, and the like. Their interest and training are not in the human relations aspects of school relationships with the public, nor are they qualified to conduct polls or to survey types of studies. Administrators generally find that they must attempt to carry the broader public relations responsibilities themselves while occasionally calling upon outside consultant help. Awareness of this problem has led to the addition of some communications courses within graduate programs for the preparation of school administrators and may eventually cause the creation of programs that will broadly train educational specialists in communications.

Responsibility of Secondary School Staff

Secondary school teachers and administrators play an important part in school-community relations. Besides their normal activities which include pupil and parent relationships, they are called upon to use their talents and interests in the planned program of public relations. Through preparation of reports and studies and participation in meetings and on committees, they make a substantive contribution to community understanding.

Secondary school principal's task in school-community relations. Although not a part of the top-level policy-making group of the school district, the secondary school principal shares the leadership and communications functions of the superintendent. Through his efforts, the professional staff of the high school is mobilized for effective work with pupils and parents. Interpretations of plans and policies to be carried out in the school are made by him or under his supervision. In the other direction, he carries the reactions of parents and staff to the policy-making level of the school organization. His function as the

[1] The National School Public Relations Association, 1201 Sixteenth Street, N.W., Washington 6, D.C., has prepared useful materials to aid schools to conduct surveys and polls, and to organize public information services.

professional leader of a school and his responsibility to coordinate and interpret the program of the school within the context of the total effect of the school district place the principal in a vital communications position. All that has been said concerning the development of community relationships applies to him.

Secondary school teacher's task in school-community relations. As a group, secondary school teachers have the largest number of direct contacts with the community. Because of their immediate impact upon the home and their close relationship to parents, either directly or through their pupils, teachers are generally regarded by school public relations experts as the most fundamental link in the entire public relations process. Unlike the members of the administrative staff, for whom the development of good relationships with the community is part of their jobs, teachers' activities have inevitable public relations implications, whether they are aware of them or not.

1. *Direct relationships with citizens.* The administrative staff must rely primarily upon mass mediums messages, but teachers can interact on a personal basis with large numbers of citizens. It is in this activity that teachers, if properly prepared, can make a distinct contribution. However, there is evidence that insufficient attention is being given to this important area of community relationships. In a study conducted under the leadership of Michigan State University, citizens were asked to whom they actually referred questions about the schools. More than 80 per cent replied that they had recently asked teachers for information. However, less than 20 per cent indicated that they had been given satisfactory help.[2] If the results of this study are an indication of a general condition, a major avenue to public understanding is not being effectively used.

2. *Work through students.* One important way in which community support for public education is developed is through the personal relationships between teachers and students. Few teachers wish merely to transmit the content of their subjects. By nature and training they become psychologically involved in the healthy development of those they instruct. This personal interest is an asset at once to good teaching and to favorable home-school relations. Parents recognize dedicated teaching, and their appreciation is reflected in the widespread moral support they have given public education. When the teacher's

[2] Reported by William Roe, Professor of Education, Michigan State University, in a seminar on communications sponsored by the University Council for Educational Administration, Columbus, Ohio, May 1960.

personal interest in students is backed up by high-quality teaching, it becomes a powerful force for public support.

3. *Community activities.* A large number of teachers regularly engage in both personal and school-related activities in the community. They contribute to the total public relations program of a school district by directly assuming public relations tasks in speaking and writing or by engaging in other community activities on behalf of the school. In a recent survey, approximately 45 per cent of the teachers questioned reported that they had delivered more than one prepared public speech during that school year.[3] In addition, the personal activities reported by teachers indicated a wide membership in community organizations. Table 19-1 shows the percentages of teachers in the sur-

Table 19-1. *Percentages of Regular Participation of Secondary School Teachers in Community Activities*

ACTIVITY	MEN	WOMEN	TOTAL
General church activities	65.9	74.3	69.9
Teach in church school	13.3	15.8	14.5
Church clubs	21.7	31.8	26.5
Fraternal or lodge activities	30.6	23.9	27.4
Service clubs	19.4	31.8	25.3
Civic welfare organizations	20.0	28.5	24.1
Social or recreational clubs	36.2	41.5	38.7
Political clubs	6.6	4.9	5.8
Others	27.2	24.7	26.0

s o u r c e : National Education Association, *The Classroom Teacher and Public Relations,* research monograph 1959-M2, Washington, D.C., 1959.

vey who reported regular participation in community activities. Teachers have an opportunity to create good will and public understanding through all their community relationships. It is reasonable to assume, however, that the nature and extent of teacher effectiveness depend largely upon whether the school leadership makes teachers understand the importance of healthy relationships and the school's interest in them.

[3] National Education Association, *The Classroom Teacher and Public Relations,* research monograph 1959-M2, Washington, D.C. (the Association), 1959, p. 37.

Contributions of Students

Students, themselves, are a powerful influence upon community attitudes toward public education. Parents are particularly sensitive to their child's reactions to his school experience, and adults frequently form attitudes about local schools from observing the activities of school-age youth about the community. All too often citizens' opinions about the schools are formed from no other contact or information than chance observations and discussions with students.

Students: a direct, regular contact between home and school. Through its students, schools have an immediate, direct, and psychologically powerful influence upon a large percentage of the families of every community. Students carry a steady stream of information between home and school. From them, parents develop predispositions to receive messages about schools in either a favorable or an unfavorable light. Teachers and counselors, particularly, are conscious of the effect of students upon parent-school relationships. In many schools students are taught about the role of the school in the life of the community and are made aware of their part in the relationships between home and school. From time to time the actions and needs of the school are explained to students, and they are given the opportunity to discuss and react. Where this is done on a regular, planned basis, schools find that students are a positive influence in the interpretation of the school program to parents. Through this process schools are also giving students some understanding about public education which they should have as future citizens.

Students as representatives to the community. Students represent the school to the community in almost everything they do. Whether through school-sponsored performances, the outside-of-school conduct of individuals and groups, or the accomplishments of talented individuals, student behavior reflects upon the school. The tendency of many adults to attribute all student conduct, good or bad, to the effect of schooling is unfortunate. Schools must accept some of the blame for this attitude and recognize the possibility of its occurrence as an element of its public relations. Schools have focused public attention upon the activities side of school life, often to the extent of interrupting the instructional program in order to do so. In many communities, schools have succeeded in putting greater emphasis on scholastic accomplishment, and in educating the public to recognize and accept scholarship as a priority in the school. Such public relations activity by schools can create a more wholesome frame of reference for public appraisal of the work of schools.

Achievement: foundation of healthy community relations. No amount of publicity can cover up an ineffective school program. Sound accomplishment, amply demonstrated, is a necessity of healthy community relations. It is by all odds the best public relations a school can have for any purpose—whether it be maintaining good parental relationships or the good will of the total community. If pupils are experiencing success in school, if they find their work challenging and important, and if their relationships with teachers are satisfying, they will exert a wholesome influence for the school.

AGENCIES AND INSTRUMENTS

Schools maintain communication with the community through the use of a great many channels. In addition to the mass mediums, regular working relationships with organized groups and with individuals provide links to the networks of interpersonal relationships which comprise the community.

Organized Community Groups

The complexity of modern society has created the need for individuals to resort to group activity in order to make their interests known and to create sources of influence to achieve what they believe to be best for the locality, the state, and the nation. In communities of any size, numerous organized groups, with at least a secondary interest in school affairs, seek to influence school programs and policies. Some groups with a primary interest in public education are encouraged and aided by the schools.

Contacts with organized groups are important to the schools. Individual opinions, attitudes, and beliefs are formed primarily in group interaction; groups facilitate communication with the public and aid in promoting public action; group activity builds individual interest in and willingness to support good schools.

The relationship of the school to the groups it encourages differs from its relationship to other organized groups. With the former, the principal objective is better relationships between school and community. There is no preconceived plan or official blueprint of a school program to be promoted. With the latter, the purpose usually is to induce some particular plan or program. Often the interests of one group are in conflict with those of another. If relationships with organized groups are to achieve the school's purpose of wider understanding, caution must be exercised by the school in both the development and use of these relationships.

School-fostered groups. Parent-teacher associations, lay advisory councils, and special citizens' committees are the vehicles for the organized participation of citizens in public education. Each has a particular function, but all provide avenues for communication and opinion formation and for the development of unified action. Despite their limitations and the reservations many professionals express concerning their activities, they have accumulated an impressive record of constructive support for public education.

1. *Parent-teacher associations.* Various local groups have sprung up with the aim of working for cooperative interaction between laymen and professionals. Interestingly, these groups have been organized primarily by laymen. Most of these local associations have become affiliated with the National Congress of Parents and Teachers which, in turn, has sponsored the further spread of local associations. Nationally the PTA has developed surprising strength (over seven million citizens currently hold membership) and its national office provides local and state units with high-quality leadership. The effectiveness of local units varies, but the PTA has demonstrated its ability to lead people in the support of sound educational improvement. At the local level, schools can well afford to encourage the PTA, for it promotes a policy of constructive participation without attempting to dominate the school leadership or dictate the school program.

2. *Lay advisory councils and special citizens' committees.* After World War II, superintendents and boards of education, plagued by mounting problems and insufficient public action, began to organize citizens' councils and committees.[4] These groups study problems, inform local citizens about school needs, and stimulate necessary action. Although both lay councils and special committees have rendered important services, experience reveals negative as well as positive results. When appropriately organized, served by able leadership, and limited to clearly defined purposes, citizens' councils and committees have generally been successful. But citizens' councils and committees are semi-official bodies. They function as extensions of the board of education, and, in one sense, are an acknowledgment that the board cannot do all

---

[4] The National Citizens' Council for Better Schools, 9 East 40 Street, New York 16, N.Y., provides many kinds of aid to interested individuals and groups.

it was elected to do. In some cases, both the boards of education and the citizens' groups have lost sight of their advisory relationship. The citizens' groups have attempted to make official decisions or have pressured boards into unwarranted action. Some boards, in turn, have used citizens' groups as "whipping boys," letting it appear that the groups have made decisions which later proved to be unpopular. Other instances have occurred in which these groups have become embroiled in intemperate debate or have been dominated by individuals interested only in airing criticism or fostering some specific measure. Because of these dangers the special committee is generally preferred to the more permanent council. However, both types have demonstrated success when, under proper conditions, they collect facts, study conditions, and prepare recommendations for the board of education.

Service, civic, and special-interest groups. Business, agriculture, labor, and veterans' organizations as well as civic, service, and fraternal clubs, have strong interests in public education. Although their primary purposes are varied, many of them have public education as a secondary concern. These groups are organized on a national basis, and they have generally formulated national policies relating to education which are promoted through local chapters. Standing committees or education representatives within the local chapters work together on education. Generally, these associations are active in three areas. First, they attempt to crystallize opinion and promote certain educational policies at the local, state, and national levels. Second, they may seek to influence the instructional programs of schools in terms of their own particular interests. This activity ranges from the use of committees to study textbooks, curriculum content, and instructional methods to the preparation of pamphlets, films, books, and other materials which are given to schools for use in instruction. Third, they directly promote student activities such as essay, debate, or similar contests, career days, and scholarships.

At times special-interest groups have worked effectively with the schools to promote needed improvements; at other times they have advocated programs or courses of action in conflict with those of the leadership of the schools. These groups will continue to exist, and they will likely increase in influence. Since they are the means by which many citizens form opinions and attitudes about public education, the schools can help these groups to obtain facts and understand problems of education. Generally, they welcome speakers, panels, and other types of programs; the schools can therefore speak directly to the membership of these groups. In addition, some members are usually available to serve on councils and committees. In many communities the schools have not taken full advantage of the possibilities offered by the development of appropriate relationships with special-interest groups.

Instruments of Communication

The previous section has dealt with the use of individuals and groups in the communications process between school and community. In addition to direct contacts, a number of other instruments of communication are available to schools. The mass mediums—visual, written, and spoken; both commercial and school-prepared—have a place in the program of public relations.

Commercial newspapers, radio, and television. Commercial communications channels in most communities reach the largest number of adults. A family, rural or urban, that did not have a radio or television set or receive a newspaper, would be an oddity indeed. These mediums can reach adults who do not attend school functions, receive school publications, or discuss school issues with others. School activities and accomplishments make attractive news stories and programs which editors and station managers realize have wide appeal. School news and features devoted to youth have an impact that goes well beyond parents of school-age children.

Obtaining the fullest use of commercial mediums of communications requires some effort and understanding on the part of professional personnel. Good working arrangements and relationships with those in charge of programming and news coverage are just as important as relationships with individuals and organized groups. Generally the school leadership—the superintendent and principals or their representatives—takes the initiative in establishing policies and guides for the preparation and clearance of materials to commercial channels. However, educators often do not realize that editors and station managers have problems and decisions to make about time or space allotments, coverage, and the like. Also, they may not understand that the staffs of newspapers, radio, and television have traditions and ethics which they regard as highly as educators do their own standards. This understanding is helpful when stories or programs critical of education appear or when carefully prepared materials are not used.

Radio, television, and newspapers require selection and preparation of material appropriate to each medium, a job which demands special training. Many excellent publications are available to guide educators in this work.[5] People in the commercial communications field can provide specific help and are usually happy to do so when they are approached in a cooperative spirit. These experts can frequently advise school personnel on how to build an integrated communications program and can give suggestions for improving its effectiveness.

School Publications

School publications serve many functions. The superintendent and the administrative staff often rely upon them to carry routine information and to announce new procedures, facts, and policies to parents, students, and staff. They may be used to build *esprit de corps* or to provide a historical record of accomplishments and activities. They may also be used to build interest in a particular part of the educational program or to increase general good will and support for the total effort of public education. Although most school publications are used primarily within the school system, some of them can be valuable adjuncts to the total program of communication between the school and community.

Values for community relations. Few school publications are prepared to serve the need for communication between school and community. Student newspapers, yearbooks, and handbooks are examples of publications used principally to service the school and its organization and are of only secondary use in community relations. Bulletins, brochures, newsletters, budgets, annual reports, and other mediums are the usual means of reaching large numbers of citizens. Experience has demonstrated that these school-published materials have special uses but are not suitable substitutes for interpersonal or mass-mediums communications.

The principal value of school publications is to supplement and reinforce other mediums. Brochures, for example, provide excellent follow-up to public meetings and mass-mediums messages reporting upon

[5] William Roe (ed.), *Schools Are News: A Manual for Educators and Editors,* East Lansing: (College of Education, Michigan State University), undated; and National School Public Relations Association, *Let's Go to Press,* Washington, D.C., 1954. For help with radio and television work see: Giraud Chester and Garnet Garrison, *Television and Radio,* New York (Appleton-Century-Crofts), 1956; and Walter Kingson, Rome Cowgill, and Ralph Levy, *Broadcasting Television and Radio,* Englewood Cliffs, N.J. (Prentice-Hall), 1955.

school needs. In the development of public opinion favorable to school building needs, for instance, a brochure can provide facts, describe possible courses of action, and indicate what public support is necessary. Newsletters and other brief printed messages can carry announcements, explain established policies, or outline action taken by the administration or the board of education.

Place in the total communications program. From the description of the community given earlier in this chapter, the part which school publications can play in community relations can be made clearer. School-published materials can service the networks of interpersonal relationships out of which opinions are formed. These materials, when well prepared, can give information about facts, plans, decisions, and contemplated actions, which will be the substance of discussion and reflection as people make up their minds about school matters. Publications coming from the school can be tailored to fit a specific communications situation, and they can be timed to be available when needed.

Importance of planning. Few schools can afford either the staff time or the funds necessary to publish large amounts of materials of many different kinds. A general publication plan is useful to avoid wasted effort. The decision to publish any material can then be based upon a serious appraisal of total communication needs. Out of a general plan specific needs can be determined. Some factors, including the "target" audience, type of publication, content, and distribution, require careful study. In this stage of planning the personnel directly involved in the preparation of materials can be helpful. In large school systems one staff member is often designated as coordinator of publications; in smaller systems a teacher or administrator usually assumes this responsibility. This person supervises the production and distribution of the material to be published, often writing and editing much of the content.

SCHOOL-COMMUNITY RELATIONS: CHALLENGE TO EDUCATION

Democracy can work only to the extent that individuals and groups have access to facts and can freely exchange ideas and opinions. In the operation of the public schools, democratic action should be at its best. How to bring this about so that schools may develop and improve to provide youth with the finest education possible is one of the most challenging problems faced by educators.

Shortcomings of Present Practices

Communication with the public through school-community relationships is central to any effort to improve public understanding of the work of schools. Educators recognize it as one of their most important problems and frankly admit that they have neglected to give it the attention it deserves. The authors have studied the reports of a number of conferences and seminars held during the past five years to consider problems of communication and school-community relations.[6] The following three areas appear to reflect serious weaknesses: First, school leaders do not recognize or understand fully the communications functions of their positions. There is a general inadequacy in communications between professional staffs and boards of education. Failure at this point weakens policy making and the ability of the staff to communicate with the public. Second, there is a general failure of administrators and teachers to understand the part played by individuals and groups outside the school in the communications process. Third, schools fail to use a major part of their potential in the development of school-community relationships. The principal shortcomings of the school appear to be not using teacher talents and not making serious efforts to confer with parents, not meeting with individuals and groups of the community and not using individuals and groups from the community in school programs.

These statements should be regarded as observations, not as conclusions or the results of research. Some school systems may be doing an excellent job in each of these areas. On the other hand, most professional personnel concerned with the problem of developing healthy community relations could profit from a serious appraisal of their present efforts in each of these areas.

Cautions

Public education has been subjected to intense scrutiny and criticism. This process is certain to increase rather than to diminish because the causes of public concern are likely to intensify. Social and

[6] Among the reports and records studied were the report of the 1956 White House Conference on Education; National Education Association centennial seminar, "New Directions in Research in Human Communication," held at the Massachusetts Institute of Technology, May 1957; statement of the Problems and Policies Committee of the American Council on Education, "Public Understanding and Support for Education," February 1958; and the University Council for Educational Administration, seminar on communications, Ohio State University, May 1960.

economic changes will continue to produce new problems, conflicts, and needs at an ever-accelerating rate. Under these conditions interest in education will increase at the same time that the problems of creating public understanding become more difficult.

One example of social change which has affected education and which involves problems of public understanding may serve to illustrate the difficulties faced by schools. Foreign languages have traditionally been taught in the secondary schools. The major emphasis has been upon giving students a reading knowledge of the language in order that they may come to appreciate the literature and the culture of a particular people. Few, if any, students were expected to use the language for communications purposes. Since World War II, this situation has changed. Students now study foreign languages to communicate, even to live, with people in other parts of the world. To meet this need, the speaking as well as the reading of foreign languages must be taught. Greater amounts of time are required for this instruction, and most students, not just the college-bound, should have it. Further, schools that have studied the problem believe that teaching the conversational aspects of languages can best be started in the elementary grades. Quite suddenly many more students wished to study foreign languages and for a different purpose than the traditional program had been designed to serve. Many citizens began to protest that foreign language instruction in public schools was inadequate, as indeed it had become. However, without proper understanding of the reason for this condition and the means to correct it, the public, too frequently, was led to believe that this part of the school program had been poorly designed and taught from the start. Certain critics immediately voiced the complaint that the youth of the country had been shortchanged, that other parts of the school program must be faulty also, and that the public schools must have been mismanaged and misled.

In communities in which the schools are out of touch with the people, irresponsible criticism is difficult to stop. There is a danger that schools will become stampeded into changes for which they are unprepared. Changing the foreign language program involves many problems and cannot be done quickly. If languages are to be introduced in the elementary schools, at which grade will they be started? Which language or languages will be taught? What materials will be used? Where will the teachers be obtained? What part of the present program should be curtailed? How will the high school program be adjusted as students who have received foreign language instruction in the elementary school reach the high school? Which students are to receive foreign language instruction? How will transfer students be placed? These and other problems must be faced in a major program change.

Even though a plan is approved, changes must be introduced gradually. Students beginning a foreign language in grade six, for example, will not reach the high school for several years. This necessarily slow but orderly change breeds impatience in the public when understanding has been lost. The only protection for schools seems to be in sound program improvement and constant attention to public information needs.

The condition illustrated by the foreign language problem described above is now being repeated in several other areas of instruction. In mathematics, the sciences, and social studies comparable problems exist and are likely to increase in the years ahead. Periods of rapid change create a dilemma for the schools. They are forced to make fundamental changes in programs in a climate which makes difficult the development of community understanding and support. Population mobility and divided interests tend to break down communications within the community; a backlog of public projects vies with schools for tax money; and other groups using skillful advertising compete with schools for public attention.

Opportunities in Change and Conflict

The conditions which have forced changes and engendered public conflicts have also created opportunities. Public interest in education is greater perhaps than at any period in the nation's history. Conflict and criticism over the issues do not imply a lack of faith in education. They do imply a need for broader understanding and more effective communications. Leaders in education can use the public's concern to achieve wider understanding and support for public education. The knowledge, techniques, and the mediums of communication are available to accomplish this task.

SELECTED REFERENCES

ANDERSON, NELS. *The Urban Community*. New York: Henry Holt, 1959.
BULLOCK, ROBERT P. *School-Community Attitude Analysis for Education Administrators*. Columbus: Ohio State University, 1959.

CIERNICK, SYLVIA, guest editor. "Public Relations for the American High School." *Bulletin of the National Association of Secondary School Principals,* September 1960.

GRIMES, ALAN P., AND ROBERT H. HORWITZ. *Modern Political Ideologies.* New York: Oxford University Press, 1959.

JONES, J. J., AND I. W. STOUT. *School Public Relations: Issues and Cases.* New York: Putnam, 1960.

KATZ, ELIHU, AND PAUL F. LAZARSFELD. *Personal Influence: the Part Played by People in the Flow of Mass Communications.* Glencoe, Illinois: The Free Press, 1955.

KNOWER, FRANKLIN H., AND PAUL H. WANER. *Communication in Educational Administration.* Columbus: Center for Educational Administration, Ohio State Univ., 1959.

McCLOSKEY, GORDON. *Education and Public Understanding.* New York: Harper, 1959.

MUELLER, HUBERT J. *Issues of Freedom: Paradoxes and Promises.* New York: Harper, 1960.

National School Public Relations Association. *Pebbles: Successful Public Relations Ideas That Start with the Teacher,* Washington, D.C.: the Association, 1960.

PIERCE, TRUMAN M., EDWARD C. MERRILL, JR., L. CRAIG WILSON, AND RALPH R. KIMBROUGH. *Community Leadership for Public Education.* Englewood Cliffs, N.J.: Prentice-Hall, 1955.

POOL, ITHIEL DESOLA. "Public Opinion and Elections." *Journal of the National Education Association,* September 1957.

STEINBERG, CHARLES S. *Public Relations, Public Opinion and Mass Media.* New York: Harper, 1958.

Dormitory life in non-public schools offers sharp contrast to day-school pattern of public secondary schools.

Nonpublic secondary boarding school provides controlled environment, academic traditions, and selected student body.

Nonpublic Secondary Schools

IT IS characteristic of secondary education in the United States that roles, functions, and balances are only temporary. Continuous change results from the multitudes of decisions made by a people who are free to choose the kinds of schools they want for their children. Nowhere is this characteristic more evident than in the roles and functions assumed by nonpublic schools.

In the United States the public character of private education always has been implicitly and explicitly recognized. The first secondary schools in colonial America were private, or nonpublic, by modern definition. Even though publicly controlled, tax-supported secondary schools have become the dominant means of educating adolescent youth, nonpublic schools have continued to play important, and strongly supported roles as optional and specialized institutions. They have increased, both in number and size of enrollments, and flourished on a pattern similar to that of the public schools. They have responded to most of the same forces that have shaped public education, adapting their goals and programs to the demands of the times and of their clientele. Such responses have produced striking differences among nonpublic schools within the same denomination, as well as among the various denominations, and between church-affiliated and independent secondary schools.

SCOPE AND GROWTH OF NONPUBLIC SECONDARY SCHOOLS

Expansions in scope and continued growth, combined with devoted loyalty of alumni and supporting groups, have given nonpublic schools a competitive relationship with public institutions out of proportion, actually, to their numerical strength. The influence of such schools is sufficient to command attention in local communities, state programs for educational support, and in efforts at the national level to strengthen public schools.

Definition of Nonpublic Secondary Schools

The term "nonpublic" as applied to a secondary school is relatively new.[1] Older terms used to designate institutions that are not supported directly by tax funds are private, parochial, sectarian, church, denominational, and independent. No agreement prevails among the various types of institutions involved as to the best common designation.

The nonpublic school is defined by Carter Good as "a private or parochial school not open to the general public for admission or not supported by public taxation."[2] The usefulness of the title "nonpublic," is that it includes both private and parochial institutions. The objection to it is that both these types of schools, like the "public schools" of England, actually serve public purposes. Some people prefer the term "independent" to suggest the nonpublic school's independence from both governmental financial support and from public controls. The term "parochial" can rarely be applied as accurately to a secondary school as it is to elementary schools because it suggests a close parish identification. High schools with religious affiliations usually have a broader base, such as a diocese or an association of congregations. Catholic high schools, for example, are usually operated by religious orders, i.e., diocese or archdiocese, rather than by individual parishes; Lutheran secondary schools are under the control of "high school associations"; while other parochial schools usually are managed by church boards or trustees, chosen in various ways.

[1] In spite of the growing popularity of the term "nonpublic," Porter Sargent's *Handbook* which presents up-to-date information on such institutions is published under the title, *The Handbook of Private Schools: An Annual Descriptive Survey of Independent Education.*

[2] Carter V. Good, *Dictionary of Education*, rev. ed., New York (McGraw-Hill), 1959.

The United States Office of Education has described the two categories of schools as follows:

> A "public" school is the creature of the State and is subject not only to the State's regulatory controls but is under the immediate operational control of a governmental agency or agent. A "public" school is supported and maintained at public expense.
>
> A "nonpublic" school, while subject to pertinent regulatory controls of the state, is under the immediate operational control of a private individual or organization. A "nonpublic" school exists apart from the public school system of the State. It may be operated as a church-related or nonsectarian institution. It may be operated on a profit or nonprofit basis. A "nonpublic" school is generally supported by private funds as distinguished from public funds raised by taxation.[3]

Nonpublic schools include both day and resident institutions, parochial, and nonchurch-related schools, and schools providing specialized programs. Some secondary schools are closely related to elementary school programs, often including kindergarten through twelfth grade; others, though basically secondary in structure, enroll pupils in the upper elementary school grades. Their quality ranges from fully accredited, highly regarded schools[4] to institutions that are hardly worthy of the name high school.

Number of Nonpublic Schools

In 1955-56, there were 3,887 nonpublic high schools in all states, including Alaska and Hawaii.[5] More recent data, for 1959-60, assembled from state departments of public instruction, the national

[3] Fred F. Beach and Robert F. Will, *The State and Nonpublic Schools,* Washington, D.C.: U.S. Department of Health, Education and Welfare, Office of Education, 1958, p. 1.

[4] Accrediting associations and other associations whose membership lists include the better nonpublic schools include California Association of Independent Schools; Cum Laude Society; Friends Council on Education; Guild of Independent Schools of New York, Inc.; Independent Schools Association of Northern New England; Middle States Association of Colleges and Secondary Schools; North Central Association of Colleges and Secondary Schools; National Council of Independent Schools; New England Association of Colleges and Secondary Schools; National Association of Principals of Schools for Girls; Private Schools Association of Central States; Secondary Education Board; Southern Association of Independent Schools.

[5] *World Almanac,* 1960, p. 496.

headquarters of various church groups, and standard references[6] are presented in Table 20-1. Not all state departments maintain records on nonpublic schools; of those that do, some list only accredited institutions. References are incomplete and disagree about the number of schools. Different definitions of secondary schools, the absence of a national record-keeping agency for independent institutions, as well as the variety of types of nonpublic educational organizations, all make identification of such high schools difficult.

Currently the United States Office of Education is undertaking a comprehensive survey to obtain up-to-date and detailed information on nonpublic schools. This agency, in the absence of established information, estimates that in 1960-61 there may have been as many as 5,000 nonpublic secondary schools in the United States, with a total enrollment as high as 1,050,000 pupils. The difference between these figures and those in Table 20-1 may be due to the exclusion from the latter tabulation of certain schools that include some secondary school grades (such as those with grades 1 through 8 or 4 through 8), and the omission from some state lists of nonaccredited high schools. The tabulations for parochial institutions, inasmuch as they were supplied by sponsoring religious bodies, are believed to be accurate; those for independent schools may be less dependable for those states that do not keep detailed records. In such instances, the number of schools had to be derived from various listings which did not always agree. Nevertheless, the distribution of parochial and independent schools by states shown in Table 20-1 is thought to provide a reasonably dependable overview of the number and types of schools operating in each state. Institutions not accounted for, if there are any, are believed to be small, and perhaps unconventional; some no doubt should not even be classified as secondary schools.

The numbers of "leading" nonpublic schools, as classified by Sargent according to states and regions in 1958,[7] and the distribution of schools that are accredited or that hold membership in a reputable regional association are shown in Table 20-2. By both classifications,

[6] A. Lyon Mansfield (ed.), *Private Independent Schools,* Wallingford, Conn. (James E. Bunting, Publisher), 1960; National Catholic Welfare Conference, *Summary of Catholic Education,* 1959, Washington, D.C. (the Conference), 1960, pp. 23-29; *National Catholic Almanac,* 1960; Porter Sargent, *The Handbook of Private Schools, 1958,* Boston (Porter Sargent), 1958.

[7] Porter Sargent, *op. cit.* These "leading" nonpublic schools were selected from a total listing of 1,848 institutions, 1,583 of which were independent and 265 parochial.

Table 20-1. *Number of U.S. Parochial and Independent Secondary Schools, by States*

STATES	PAROCHIAL	INDEPENDENT	TOTAL
Alabama	70	15	85
Alaska	11	—	11
Arizona	11	11	22
Arkansas	14	3	17
California	165	99	264
Colorado	25	10	35
Connecticut	53	64	117
Delaware	12	5	17
Washington, D.C.	19	19	38
Florida	37	43	80
Georgia	11	16	27
Hawaii	39	8	47
Idaho	6	—	6
Illinois	152	36	188
Indiana	36	10	46
Iowa	108	11	119
Kansas	41	—	41
Kentucky	76	9	85
Louisiana	93	33	126
Maine	25	37	62
Maryland	50	45	95
Massachusetts	142	102	244
Michigan	176	63	239
Minnesota	88	7	95
Mississippi	43	4	47
Missouri	79	16	95
Montana	19	2	21
Nebraska	262	2	264
Nevada	2	—	2
New Hampshire	23	19	42
New Jersey	103	26	129
New Mexico	25	5	30
New York	270	128	398
North Carolina	31	24	55
North Dakota	20	1	21
Ohio	141	18	159
Oklahoma	28	6	34
Oregon	36	3	39
Pennsylvania	209	90	299
Rhode Island	26	9	35
South Carolina	12	8	20
South Dakota	21	4	25
Tennessee	23	17	40
Texas	81	41	122
Utah	9	—	9
Vermont	13	12	25
Virginia	45	11	56
Washington	31	3	34
West Virginia	21	33	54
Wisconsin	67	8	75
Wyoming	5	—	5
TOTALS	3,105	1,136	4,241

Table 20-2. *Distribution of 934 "Leading" and Accredited Nonpublic Schools, by States and Regions*

REGION AND STATES	NUMBER OF LEADING SCHOOLS [a]	NUMBER OF ACCREDITED SCHOOLS [b]
New England:		
Maine	15	20
New Hampshire	17	15
Vermont	6	6
Massachusetts	100	87
Rhode Island	14	13
Connecticut	57	57
New York	159	118
New Jersey	55	51
REGIONAL TOTAL	423	367
Middle States:		
Pennsylvania	70	80
Delaware	6	8
Maryland	36	31
Washington, D.C.	16	16
REGIONAL TOTAL	128	135
South Atlantic:		
Virginia	33	27
West Virginia	5	2
North Carolina	13	8
South Carolina	6	4
Georgia	7	8
Florida	27	24
REGIONAL TOTAL	91	73
South Central:		
Kentucky	8	11
Tennessee	19	31
Alabama	6	5
Mississippi	4	4
Louisiana	6	19
Texas	14	19
REGIONAL TOTAL	57	89
East North Central:		
Ohio	24	16
Indiana	5	4
Michigan	10	8
Illinois	33	26
Wisconsin	8	7
REGIONAL TOTAL	80	61
West North Central:		
Minnesota	12	9
Iowa	4	2

Table 20–2. *(continued)*

REGION AND STATES	NUMBER OF LEADING SCHOOLS a	NUMBER OF ACCREDITED SCHOOLS b
Missouri	17	6
Arkansas	2	—
North Dakota	2	—
South Dakota	3	3
Nebraska	2	1
Kansas	4	1
Oklahoma	2	2
REGIONAL TOTAL	48	24
Mountain:		
Colorado	7	7
Idaho	1	—
Utah	3	1
Arizona	10	6
Nevada	—	—
New Mexico	2	1
Wyoming	—	—
REGIONAL TOTAL	23	15
Pacific:		
Alaska	—	—
Washington	6	5
Oregon	3	2
California	70	48
Hawaii	5	4
REGIONAL TOTAL	84	59
TOTALS: "Leading" schools	934	—
Accredited schools	—	823

a As classified by Porter Sargent, *The Handbook of Private Schools,* Boston (Porter Sargent), 1958, pp. 3-576.
b Institutions listed by Sargent as holding membership in an Accrediting or Regional Association with standards for membership.

which are based on qualitative considerations, 60 per cent of the institutions are in Washington, D.C., and in eleven New England and Middle Atlantic states.

Location of Nonpublic Schools

One distinguishing characteristic of nonpublic secondary schools, reflected in Table 20-2, is their geographical concentration. Whereas public high schools serve city, hamlet, and rural countryside, nonpublic institutions are more common in some parts of the nation than in others. Various factors help to explain this uneven distribution. They include the historical pattern of educational development; economic, cultural, and family traditions; dominance of particular schools; climate; and the religious, national, and social composition of the particular community.

Nonpublic secondary schools were established first in the original thirteen states. They were subsequently founded in some of the newer states in the Midwest as intellectual and religious groups moved across the Appalachian Mountains, taking with them their dedication to education and to the types of schools they had known. Until the latter part of the nineteenth century, nonpublic schools, although relatively few in number, predominated in the South where "free schools" were maintained only for children of indigent families. By the time the states west of the Mississippi were developed, the public school movement had so captured the imagination and enthusiasm of the people that state school systems advanced with great momentum. The nonpublic schools, except the parochial, did not seem to be needed in the West, partly because of the strength of the new public high schools, and partly because parents who could afford to send their sons and daughters to boarding institutions preferred the better known Eastern preparatory schools. The first nonpublic, nonparochial school west of the Rocky Mountains, in fact, was the Punahou School in Honolulu, Hawaii, established by missionaries from New England states to provide for their children the type of college preparation they had known in the East.

Another index of the geographical concentration of nonpublic schools is the proportion of secondary school enrollments served in the various states. Figure 20-1 shows the percentages of high school students enrolled in nonpublic schools in each state for 1953-54 and 1959-60. Hawaii, the newest state, was highest with 40.3 per cent. Tennessee, North Carolina, and Wyoming, each with 1 per cent, were low. The over-all national average dropped slightly from 11.88 to 11.27 during this six-year period. By states, however, percentages enrolled in nonpublic schools ranged from an increase from 14 per cent to 30 per cent in Ohio to a decrease from 46 per cent to 30 per cent in Rhode Island.

The general decrease in percentages enrolled in nonpublic schools suggests that expanding secondary school populations are being cared for more by public institutions. It will be noted that only three states west of the Mississippi: Minnesota, Missouri, and Louisiana, exceeded the national average in 1959-60. East of the Mississippi, the traditional Southern and borderline states, except Delaware and Indiana, show percentages below the national average. The highest concentration of

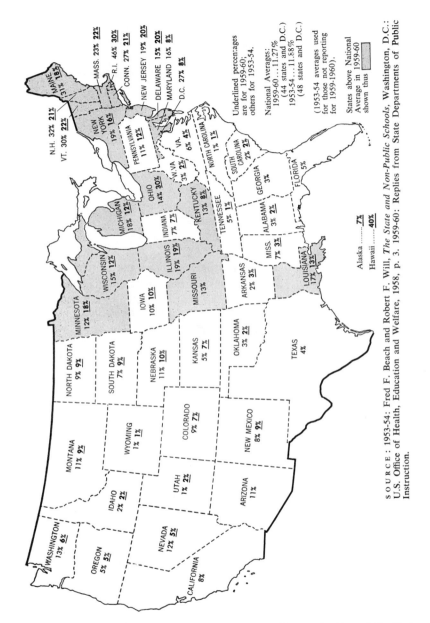

N.H. 32% <u>21%</u>
VT. 30% <u>22%</u>
MAINE 31% <u>18%</u>
MASS. 23% <u>22%</u>
R.I. 46% <u>30%</u>
CONN. 27% <u>21%</u>
NEW JERSEY 19% <u>20%</u>
DELAWARE 15% <u>20%</u>
MARYLAND 16% <u>8%</u>
D.C. 27% <u>8%</u>
NEW YORK 19% <u>15%</u>
PENNSYLVANIA 11% <u>12%</u>
W.VA. 3% <u>2%</u>
VA. 6% <u>4%</u>
NORTH CAROLINA 1% <u>1%</u>
SOUTH CAROLINA 2% <u>2%</u>
GEORGIA 3%
FLORIDA 5%
OHIO 14% <u>30%</u>
KENTUCKY 13% <u>8%</u>
TENNESSEE 5% <u>1%</u>
ALABAMA 3% <u>2%</u>
MICHIGAN 18% <u>12%</u>
INDIANA 7% <u>7%</u>
ILLINOIS 19% <u>19%</u>
MISSOURI 13%
MISS. 7% <u>3%</u>
LOUISIANA 17% <u>13%</u>
WISCONSIN 15% <u>12%</u>
IOWA 10% <u>10%</u>
ARKANSAS 2% <u>3%</u>
MINNESOTA 12% <u>18%</u>
NORTH DAKOTA 9% <u>9%</u>
SOUTH DAKOTA 7% <u>9%</u>
NEBRASKA 11% <u>10%</u>
KANSAS 5% <u>7%</u>
OKLAHOMA 3% <u>2%</u>
TEXAS 4%
MONTANA 11% <u>9%</u>
WYOMING 1% <u>1%</u>
COLORADO 9% <u>7%</u>
NEW MEXICO 8% <u>9%</u>
IDAHO 2% <u>2%</u>
UTAH 1% <u>2%</u>
ARIZONA 11%
WASHINGTON 13% <u>6%</u>
OREGON 5% <u>5%</u>
NEVADA 12% <u>5%</u>
CALIFORNIA 8%

Underlined percentages
are for 1959-60;
others for 1953-54.

National Averages:
1959-60....11.27%
(44 states and D.C.)
1953-54....11.88%
(48 states and D.C.)

(1953-54 averages used
for those not reporting
for 1959-1960).

States above National
Average in 1959-60
shown thus

Alaska .... <u>7%</u>
Hawaii ...... <u>40%</u>

SOURCE: 1953-54: Fred F. Beach and Robert F. Will, *The State and Non-Public Schools*, Washington, D.C.: U.S. Office of Health, Education and Welfare, 1958, p. 3. 1959-60: Replies from State Departments of Public Instruction.

Fig. 20–1. Percentage of Secondary School Enrollments in Nonpublic High Schools, 1953–54 and 1959–60

nonpublic school enrollments was in the New England states, the home of the outstanding independent schools and the region where parochial school commitments originated.

Nonpublic schools tend also to be unevenly distributed within the various states, clustering in the largest cities. The Chicago archdiocese of the Catholic Church, for example, had 91 secondary schools in and about the city in 1958 with a total enrollment of 54,000, which was perhaps 85 to 90 per cent of the total nonpublic school enrollment for the state of Illinois. This city system of parochial schools had at that time just completed an expenditure of $37 million during a five-year program of expansion and was preparing to spend another $40 million in anticipation of a combined high school enrollment of 75,000 by 1963.

Enrollments

The period of 1800-1870 was the heyday of the private academy; private secondary schools served 40 per cent of the high school enrollments as late as 1890, the eve of their eclipse by the public high school. The turn of the twentieth century saw the nonpublic secondary school begin to decline in influence, while its enrollments continued to increase. The loss of prominence was due to the rapid expansion of public high schools, rather than to any retrenchment of nonpublic secondary schools.

The total enrollment of pupils in nonpublic secondary schools in 1953-54 was 747,323.[8] Almost 70 per cent of these pupils were attending school in only twelve states: New York, Pennsylvania, Illinois, Michigan, Ohio, California, Massachusetts, New Jersey, Wisconsin, Missouri, Connecticut, and Louisiana. Such a distribution might be expected inasmuch as all of these states, except Connecticut and Louisiana, have relatively large high school populations. However, these same states enrolled only about 50 per cent of the total 6,290,245 students who were that year attending public schools.

Growth in enrollments. The increase in nonpublic, as compared to public, secondary school enrollments from 1900 to 1960 is shown in Figure 20-2. During these years nonpublic high schools have expanded enrollments significantly in every decade, including the years from 1940-1950 during which public high school enrollments took a substantial drop. Actually, nonpublic high school enrollments increased over 800 per cent during the first half of this century. But an even

---

[8] Fred F. Beach and Robert F. Will, *op. cit.,* p. 3.

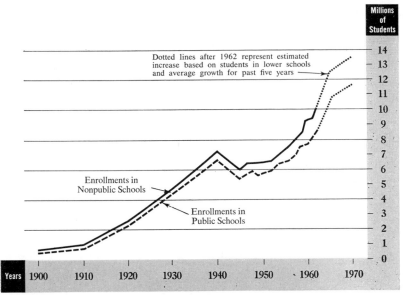

Fig. 20–2. *Enrollments in Public and Nonpublic Secondary Schools, 1900–1970, Grades 9–12*

SOURCE: Research Division, NEA, *Status and Trends: Vital Statistics, Education, and Public Finance,* Washington, D.C. (National Education Association), 1959, p. 9.

greater increase of over 1,400 per cent for public high schools reduced the percentage of high school students in nonpublic schools. Nevertheless, if present trends continue, the enrollments of nonpublic secondary schools will be approaching two million by 1970, which is predicted to be about 14 per cent of the total high school population at that time.

The pattern of the nonpublic secondary school's enrollments over the first half of this century can be shown in one way by the percentage of high school students served by such institutions for the nation as a whole. Table 20-3 indicates that in 1900, 18 per cent of all secondary school students were attending nonpublic schools. The percentage in these institutions dropped to a low of 6 per cent in 1940, but it had climbed back to an estimated 12 per cent in 1960. Strong enthusiasm for the public high school, combined with economic reverses during the 1930's, is believed to be responsible for the drop in percentages that took place from 1920-1940. Improved economic conditions, a nationwide revival of interest in religion and parochial education, and wider interest in college preparation are factors that possibly contributed to the reversal of the downward trend since 1940.

Table 20-3. *Percentage of Enrollments in Nonpublic Schools, 1900–1960*

YEAR	GRADES K-12	GRADES 9-12
1900	8	18
1910	9	11
1920	7	9
1930	9	8
1940	9	6
1950	12	10
1954	13	11
1960	14[a]	12[a]

[a] Estimated.

SOURCE: Research Division, NEA, *op. cit.,* p. 9.

Types of Institutions

Nonpublic schools may be classified according to their sponsorship or affiliation, e.g., parochial or independent; scope of service—day or boarding schools; or nature of programs—college preparation, tutorial, remedial, or general.

Sponsorship or affiliation. The relative size of nonpublic schools, in terms of their sponsorship or affiliation, is shown in Table 20-4 which classifies all such institutions according to numbers and enrollments. The largest group is composed of those high schools sponsored by or affiliated with the Catholic Church and its various dioceses and organizations. This category included 2,390 out of the total of 4,241 schools, or 57 per cent, in 1959-60. Enrollment for Catholic schools that year was 825,077, almost 79 per cent of the total estimated enrollments in nonpublic schools. This figure, a new high in Catholic secondary school enrollments, represented a 70.9 per cent increase from 1947-48. These institutions produced a total of 123,690 high school graduates in 1959.[9]

The 1,136 independent schools comprise the next largest group of nonpublic high schools. Although they represent over 26 per cent of the institutions, their enrollments are estimated to be only about 12 per cent of the total because, being boarding schools for the most part, they tend to be smaller than the church-related high schools which are largely day schools.

[9] National Catholic Welfare Conference, *op.cit.,* pp. 28-29.

Table 20-4. *Number and Enrollments of Nonpublic Secondary Schools by Control or Affiliation, 1959–60*

CONTROL OR AFFILIATION	NUMBER	PER CENT OF NONPUBLIC SCHOOLS	ENROLLMENTS	PER CENT OF NONPUBLIC ENROLLMENTS
PAROCHIAL:				
Roman Catholic	2,390	56.355	825,077	78.429
Episcopalian	108	2.546	19,459	1.850
Seventh Day Adventist	82	1.934	13,685	1.301
Lutheran	42	.990	13,140	1.249
Christian	36	.849	9,190	.874
Jewish	35	.825	6,000[a]	.570
Friends	23	.542	5,567	.529
Methodist	13	.307	3,741	.356
Baptist	13	.307	3,914	.372
Presbyterian	8	.187	2,070	.197
Other and Non-denominational	355	8.371	24,514[a]	2.330
Subtotal	3,105	73.213	926,357[a]	88.057
INDEPENDENT:				
All types	1,136	26.786	125,643[a]	11.943
Total	4,241	100	1,052,000[a]	100

[a] Partially estimated.

SOURCES: Returns from questionnaries to State Departments of Education; Porter Sargent, *The Hand Book of Private Schools,* Boston: Porter Sargent, 1958; and, National Catholic Welfare Conference, *Summary of Catholic Education,* Washington D.C.: The Conference, 1959. Information provided by various Protestant and Jewish school associations and churches.

Scope of service. Sargent's *Handbook* classifies 1,731 schools[10] on the basis of services they provide in the following categories: boarding schools, 977; day schools, 502; home schools, 157; and tuition and remedial schools, 95. Because this publication aims at helping parents select suitable nonpublic schools for their children, it is to be expected that more boarding schools would be listed than other kinds. Home schools include institutions that serve handicapped youth. Tutorial and remedial schools enroll students who require or desire special help, usually to qualify for college entrance.

[10] This number does not include an additional 133 for which insufficient information made classification by type impossible.

Nature of program. Nonpublic secondary schools often classify themselves by the nature of their programs. Such specializations are advertised in campaigns to increase endowments. In 1958, Sargent listed 931 boarding schools in accordance with the specialties shown in Table 20-5. The tendency of nonpublic schools to specialize or be

Table 20-5. Nonpublic Boarding Schools Classified According to Strength of Programs

PROGRAM STRENGTHS	NUMBER SCHOOLS CLASSIFIED
Academic Schools:	
Languages	96
Mathematics	83
Science	94
Honors Courses	38
	311
Specialized Schools:	
Remedial Reading	218
Developmental Reading	115
Tutorial and Make-up	119
	452
General Curriculum	168
TOTAL	931[a]

a Not included are 46 unclassified boarding schools.
SOURCE : Sargent, *op. cit.,* pp. 879-901.

strong in particular academic subject fields and in remedial or developmental reading contrasts with the aim of most public schools to be as comprehensive as possible.

THE GROWTH OF NONPUBLIC SECONDARY SCHOOLS

In view of the obstacles which have confronted nonpublic education, its growth, particularly at the elementary school level, has been phenomenal. Not all of the denominational groups that have sponsored nonpublic schools, however, have exerted vigorous efforts to expand their services. Independent schools also have often not attempted to increase their enrollments since their objectives center around giving high-quality instruction on an individual or small-group basis; nor have their boards of control sought to establish additional schools. But two denominational bodies, the Roman Catholic church and the Lutheran church, have vigorously attempted to expand the influence and services of their schools. From their efforts and experiences, insights into the difficulties faced by nonpublic schools can be gained.

The Growth of Various Types of Schools

Catholic secondary schools. Motivated by church doctrines that make attendance at church-sponsored schools mandatory if facilities are available, the Catholic church has endeavored to provide schools wherever the membership was large enough to warrant them. As is to be expected, these nonpublic schools grew first in cities and states where the Catholic population was greatest. Their success is reflected in the following statement:

> Fifty years ago Catholic education was a buyer's market: The hierarchy and the pastors begged the laity to support and utilize our struggling school system. Now it is a seller's market: the Church strains every sinew to meet the increasing demand for a Catholic education at every level.
>
> This fall, for the first time, the number of students in our Catholic elementary and secondary schools, colleges and universities will perhaps top five million. Official figures for 1958 show that in the last decade Catholic elementary school registration leaped almost 70 per cent; enrollment in our secondary schools jumped some 15 per cent, and in the colleges and universities, approximately 24 per cent.[11]

Yet in spite of this success, the Church still confronts difficulties in providing nonpublic schools for a spiraling population. A Catholic journal reported recently that two-thirds of Catholic children of high school age are not in church schools. As a result, the editor raises for consideration the possibility of concentrating church resources on secondary education alone. "It can be argued that the objectives of the Council of Baltimore—the strengthening of the faith, the development of lay leadership and the multiplication of vocations—can be better achieved through high schools and colleges than through elementary schools."[12]

[11] "Rising Tide of Pupils," *America,* September 6, 1958, p. 565.
[12] "New Pattern for Catholic Education?", *America,* May 7, 1960, p. 213.

Another aspect of this problem is that the Church relies heavily upon teaching sisters to provide instructional staffs. There is a continuous need to recruit from student ranks those who will enter religious educational work.[13]

Lutheran church schools. Of the Protestant denominations, the Lutheran church has exhibited the strongest commitment to nonpublic schools. Although considerably smaller and less well known than the Catholic church system of education, the Lutheran secondary schools have faced similar difficulties in their growth. Particularly does their story emphasize the obstacles encountered by a church school when the diversity of religious groups in a community, combined with the drawing power of the public schools, makes it impossible to assemble enough children of one faith to maintain a school.

Perhaps the earliest Lutheran school in America was founded by a Swedish Lutheran colony in 1638 on the Delaware.[14] Another was opened in Dutch New Amsterdam in 1648; Lutheran Salzburgers from Austria founded still another near Savannah, Georgia, in 1734. As Lutheran immigrants became more numerous, they united into larger church bodies, and the number of schools soon exceeded the number of churches. By 1829, 84 parishes were operating 206 schools. With the expansion of public schools, these early denominational schools virtually disappeared.

The Lutheran Church-Missouri Synod was a later organization established by new immigrants who had come to the United States partly because of dissatisfaction with a state church. They were eager to maintain control over the education of their own youth. "One of their main objects was the proper indoctrination and training of the youth in Lutheran elementary and secondary schools; and their expressed ideal was to have a Lutheran parish school next to every Lutheran church, with high schools in larger centers."[15]

From its beginning this religious body had its own teacher training institutions and seminaries; separate high schools date from 1903. Since that time nineteen Lutheran high schools have been established, sixteen of them in the last twenty-five years. In 1937 the Lutheran

---

[13] For a discussion of this problem related to the issue of where emphasis should be placed in Catholic schools—at the elementary or secondary school level, see Walter E. Stokes, Society of Jesus, "100,000 Valiant Women," *America,* April 23, 1960, pp. 132-34.

[14] A. C. Stellhorn, "Schools of the Lutheran Church-Missouri Synod," *School and Society,* May 9, 1959, pp. 225-27.

[15] *Ibid.,* p. 226.

Church-Missouri Synod had three high schools with 734 students; in 1947, eight schools with 2,916 students; in 1957, fourteen schools with 7,345 students.[16] Enrollment in the elementary schools of the same body grew from 75,271 in 1937, to 140,622 in 1957. Rapid as the growth has been, only a small fraction of Lutheran youth attend nonpublic high schools, but Lutheran efforts to persuade members to maintain their own church high schools have many interesting parallels to and contrasts with Catholic schools.

Independent schools. Independent schools, particularly the well-known, long-established ones, base their appeal on quality and specialized services to students. Their major objective always has been college preparation. The remedial programs they offer are usually directed toward helping pupils overcome academic difficulties so that college work will be possible.

To accomplish such objectives student-faculty ratios are kept low—below eleven students to each teacher in leading independent schools. Individual help, coaching, supervised study, and regulated daily schedules, particularly in boarding schools, are practices by which high academic attainment is encouraged. In addition, so far as they can, such schools attempt to select students on the basis of academic qualifications.

Increasing costs, teacher shortages, need for plant expansion, providing scholarships, adapting curriculum to new knowledge, and utilizing up-to-date instructional resources are all problems that bear heavily upon independent schools. Without support from a church group, they must rely entirely upon endowments and tuition. Tuition (which usually includes board and room) ranges in the leading boarding schools from $1,500 to more than $2,000 a year. As the almost annual necessity to increase rates continues, independent schools find expansions in size of enrollments difficult.

Problems of Growth

Matching public school services. All nonpublic schools face the task of keeping abreast of rapid advances in public education. Even the independent preparatory school, which historically has marketed its program under the banner of "academic quality," is often hard pressed to prove that it does a superior job as compared to better public schools. Whereas at one time the nonpublic school looked upon itself

[16] O. A. Dorn, *The Lutheran Annual,* 1959, St. Louis, Mo. (Concordia Publishing House), 1958, p. 63.

as the pace-setter for public institutions, the situation is now rapidly reversing.

An obvious problem of the nonpublic school is the provision of buildings and facilities comparable to new public school plants. In New York City, for example, it has been estimated that each public school child is provided with 94 square feet of space in elementary schools, and 115 in high schools; but the parochial school student may have as little as 50 square feet or less, at either level.[17] Libraries, laboratories, auditoriums, gymnasiums, cafeterias, shops, and special-purpose rooms are other facilities in public schools that nonpublic institutions often feel compelled to provide. Similarly, audio-visual aids and other types of special instructional supplies have become necessities in nonpublic as well as public secondary schools.

The challenge of matching curricular offerings is one that most nonpublic schools have elected to bypass. They do this by restricting their emphasis to specific educational objectives, and by selecting students whose aims coincide with the school's program. For the independent school, this solution may work reasonably well. The parochial institution, however, is usually expected to serve all members of the faith, regardless of their educational plans. Such an objective often forces the nonpublic school to attempt to emulate the comprehensive public high school, an assignment that may be beyond its capacity.

Higher standards for teachers, increased student services in such areas as guidance, special education, extracurricular activities, and remedial work are other examples of practices in public high schools that nonpublic institutions may be expected to match. Their inability to do so may weaken public confidence and tend to cause students to elect to attend public secondary schools.

Financial burdens. Nonpublic schools are a financial burden both on the sponsoring body and on the individual families who send their children to them. Only a few such institutions are so heavily endowed or so well supported by a sponsoring agency that they do not have to charge tuition. Even church day schools are being forced to charge tuition which may run from $300 a year up.

Parochial schools are sometimes able to apportion the cost of their programs among the members of the parish. In most cases, however, all nonpublic schools must undertake annual fund-raising campaigns to help meet expanding budgets.

[17] Roger A. Freeman, "The Classroom Shortage," *America,* April 4, 1959, p. 28.

SPECIAL PURPOSES OF NONPUBLIC SCHOOLS

The purposes for which nonpublic schools exist go beyond those of the public schools. The nonpublic institutions are expected to achieve the goals of the public schools as well as other goals that provide the special reason for their existence. These latter may include religious indoctrination, specialized education, experimentation and research, or the provision of model programs for teacher training.

Religious Indoctrination

The foremost purpose of most parochial schools is religious indoctrination. While a few church-related institutions attempt to fulfill this function by emphasizing general moral and spiritual training in a Christian atmosphere, the nonpublic schools that have expanded the most have adhered to the principle of providing specific religious indoctrination.

Only in the teaching of religion, per se, does the nonpublic school perform a function that is entirely different from any function of the public schools. The public school must emphasize moral and spiritual values as products of various religious systems, established law, and the thinking of civilized men; the parochial school, on the other hand, is committed to a specific religion and its system of values. This difference, which is deeply rooted in the constitutional provision for separation of church and state, has been the basis for heated debate and extended legal battles in recent years.[18]

Church-related schools, for the most part, attempt to capitalize on the public schools' inability to teach moral and spiritual values from the point of view of a specific religious commitment. They believe that religious training and education generally cannot be separated. In such schools, religious education is usually not restricted to the study about religion as is done in public schools; it includes religious exercises and indoctrination in a particular faith. Most religious bodies feel a divine obligation to "lead the young upon the way of the Lord." Nonpublic schools are viewed by some such groups as the natural and most efficient means for achieving this objective.

Specialized Education

Two traditional and sometimes closely related goals of nonpublic

[18] For one of the most careful analyses of this problem see V. T. Thayer, *The Role of the School in American Society,* New York (Dodd, Mead), 1960, pp. 353-427.

schools are college preparation and training for a religious vocation. In early times, these objectives were often inseparable, inasmuch as the principal function of colleges, for which high schools prepared students, was to train ministers. Nonpublic schools often existed as satellites of particular institutions of higher learning to prepare students for specific programs and standards. To some extent this pattern still prevails today; it is not likely to disappear completely as long as certain colleges continue to restrict their student body to students with highly similar goals.

A few nonpublic secondary schools have as objectives other types of specialization. One of the aims of the recently founded Indian Springs School, in Helena, Alabama, is to give boys of superior intelligence opportunities to develop independence in learning through "self-instruction." The generously endowed Kamehameha Schools of Honolulu, Hawaii, have the unique goal of preparing descendants of the Hawaiian race for vocations and academic advancement. A number of military high schools, such as Staunton Military Academy in Virginia and the New Mexico Military Institute, prepare young men for military careers. Some schools specialize in the fine arts; others, in training for business positions; a few still function as "finishing schools" for young women.

Research and Experimentation

Some nonpublic schools have given leadership to all secondary education through their programs of research and experimentation. The famous "Eight-Year Study" sponsored by the Progressive Education Association included a disproportionately large number of nonpublic schools in the 200 high schools that experimented with ways to prepare for college. In fact, in the forefront of nearly every new development in secondary education in the United States are to be found nonpublic schools whose faculties have the vision and freedom to try new ventures.

Research and experimentation in the nonpublic secondary school are encouraged by its freedom from local control and public opinion in general. It can, if it desires, test theories and improve procedures without endangering its relationship with the community in which it exists. Independent schools can even select a student body suited to its research purposes, for example, for studies of the academically talented.

However, few nonpublic schools, regretfully, accept the challenge to experiment. Parochial institutions often are committed to established patterns that are closely related to religious rituals, doctrines, and traditions. Independent schools, too, may be dedicated to inflexible programs and procedures.

Model Programs for Teacher Training

Nonpublic secondary schools closely associated with teacher education institutions customarily are expected to provide model programs as exhibits to prospective teachers and to other high schools. Typically, their resources are made available for both observation and practice teaching. The University High School of Chicago University, and the old Lincoln School of Teachers College, Columbia University, are examples of laboratory schools whose research and demonstration programs have had nation-wide influence on secondary schools.

STRENGTHS OF THE NONPUBLIC SCHOOLS

In a land where uniformity is often prized, many people feel that the variety contributed by the existence of nonpublic schools represents a form of insurance against a stultifying sameness of educational goals and programs. In presenting the case for the private school Heely listed its advantages as:

(a) Independence
(b) Selectivity
(c) Freedom to decide who shall teach and not teach
(d) Freedom of speech and opinion immune to public regulation
(e) Ability to provide instruction in small groups[19]

Looking toward the expanding high school population, he indicated the problem of mass education to which the nonpublic school can provide one alternative:

> Can the public school realistically hope that it can increasingly develop capacities on an individual basis? There is no reason to believe that it can reduce even its present population to comfortable limits, and, once the irresistible expansion has established itself, it is scarcely to be hoped that it will recede.[20]

One advantage of the nonpublic school usually conceded by both its adherents and opponents is firm control of pupil behavior. Leighton Johnson, a college educator, stresses this point.

[19] Allen V. Heely, *Why the Private School?*, New York (Harper), 1951, p. 32.

[20] *Ibid.*, p. 32.

One generalization, though, which can be supported is that in most cases the private school, when overtaxed by student behavior which is unacceptable to it, can slough off the offender to the public school. The public school is often required to accept the discarded, and usually finds it more difficult to suspend or expel the student who fails to measure up to expected standards of conduct. It is ironic that, in some situations, the pupil who is expelled from the private school and must be accepted by the public schools is a difficult pupil to work with because his problems were caused by, or exacerbated by, the private school which so easily dropped him.[21]

Nonpublic schools at times undertake programs and services that public schools avoid. They have frequently pioneered for social justice for minority groups. Religious denominations, for example, established the first schools to serve American Indians. In the perplexing field of racial integration, nonpublic schools have been leaders; Friends schools were serving Negroes before 1860, and Catholic efforts toward integration have attracted attention in recent years. Henry Barnard reports that Catholic schools were the first to integrate in Washington, D.C.[22] The seventeen Catholic schools in Northern Virginia have been integrated since May 1954.[23]

Efforts have been made in the South to use private schools as devices to nullify the effect of the Supreme Court decisions compelling integration. In Virginia a system of state and local "tuition grants" helps to provide support for schools in Charlottesville, Front Royal, Prince Edward County, and Norfolk.[24] Little Rock, Arkansas, has also opened this type of private nonsegregated school.

Religious groups believe, of course, that the major strength of parochial schools is their ability to integrate instruction in doctrine into their educational programs. The Catholic position on this matter is well known. A recent illustration of the reasons for preferring church-controlled schools to public schools comes from representatives of the Jewish religion, a group with a distinguished record for supporting public education. Himmelfarb enumerates various reasons why some members of this faith are now establishing their own parochial day

[21] Leighton H. Johnson, "Unemphasized Aspects of the Independent-School Question," *School and Society,* May 23, 1959, p. 240.

[22] Henry Barnard, *Barnard's American Journal of Education,* Vol. XIX, 1870, p. 217.

[23] Wilfred Parsons, "Desegregation: Virginia Background," *America,* September 28, 1958, p. 637.

[24] "Private (Unmixed) Schools: How They're Working Out," *U.S. News and World Report,* September 26, 1960.

schools.[25] They include the desire to provide the Jewish community with learned laymen and professionals; disappointment with the lack of intellectual emphasis in public schools, and a feeling that through Jewish schools they can promote confidence in the Jewish people that they have "arrived as Americans." These feelings are growing in spite of strong objections from some members of the Jewish faith that parochial schools weaken public institutions and against their long-advanced position that children should learn in public schools by experience to get along with people who are racially, religiously, and ethnically different.

OBJECTIONS TO NONPUBLIC SCHOOLS

As is true of many public problems in this nation, the nonpublic school is often a controversial subject. In recent years, conflicts between supporters of nonpublic and public educational institutions have aired generously their objections to each other.[26] Although the offensive in this debate is most frequently taken by the champions of parochial or independent schools, supporters of public education have recently raised certain objections to the role of nonpublic institutions in secondary education in the United States.

While the right of parents to maintain nonpublic schools and to send their children to them is not seriously questioned anywhere in the United States, there are two key objections to nonpublic schools. One is that a dual school system destroys democratic unity and thereby weakens community, state, and national life; the other is that efforts to support nonpublic schools tend to undermine public confidence in, financial support for, and dedication to public schools.

The first issue is brought clearly into the open by Conant's careful analysis:

> The greater the proportion of our youth who fail to attend our public schools and who receive their education elsewhere, the greater the threat to our democratic unity. . . .
> If one accepts the ideal of a democratic, fluid society with a minimum of class distinction, the maximum of fluidity, the maximum of

[25] Milton Himmelfarb, "Reflections on the Jewish Day School," *Commentary*, July 1960, pp. 29-36.

[26] See V. T. Thayer, *op. cit.*, pp. 315-427; V. T. Thayer, *Public Education and Its Critics*, New York (Macmillan), 1954. Also, Freeman R. Butts, *The American Tradition in Religion and Education*, Boston (Beacon Press), 1950.

understanding between different vocational groups, then the ideal secondary school is a comprehensive public high school. Of this much there can be no doubt: If one wished generation after generation to perpetuate class distinction based on hereditary status in a given society, one would certainly demand a dual system of schools; this is the case in the Province of Quebec where a majority of the people wish to perpetuate two different cultural groups.[27]

The multiple systems of education in other nations, such as England, Australia, or Spain, with their various types of independent, aided, and public schools, are viewed without envy by informed citizens of the United States. They recall how neighboring Canada has been divided over support of Catholic and Protestant schools, and how France has struggled with the problem of maintaining both public and nonpublic schools since the time of Napoleon. A similar question plagues Belgium and increases animosities between religious groups in Holland and other European nations.[28] For this reason, many public school leaders and citizens fear that the nonpublic school, if it increases in strength and aggressiveness, will ultimately weaken democratic unity in the United States. Also, some students of education agree with Conant that it is unfortunate to separate youth during the secondary school years which are so important to their civic-social development.

Those whose children attend independent or parochial schools often do not maintain as vital a concern for public education as is desirable. Nor do adults who are products of nonpublic schools feel strong commitments to support public high schools. Such a lack of ties with the public schools may prompt proponents of nonpublic secondary schools to oppose expenditures for public schools. When such action occurs, it encourages counterreactions against nonpublic schools in general.

REGULATION OF NONPUBLIC SCHOOLS

Two decisions of the Supreme Court of the United States have had far-reaching consequences in defining the rights of nonpublic schools. In the Dartmouth College case, in 1819, the Court held that an educational institution has a right to exist as a private corporation and is not

[27] James Bryant Conant, *Education and Liberty,* Cambridge, Mass. (Harvard Univ. Press), 1953, pp. 81-82.
[28] Edmund J. King, *Other Schools and Ours,* New York (Rinehart), 1958, p. 43.

a state monopoly. The Oregon case in 1925 upheld the right of parents to send children to proper private schools. The state, however, exercises a right to regulate nonpublic schools through a variety of lawful devices. These devices include laws applying generally to individuals or organizations conducting businesses or charitable undertakings, laws applying to nonpublic schools explicitly under the state's authority to ensure an educated citizenry, and regulatory measures.

The state may regulate nonpublic schools through incorporation. In a number of states, in fact, the first corporations under state constitutions were educational institutions. Regulation may also be accomplished by requiring state approval of school programs and state recognition of schools. One state, Alabama, requires church-affiliated schools to have state approval in order to admit pupils. A state may also regulate nonpublic schools by establishing standards to be met by compulsory education; some states may deny the right of a school to serve youth of compulsory school age if it fails to comply with established standards.

Certain kinds of public support may be used as regulatory devices. These may include services to particular groups of students, such as handicapped pupils or delinquents. Some states provide scholarships or tuition allowances for pupils in nonpublic schools under special circumstances. Four states[29] provide free textbooks to students in such schools. The meeting of certain conditions by the school is essential to the receipt of these benefits. Provision of tax exemption is another regulatory mechanism. Schools may be required to meet certain criteria in order to qualify for tax exemption.

States also have the authority to license both schools and teachers. Neither in the United States nor in other nations is it customary for the certification requirements for teachers to be as strictly applied to teachers in nonpublic schools as they are to those in public schools.

It is fair to say that regulation of nonpublic schools, both by state and voluntary agencies, is neither so strictly nor so consistently applied as is that of public schools. The effort made by many of these institutions to achieve excellence, consequently, is all the more to their credit.

The roles of nonpublic schools have changed in the past and are changing now. Their place in the over-all design of secondary education is and will continue to be of vital interest to the public at large.

[29] Alabama, Louisiana, Mississippi, and New Mexico. Fred F. Beach and Robert F. Will, *op. cit.*, p. 270.

SELECTED REFERENCES

BARRAT, ROBERT. "The School Question in France." *Commonweal,* December 25, 1959.

BEACH, FRED F., AND ROBERT F. WILL. *The State and Nonpublic Schools.* Washington, D.C.: U.S. Department of Health, Education and Welfare, Office of Education, 1958.

BUTTS, R. FREEMAN. *The American Tradition: Religion and Education.* Boston: Beacon Press, 1950.

FUESS, CLAUDE M. *Independent Schoolmaster.* Boston: Little, Brown, 1952.

HECHINGER, GRACE, AND FRED M. HECHINGER. "The Key Role of the Private School." *New York Times Magazine,* May 10, 1959.

HEELY, ALLAN V. "The Case for Private Schools." *School Executive,* October 1955.

JOHNSON, LEIGHTON H. "Unemphasized Aspects of the Independent School Question." *School and Society,* May 23, 1959.

KERWIN, JEROME G. *Catholic Viewpoint on Church and State.* Garden City, N. Y.: Hanover House, 1960.

KOHLBRENNER, BERNARD J. "Some Practical Aspects of the Public Character of Private Education." *School and Society,* October 11, 1958.

LIEBERMAN, MYRON. "Diplomas for Sale." *Nation,* December 26, 1959.

MCCLUSKEY, NEIL G. "How Much State Support?" *America,* September 19, 1959.

National Catholic Welfare Conference. *Summary of Catholic Education, 1959.* Washington, D.C.: the Conference, Department of Education, 1960.

Foreign exchange students to high schools in the United States have both increased scholastic competition and decreased international differences.

Images of rigid discipline and high academic achievement in schools abroad cause some to advocate that secondary schools in the United States should adopt European and Russian methods and programs.

CHAPTER 21

Competition from Abroad

AMERICANS are proud competitors; they strive to excel in every endeavor. In government, economic system, public institutions, creative genius, they have long recognized no other country as their equal. The habit of success, established in industrial development, business ingenuity, world trade, standards of living, individual and group sports, and in two world wars, cultivated illusions of invincibility in the minds of all.

These illusions suffered sorely in the postwar international tensions, especially in the Korean conflict, in which the United States carried the brunt of the fighting for the United Nations, and which ended in a stalemate and negotiated cessation rather than a clear-cut victory. The prolonged frustration, and at times humiliation, which tedious, indecisive international diplomacy produced in a people oriented to forthright, successful action laid the foundation for the near-hysteria that developed when the Soviet Union, on the eve of the geophysical year, achieved the technological victory of placing the first man-made satellite into orbit around the earth.

The sudden awareness that a competing world power had educated and utilized the brain power of its scientists to greater advantage in the space field set in motion widespread efforts to discover the reason for the apparent failure of the United States. Inasmuch as the Russian achievement was intellectual, it was only natural that people should turn the inquiry toward the institution most responsible for refining mental resources—public education. Because secondary schools play a key role in the initial discovery and development of intellectual talent, and because they are close to the people, they soon became a focus of public criticism.

The Russian achievement, some held, must have been due to their superior system of education. This proposition set into motion appeals for secondary schools in the United States to emulate Soviet educational practices. The suggestion was strongly advanced, also, that other European schools might provide a model of the type of quality education needed in this country.[1] Such proposals were often recognized as the result of fear and anxiety at home rather than of the demonstrated superiority of educational practices of other nations. Nevertheless, they have stimulated the widest interest in comparative secondary education that has existed since the days of Horace Mann's study of the German school system. They make appropriate a brief consideration of the challenges coming from abroad as the final chapter in a text that deals with the current concerns of secondary education in the United States.

COMMITMENTS TO EDUCATION

Any comparison of national systems of education must focus attention on each nation's commitment to education, both that of the government and that of individuals. The belief of a country in its system of schooling, and the faith its citizens place in educational development go far to shape the quality of education.

National Commitment

Striking differences are found between the United States and most other leading nations of the world in the national commitment made to education. These differences include the constitutional provisions for education on a nation-wide basis, the amount of support, the belief in the importance of education to the nation's destiny, and the general status accorded to education.

Constitutional provisions. No mention is made of education in the

---

[1] H. G. Rickover, *Education and Freedom*, New York: (Dutton), 1959.

federal Constitution of the United States. Responsibility for providing schools is left to individual states. As a consequence, except on military reservations and in territorial provinces, Congress and the President can only encourage and stimulate educational efforts. The U.S. Office of Education has no authority to establish programs, prescribe curriculums, set standards, apportion students, or certify teachers. It can influence education only through research and various types of indirect leadership activities.

In contrast, other nations have definite commitments to education at the national level. The "Stalin Constitution" adopted by the U.S.S.R. in 1936 proclaimed the right of all citizens of Russia to an education, and asserted:

> This right is ensured by universal and compulsory education; by free education up to and including the seventh grade; by a system of state stipends for students of higher educational establishments who excel in their studies; by instruction in schools being conducted in the native language, and by the organization in the factories, state farms, machine and tractor stations, and collective farms of free vocational, technical and agronomic training for the working people.[2]

When adopted in 1947, the Constitution of India specified that universal, compulsory, and free education must be provided within ten years for all children under the age of fourteen.[3] The events that have shaken India since her independence have extended the time needed to achieve this objective; nevertheless, the progress made and planned is almost unmatched in the history of the world.

Similarly, in the older European nations—England, France, Italy, Germany, Norway, Sweden, Denmark, to list a few examples—constitutional commitments to education gave direction to the nature and quality of programs provided in schools. Compared with nations able to marshal educational resources to serve national needs much as military forces can be marshaled, the United States must depend upon fifty separate states, and numerous counties and local school districts in each, to determine the nature and course of education. The cumbersomeness of this process has prompted proposals for the establishment of a national board of education or a national commission on the cur-

[2] George Z. F. Bereday, William W. Brickman, and Gerald H. Read (eds.), *The Changing Soviet School,* Cambridge, Mass. (Riverside Press), 1960, p. 69.
[3] Humayun Kabir, *Education in New India,* New York (Harper), 1957, p. 1.

riculum, either of which might give some direction, or guidance, to local school systems.[4]

In spite of the challenges from abroad, efforts to develop a national commitment to education in the United States meet with vigorous opposition. Appropriations by Congress for education are fought bitterly by various types of interest groups, usually under the slogans, "states' rights," or "preservation of local autonomy." Thoughtful students of education and political science as well as leaders in other fields have concluded that failure to utilize the total resources of the federal government to strengthen schools leaves education dependent upon insufficient financial support and contributes to uneven standards and unsatisfactory educational outcomes.[5]

Financial support. Another measure of a country's commitment to education is the share of its total national income that is invested in its schools. Accurate comparisons of the proportion of annual incomes invested in education are made difficult by the multiple sources of support for education. These sources are both private and public and income may be collected at local, state, and national levels. The two nations whose investments in education are most frequently compared are the United States, which allocates 3.5 per cent of its national income, and Russia, which assigns more than 6 per cent.[6] Most European nations which do not attempt to maintain universal education beyond the elementary school put from 2.5 to 3.5 per cent of their income into education, including contributions to both public and private schools. India, a new democracy, is estimated to assign as much as 4 to 6 per cent of its total national income to education.

Education and the national destiny. Until recent years, the people of the United States have not believed that secondary education is solidly linked to the destiny of the nation, as do citizens of certain other nations. Instead, education at this level has been looked upon as a contribution to the individual. High school attendance has been legislated and encouraged more for social and vocational reasons than for national security.

4 H. G. Rickover, *The Truth Shall Make You Free,* Brooklyn (Polytechnic Institute of Brooklyn, Speech for Dedication-Inauguration Ceremonies), April 19, 1958, p. 7. Also, F. M. King, "National Curriculum," *Minnesota Journal of Education,* April 1959.

5 Robert Shayon, "Let the Debate Be Honest," *National Education Association Journal,* February 1959.

6 Some experts estimate that Russia may invest as much as 12 per cent of its total income in education, but these percentages should be considered in the light of the greater total income of the United States.

In the ideological struggle in which the United States is now engaged, however, the competition comes from nations that see education as the key instrument for the achievement of national goals. The central government of the People's Republic of China, for example, issued in 1954 a policy statement that assigned secondary education a vital role in accomplishing the communization of China. As reported by Chu, "the aim of secondary education was to educate students through the socialist ideology for their all-round development as future members of a socialist society."[7] The Russian position was expressed in 1958 by N. S. Khrushchev when he explained the need for educational reforms that would relate school learning more closely to productive labor: "The Soviet school must prepare an all-round educated person, well versed in the sciences as well as being able to labour systematically, a person who wishes to be useful to society, to participate actively in productive labour necessary for that society."[8]

The emphasis given by competing nations to the importance of secondary education for the national destiny gives meaning and purpose to education beyond the individual's right and natural desire to develop his talents. It places squarely on the high school responsibility for developing skills and scholarship that are essential to national well-being.

The status of education. The status a nation accords to education is shown in a variety of ways: in the emphasis placed on intellectual attainments; in the respect and salaries given to teachers; and in the priorities assigned to educational activities in community, state, and national life. Americans have exhibited a continuing faith in education. Each generation has reached beyond the last to extend educational benefits to increasing numbers of children, for longer periods of schooling. Yet, ironically enough, education has never been accorded a high status in the prestige scale of community life.

Compared to other nations where intellectual development is held in high regard, the United States has tended to pay tribute to material accomplishments, to social relationships, to recreational pursuits, and to entertainment. Such attitudes carry over into high schools where academic achievement has been rated below athletic competition, and social activities have usurped time that should go to study.

[7] S. Y. Chu, "Secondary Education in New China," *The Secondary School Curriculum, The Year Book of Education,* George Z. F. Bereday and Joseph A. Lauwerys (eds.), Tarrytown, N.Y.: (World Book Company), 1958, p. 146.

[8] Deana Levin, *Soviet Education Today,* London (Staples Press), 1959, p. 121.

Perhaps the clearest evidence that low status is accorded to education in the United States as compared to other nations is the level of salaries paid to teachers. Here, the auto mechanic, the blast furnace operator, construction worker, plumber, electrician, painter, and members of all other professions are rewarded more highly for their services than are high school teachers.[9]

Individual Dedication

The challenge of foreign educational systems to secondary education in the United States does not come entirely from national commitments or the structure of education itself. It is derived, in part, from their students' zeal and respect for learning, their strong motivation for learning, and their determination to advance by intellectual means. To be sure, it is easy to depreciate high school youth in this country by comparing the gifted in other nations with the average in the United States, as some critics have done.[10] It is also possible to forget that students in high schools of many other nations are selected on the basis of academic success and interest. Nevertheless, respected observers of Russian youth, such as Dr. Lawrence Derthick, United States Commissioner of Education, attest that they exhibit more individual dedication to learning than do high school students in the United States.

In an open society that has worshiped the pioneer, the self-made man, and the nonintellectual, education—beyond the skills necessary for literacy—has always been treated more or less as a luxury. Graduation from high school often is looked upon as a community custom, if not a personal right, which is part of the ritual of induction into adult life. For all too many, college attendance has been nothing more than a response to the expectations of family, or social or economic class. Under such circumstances, zeal and respect for learning have not thrived as much as in less privileged nations.

With education only one of several avenues to personal social and economic success, the American high school student may not be as highly motivated to excel in school as his Russian counterpart who must learn or leave school to work. The absence of rigid standards for advancement from one level of the school system to another may in itself, many believe, have contributed to lowering the motivation of many students in the United States. In addition, the commitment "to

[9] Maurice J. Thomas, *The Concern of All,* Pittsburgh: (Tri-State Area School Council, Univ. of Pittsburgh), 1960, p. 19.

[10] See *Life*, March 24, 1958, pp. 27-35.

live for the state" with which students in Communist countries are indoctrinated may give them a drive toward academic accomplishment that is not found in a democracy.

The motivation of the individual to learn is a prime factor in the success of any system of education. The roots of such inspiration are in the home, the community, and the traditions of the society. The goals endorsed by a people, the type of youth activities that are rewarded, the relationship between education and vocational and economic success—all help set the level of motivation that students bring to high school.

ORGANIZATION OF SECONDARY SCHOOLS

In addition to the national and individual commitment to education in other countries, the secondary schools in the United States are being challenged by differences between their organization and that of schools abroad. These are mainly in the centralized control of educational programs, the dual systems that segregate youth on the basis of ability, the shorter periods of education with what is alleged to be greater achievement, and the programs of selective admission to high schools.

Centralized National Control

Just as the United States has no formal national constitutional commitment to education, so it has no national control. In fact, a long-standing argument about the dangers of federal control of education flares up in each Congressional session when federal appropriations to education are proposed. In contrast, most of the other countries of the world, as well as all those under Communist domination, maintain centralized control over education in the same fashion that power is exercised over their armed forces. The ministry of education in such nations has the power to prescribe educational programs and curriculums, establish and enforce standards, recruit, train, and certify teachers, decree student quotas for different schools, and appraise the results of the educational effort in terms of its contribution to state goals.

The frustrating and time-consuming processes involved in strengthening or redirecting education in the United States, wherein each community sets policy for its own schools[11] with varying degrees of control

[11] Hawaii, a state that has not yet abandoned the centralized state control developed during its territorial status, is an exception to this pattern.

Selective Admission

The "ladder" system of education in the United States permits any pupil who completes one level successfully to pass on to the next. A similar practice prevails, interestingly enough, in Russia and Communist China, where the goal is to provide elementary and secondary education to every student of normal capacities.

A contrasting system long popular in Europe for selecting students for high school admission is one based on national examinations. Under such a plan students undertake examinations at about age 11 or 12 to determine their eligibility for secondary education. On the basis of their scores, they are assigned to schools appropriate to their talents. This practice closely resembles the dual school system found in a few schools in this country that seeks to select homogeneous groups for particular types of schools. Table 21-2 shows the selectivity of secondary schools in sample nations.

Table 21-2. *Selectivity of Secondary Schools*

| | BASIS FOR ADMISSION TO SECONDARY SCHOOL | |
NATION	ELEMENTARY SCHOOL COMPLETION	EXAMINATION
Canada	X	
China	X	
France		X
Great Britain		X
India		X
Peru		X
Soviet Union	X	
Sweden		X
Switzerland		X
United States	X	

STRENGTH OF CURRICULUM

Perhaps the greatest challenge coming from abroad to secondary schools in the United States is that to the curriculum itself. Americans sense that other nations may be doing a superior job preparing scientists, and they suspect that their high school programs are not equal to those of other nations, particularly Russia, in subject concentration, curricular depth, emphasis on specialization, control of talent development, and possibly teacher scholarship.

Concentration on Academic Subjects

The suspicion that the elective system and the wide range of high school offerings has produced a type of secondary education that permits students to avoid the more rigorous basic subjects of the curriculum has led to comparisons with other national high schools.[16] The focus of such investigations has been on the differences from nation to nation in emphasis on secondary school subjects. Efforts have been made to gauge the extent of concentration on certain subjects both by their inclusion in required programs and the amount of time devoted to their study. Specifically, the interest has been in science, mathematics, foreign language, history, and the native language—the basic academic subjects. The investigations have dealt almost exclusively with the academic concentrations of gifted and college-bound youth.

Some expected difficulties are encountered in comparing subject concentrations of high school pupils in different countries. One is that other countries maintain various types of dual schools; whereas the United States incorporates all subjects in the curriculum of the comprehensive high school. The casual observer may examine the curriculum of an academic high school of another country, without studying the program offered by its technical schools, and conclude that the nation's concentration on academic subjects, as compared to applied fields, is far greater than that found in the United States. Another problem is the one that Conant approached when he prepared an academic inventory for the brighter students to ascertain which subjects they elect beyond those specifically required by the school or a particular curricular pattern. The differences between secondary schools within the United States itself also make reliable comparisons with other nations difficult. For example, Conant, in applying his academic inventory to twenty-two comprehensive high schools, found the percentage of academically talented boys who were enrolled in the fourth year of high school mathematics (counting from grade 9),

[16] Rickover, *Education and Freedom*, pp. 229-49; Bereday, Brickman, and Read (eds.), *The Changing Soviet School*, pp. 213-39; and Bereday and Lauwerys (eds.) *The Year Book of Education*, 1958.

ranged from a high of 100 per cent to a low of 35 per cent.[17] The number of students taking the fourth year of a foreign language varied from 55 per cent to zero. In the fourth year of science, the range was from 70 per cent to zero. Only in English were 100 per cent enrollments in fourth-year work common; yet even here, one school had only 35 per cent of its brightest students continuing the study of their native language and literature.

In nations in which the program for all youth is prescribed by the central government, it is somewhat easier to study the concentration of subjects in the secondary school. A recent study of the general high school program in Communist China in 1957-58, for example, revealed an apportionment of students' time to different subjects as shown in Table 21-3. Data on Communist China were selected for comparison because of their recency and current interest and the similarity between this nation and Soviet Russia. Several striking differences from the typical pattern found in secondary schools in the United States will be noted. One is the distribution of the student's weekly time among as many as fourteen subjects; in no year does the number of subjects studied drop below ten. To achieve this breadth of study, one-, two-, and three-hour courses—similar to the college plan in this country—are scheduled; this contrasts to the five-hour courses popular in secondary schools in the United States.[18]

There are also great differences between the times devoted to specific subjects. For example, in most high schools in the United States all students are required to take science in the seventh, eighth, and ninth grades. The proportion of time devoted to physics during these years is estimated to be 25 per cent, or 44 hours, during the seventh grade; 35 per cent, or 61 hours, during the eighth grade, and 60 per cent, or 105 hours, in the ninth-grade science course. Thus, a total of 210 hours of physics is required of all students by the conclusion of the ninth grade. If the student elects physics in the eleventh year, after taking biology in the tenth, he will add another 175 hours to this amount, making a total of 385 hours. In some schools, students who do not elect physics are required to enroll for a course in physical science in which about 60 per cent of the content belongs to the field of

[17] Conant, *op. cit.*, p. 114.

[18] The assumption that every subject should be accorded equal time in the school week is rooted in the recommendations of the Committee of Ten which held, in 1893, that any subject studied with equal time, intensity, and under equally competent instruction should be judged of equal worth in the school curriculum.

Table 21-3. New Curriculum for Secondary Schools of Communist China Showing Concentration on Various Subjects

SUBJECTS	FIRST YEAR	SECOND YEAR	THIRD YEAR	FOURTH YEAR	FIFTH YEAR	SIXTH YEAR	TOTAL NUMBER OF HOURS
Chinese language	2	2	2	–	–	–	204
Literature	5	5	5	5	5	5	1,010
Arithmetic	6/5	–	–	–	–	–	187
Algebra	–	4	2	4/3	2	2	455
Geometry	–	2	3	2/3	2	2	389
Trigonometry	–	–	–	–	2	2	134
History of China	3/2	3	–	–	3	3	385
World history	–	–	3	–	–	–	102
New and newest world history	–	–	–	3	–	–	102
Politics	2	1	1	2	2	2	336
Physical geography	3/2	–	–	–	–	–	85
World geography	–	2/3	–	–	–	–	85
Chinese geography	–	–	3/2	–	–	–	85
Economic geography of China	–	–	–	–	2	–	68
Botany	3	2	–	–	–	–	170
Zoology	–	2/4	2	–	–	–	170
Human anatomy and physiology	–	–	–	2	–	–	68
Physics	–	3/2	2	3	3	4	485
Chemistry	–	–	2/3	2	2	3	317
Foreign language	3	–	–	4	4	4	510
Physical culture	2	2	2	2	2	2	404
Music	1	1	1	–	–	–	102
Drawing	1	1	1	–	–	–	102
Basic agriculture	–	–	2	–	–	–	68
WEEKLY LOAD	28/29	30	31	29	29	29	6,023

SOURCE: V. Klepikov (translated by Ina Schlesinger), "The New Curricula of the General Education Schools of China," *School and Society*, February 13, 1960, p. 73. Reprinted by permission of *School and Society*.

physics. For such students, an additional 105 hours should be added to the 210 previously required to make a total of 315 hours. These three figures—385 hours for the student who elects physics, 315 hours for the student who takes physical science in the eleventh grade, and 210 hours for students who do not take physics beyond the ninth grade— can be compared to the 485 hours devoted by all students to this subject in the general-education high schools in Red China. Similar comparisons can be made with other subjects.

Curricular Depth

Another fear of American citizens concerns the depth of curricular treatment in secondary schools. This anxiety springs from the suspicion that some subjects, as presented in some schools, merit their titles in name only. Questions are being raised about the up-to-dateness and appropriateness of content; people are asking whether a tendency to emphasize the current, the superficial, the popular topics has not "watered down" the content to the point where its basic value as an academic discipline has been lost. In effect, secondary schools are charged with adapting the content of subjects to fit pupils instead of challenging students to measure up to the exacting scholarship required to master the subjects.

No subject field is safe from being challenged to prove that it offers sufficient and appropriate depth. Teachers are accused of teaching "about" subjects, rather than teaching basic principles and the structure of knowledge. The charges and countercharges have been widely publicized in the public press as well as in the professional literature. They, like the other problems that confront secondary education, stem largely from the challenges from high school programs in other nations. Already, they have set in motion efforts to reorganize the curricular content of high school subjects.[19] Educational leaders report that high school work is being "toughened" with a deeper emphasis on content, with longer school days being scheduled, and more homework assigned.[20] At the same time, attention is being given to the problem of strengthening the foundations of scholarship in the elementary schools. The introduction of the study of foreign language into the curriculum of primary schools may force a complete reorgani-

---

[19] Robert E. K. Rourke, "Some Implications of Twentieth Century Mathematics for High Schools," *Mathematics Teacher,* February 1958, pp. 74-86.

[20] Robert E. K. Rourke, "Extending School Services for Children," Appleton, Wisc. (Appleton Public Schools), January 19, 1959.

zation of such instruction throughout the subsequent years of the public school system. Similar problems are being confronted in science, mathematics, history, geography, and world literature.

In the achievement of greater curricular depth, the emphasis is largely, as yet, on designing programs of education suited to the academically talented students. Yet some parents and educators feel that even students of average capacity can deal with more difficult content in the elementary school grades and in high school than has been provided for them. Such attitudes receive reinforcement from the patterns of curricular depth that are found in other nations.

Control of Talent Development

Communist nations have little difficulty with the regulation of talent development. They simply admit to advanced schools, and schools that emphasize particular programs, students whose intellectual capacities and political loyalties best suit them for such training. In addition, they can guarantee that talent is not wasted by compelling students to continue their studies. Economic need is never a factor since the government pays the student to go to school. Other countries with centralized control of educational programs can, by the use of state-administered entrance examinations, select for training young people whose talent promises to be a good investment for the state.

The United States, on the other hand, faces a difficult challenge to conserve talent, to develop it in quantities and to degrees of excellence required for both private enterprise and national purposes. Where other nations can control and command the development of talent, a democracy must stimulate and guide. Awareness of this difference led Conant to recommend the establishment of a satisfactory system of counseling, beginning in the elementary school and continuing throughout subsequent years of schooling.[21] When the United States Congress established the National Defense Education Act in 1958 to strengthen the preparation of students in mathematics, science, and foreign language—for national security reasons—it appropriated funds to prepare guidance counselors and to help improve counseling programs for gifted students in elementary and secondary schools.

The challenge to meet compulsory controls over talent with guided choices imposes upon high school teachers, counselors, and administrators, as well as on parents, a continuing responsibility. Only as young

[21] Conant, *op. cit.*, p. 44.

people can be brought to appraise accurately their own potentialities and to undertake educational programs appropriate in quality and duration to bring their talents to maximum fruition will the United States be able to compete successfully.

Early Specialization

One significant difference between traditional European secondary education and that in the United States is in the beginning of specialization. Education in this country, at all levels, has tended to emphasize broad preparation in many fields, with specialization being postponed to the post-high school years and, in the professional fields, even beyond undergraduate college years. Most foreign school systems, in contrast, begin specialization early, usually during the first years of the high school.

England has long required specialization in the secondary school program, beginning at age eleven. *The Regulations for Secondary Schools,* of 1924, recognized five groups of subjects in which students could prepare for examinations: science and mathematics, classics, modern studies, classics with modern studies, and geography with other combinations of subjects.[22] These classifications were liberalized over the succeeding twenty-five years until in 1950 a "General Certificate of Education" was created to permit noncollege-bound youth to study subjects best suited to their abilities and interests. Those planning to enter college must still conform to the pattern of early specialization.

As is to be expected, students who have specialized early are much more advanced in their field of specialization than students in the United States. That they have less breadth of knowledge is frequently overlooked when the focus is on the development of highly trained scientists, linguists, mathematicians, or military experts. That bright students in the United States, when they reach the stage of specialization, do overtake their counterparts from other countries does not seem to some an adequate reason for postponement of specialization. As a consequence, secondary schools face pressures to reduce the breadth of subject selection by students in order to permit earlier specialization.

Scholarship of Teachers

Challenges to improve the quality of secondary education in the

[22] W. A. C. Steward, "Curriculum Continuity and Development at the Secondary Level in England," The Year Book of Education, Bereday and Lauwerys (eds.), 1958, pp. 74-75.

United States are raising questions about the scholarship of high school teachers. The question is asked, first of all, whether teachers have sufficient preparation in the content of the subject fields they teach. The charge is often made that teacher education programs and requirements for certification overemphasize methodology to the detriment of preparation in content areas. Numerous critics of the preparation of high school teachers in the United States seem to be in accord with a statement made by the head of the natural science faculties of the University of Moscow: "Methods-of-teaching courses are not necessary in the secondary grades; it will be enough if the teacher knows his subject well. Practice will teach him how to teach."[23]

The fact is that Russian high school teachers usually have more preparation in pedagogy than do teachers in the United States; but they also have more extensive specialization in the subjects they teach. This is because, first, the length of the training program in Russia is five years, as compared to four here; and second, the Russian teacher specializes in only one teaching field, whereas teachers in the United States are usually required to be qualified to teach two or three subjects. The resulting differences in levels of scholarship, many feel, may be significant in terms of quality of instruction, particularly for academically talented youth.

Another question about the scholarship of secondary school teachers concerns their continued study and research while on the job. Here again, contrasts with practices in Russia are worth notice. The high school teacher in Russia is expected to engage in research and to keep abreast of his subject. He is a specialist, with scholarly obligations similar to those assumed by university professors in this country. To assure that his scholarship will not suffer, his teaching load consists of only 18 hours of teaching a week, three hours a day for the six days per week schools are in session. This load compares with 25-30 class hours of teaching required of high school teachers in the United States, not including extra duties connected with the supervision of study halls, lunchrooms, playgrounds, and extracurricular activities. The United States has never envisioned the secondary school teacher as a scholar; yet it expects him to promote scholarship in his students, apparently by precept rather than example. Comparisons with attitudes toward the teacher's role in other nations raise questions about the validity of such points of view.

[23] Bereday, Brickman, and Read (eds.), *The Changing Soviet School*, p. 294.

CHALLENGE TO THE UNITED STATES

From abroad, as well as within, the challenges to secondary education in the United States are becoming clearer. In recent years, the efforts by schools throughout the nation to face squarely comparisons with other countries and to remedy revealed weaknesses have gone far to preserve confidence in the adaptability of secondary schools. Teachers and school leaders have traveled extensively to study educational programs of other nations. Visitors from foreign countries have been called upon to criticize our schools freely as an aid to the effort. Furthermore, the public is becoming better informed about other secondary school systems, their purposes, strengths, and weaknesses. Along with better information, there seem to be developing in the public mind certain convictions about education in the United States as compared with that in other countries.

The Importance of Comparing School Systems

Although programs of education are more or less indigenous to the societies that create them and, therefore, are neither exportable or importable, it is possible by comparison to identify strengths and weaknesses of a nation's system of education. In addition, certain educational practices in one country may be adapted to suit similar problems in others. The more that is known about educational programs in other countries, the better able the people of the United States will be to improve their own.[24]

Reliable knowledge about other people's schools will help the United States to appraise accurately the educational structures and procedures that some critics wish to see adopted. Many of the European practices that are currently being eulogized, for example, have been or are being abandoned by their own nations. Leaders in secondary education have a responsibility to know about schools in other leading nations and to keep citizens informed about them.

Above all, knowledge of secondary schools in other countries is vital because of the role education must play in national defense. The strength of a nation rests heavily upon the kind and quality of education it provides to its future generations. It is impossible to appraise accurately the progress another nation is making without knowing what is happening in its program of education. In fact, perhaps the

[24] Thomas Woody, "The Significance of Knowing About Soviet Education," *School and Society,* November 8, 1958, pp. 3-9.

best indicator of a nation's advancement is the nature and extent of |
educational services it provides.

Refinement and Rededication

To ignore the challenges coming to secondary education from abroad
may well lead to disaster; to attempt to copy educational programs
and practices, or to superimpose aspects of other systems on the
United States may be equally fatal. Educational advances in other
nations must not be allowed to undermine confidence in the system of
schools that is a unique creation of the United States. The success of
others, rather, should serve to stimulate vigorous efforts to refine and
strengthen secondary education here. Out of an awareness of the educational gains abroad and the study of other types of systems of schooling should come a rededication to education in the United States. The
impetus from the discovery that other nations are attempting through
education to "reach and overreach" America may well stimulate the
greatest educational revival that the nation has ever known.

United States Schools as a World Model

The free world looks to the United States for leadership in all fields,
but particularly in education. The role of "world model" places new
and heavy responsibilities on secondary schools. They stand as demonstrations of the kind of educational programs and opportunities that
freedom and private enterprise can provide. The image they create
may well be reflected around the earth.

At no time in the history of the world have so many underprivileged
people, in underdeveloped as well as in major nations, reached so
hungrily for the benefits of education. Inspired by new freedoms and
the spirit of democracy that the United States has popularized, they
struggle to achieve within a decade all the educational advances that
have taken centuries in older nations. In this mission, they do not have
the time for trial and error, nor do they have the resources for their
own educational research; instead they borrow with confidence the
educational experiences of other nations.

Secondary schools in the United States are challenged to demonstrate how the world's youth should best be educated. Those who argue
for the adoption of an old-world, dual system that will separate the
intellectual elite from the rest fail to see that such a plan would serve
only to destroy the faith of the common people throughout the world

in our democratic system of education. On this point L. G. Derthick, United States Commissioner of Education, comments:

> Each month visitors from all over the world come to study our comprehensive schools. Without doubt, they see two distinct advantages in them: (1) the building of social unity by lowering traditional class barriers and (2) the preparation of more young people for life in societies which, like our own, are demanding increasing numbers of secondary school graduates. They know that the American high school has helped young people of all creeds and classes learn how to live together in the United States. They know also that a traditional 19th century educational system cannot prepare the great body of youth to work and live in a 20th century industrial society where each citizen must vote intelligently and be an efficient worker. It is significant that England and Sweden have taken steps to establish comprehensive schools.[25]

The comprehensive high school is a unique feature of secondary education in the United States that appeals to other nations of the world who are striving to achieve universal education for newly freed people. Yet this institution must achieve high standards of excellence for all, and particularly for the academically talented students; otherwise, the example it sets will be one of mass educational mediocrity, a poor model for the world's underdeveloped nations which are so desperately in need of intellectual competence.

Meeting New Competition with Traditional Values

The challenge of the times to secondary education is to demonstrate that universality, quality, and efficiency can be achieved within one comprehensive school. To attain this objective, rigorous efforts will be required to eliminate identified weaknesses while preserving proved strengths. The old as well as the new must be subject to objective appraisal, as educational programs and practices are built on the results of research rather than the advice of advocates. A constant directive for all engaged in educational leadership might well be to strengthen high schools to meet the future without sacrificing past gains or mutilating the distinctive character of secondary education in the United States.

[25] Lawrence G. Derthick, "Review of the American Educational System," *Hearings,* Subcommittee of the Committee on Appropriations, House of Representatives, 86th Congress, 2nd Session, Washington, D.C. (Government Printing Office), 1960, p. 10.

SELECTED REFERENCES

BEREDAY, GEORGE Z. F., WILLIAM W. BRICKMAN, AND GERALD H. READ, eds. *The Changing Soviet School.* Cambridge, Mass.: Riverside Press, 1960.

BEREDAY, GEORGE Z. F., AND JOSEPH LAUWERYS, eds. *The Secondary School Curriculum.* The Year Book of Education, Tarrytown, N. Y.: World Book Company, 1958.

DERTHICK, LAWRENCE G. "Review of the American Educational System," *Hearings,* Subcommittee of the Committee on Appropriations, House of Representatives, 86th Congress, 2nd Session, Washington, D.C.: Government Printing Office, 1960.

ELAM, STANLEY, ed. "Problems and Promises of Education in Asia," *Phi Delta Kappan,* special issue, December 1957.

KABIR, HUMAYUN. *Education in New India,* New York: Harper, 1957.

LEVIN, DEANA. *Soviet Education Today.* London: Staples Press, 1959.

MEDLIN, W. K., C. B. LINDQUIST, AND M. L. SCHMITT. *Soviet Educational Programs.* Washington, D.C.: U.S. Office of Education, 1960.

PASSOW, HARRY A. *Secondary Education for All: The English Approach.* New York: Ronald Press, 1961.

RICKOVER, H. G. *Education and Freedom.* New York: Dutton, 1959.

ULRICH, ROBERT. *The Education of Nations.* Cambridge, Mass.: Harvard Univ. Press, 1961.

UNESCO, *XXIInd International Conference on Public Education.* Geneva: International Bureau of Education, 1959.

WOODRING, PAUL, ed. "Education in America," *Saturday Review,* monthly supplement, September 17, 1960.

Index

Ability grouping, see Grouping
Academic curriculum, 214
  history of, 215
Academy
  English, 62
  Philadelphia, 64
  purpose of, 47
Acceleration, 405
Activities, problems in conducting, 293
Activity curriculum, 202
Adams, John, 34
Administration
  responsibilities of, 194
  student-staff participation in, 194
  teacher participation in, 195
Adolescence, 131
Albright, A. D., 323
Alcorn, Marvin, 224
Allen, William H., 232
Allport, Gordon W., 205
American Association of School Administrators, 310, 323, 375
American creed, 83
Ames, Louise Bates, 169
Anderson, Harold, 111, 122
Anderson, Nels, 462
Anglican church, 60
Anti-intellectualism, 122
Armstrong, W. Earl, 320
Association for Supervisors and Curriculum Development, 263
Audio-visual aids, 231, 381
Audio-visual specialist, 190
Automation, 11

Babian, Haig, 17
Barnard, Henry, 63
Barnard, Wilfred, 486
Barrat, Robert, 490
Bauer, Raymond, 85
Beach, Fred F., 56, 467, 474, 490
Beard, Charles, 48
Beard, Mary, 48
Beatty, John L., 100
Beberman, Max, 409
Beekman, Marvin, 434
Beginning teachers, 193
Behavior outcomes, emphasis on, 106
Behavioral sciences, 9
Behaviorism, 164
Bello, Francis, 141
Bennis, Warren G., 197
Bent, Rudyard K., 323
Bereday, George Z. F., 495, 497, 503, 509, 513
Bidwell, Charles E., 305
Birch, J. W., 394
Birth rate, 22, 24
Bissex, Henry S., 229
Block-time curriculum, 221
Bloom, Benjamin, 204, 224
Bloomgarten, Lawrence, 126
Bogue, David J., 31
Bosch, Gerald, 321
Bossing, Nelson, 221
Bowman, Fred Q., 270
Broudy, Harry, 412
Brainwashing, 85
Brickman, William W., 495, 503, 509, 513

Bridenbaugh, Carl, 79
Bridenbaugh, Jessica, 79
Brinton, Crane, 128, 151, 152, 172
Brown, Edwin, 245
Broyles, Robert E., 317
Brsacker, William E., 270
Bryan, J. Ned, 137
Bullock, Robert P., 462
Bureau of Indian Affairs, 37
Burns, Edward McNall, 172
Buros, Oscar K., 258
Bursch, Charles W., 384
Butts, R. Freeman, 79, 490
Buildings, 346
  early, 348
  economy of, 370
  educational utility of, 369
  efforts to provide, 356
  impact of, 357
  influence of vocational education
    on, 355
  modern examples of, 348, 349,
    358, 359, 367, 368, 369, 372,
    377, 378, 379, 382
  multiuse areas of, 367, 368
  obsolescence of, 356
  scope of, 356
  shortage of, 349, 350, 351, 352,
    353
  see also School plant
Bydslek, Grace, 296

Cain, Leo F., 428, 431
Caldwell, Edson, 270
Camp, Dolph, 258
Campbell, Arthur A., 24, 31
Campbell, Roald F., 197, 323
Campus plan, see School plant
Capacities
  generalized, 138, 139
  individual, 105
  specialized, 138, 139
Cardinal Principles of Secondary
  Education, 70, 74
Career orientation, 291
Career teachers, 230
Carnegie units, 210

Carter, Harold D., 386
Case studies, 259
Caswell, Hollis, 69
Catholic secondary schools, 479
Centralization, 176
Chalmers, Randolph C., 100
Chamberlin, Leo M., 197, 345
Chandler, B. J., 245, 345
Charles II, 61
Chase, Francis S., 111, 122
Chauncey, Henry, 396
Cheating, 171
Chester, Giraud, 458
Chief state school officer, 177
Chu, S. Y., 497
Church-related schools, 483
Church and state, separation of, 42,
  99
Ciernick, Sylvia, 463
Civic groups, 455, 456
Classroom management, 238
Classroom presentations, teacher's
  role in, 240
Clay, George R., 163
Cloyd, David Excelmons, 65
Cocking, Walter D., 370
Cold War, 7
Cole, William Graham, 171
College Board Mathematics
  Achievement tests, 214
Commager, Henry S., 100
Competition from abroad, 492, 512
Commission on the Reorganization
  of Secondary Education, 51
Common heritage, 81, 82
  components of, 83
  modern problems in, 98
  nature of, 82
  role of curriculum in, 96, 97
  sources of, 83
  transmittal of, 92, 93
Common learnings, see General
  education
Communications, see School-com-
  munity communications
Communist China, 505
Community attitudes toward education, 449

Community responsibility in education, 440

Conant, James B., 4, 5, 6, 17, 50, 51, 63, 70, 122, 143, 237, 248, 288, 352, 405, 412, 488, 500, 504, 507

Concentration in depth of curriculum, 119

Conger, Louis H., Jr., 303

Connors, Donald F., 97

Consolidation of schools, 54

Constitution of India, 495

Controversy in democracy, 72

Cook, Walter W., 412

Cooper, Bernice L., 318

Core curriculum, 203

Cornell, Francis G., 127, 195

Cornog, William H., 405

Council for Basic Education, 281

Counseling, 257, 260, 426

Counselors, number of, 261

Counts, George S., 90

Cowgill, Rome, 458

Cox, Catherine, 391

Cremin, Lawrence A., 79

Cromwell, Oliver, 61

Cross, A. J., 245

Crowder, Thora, 412

Crowther, Geoffrey, 127

Cubberley, Ellwood P., 68, 79, 126

Culbertson, Jack A., 323

Cultural heritage, curriculum treatment of, 95

Cultural lag, 90

Cumulative records, 258
    use of, 145

Curriculum
    activity pattern of, 202
    bases of, 204
    competing designs of, 202
    conflicts of, 201
    core pattern of, 203
    development of, 199
    diluted, 202
    effects of administrative patterns on, 210
    effects of pupil choices on, 209
    learning experiences of, 201

Curriculum—(*Continued*)
    legal controls on, 206
    meaning of, 200
    measuring effectiveness of, 213
    offerings of, 214
    omnibus quality of, 200
    patterns of, 220, 221, 222
    planning of, 199, 210, 211, 213
    prescribed-content approach of, 201
    school-board control of, 209
    school-planned activities of, 201
    societal goals of, 206

Cypher, Irene F., 245

Dabelstein, Donald H., 435

Dabney, Charles William, 67, 79

Daly, Flora M., 428

Damrin, Dora E., 270

Darden, Colgate W., Jr., 47

Davies, Daniel R., 197

Deering, Elmer C., 356, 384

Deevy, Edward S., Jr., 31

DeHaan, Robert F., 146, 392, 412

Democracy
    controversy in, 92
    decay of, 85, 86
    as political theory, 82
    self-destination within, 84
    as way of life, 82

Democratic organization, key to, 195

Derthick, Lawrence G., 44, 512, 513

Dewey, John, 158, 201

Diplomas, 434

Discipline, 266

Discrimination in public schools, 135

Divine Gifts Concept, 128

Dorn, O. A., 481

Dorsey, Mattie F., 213, 236, 335

Douglas, Paul, 345

Drews, Elizabeth, 472

Dropouts, 41

Dual systems, 500

Dunn, Lloyd, 423, 435

Durant, Will, 151

Dutch Reformed church, 60

Ebenstein, William, 141
Economic conditions, relationship
  to talent of, 134
Education
  basic, 73
  character of, 42
  compared to other professions, 13
  definition of, 199
  efficiency in, 16
  emotions in, 163
  excellence in, 15
  expanding services of, 189
  as function of church, 42
  land grants and, 60
  length of, 249
  local controls upon, 440
  objectives of, 99, 104, 113
  population and, 20-28
  public, see Public education
  religion and, 60
  role of electronics in, 13
  sectarianism in, 63
  state systems of, 176
  and will of the people, 60
Edwards, Newton, 35, 56
Efficiency
  in education, 16
  test of, 16
Ehrenkrantz, Ezra, 380
Elam, Stanley, 513
Electronics, 13
Emotional stability as function of
  secondary school, 76
English classical school, 68
Excellence in education, 227
Exceptional education, 416; see also
  Handicapped
Experience-centered core curriculum, 222
Evaluation
  agents of, 242
  criteria for, 242
  judgment of evidence in, 244
  procedures in, 243
Everett, Samuel, 412
Eye, Glen G., 323

Fadiman, Clifton, 156
Family traditions, relation to social
  customs of, 133
Farwell, Gail F., 262
Faunce, Ronald C., 289
Federal aid, see Federal funds
Federal assistance, 9
Federal funds in education, 43, 44
Films, 13
Finance, see School finance
First law of life, 205
Fitzwater, C. O., 56
Flat grants in school finance, 39, 40
Follow-up in guidance, 260
Ford, Edmund A., 54
Ford Foundation, 245
Foreign challenge to education, 496
Foreign education system
  as challenge to U.S., 510
  compared to U.S., 510
  control of talent in, 507
  dedication to, 498
  dual, 500
  early specialization in, 508
  length of attendance in, 500
  national control of, 499
  organization of, 499
  selective admission in, 502
  status of, 497
  strength of curriculum in, 503
  stress on academic subjects in,
    503
  teacher preparation in, 509
Foreign languages in secondary
  school, 461
Foundation principle, 40
Franklin, Benjamin, 46, 64, 65, 71
"Free cats," 47
Freedman, Francis, 201
Freedman, Roger A., 482
Freedman, Ronald F., 24, 31
French, Will, 54, 203, 224
Fuess, Claude M., 490

Gallagher, James J., 402, 406, 408,
  412
Gardiner, Lyceum, 66
Gardner, John W., 146

Garrison, Garnet, 458
Garrison, J. K., 435
Gaumnitz, Walter H., 189
General education, defined, 54
Gesell, Arnold, 169
Getzels, Jacob W., 161, 166
Ghiselin, Brewster, 108, 123
G.I. Bill, 135
Gideonse, Harry D., 17
Gifted student, 386
    ability grouping of, 403
    acceleration of, 405
    administrative provisions for, 402, 403
    characteristics of, 393, 397, 398
    considerations for, 391
    demand for, 389
    evaluation of, 410, 411
    false assumptions about, 390
    flexible grouping of, 405
    interests of, 399
    motivation for, 399
    neglect of, 388
    planning for, 401
    program for, 15
    provision for, 9
    secondary school programs for, 400
    separation of, 404
    small school's provision for, 406
    special abilities of, 396
    special programs for, 407
    use of group tests for, 396
    use of standard tests with, 395
Ginsberg, Eli, 172
Gladwin, Thomas, 417, 435
Glazer, R., 232
Goldberg, Miriam, 400, 412
Goldstein, Herbert, 427, 430
Good, Carter V., 274, 466
Good, H. G., 56
Goodlad, John I., 245
Graduation, requirements for, 208
Graham, G., 296
Grant, W. Vance, 30, 36
Gregg, Russell, 180, 197, 323
Grimes, Alan P., 463
Griswold, A. Whitney, 170

Gross, Richard, 96
Group guidance, 263
Grouping, 118, 187, 188, 191, 212, 269
    by ability, 403, 429
    flexible, 405
Groups, teachable, *see* Teachable groups
Guba, Egon G., 305, 318
Guidance, 121
    in career decisions, 256
    director of, 262
    in educational plans, 255
    group, *see* Group guidance
    increasing emphasis on, 248
    informational resources for, 268
    and learning process, 264
    meaning of, 257
    objectives of, 260, 265
    as opposed to compulsion, 248
    in personal adaptations to environment, 256
    programs of, 248, 266
    relationship of, to instruction, 264
    role of, 270
    services of, 55, 56
    teamwork in, 267
Guilford, J. P., 412
Gulick, Luther H., 186
Gwynn, John Minor, 221, 224

Habit, 164
Hamilton, Homer, 296
Hand, Harold C., 41, 217
Handicapped
    ability grouping of, 429
    classification of, 424
    counseling of, 426
    defined, 416
    diagnosis of, 424
    differential training for, 425
    distribution of, 420
    education for, 414, 422
    federal assistance of, 432
    future of education of, 435
    hospital instruction for, 431
    instructional provisions for, 428

Handicapped—(*Continued*)
  integrated programs for, 430
  number of, 420, 421
  programs for, 56
  in regular classrooms, 428
  relation of academic standards
    to, 433
  responsibility of secondary school
    for, 422
  role of small school in education
    of, 433
  secondary school program for,
    431
  separate schools for, 430
  society's concern for, 416
  standards for graduation of, 434
  state assistance of, 432
  Swedish approach to, 423
  teachers for, 432
  vocational training for, 427
  see also Educational therapy
Hansford, Byron W., 323
Hanson, O. A., 45
Harrington, Alan, 253
Harvard Report, 54
Hauser, Philip M., 31
Havighurst, Robert J., 70, 146, 205,
  392, 412
Heber, Rick, 418, 426, 427, 430,
  435
Hechinger, Fred M., 490
Hechinger, Grace, 490
Heely, Allen V., 485, 490
Henricks, Marvin L., 171
Henry, Nelson B., 270
Hersey, John, 412
High school
  comprehensive, 6, 51, 94
  development of, 59
  differentiated, 6, 126, 145
  English, 68, 69
  enrollments in, 26-30
  graduation, *see* Graduation
  organization of, 183, 184
  planning, 271, 374, 383
  programs, balance in, 283
  role of community in, 373

High school—(*Continued*)
  role of teacher in, 373
  standards in, 121
  student, 166-67
  task of, 92
  see also Secondary school
Hill, Arthur S., 420, 435
Hill, C. M., 56
Hillfish, H. Gordon, 241
Himmelfarb, Milton, 487
Hlavaty, Julius H., 131
Holton, Gordon, 17
Home-school relationship in educa-
  tion, 441
Hollingshead, August B., 288
Hollingworth, Leta, 398
Hoppy, Arthur A., 224
Horwitz, Robert H., 463
Hughes, Everett Cherrington, 172
Hull, J. H., 354
Humanities, 9
Hutchin, Clayton D., 356, 384
Hutchins, Robert M., 106, 129

Ilg, Frances L., 169
Imposition v. self-direction, 162
Inaugural address of President Ken-
  nedy, 89
Independent schools, 48
  number of, 469, 470
  see also Nonpublic secondary
    schools
Individual commitment to scholar-
  ship, 221
Input, 418
Integrative process, 418
Intellectual development in second-
  ary school, 73, 104
Interests of students, 284
Intermediate school districts, value
  of, 180
Interns, 230
Instruction
  aspects of, 236
  impact of technology upon, 190
  methods of gathering evidence
    about, 243
  obligations of, 265

Instruction—(*Continued*)
  its relationship to guidance, 264
  use of staff in, 228
Instructional resources, organization of, 228
Instructional secretary, 230
Instructional teams, 229
  composition of, 230
  guidance in, 269
Itinerant specialists, 418

Jackson, P. W., 138
Jacobson, Paul B., 323
James, William, 164
Jannoccone, Lawrence, 197
Jefferson, Thomas, 67, 68, 71, 126
Jefferson's Plan for Education in Virginia, 67, 126
Johnson, Edgar G., 270
Johnson, Leighton H., 486, 490
Johnson, Mauritz J., 270
Johnson, Nora, 162
Jones, Howard Mumford, 100
Jones, J. J., 463
Josephs, Devereux C., 4, 17, 130, 248
Junior high school, organizational patterns of, 52

Kabir, Humayun, 495, 513
Kalamazoo case, 38
Katz, Elihu, 463
Kay, John K., 380
Keats, John, 79
Keller, Robert J., 315, 319
Kennedy, John F., 89
Kents Hill School, 65
Kerwin, Jerome G., 490
Kiehl, Robert, 250
Kilzer, Louis R., 296
Kimbrough, Ralph R., 463
Kindred, Leslie W., 197, 345
King, Edmund J., 225, 488
King, F. M., 496
Kingsley, Howard L., 165
Kingson, Walter, 458
Kinkead, Eugene, 85, 172
Klausmeir, Herbert J., 345

Knower, Franklin H., 463
Knowledge, 390
  advance of, 390
  avenues to, 114
  discovery of, 113
  function of, 111
  mastery of, 114
  organization of, 110
  use of, 113, 116
Koerner, James D., 110, 123
Kohlbrenner, Bernard J., 490
Koos, Leonard V., 69, 70, 79
Koral, Alexander G., 412
Korean G.I. Bill, 135
Kornberg, Leonard, 435
Kough, Jack, 146
Krug, Edward A., 225, 271
Krugman, Morris, 252

Laboratory teaching, 234
Ladder system of education, 502
Lane, Willard R., 323
Latin grammar school, 63, 64
  function of, 71
  purpose of, 47
Lauwerys, Joseph A., 497, 503, 513
Lay advisory councils, as related to schools, 455
Lay readers, 230
Lazarsfeld, Paul F., 463
Leadership for the secondary school, 299
  dilemmas of, 313
  elements contributing to, 304
  function of, 301
  image, 304
  impact of, 302
  lengthening shadow concept of, 307
  means of accomplishing, 301
  nature of, 300
  new assignments for, 315
  new demands on, 311
  opportunities in secondary schools in, 316
  principle of education, 141
  source of authority for, 300
  teacher's role in, 322

Leadership for the secondary school
—(*Continued*)
  team, 310
  test of, 303
Learning laboratory
  history of, 354
  significance of, 355
Learning skills
  development of, 109
  maturation of, 109
Lessinger, L. M., 412
Leven, Charles L., 27
Levin, Deana, 497, 513
Levy, Ralph, 458
Lieberman, Myron, 470
Life adjustment, 73
Lindquist, C. B., 513
Linley, James M., 224
Lipham, James M., 323
Little, J. Kenneth, 134
Local school districts, 181
Locke, John, 62
Lockwood, William V., 251
Long, Charles M., 316
Lorge, Irving, 406
Lovett, Abercrombie, 87
Loyalty oaths, 86
Luecking, Evelyn, 413
Lumsdaine, A. A., 232
Lunch program, cost of federal, 38
Luther, Martin, 62, 155
Lutheran church schools, 480

McCann, Lloyd E., 323
McCleary, Lloyd E., 281
McCloskey, Gordon, 463
McClusky, Neil G., 490
McCollum case, 42
Mackie, Romaine P., 435
McLeod, John W., 380
McLure, William P., 180
McPartland, John, 389
Madison, James, 34
Magnifico, L. X., 436
Malthus, Thomas R., 21, 31
Manpower shortage, 250
Mansfield, A. Lyon, 468
Marr, Harriet, 79

Marson, Philip, 345
Martinson, Ruth, 412
Martyn, K. A., 398
Masland, Richard L., 417, 435
Massachusetts High School Law, 69
Mathematics, emphasis on, 218
Mathis, Claude, 245
Mayor, Frederick, 100
Medlin, W. K., 513
Meil, Alice, 235
Melancthon, Philipp, 62
Merrill, Edward C., Jr., 320, 463
Merit salary, 342
Methods of instruction, 120
Miller, Carroll, 271
Miller, J. Erwin, 309
Miller, Van, 56, 323
Millet, John D., 197
Mills, Charles L., 380
Milton, John, 62
Mobility
  impact of, 28
  trends in, 27
Monroe, Paul, 61
Moore, Hollis, Jr., 320, 321
Moral training in secondary schools, 73
Mort, Paul R., 127
Moser, Leslie, 132
Motivation, 236
Mowrer, Hobart O., 225
Mueller, William J., 260
Muller, Herbert J., 100, 159, 160, 463
Multiuse areas, 367
Multiple-track plan, 404
Myrdal, Gunnar, 83

Nagle, A. J., 245
National Association of Secondary School Principals, 197, 296
National Catholic Welfare Conference, 476, 490
National Citizens' Council for Better Schools, 455
National commitment to education, 494

National Defense Education Act, 9, 43, 44, 507
National Education Association, 245, 282
National examinations, 213
National School Public Relations Association, 450, 463
National Society for the Study of Education, 392
National systems of education, 494, 495
  financial support for, 496
  see also Foreign education
Needs of students, 284
Newgarten, Bernice L., 100
Newspapers, as related to school-community communication, 457
Noall, Mathew F., 228
Nonpublic secondary schools, 464
  current survey of, 468
  defined, 466, 467
  enrollment in, 473–77
  experimentation in, 484
  financial problems in, 482
  growth of, 466, 479
  location of, 471
  number of, 467
  objectives of, 487
  problems of, 481
  purposes of, 483
  regulation of, 488
  religious indoctrination in, 483
  research in, 484
  scope of, 466
  services of, 477
  strengths of, 485, 486
  teacher training programs for, 485
  types of, 476
Nordberg, H. Orville, 296
Novak, Benjamin, 225

Occupational choices, 249
Occupational information and guidance service, 248
Oden, Melita H., 136, 138, 147, 413
Ogburn, William F., 90

Ohlsen, Merle M., 338, 400
Oregon case, 489
Organization, democratic, *see* Democratic organization
Output, 418

Parable of the Lamp, 77
Parent-Teacher Associations, 455
Parochial schools, 99
  number of, 469, 470
  transportation for, 43
  see also Nonpublic schools
Parsons, Wilford, 486
Pasch, Dorothy F., 430
Passow, Harry A., 392, 412, 513
Paternalism, decline of, 253
Patterson, C. H., 426, 435
Patterson, Franklin, 92, 95, 100, 263
Pegnato, C. W., 394
Penn, William, 64
Personal-social development of students, 290
Phelps, A. T., 245
Philadelphia Academy, 64
Pierce, Truman M., 320, 323, 463
Platt, John Rader, 24
Politics and administration, 314
Pool, Ithiel DeSola, 463
Population
  effect of depression upon, 22
  growth of, 19-23
  effect of immigration upon, 22
  mobility of, 27
Prestwood, Elwood, L., 197
Principal, 321
  competencies necessary for, 321
  duties of, 306, 308, 309, 311
  opportunities offered by, 321
  personal traits of, 319
  professional, 317, 320
  qualifications for, 319
  status of, 318
Pritzkow, Philo T., 212, 225
Private education, *see* Nonpublic secondary schools, Private schools
Private schools, 45
Professional associations

Professional associations—(*Cont.*)
  membership in, 345
  types and purposes of, 344
Proff, Fred, 400
Progressive Education Movement,
  origin of, 122
Project areas, 189
Project for the Improvement of
  Thinking, 112
Public education, 32
  attacks upon, 441
  for the common good, 32
  decentralization of, 49, 176
  early concepts of, 36
  early standards of, 35, 36
  federal participation in, 37, 38
  financing of, 38
  local-state relationship in, 36, 37
  organization, transition of, 181
  role of professional personnel in,
    442, 443
  role of public in, 440
  slow growth of, 48
  state responsibility for, 34
  unique features of, 49
Public high school, 127
  characteristics of, 127
  purpose of, 47
Public school, defined, 467
  English, 61
  secondary, enrollment of, 475
Puritan church, 60

Quakers, 60
Quality teaching, 244

Rabi, I. I., 141
Racial segregation, *see* Segregation
Radio, 457
Randall, John Herman, Jr., 104
Rate bill, 39
Read, Gerald H., 495, 509, 513
Redefer, F. L., 345
Reeves, Dorothy, 345
Regulations for secondary schools,
  508
Reid, John Lyon, 369, 384
Religion of early settlers, 42

Reller, Theodore, 323
Remuneration in teaching, 341-43
Resource-room teachers, 418
Retention of high school youth, 29
Reynolds, George F., 97
Rice, Mabel C., 420, 435
Richey, Herman, 35, 56
Rickover, Hyman G., 4, 5, 6, 17,
  84, 494, 496, 500, 503, 513
Riesman, David, 161, 256, 313
Riesman, Whyte, 161
Roe, Anna, 144
Roe, William, 452, 458
Rogers, Carl R., 271
Rogers, Jack, 345
Rogers, Virgil, 345
Romine, Stephen, 318
Roosevelt, Franklin D., 160
Rothney, J. W. M., 260
Rothstein, Jerome H., 435
Rourke, Robert E. K., 506
Runkel, Philip, 270
Russia, competition from, 7, 8
Russian education, differences be-
  tween U.S. and, 494
Ryans, David G., 245, 336, 345

Salaries, *see* Remuneration
Sarason, Seymour B., 417, 435
Sargent, Porter, 466, 468, 471, 497
Satisfaction, as basis for scholarship, 122
Sax, Karl, 31
Schein, Edgar H., 85
Schmitt, M. L., 513
Scholarship, 103
  community support of, 117
  conditions required for, 117
  meaning of, 108
  nature of, 107
Scholastic standards, 121
School atmosphere, 290
School-community relations, 438,
  444, 447, 448
  cautions concerning, 460, 461
  as challenge to education, 459
  groups as related to, 454
  principal's task in, 450

School-community relations—
(*Continued*)
  principles of program for, 449
  publications as related to, 458
  responsibility of staff in, 450
  shortcomings of, 460
  student's role in, 451, 453
  teacher's role in, 451, 452
  use of specialists in, 450
School consolidation, *see* Consolidation
School finance, 37
  flat grants in, 37
  foundation principle in, 40
  history of, 38
  local-state partnership in, 39
  state aid in, 41
School-fostered groups, 455
School-individual contacts, 446
School management, participation of students in, 95
School organization, 181
  conditions of, 182
  elements of, 182
  formal structure of, 182, 185
  specialists in, 190
  teacher contributions to, 192
  trends in, 194
School plant, 360-84
School service activities, 277
Schools
  democratic opposition to, 5
  local control of, 35
  size of, 189
  tasks of, 170
Schools-within-schools, 268, 376, 378, 380
Schultz, Raymond E., 338
Science, 157
  age of, 10
  as an answer to truth, 158
  of conduct, 158
Science programs, 218
  emphasis on, 218
  weaknesses of, 98
  in U.S. vs. foreign secondary schools, 504
Scientific method, 120

Scott, C. W., 56
"Search for the sun" trend, 27
Secondary education, 4
  academic standards of, 121, 433
  characteristics of, 7, 50, 51
  comprehensive, 6
  controversy about, 3, 4, 49
  curricular depth of, 506
  democratic, 91
  differentiation in, 6, 126
  early American, 63
  emotional stability in, 76
  English influence upon, 61, 62
  first public, 68
  functions of, 59, 69-75, 77, 79
  German influence upon, 61, 62
  goals of, 14
  grade patterns of, 187
  hidden costs of, 41
  intellectual development in, 73, 104
  limitations of, 5
  mission of, 17
  moral training in, 73
  organization of, 52, 175, 181-94
  physical well-being in, 75
  quality in, 15
  social proficiency in, 74
  and specialization, 12
  unity in, 91
  and value development, 167
  and world affairs, 6
Secondary school program, 54
  balance in, 223
  challenge of, 224
  depth of, 118
  federal assistance to, 9
  flexibility of, 223
  over-all design of, 223
  prospects of, 54
  as protest of people, 46
  role of humanities in, 9
  shortcomings of, 187
  student behavior in, 166
  types of, 77
  variety in, 244
Segre, Emilio G., 141
Segregation, racial, 44

Selectivity, 502
Self-destruction in democracy, 84
Self-direction in guidance, 266
Self-evaluation in guidance, 265
Self-made man, 128
Separate subject curriculum, 220
Serling, Robert J., 131
Shaw, George Bernard, 154
Shayon, Robert, 496
Shea, Arthur V., 172
Shores, J. Harlan, 123
Shuster, G. N., 100
Shutzer, Bruce, 137
Simpson, Richard L., 197
Singleton, M. D., 296
Skinner, B. F., 232
Smith, B. O., 112, 123
Smith, C. Currien, 242
Smith, George Cline, 360
Smith, Philip G., 241
Smith, Rose Marie, 30, 36
Smith, William, 66
Social customs, relation to education of, 133
Social maladjustment, 419
Social proficiency in secondary education, 74
Soviet Union, 492
Spalding, Willard, 56, 323
Special education, 55, 416, 417; *see also* Handicapped
Specialization, 130, 190
Spindler, George, 100
Sputnik, 8, 9, 77, 492, 494
Staff Utilization Project, 191, 361
Stalin Constitution, 495
Stanford-Binet I.Q. Test, 394
Stanley, William O., 56, 123
State boards of education, 177
State departments of education, organization of, 178, 179
Status leaders, 183
Steinberg, Charles S., 463
Stellhorn, A. C., 480
Stephenson, Harold H., 296
Steward, W. A. C., 508
Stewart, C. C., 271

Stiles, Lindley J., 77, 201, 213, 229, 236, 237, 245, 335, 345, 363
Stinnett, T. M., 320
Stoddard, Alexander, 197, 274
Stoddard, George D., 104
Stokes, Walter E., 480
Stout, I. W., 463
Strang, Ruth, 345, 391
Strauss, Lewis L., 17
Strodtbeck, F. L., 400
Student activities, 272
    appraisal of, 286
    attitudes toward, 279
    characteristics of, 274
    coordination with education programs of, 287
    cultural, 278
    definition of, 274
    development of, 278, 279
    educational, 278
    faculty-student cooperation in, 287
    future of, 295
    nature of, 272
    organization of, 282
    as public entertainment, 276
    recreational, 277
    social, 278
    and teaching activities, 292
    types of, 276
    values of, 289
Student-teacher, traits of, 339
Study habits, 110
Subject-centered block-time curriculum, 221
Subject-centered core curriculum, 222
Subject-matter curriculum, 202
Sumpton, Merle R., 413
Symbols, systems of, 109

Taba, Hilda, 70, 167
Talent, 141
    adaptability of, 141
    competition for, 131
    conservation of, 146
    cultivation of, 130
    development of, 125, 132, 140

Talent—(*Continued*)
  discovery of, 125
  identification of, 138, 144
  nature of, 136
  relationship of intelligence to, 137
  traits, 139
  use of, 142
Tannenbaum, Robert, 323
Tape recordings, use of, 13
Tarlet, Donald G., 245
Taylor, Calvin W., 147
Teachable groups, 191
Teacher competence, 312
Teachers, 337, 340
  beginning, *see* Beginning teachers
  factors influencing performance
    of, 195
  as leaders, 322
  as part of community, 341
  prospective, 330
  qualities of, 337, 338
  role in community of, 452
  salaries of, *see* Remuneration
  secondary, 324
  shortage of, 24, 26, 326-31
  specialization of, 11, 12, 130
  student, *see* Student teacher
Teacher-centered schools, 195
Teacher-counselors, 262
Teacher-student planning, 235
Teaching, 333
  federal interest in, 336
  overorganization of, 192
  overscheduling in, 192
  perceptions of, 191
  as a profession, 333, 334, 339
  qualifications for, 335, 337, 338
  recruitment of, 332
  status in, 334
  teams, 231, 381
  traditional, 192
Technology
  developments in, 10
  influence on talent of, 131
Tead, Ordway, 197, 309, 311, 323
Teahan, J. E., 412
Team leader, 230

Team teaching, nature of, 231
Telemation, use of, 13
Television
  closed-circuit, 16, 239, 381
  as related to school, 457
  see also School-community com-
    munications
Terman, Lewis M., 136, 138, 147,
  388, 391, 394, 398, 399, 413
Testing, 257
  purposes of, 258
Thayer, V. T., 17, 73, 100, 172,
  487
Thelan, Herbert, 191
Therapy, educational, 418
Thirring, Hans, 79
Thomas, Maurice J., 498
Tiedeman, David V., 244
Torrance, E. P., 400
Totalitarianism, challenge of, 252
Traxler, Arthur E., 147, 258
Trump, J. Lloyd, 228, 245, 274,
  375, 384
Turner, Frederick J., 31, 68
Tyler, Ralph W., 388

Ulrich, Robert, 513
UNESCO, 513
Unified studies curriculum, 222
Universal education, need for, 47
Universality in education, 14
United States, 6
  leadership of, 6
  schools, 511
  world image of, 88, 89
Up-through-the-ranks concept, 129
Urbanization, 157
Urwick, Lyndall, 186

Value development, factors in, 162
Value system, 168
Values, 156
  conception of, 156
  development of, 149
  and folklore, 152
  historical emphasis upon, 150
  impact of contemporary forces
    on, 156

Values—(*Continued*)
  increasing depth of, 170
  and philosophy, 153
  plural nature of, 155
  and political theory, 153
  and racial traditions, 152
  and religion, 153
  and science, 154
  and social theory, 153
  sources of, 152
  transition in, 161
Vekich, Anne M., 262
Vocational education, 355, 427

Waddington, C. H., 172
Walsh, Michael P., 172
Waner, Paul H., 463
Warner, W. Lloyd, 133
Washington, George, 34
Watson, George, 180
Wechsler, David, 105
Welty, M. L., 296
Wertenbaker, Thomas Jefferson, 79
Wetzler, Wilson F., 318

Whelpton, Pascal K., 24, 31
Whitehead, Alfred North, 108, 111, 123
Whyte, William H., Jr., 161, 170
Wiles, Kimball, 263
Will, Robert F., 56, 467, 474, 490
Wilson, Charles E., 326
Wilson, Craig, 463
Wilson, Parry, 228
Wingo, G. Max, 235, 245
Wisdom, achievement of, 116
Wittich, Walter A., 232, 407
Witty, Paul, 147
Wolfle, Dael, 142
Woodard, Prince B., 319
Woodring, Paul, 245, 404, 513
Woody, Thomas, 510
Wright, E. Wayne, 260
Wright, Grace S., 221
Wriston, Henry M., 143
Wright, Louis B., 64

Zeleny, Leslie, 96, 100
Zirbes, Laura, 296

B 3
C 4
D 5
E 6
F 7
G 8
H 9
I 0
J 1